75 Readings

An Antholgy

75 Readings

An Anthology

Tenth Edition

Santi V. Buscemi
Middlesex County College

Charlotte Smith
Adirondack Community College

Boston Burr Ridge, IL Dubuque, IA Madison, WI New York
San Francisco St. Louis Bangkok Bogotá Caracas Kuala Lumpur
Lisbon London Madrid Mexico City Milan Montreal New Delhi
Santiago Seoul Singapore Sydney Taipei Toronto

The *McGraw·Hill* Companies

Higher Education

75 READINGS: AN ANTHOLOGY

Published by McGraw-Hill, a business unit of The McGraw-Hill Companies, Inc., 1221
Avenue of the Americas, New York, NY, 10020. Copyright © 2007, 2004, 2001, 1999, 1997,
1995 by The McGraw-Hill Companies, Inc. All rights reserved. No part of this publication
may be reproduced or distributed in any form or by any means, or stored in a database or
retrieval system, without the prior written consent of The McGraw-Hill Companies, Inc.,
including, but not limited to, in any network or other electronic storage or transmission, or
broadcast for distance learning.

Some ancillaries, including electronic and print components, may not be available to
customers outside the United States.

This book is printed on acid-free paper.

2 3 4 5 6 7 8 9 0 DOC/DOC 0 9 8 7

ISBN-13: 978-0-07-312513-8
ISBN-10: 0-07-312513-X

Vice President and Editor-in-Chief: *Emily Barrosse*
Publisher: *Lisa Moore*
Sponsoring Editor: *Victoria Fullard*
Freelance Developmental Editor: *Beth Baugh*
Marketing Manager: *Lori DeShazo*
Permissions Coordinator: *Karyn Morrison*
Managing Editor: *Jean Dal Porto*
Project Manager: *Emily Hatteberg*
Art Director: *Jeanne Schreiber*
Designer: *Marianna Kinigakis*
Senior Media Project Manager: *Alexander Rohrs*
Production Supervisor: *Janean A. Utley*
Cover Image: © *Getty Images/Joanna McCarthy*
Composition: *10/12 Palatino by International Typesetting and Composition*
Printing: *45# New Era Matte, R. R. Donnelley & Sons*

Credits: The credits section for this book begins on page 435 and is considered an extension
of the copyright page.

Library of Congress Cataloging-in-Publication Data

75 readings : an anthology / [edited by] Santi V. Buscemi, Charlotte Smith.—10th ed.
    p.   cm.
  Includes bibliographical references and index.
  ISBN-13: 978-0-07-312513-8 (pbk. : acid-free paper)
  ISBN-10: 0-07-312513-X (pbk. : acid-free paper)
  1. College readers. 2. English language—Rhetoric—Problems, exercises, etc.
I. Buscemi, Santi V. II. Smith, Charlotte. III. Title: Seventy-five readings.
  PE1417.A13 2007
  808'.0427—dc22   2006012764

The Internet addresses listed in the text were accurate at the time of publication. The inclusion
of a Web site does not indicate an endorsement by the authors or McGraw-Hill, and
McGraw-Hill does not guarantee the accuracy of the information presented at these sites.

www.mhhe.com

About the Authors

SANTI BUSCEMI is a professor of English at Middlesex County College in Edison, New Jersey. He teaches developmental and first-year composition.

CHARLOTTE SMITH is a professor of English at Adirondack Community College in Queensbury, New York, where she teaches technical writing and directs the writing center.

Contents

Chapter 3
PROCESS ANALYSIS   59

Chapter 4
DEFINITION   91

Chapter 5
CLASSIFICATION AND DIVISION   115

Chapter 6
COMPARISON AND CONTRAST   152

Chapter 7
EXAMPLE AND ILLUSTRATION   185

Chapter 10
ARGUMENT AND PERSUASION   294

Chapter 11
MIXED STRATEGIES   382

THEMATIC CONTENTS

Rites of Passage

Aging

Global Issues

Gender Politics

Education

CONTENTS GROUPED BY GENRE AND DISCIPLINE

GENRES

Autobiography and Memoir

Arts and Humanities

Education

Ethnic Studies

History

International Studies

Law

Linguistics/Communication

Natural Sciences

Biological Sciences

Philosophy/Ethics

Sociology

Joan Didion: *Marrying Absurd*   38

Ellen Goodman: *The Company Man*   98

Edward T. Hall: *The Anthropology of Manners*   188

Philip Meyer: *If Hitler Asked You to Electrocute a Stranger, Would You? Probably*   234

Jessica Mitford: *Behind the Formaldehyde Curtain*   63

Jo Goodwin Parker: *What Is Poverty?*   94

Gail Sheehy: *Predictable Crises of Adulthood*   115

Susan Sontag: *Women's Beauty: Put Down or Power Source?*   91

Deborah Tannen: *Talk in the Intimate Relationship: His and Hers*   156

Judith Viorst: *The Truth about Lying*   136

Preface

75 Readings: An Anthology introduces students to a range of classic and contemporary essays. The text also exposes them to a variety of rhetorical strategies, writing styles, themes, and topics. At the same time, it retains maximum flexibility for the instructor. We have continued to look for essays that provide good structural models for rhetorical techniques and that raise complex questions about current and enduring issues. Thus, the selections in this text need not be used merely to illustrate form.

For instructors who like the selections but do not organize their classes around rhetorical modes, we have included two alternate tables of contents, which arrange selections by themes and genres. Moreover, because there is no pedagogical apparatus in the text itself to direct its use, *75 Readings* is particularly adaptable to a variety of teaching approaches. However, for instructors who desire apparatus, the instructor's manual provides, for each selection, a brief author biography, comments introducing the essay, questions for discussion, prompts for responding to and engaging the text, and suggestions for sustained writing.

As with previous editions, we have sought the advice of many colleagues across the country to determine changes that would make this book even more effective and appealing as a learning tool for college readers and writers. Many of these professionals have put both the new and the old selections in this book to the ultimate test by using them in their classrooms. They have also provided helpful suggestions that have enabled us to fashion a new table of contents that makes *75 Readings* more versatile and more representative of contemporary American cultures than ever before.

CHANGES IN THE TENTH EDITION

Based on reviewers' suggestions, we designed the tenth edition to include:

- A new essay pairing on "cloning" in the chapter on argument and persuasion.
- Twenty new readings that add depth, diversity, and interest to the text:

Edward Abbey: *The Serpents of Paradise*

Frank Bures: *Test Day*

Michael Byers: *Monuments to Our Better Nature*

Annie Dillard: *Living Like Weasels*

David Ewing Duncan: *DNA as Destiny*

Joseph Epstein: *The Green-Eyed Monster: Envy Is Nothing to Be Jealous Of*

Martin Gansberg: *37 Who Saw Murder Didn't Call the Police*

James Greenwood and Sam Brownback: *Symposium: Should Congress Use Tax Dollars to Fund Therapeutic Cloning?*

Tom Haines: *Facing Famine*

Brendan I. Koerner: *Embryo Police*

Medicine Grizzlybear Lake: *An Indian Father's Plea*

John (Fire) Lame Deer and Richard Erdoes: *Alone on the Hilltop*

Alan Lightman: *Smile*

John McPhee: *Silk Parachute*

N. Scott Momaday: *Revisiting Sacred Ground*

Bharati Mukherjee: *Two Ways to Belong in America*

Paul Salopek: *Shattered Sudan*

Bailey White: *Forbidden Things*

Virginia Woolf: *Shakespeare's Sister*

William Zinsser: *Clutter*

SUPPLEMENTS

75 Readings gives students and instructors access to a Catalyst 2.0–powered Web site at www.mhhe.com/. Go online to find:

- Additional resources that complement selected readings in *75 Readings*
- Tutorials for document design and visual rhetoric
- Guides for avoiding plagiarism and evaluating sources
- Bibliomaker software for MLA, APA, Chicago, and CSE styles of documentation
- Many more tools that support students with their writing

Delivered in a new, state-of-the-art course management system featuring online peer-review utilities, a grade book, and communication tools, Catalyst 2.0 is available free with *75 Readings*.

Please consult your local McGraw-Hill representative or consult McGraw-Hill's Web site at www.mhhe.com/english for more information on the supplements that accompany *75 Readings*, 10E.

ACKNOWLEDGMENTS

Special thanks are due to those instructors who reviewed and helped us shape this anthology with their suggestions, particularly:

Robert Akin, Houston Community College System
Marc Arnold, University of Arkansas at Little Rock
Margaret Bartelt, Owens Community College
Carole Beasley, East Mississippi Community College
Kristina E. Benson, Jamestown Community College
Rebecca Blair, Wartburg College
Robinson Blann, Trevecca Nazarene University
Diane Whitley Bogard, Austin Community College
Bradley R. Bowers, Barry University
Regina Briefs-Elgin, New Mexico Highlands University
Polly Buckingham, Eastern Washington University
Mary V. Cantrell, Tulsa Community College
Ursula Carlson, Western Nevada Community College

Christine Caver, University of Texas at San Antonio
Ken Claney, Tulsa Community College
Richard A. Clark, Seattle Central Community College
Sarah V. Clere, Mount Olivet College
Walter P. Collins, University of South Carolina at Lancaster
Brenda Cornell, Central Texas College
Jonathan Dallas, Hibbing Community College
Dani Day, Cisco Junior College
Elizabeth A. Desy, Southwest Minnesota State University
Susan L. Dunston, New Mexico Tech
Tim Emerson, Onondaga Community College/SUNY Cortland
Janice Gardner, Peninsula College
Judy Glueckstein, University of Wisconsin–Green Bay
Dawn M. Hendrix, Central Oregon Community College
Jeff Kosse, Iowa Western Community College
Roba Kribs, Ancilla College
Henry Marchand, Cedar Crest College
Dorothy M. Martelle, Alfred University
Jeannine McDevitt, Pennsylvania Highlands Community College
Melaney Moisan, Chemeketa Community College
Julie Odell, Community College of Philadelphia
Ann Rayson, University of Hawaii at Manoa
Monika Riney, Thomas College
Joseph Turner, Johnson C. Smith University
Worth Weller, Indiana–Purdue University Fort Wayne

We also thank our friends at McGraw-Hill—Tori Fullard and Emily Hatteberg—and at Carlisle Publishing Services—Beth Baugh—who encouraged us and helped us continue these projects.

Finally, we want to hear what you think about this text. Please visit McGraw-Hill's English Garden Web site (www.mhhe.com/english) or e-mail english@mcgraw-hill.com to make suggestions or comments about *75 Readings* or to ask any questions about its use.

Santi Buscemi
Charlotte Smith

Narration

Shooting an Elephant

George Orwell

In Moulmein, in Lower Burma, I was hated by large numbers of 1 people—the only time in my life that I have been important enough for this to happen to me. I was sub-divisional police officer of the town, and in an aimless, petty kind of way anti-European feeling was very bitter. No one had the guts to raise a riot, but if a European woman went through the bazaars alone somebody would probably spit betel juice over her dress. As a police officer I was an obvious target and was baited whenever it seemed safe to do so. When a nimble Burman tripped me up on the football field and the referee (another Burman) looked the other way, the crowd yelled with hideous laughter. This happened more than once. In the end the sneering yellow faces of young men that met me everywhere, the insults hooted after me when I was at a safe distance, got badly on my nerves. The young Buddhist priests were the worst of all. There were several thousands of them in the town and none of them seemed to have anything to do except stand on street corners and jeer at Europeans.

All this was perplexing and upsetting. For at that time I had 2 already made up my mind that imperialism was an evil thing and the sooner I chucked up my job and got out of it the better. Theoretically—and secretly, of course—I was all for the Burmese and all against their oppressors, the British. As for the job I was doing, I hated it more bitterly than I can perhaps make clear. In a job like that you see the dirty work of Empire at close quarters. The wretched prisoners huddling in the stinking cages of the lock-ups, the grey, cowed faces of the long-term convicts, the scarred buttocks of the men who had been Bogged with bamboos—all these oppressed me with an intolerable sense of guilt. But I could get nothing into perspective. I was young and ill-educated and I had had to think out my problems in the utter silence that is imposed on every Englishman in the East. I did not even know that the British Empire is dying, still less did I know that it is a great deal better than the younger empires that are going to supplant it. All I knew was that I was stuck between my hatred of the empire I served and my rage against the evil-spirited little beasts who tried to make my job impossible. With one part of my mind I thought of the British Raj as an unbreakable tyranny, as something clamped down, in *saecula saeculorum,* upon the will of prostrate peoples; with another part I thought that the greatest joy in the world would be to drive a bayonet into a Buddhist priest's guts. Feelings like these are the normal by-products of imperialism; ask any Anglo-Indian official, if you can catch him off duty.

3   One day something happened which in a roundabout way was enlightening. It was a tiny incident in itself, but it gave me a better glimpse than I had had before of the real nature of imperialism—the real motives for which despotic governments act. Early one morning the subinspector at a police station the other end of the town rang me up on the phone and said that an elephant was ravaging the bazaar. Would I please come and do something about it? I did not know what I could do, but I wanted to see what was happening and I got on to a pony and started out. I took my rifle, an old .44 Winchester and much too small to kill an elephant, but I thought the noise might be useful *in terrorem.* Various Burmans stopped me on the way and told me about the elephant's doings. It was not, of course, a wild elephant, but a tame one which had gone "must." It had been chained up, as tame elephants always are when their attack of "must" is due, but on the previous night it had broken its chain and escaped. Its mahout, the only person who could manage it when it was in that state, had set out in pursuit, but had taken the wrong direction and was now twelve hours' journey away, and in the morning the elephant had suddenly reappeared in the town. The Burmese

population had no weapons and were quite helpless against it. It had already destroyed somebody's bamboo hut, killed a cow and raided some fruit-stalls and devoured the stock; also it had met the municipal rubbish van and, when the driver jumped out and took to his heels, had turned the van over and inflicted violences upon it.

   The Burmese sub-inspector and some Indian constables were waiting for me in the quarter where the elephant had been seen. It was a very poor quarter, a labyrinth of squalid bamboo huts, thatched with palmleaf, winding all over a steep hillside. I remember that it was a cloudy, stuffy morning at the beginning of the rains. We began questioning the people as to where the elephant had gone and, as usual, failed to get any definite information. That is invariably the case in the East; a story always sounds clear enough at a distance, but the nearer you get to the scene of events the vaguer it becomes. Some of the people said that the elephant had gone in one direction, some said that he had gone in another, some professed not even to have heard of any elephant. I had almost made up my mind that the whole story was a pack of lies, when we heard yells a little distance away. There was a loud, scandalized cry of "Go away, child! Go away this instant!" and an old woman with a switch in her hand came round the corner of a hut, violently shooing away a crowd of naked children. Some more women followed, clicking their tongues and exclaiming; evidently there was something that the children ought not to have seen. I rounded the hut and saw a man's dead body sprawling in the mud. He was an Indian, a black Dravidian coolie, almost naked, and he could not have been dead many minutes. The people said that the elephant had come suddenly upon him round the corner of the hut, caught him with its trunk, put its foot on his back and ground him into the earth. This was the rainy season and the ground was soft, and his face had scored a trench a foot deep and a couple of yards long. He was lying on his belly with arms crucified and head sharply twisted to one side. His face was coated with mud, the eyes wide open, the teeth bared and grinning with an expression of unendurable agony. (Never tell me, by the way, that the dead look peaceful. Most of the corpses I have seen looked devilish.) The friction of the great beast's foot had stripped the skin from his back as neatly as one skins a rabbit. As soon as I saw the dead man I sent an orderly to a friend's house nearby to borrow an elephant rifle. I had already sent back the pony, not wanting it to go mad with fright and throw me if it smelt the elephant.

5   The orderly came back in a few minutes with a rifle and five cartridges, and meanwhile some Burmans had arrived and told us that the elephant was in the paddy fields below, only a few hundred yards away. As I started forward practically the whole population of the quarter flocked out of the houses and followed me. They had seen the rifle and were all shouting excitedly that I was going to shoot the elephant. They had not shown much interest in the elephant when he was merely ravaging their homes, but it was different now that he was going to be shot. It was a bit of fun to them, as it would be to an English crowd; besides they wanted the meat. It made me vaguely uneasy. I had no intention of shooting the elephant—I had merely sent for the rifle to defend myself if necessary—and it is always unnerving to have a crowd following you. I marched down the hill, looking and feeling a fool, with the rifle over my shoulder and an ever-growing army of people jostling at my heels. At the bottom, when you got away from the huts, there was a metalled road and beyond that a miry waste of paddy fields a thousand yards across, not yet ploughed but soggy from the first rains and dotted with coarse grass. The elephant was standing eight yards from the road, his left side towards us. He took not the slightest notice of the crowd's approach. He was tearing up bunches of grass, beating them against his knees to clean them and stuffing them into his mouth.

6   I had halted on the road. As soon as I saw the elephant I knew with perfect certainty that I ought not to shoot him. It is a serious matter to shoot a working elephant—it is comparable to destroying a huge and costly piece of machinery—and obviously one ought not to do it if it can possibly be avoided. And at that distance, peacefully eating, the elephant looked no more dangerous than a cow. I thought then and I think now that his attack of "must" was already passing off; in which case he would merely wander harmlessly about until the mahout came back and caught

him. Moreover, I did not in the least want to shoot him. I decided that I would watch him for a little while to make sure that he did not turn savage again, and then go home.

But at that moment I glanced round at the crowd that had fol- 7 lowed me. It was an immense crowd, two thousand at the least and growing every minute. It blocked the road for a long distance on either side. I looked at the sea of yellow faces above the garish clothes—faces all happy and excited over this bit of fun, all certain that the elephant was going to be shot. They were watching me as they would watch a conjurer about to perform a trick. They did not like me, but with the magical rifle in my hands I was momentarily worth watching. And suddenly I realized that I should have to shoot the elephant after all. The people expected it of me and I had got to do it; I could feel their two thousand wills pressing me forward, irresistibly. And it was at this moment, as I stood there with the rifle in my hands, that I first grasped the hollowness, the futility of the white man's dominion in the East. Here was I, the white man with his gun, standing in front of the unarmed native crowd—seemingly the leading actor of the piece; but in reality I was only an absurd puppet pushed to and fro by the will of those yellow faces behind. I perceived in this moment that when the white man turns tyrant it is his own freedom that he destroys. He becomes a sort of hollow, posing dummy, the conventionalized figure of a sahib. For it is the condition of his rule that he shall spend his life in trying to impress the "natives," and so in every crisis he has got to do what the "natives" expect of him. He wears a mask, and his face grows to fit it. I had got to shoot the elephant. I had committed myself to doing it when I sent for the rifle. A sahib has got to act like a sahib; he has got to appear resolute, to know his own mind and do definite things. To come all that way, rifle in hand, with two thousand people marching at my heels, and then to trail feebly away, having done nothing—no, that was impossible. The crowd would laugh at me. And my whole life, every white man's life in the East, was one long struggle not to be laughed at.

But I did not want to shoot the elephant. I watched him beat- 8 ing his bunch of grass against his knees, with that preoccupied grandmotherly air that elephants have. It seemed to me that it would be murder to shoot him. At that age I was not squeamish about killing animals, but I had never shot an elephant and never wanted to. (Somehow it always seems worse to kill a *large* animal.) Besides, there was the beast's owner to be considered. Alive, the elephant was worth at least a hundred pounds; dead, he would only be worth the value of his tusks, five pounds, possibly. But I had got to act quickly. I turned to some experienced-looking Burmans who had been there when we arrived, and asked them how the elephant had been behaving. They all said the same thing: he took no notice of you if you left him alone, but he might charge if you went too close to him.

9   It was perfectly clear to me what I ought to do. I ought to walk up to within, say, twenty-five yards of the elephant and test his behavior. If he charged, I could shoot; if he took no notice of me, it would be safe to leave him until the mahout came back. But also I knew that I was going to do no such thing. I was a poor shot with a rifle and the ground was soft mud into which one would sink at every step. If the elephant charged and I missed him, I should have about as much chance as a toad under a steam-roller. But even then I was not thinking particularly of my own skin, only of the watchful yellow faces behind. For at that moment, with the crowd watching me, I was not afraid in the ordinary sense, as I would have been if I had been alone. A white man mustn't be frightened in front of "natives"; and so, in general, he isn't frightened. The sole thought in my mind was that if anything went wrong those two thousand Burmans would see me pursued, caught, trampled on and reduced to a grinning corpse like that Indian up the hill. And if that happened it was quite probable that some of them would laugh. That would never do. There was only one alternative. I shoved the cartridges into the magazine and lay down on the road to get a better aim.

10   The crowd grew very still, and a deep, low, happy sigh, as of people who see the theatre curtain go up at last, breathed from innumerable throats. They were going to have their bit of fun after all. The rifle was a beautiful German thing with cross-hair sights. I did not then know that in shooting an elephant one would shoot to cut an imaginary bar running from ear-hole to ear-hole. I ought,

therefore as the elephant was sideways on, to have aimed straight at his ear-hole, actually I aimed several inches in front of this, thinking the brain would be further forward.

When I pulled the trigger I did not hear the bang or feel the kick—one never does when a shot goes home—but I heard the devilish roar of glee that went up from the crowd. In that instant, in too short a time, one would have thought, even for the bullet to get there, a mysterious, terrible change had come over the elephant. He neither stirred nor fell, but every line of his body had altered. He looked suddenly stricken, shrunken, immensely old, as though the frightful impact of the bullet had paralysed him without knocking him down. At last, after what seemed a long time—it might have been five seconds, I dare say—he sagged flabbily to his knees. His mouth slobbered. An enormous senility seemed to have settled upon him. One could have imagined him thousands of years old. I fired again into the same spot. At the second shot he did not collapse but climbed with desperate slowness to his feet and stood weakly upright, with legs sagging and head drooping. I fired a third time. That was the shot that did for him. You could see the agony of it jolt his whole body and knock the last remnant of strength from his legs. But in falling he seemed for a moment to rise, for as his hind legs collapsed beneath him he seemed to tower upward like a huge rock toppling, his trunk reaching skyward like a tree. He trumpeted, for the first and only time. And then down he came, his belly towards me, with a crash that seemed to shake the ground even where I lay.

I got up. The Burmans were already racing past me across the mud. It was obvious that the elephant would never rise again, but he was not dead. He was breathing very rhythmically with long rattling gasps, his great mound of a side painfully rising and falling. His mouth was wide open—I could see far down into caverns of pale pink throat. I waited a long time for him to die, but his breathing did not weaken. Finally I fired my two remaining shots into the spot where I thought his heart must be. The thick blood welled out of him like red velvet, but still he did not die. His body did not even jerk when the shots hit him, the tortured breathing continued without a pause. He was dying, very slowly and in great agony, but in some world remote from me where not even a bullet could damage him further. I felt that I had got to put an end to that dreadful noise. It seemed dreadful to see the great beast lying there, powerless to move and yet powerless to die, and not even to be able to finish him. I sent back for my small rifle and poured shot after shot into his heart and down his throat. They seemed to make no impression. The tortured gasps continued as steadily as the ticking of a clock.

13   In the end I could not stand it any longer and went away. I heard later that it took him half an hour to die. Burmans were bringing dahs and baskets even before I left, and I was told they had stripped his body almost to the bones by the afternoon.

14   Afterwards, of course, there were endless discussions about the shooting of the elephant. The owner was furious, but he was only an Indian and could do nothing. Besides, legally I had done the right thing, for a mad elephant has to be killed, like a mad dog, if its owner fails to control it. Among the Europeans opinion was divided. The older men said I was right, the younger men said it was a damn shame to shoot an elephant for killing a coolie, because an elephant was worth more than any damn Coringhee coolie. And afterwards I was very glad that the coolie had been killed; it put me legally in the right and it gave me a sufficient pretext for shooting the elephant. I often wondered whether any of the others grasped that I had done it solely to avoid looking a fool.

1936

Salvation

Langston Hughes

1   I was saved from sin when I was going on thirteen. But not really saved. It happened like this. There was a big revival at my Auntie Reed's church. Every night for weeks there had been much preaching, singing, praying, and shouting, and some very hardened sinners had been brought to Christ, and the membership of

the church had grown by leaps and bounds. Then just before the revival ended, they held a special meeting for children, "to bring the young lambs to the fold." My aunt spoke of it for days ahead. That night I was escorted to the front row and placed on the mourners' bench with all the other young sinners, who had not yet been brought to Jesus.

My aunt told me that when you were saved you saw a light, 2 and something happened to you inside! And Jesus came into your life! And God was with you from then on! She said you could see and hear and feel Jesus in your soul. I believed her. I had heard a great many old people say the same thing and it seemed to me they ought to know. So I sat there calmly in the hot, crowded church, waiting for Jesus to come to me.

The preacher preached a wonderful rhythmical sermon, all 3 moans and shouts and lonely cries and dire pictures of hell, and then he sang a song about the ninety and nine safe in the fold, but one little lamb was left out in the cold. Then he said: "Won't you come? Won't you come to Jesus? Young lambs, won't you come?" And he held out his arms to all us young sinners there on the mourners' bench. And the little girls cried. And some of them jumped up and went to Jesus right away. But most of us just sat there.

A great many old people came and knelt around us and 4 prayed, old women with jet-black faces and braided hair, old men with work-gnarled hands. And the church sang a song about the lower lights are burning, some poor sinners to be saved. And the whole building rocked with prayer and song.

Still I kept waiting to *see* Jesus. 5

Finally all the young people had gone to the altar and were 6 saved, but one boy and me. He was a rounder's son named Westley. Westley and I were surrounded by sisters and deacons praying. It was very hot in the church, and getting late now. Finally Westley said to me in a whisper: "God damn! I'm tired o' sitting here. Let's get up and be saved." So he got up and was saved.

Then I was left all alone on the mourners' bench. My aunt 7 came and knelt at my knees and cried, while prayers and songs swirled all around me in the little church. The whole congregation prayed for me alone, in a mighty wail of moans and voices. And I kept waiting serenely for Jesus, waiting, waiting—but he didn't come. I wanted to see him, but nothing happened to me. Nothing! I wanted something to happen to me, but nothing happened.

8   I heard the songs and the minister saying: "Why don't you come? My dear child, why don't you come to Jesus? Jesus is waiting for you. He wants you. Why don't you come? Sister Reed, what is this child's name?"

9   "Langston," my aunt sobbed.

10   "Langston, why don't you come? Why don't you come and be saved? Oh, Lamb of God! Why don't you come?"

11   Now it was really getting late. I began to be ashamed of myself, holding everything up so long. I began to wonder what God thought about Westley, who certainly hadn't seen Jesus either, but who was now sitting proudly on the platform, swinging his knickerbockered legs and grinning down at me, surrounded by deacons and old women on their knees praying. God had not struck Westley dead for taking his name in vain or for lying in the temple. So I decided that maybe to save further trouble, I'd better lie, too, and say that Jesus had come, and get up and be saved.

12   So I got up.

13   Suddenly the whole room broke into a sea of shouting, as they saw me rise. Waves of rejoicing swept the place. Women leaped in the air. My aunt threw her arms around me. The minister took me by the hand and led me to the platform.

14   When things quieted down, in a hushed silence, punctuated by a few ecstatic "Amens," all the new young lambs were blessed in the name of God. Then joyous singing filled the room.

15   That night, for the last time in my life but one—for I was a big boy twelve years old—I cried. I cried, in bed alone, and couldn't stop. I buried my head under the quilts, but my aunt heard me. She woke up and told my uncle I was crying because the Holy Ghost had come into my life, and because I had seen Jesus. But I was really crying because I couldn't bear to tell her that I had lied, that I had deceived everybody in the church, that I hadn't seen Jesus, and that now I didn't believe there was a Jesus any more, since he didn't come to help me.

1940

Grandmother's Victory

Maya Angelou

"Thou shall not be dirty" and "Thou shall not be impudent" were 1
the two commandments of Grandmother Henderson upon which
hung our total salvation.

Each night in the bitterest winter we were forced to wash 2
faces, arms, necks, legs, and feet before going to bed. She used to
add, with a smirk that unprofane people can't control when ven-
turing into profanity, "and wash as far as possible, then wash
possible."

We would go to the well and wash in the ice-cold, clear water, 3
grease our legs with the equally cold stiff Vaseline, then tiptoe into
the house. We wiped the dust from our toes and settled down for
schoolwork, cornbread, clabbered milk, prayers, and bed, always
in that order. Momma was famous for pulling the quilts off after we
had fallen asleep to examine our feet. If they weren't clean enough
for her, she took the switch (she kept one behind the bedroom door
for emergencies) and woke up the offender with a few aptly placed
burning reminders.

The area around the well at night was dark and slick, and 4
boys told about how snakes love water, so that anyone who had
to draw water at night and then stand there alone and wash knew
that moccasins and rattlers, puff adders, and boa constrictors
were winding their way to the well and would arrive just as the
person washing got soap in her eyes. But Momma convinced us
that not only was cleanliness next to Godliness, dirtiness was the
inventor of misery.

The impudent child was detested by God and a shame to its 5
parents and could bring destruction to its house and line. All
adults had to be addressed as Mister, Missus, Miss, Auntie,
Cousin, Unk, Uncle, Buhbah, Sister, Brother, and a thousand other
appellations indicating familial relationship and the lowliness of
the addressor.

Everyone I knew respected these customary laws, except for 6
the powhitetrash children.

Some families of powhitetrash lived on Momma's farmland 7
behind the school. Sometimes a gaggle of them came to the Store,

filling the whole room, chasing out the air, and even changing the well-known scents. The children crawled over the shelves and into the potato and onion bins, twanging all the time in their sharp voices like cigar-box guitars. They took liberties in my Store that I would never dare. Since Momma told us that the less you say to whitefolks (or even powhitetrash) the better, Bailey and I would stand, solemn, quiet, in the displaced air. But if one of the playful apparitions got close to us, I pinched it. Partly out of angry frustration and partly because I didn't believe in its flesh reality.

8   They called my uncle by his first name and ordered him around the Store. He, to my crying shame, obeyed them in his limping dip-straight-dip fashion.

9   My grandmother, too, followed their orders, except that she didn't seem to be servile because she anticipated their needs.

10   "Here's sugar, Miz Potter, and here's baking powder. You didn't buy soda last month, you'll probably be needing some."

11   Momma always directed her statements to the adults, but sometimes, Oh painful sometimes, the grimy, snotty-nosed girls would answer her.

12   "Naw, Annie . . ."—to Momma? Who owned the land they lived on? Who forgot more than they would ever learn? If there was any justice in the world, God should strike them dumb at once!—"Just give us some extra sody crackers, and some more mackerel."

13   At least they never looked in her face, or I never caught them doing so. Nobody with a smidgen of training, not even the worst roustabout, would look right in a grown person's face. It meant the person was trying to take the words out before they were formed. The dirty little children didn't do that, but they threw their orders around the Store like lashes from a cat-o'-nine-tails.

14   When I was around ten years old, those scruffy children caused me the most painful and confusing experience I had ever had with my grandmother.

15   One summer morning, after I had swept the dirt yard of leaves, spearmint-gum wrappers and Vienna-sausage labels, I raked the yellow-red dirt, and made half-moons carefully, so that the design stood out clearly and mask-like. I put the rake behind

the Store and came through the back of the house to find
Grandmother on the front porch in her big, wide white apron.
The apron was so stiff by virtue of the starch that it could have
stood alone. Momma was admiring the yard, so I joined her. It
truly looked like a flat redhead that had been raked with a big-
toothed comb. Momma didn't say anything but I knew she liked
it. She looked over toward the school principal's house and to the
right at Mr. McElroy's. She was hoping one of those community
pillars would see the design before the day's business wiped it
out. Then she looked upward to the school. My head had swung
with hers, so at just about the same time we saw a troop of
powhitetrash kids marching over the hill and down by the side of
the school.

I looked to Momma for direction. She did an excellent job of 16
sagging from her waist down, but from the waist up she seemed
to be pulling for the top of the oak tree across the road. Then she
began to moan a hymn. Maybe not to moan, but the tune was so
slow and the meter so strange that she could have been moaning.
She didn't look at me again. When the children reached halfway
down the hill, halfway to the Store, she said without turning,
"Sister, go on inside."

I wanted to beg her, "Momma, don't wait for them. Come on 17
inside with me. If they come in the Store, you go to the bedroom
and let me wait on them. They only frighten me if you're around.
Alone I know how to handle them." But of course I couldn't say
anything, so I went in and stood behind the screen door.

Before the girls got to the porch I heard their laughter crack- 18
ling and popping like pine logs in a cooking stove. I suppose my
lifelong paranoia was born in those cold, molasses-slow minutes.
They came finally to stand on the ground in front of Momma. At
first they pretended seriousness. Then one of them wrapped her
right arm in the crook of her left, pushed out her mouth and
started to hum. I realized that she was aping my grandmother.
Another said, "Naw, Helen, you ain't standing like her. This
here's it." Then she lifted her chest, folded her arms and mocked
that strange carriage that was Annie Henderson. Another
laughed, "Naw, you can't do it. Your mouth ain't pooched out
enough. It's like this."

19   I thought about the rifle behind the door, but I knew I'd never be able to hold it straight, and the .410, our sawed-off shotgun, which stayed loaded and was fired every New Year's night, was locked in the trunk and Uncle Willie had the key on his chain. Through the fly-specked screen door, I could see that the arms of Momma's apron jiggled from the vibrations of her humming. But her knees seemed to have locked as if they would never bend again.

20   She sang on. No louder than before, but no softer either. No slower or faster.

21   The dirt of the girls' cotton dresses continued on their legs, feet, arms, and faces to make them all of a piece. Their greasy uncolored hair hung down, uncombed, with a grim finality. I knelt to see them better, to remember them for all time. The tears that had slipped down my dress left unsurprising dark spots, and made the front yard blurry and even more unreal. The world had taken a deep breath and was having doubts about continuing to revolve.

22   The girls had tired of mocking Momma and turned to other means of agitation. One crossed her eyes, stuck her thumbs in both sides of her mouth and said, "Look here, Annie." Grandmother hummed on and the apron strings trembled. I wanted to throw a handful of black pepper in their faces, to throw lye on them, to scream that they were dirty, scummy peckerwoods, but I knew I was as clearly imprisoned behind the scene as the actors outside were confined to their roles.

23   One of the smaller girls did a kind of puppet dance while her fellow clowns laughed at her. But the tall one, who was almost a woman, said something very quietly, which I couldn't hear. They all moved backward from the porch, still watching Momma. For an awful second I thought they were going to throw a rock at Momma, who seemed (except for the apron strings) to have turned into stone herself. But the big girl turned her back, bent down and put her hands flat on the ground—she didn't pick up anything. She simply shifted her weight and did a hand stand.

24   Her dirty bare feet and long legs went straight for the sky. Her dress fell down around her shoulders, and she had on no drawers. The slick pubic hair made a brown triangle where her

legs came together. She hung in the vacuum of that lifeless morning for only a few seconds, then wavered and tumbled. The other girls clapped her on the back and slapped their hands.

Momma changed her song to "Bread of Heaven, Bread of 25
Heaven, feed me till I want no more."

I found that I was praying too. How long could Momma hold 26
out? What new indignity would they think of to subject her to?
Would I be able to stay out of it? What would Momma really like
me to do?

Then they were moving out of the yard, on their way to town. 27
They bobbed their heads and shook their slack behinds and
turned, one at a time:

"'Bye, Annie."   28

"'Bye, Annie."   29

"'Bye, Annie."   30

Momma never turned her head or unfolded her arms, but she 31
stopped singing and said, "'Bye, Miz Helen, 'bye, Miz Ruth, 'bye,
Miz Eloise."

I burst. A firecracker July-the-Fourth burst. How could 32
Momma call them Miz? The mean nasty things. Why couldn't she
have come inside the sweet, cool store when we saw them breasting the hill? What did she prove? And then if they were dirty,
mean, and impudent, why did Momma have to call them Miz?

She stood another whole song through and then opened the 33
screen door to look down on me crying in rage. She looked
until I looked up. Her face was a brown moon that shone on me.
She was beautiful. Something had happened out there, which I
couldn't completely understand, but I could see that she was
happy. Then she bent down and touched me as mothers of the
church "lay hands on the sick and afflicted" and I quieted.

"Go wash your face, Sister." And she went behind the candy 34
counter and hummed, "Glory, glory, hallelujah, when I lay my
burden down."

I threw the well water on my face and used the weekday 35
handkerchief to blow my nose. Whatever the contest had been
out front, I knew Momma had won.

I took the rake back to the front yard. The smudged footprints 36
were easy to erase. I worked for a long time on my new design

and laid the rake behind the wash pot. When I came back in the Store, I took Momma's hand and we both walked outside to look at the pattern.

37   It was a large heart with lots of hearts growing smaller inside, and piercing from the outside rim to the smallest heart was an arrow. Momma said, "Sister, that's right pretty." Then she turned back to the Store and resumed, "Glory, glory, hallelujah, when I lay my burden down."

1970

Coming to an Awareness of Language

Malcolm X

1   I've never been one for inaction. Everything I've ever felt strongly about, I've done something about. I guess that's why, unable to do anything else, I soon began writing to people I had known in the hustling world, such as Sammy the Pimp, John Hughes, the gambling house owner, the thief Jumpsteady, and several dope peddlers. I wrote them all about Allah and Islam and Mr. Elijah Muhammad. I had no idea where most of them lived. I addressed their letters in care of the Harlem or Roxbury bars and clubs where I'd known them.

2   I never got a single reply. The average hustler and criminal was too uneducated to write a letter. I have known many slick, sharp-looking hustlers, who would have you think they had an interest in Wall Street; privately, they would get someone else to read a letter if they received one. Besides, neither would I have replied to anyone writing me something as wild as "the white man is the devil."

3   What certainly went on the Harlem and Roxbury wires was that Detroit Red was going crazy in stir, or else he was trying some hype to shake up the warden's office.

4   During the years that I stayed in the Norfolk Prison Colony, never did any official directly say anything to me about those

letters, although, of course, they all passed through the prison censorship. I'm sure, however, they monitored what I wrote to add to the files which every state and federal prison keeps on the conversion of Negro inmates by the teachings of Mr. Elijah Muhammad.

But at that time, I felt that the real reason was that the white 5 man knew that he was the devil.

Later on, I even wrote to the Mayor of Boston, to the Governor 6 of Massachusetts, and to Harry S. Truman. They never answered; they probably never even saw my letters. I handscratched to them how the white man's society was responsible for the black man's condition in this wilderness of North America.

It was because of my letters that I happened to stumble upon 7 starting to acquire some kind of a homemade education.

I became increasingly frustrated at not being able to express 8 what I wanted to convey in letters that I wrote, especially those to Mr. Elijah Muhammad. In the street, I had been the most articulate hustler out there—I had commanded attention when I said something. But now, trying to write simple English, I not only wasn't articulate, I wasn't even functional. How would I sound writing in slang, the way I would *say* it, something such as, "Look, daddy, let me pull your coat about a cat, Elijah Muhammad—"

Many who today hear me somewhere in person, or on tel- 9 evision, or those who read something I've said, will think I went to school far beyond the eighth grade. This impression is due entirely to my prison studies.

It had really begun back in the Charlestown Prison, when 10 Bimbi first made me feel envy of his stock of knowledge. Bimbi had always taken charge of any conversation he was in, and I had tried to emulate him. But every book I picked up had few sentences which didn't contain anywhere from one to nearly all of the words that might as well have been in Chinese. When I just skipped those words, of course, I really ended up with little idea of what the book said. So I had come to the Norfolk Prison Colony still going through only book-reading motions. Pretty soon, I would have quit even these motions, unless I had received the motivation that I did.

11   I saw that the best thing I could do was get hold of a dictionary—to study, to learn some words. I was lucky enough to reason also that I should try to improve my penmanship. It was sad. I couldn't even write in a straight line. It was both ideas together that moved me to request a dictionary along with some tablets and pencils from the Norfolk Prison Colony school.

12   I spent two days just riffling uncertainly through the dictionary's pages. I'd never realized so many words existed! I didn't know *which* words I needed to learn. Finally, just to start some kind of action, I began copying.

13   In my slow, painstaking, ragged handwriting, I copied into my tablet everything printed on that first page, down to the punctuation marks.

14   I believe it took me a day. Then, aloud, I read back, to myself, everything I'd written on the tablet. Over and over, aloud, to myself, I read my own handwriting.

15   I woke up the next morning, thinking about those words—immensely proud to realize that not only had I written so much at one time, but I'd written words that I never knew were in the world. Moreover, with a little effort, I also could remember what many of these words meant. I reviewed the words whose meanings I didn't remember. Funny thing, from the dictionary first page right now, that "aardvark" springs to my mind. The dictionary had a picture of it, a long-tailed, long-eared, burrowing African mammal, which lives off termites caught by sticking out its tongue as an anteater does for ants.

16   I was so fascinated that I went on—I copied the dictionary's next page. And the same experience came when I studied that. With every succeeding page, I also learned of people and places and events from history. Actually the dictionary is like a miniature encyclopedia. Finally the dictionary's A section had filled a whole tablet—and I went on into the B's. That was the way I started copying what eventually became the entire dictionary. It went a lot faster after so much practice helped me to pick up handwriting speed. Between what I wrote in my tablet, and writing letters, during the rest of my time in prison I would guess I wrote a million words.

17   I suppose it was inevitable that as my word-base broadened, I could for the first time pick up a book and read and now begin to

understand what the book was saying. Anyone who has read a great deal can imagine the new world that opened. Let me tell you something: from then until I left that prison, in every free moment I had, if I was not reading in the library, I was reading on my bunk. You couldn't have gotten me out of books with a wedge. Between Mr. Muhammad's teachings, my correspondence, my visitors . . . and my reading of books, months passed without my even thinking about being imprisoned. In fact, up to then, I never had been so truly free in my life.

1965

Me Talk Pretty One Day

David Sedaris

Welcome to French class, where you must learn to juggle irregular verbs, flying chalk, and the constant threat of bodily harm. At the age of forty-one, I am returning to school and having to think of myself as what my French textbook calls "a true debutant." After paying my tuition, I was issued a student ID, which allows me a discounted entry fee at movie theaters, puppet shows, and Festyland, a far-flung amusement park that advertises with billboards picturing a cartoon stegosaurus sitting in a canoe and eating what appears to be a ham sandwich.   1

I've moved to Paris in order to learn the language. My school is the Alliance Francaise, and on the first day of class, I arrived early, watching as the returning students greeted one another in the school lobby. Vacations were recounted, and questions were raised concerning mutual friends with names like Kang and Vlatnya. Regardless of their nationalities, everyone spoke what sounded to me like excellent French. Some accents were better than others, but the students exhibited an ease and confidence I found intimidating. As an added discomfort, they were all young, attractive, and well dressed, causing me to feel not unlike Pa Kettle trapped backstage after a fashion show.   2

3   I remind myself that I am now a full-grown man. No one will ever again card me for a drink or demand that I weave a floor mat out of newspapers. At my age, a reasonable person should have completed his sentence in the prison of the nervous and the insecure—isn't that the great promise of adulthood? I can't help but think that, somewhere along the way, I made a wrong turn. My fears have not vanished. Rather, they have seasoned and multiplied with age. I am now twice as frightened as I was when, at the age of twenty, I allowed a failed nursing student to inject me with a horse tranquilizer, and eight times more anxious than I was the day my kindergarten teacher pried my fingers off my mother's ankle and led me screaming toward my desk. "You'll get used to it," the woman had said. I'm still waiting.

4   The first day of class was nerve-racking, because I knew I'd be expected to perform. That's the way they do it here—everyone into the language pool, sink or swim. The teacher marched in, deeply tanned from a recent vacation, and rattled off a series of administrative announcements. I've spent some time in Normandy, and I took a monthlong French class last summer in New York. I'm not completely in the dark, yet I understood only half of what this teacher was saying.

5   "If you have not meismslsxp by this time, you should not be in this room. Has everybody apzkiubjxow? Everyone? Good, we shall proceed." She spread out her lesson plan and sighed, saying, "All right, then, who knows the alphabet?"

6   It was startling, because a) I hadn't been asked that question in a while, and b) I realized, while laughing, that I myself did not know the alphabet. They're the same letters, but they're pronounced differently.

7   "Ahh." The teacher went to the board and sketched the letter a. "Do we have anyone in the room whose first name commences with an ahh?"

8   Two Polish Annas raised their hands, and the teacher instructed them to present themselves, giving their names, nationalities, occupations, and a list of things they liked and disliked in this world. The first Anna hailed from an industrial town outside of Warsaw and had front teeth the size of tombstones. She worked as a seamstress, enjoyed quiet times with friends, and hated the mosquito.

"Oh, really," the teacher said. "How very interesting. I ₉ thought that everyone loved the mosquito, but here, in front of all the world, you claim to detest him. How is it that we've been blessed with someone as unique and original as you? Tell us, please."

The seamstress did not understand what was being said, but ₁₀ she knew that this was an occasion for shame. Her rabbity mouth huffed for breath, and she stared down at her lap as though the appropriate comeback were stitched somewhere alongside the zipper of her slacks.

The second Anna learned from the first and claimed to love ₁₁ sunshine and detest lies. It sounded like a translation of one of those Playmate of the Month data sheets, the answers always written in the same loopy handwriting: "Turn-ons: Mom's famous five-alarm chili! Turnoffs: Insincerity and guys who come on too strong!!!"

The two Polish women surely had clear notions of what ₁₂ they liked and disliked, but, like the rest of us, they were limited in terms of vocabulary, and this made them appear less than sophisticated. The teacher forged on, and we learned that Carlos, the Argentine bandonion player, loved wine, music, and, in his words, "Making sex with the women of the world." Next came a beautiful young Yugoslavian who identified herself as an optimist, saying that she loved everything life had to offer.

The teacher licked her lips, revealing a hint of the sadist we ₁₃ would later come to know. She crouched low for her attack, placed her hands on the young woman's desk, and said, "Oh, yeah? And do you love your little war?"

While the optimist struggled to defend herself, I scrambled to ₁₄ think of an answer to what had obviously become a trick question. How often are you asked what you love in this world? More important, how often are you asked and then publicly ridiculed for your answer? I recalled my mother, flushed with wine, pounding the table late one night, saying, "Love? I love a good steak cooked rare. I love my cat, and I love . . ." My sisters and I leaned forward, waiting to hear our names. "Tums," our mother said. "I love Tums."

15   The teacher killed some time accusing the Yugoslavian girl of masterminding a program of genocide, and I jotted frantic notes in the margins of my pad. While I can honestly say that I love leafing through medical textbooks devoted to severe dermatological conditions, it is beyond the reach of my French vocabulary, and acting it out would only have invited unwanted attention.

16   When called upon, I delivered an effortless list of things I detest: blood sausage, intestinal pate, brain pudding. I'd learned these words the hard way. Having given it some thought, I then declared my love for IBM typewriters, the French word for "bruise," and my electric floor waxer. It was a short list, but still I managed to mispronounce IBM and afford the wrong gender to both the floor waxer and the typewriter. Her reaction led me to believe that these mistakes were capital crimes in the country of France.

17   "Were you always this palicmkrexjs?" she asked. "Even a fiuscrzsws tociwegixp knows that a typewriter is feminine."

18   I absorbed as much of her abuse as I could understand, thinking, but not saying, that I find it ridiculous to assign a gender to an inanimate object incapable of disrobing and making an occasional fool of itself. Why refer to Lady Flesh Wound or Good Sir Dishrag when these things could never deliver in the sack?

19   The teacher proceeded to belittle everyone from German Eva, who hated laziness, to Japanese Yukari, who loved paintbrushes and soap. Italian, Thai, Dutch, Korean, Chinese—we all left class foolishly believing that the worst was over. We didn't know it then, but the coming months would teach us what it is like to spend time in the presence of a wild animal. We soon learned to dodge chalk and to cover our heads and stomachs whenever she approached us with a question. She hadn't yet punched anyone, but it seemed wise to prepare ourselves against the inevitable.

20   Though we were forbidden to speak anything but French, the teacher would occasionally use us to practice any of her five fluent languages.

21   "I hate you," she said to me one afternoon. Her English was flawless. "I really, really hate you." Call me sensitive, but I couldn't help taking it personally.

22   Learning French is a lot like joining a gang in that it involves a long and intensive period of hazing. And it wasn't just my

teacher; the entire population seemed to be in on it. Following brutal encounters with my local butcher and the concierge of my building, I'd head off to class, where the teacher would hold my corrected paperwork high above her head, shouting, "Here's proof that David is an ignorant and uninspired ensigiejsokhjx."

Refusing to stand convicted on the teacher's charges of lazi- 23 ness, I'd spend four hours a night on my homework, working even longer whenever we were assigned an essay. I suppose I could have gotten by with less, but I was determined to create some sort of an identity for myself. We'd have one of those "complete the sentence" exercises, and I'd fool with the thing for hours, invariably settling on something like, "A quick run around the lake? I'd love to. Just give me a minute to strap on my wooden leg." The teacher, through word and action, conveyed the message that, if this was my idea of an identity, she wanted nothing to do with it.

My fear and discomfort crept beyond the borders of my class- 24 room and accompanied me out onto the wide boulevards, where, no matter how hard I tried, there was no escaping the feeling of terror I felt whenever anyone asked me a question. I was safe in any kind of a store, as, at least in my neighborhood, one can stand beside the cash register for hours on end without being asked something so trivial as, "May I help you?" or "How would you like to pay for that?" My only comfort was the knowledge that I was not alone.

Huddled in the smoky hallways and making the most of our 25 pathetic French, my fellow students and I engaged in the sort of conversation commonly overheard in refugee camps.

"Sometimes me cry alone at night." 26

"That is common for me also, but be more strong, you. Much 27 work, and someday you talk pretty. People stop hate you soon. Maybe tomorrow, okay?"

Unlike other classes I have taken, here there was no sense 28 of competition. When the teacher poked a shy Korean woman in the eyelid with a freshly sharpened pencil, we took no comfort in the fact that, unlike Hyeyoon Cho, we all knew the irregular past tense of the verb "to defeat." In all fairness, the teacher hadn't meant to hurt the woman, but neither did she spend much time apologizing, saying only, "Well, you should have been paying more attention."

29   Over time, it became impossible to believe that any of us would ever improve. Fall arrived, and it rained every day. It was mid-October when the teacher singled me out, saying, "Every day spent with you is like having a cesarean section." And it struck me that, for the first time since arriving in France, I could understand every word that someone was saying.

30   Understanding doesn't mean that you can suddenly speak the language. Far from it. It's a small step, nothing more, yet its rewards are intoxicating and deceptive. The teacher continued her diatribe, and I settled back, bathing in the subtle beauty of each new curse and insult.

31   "You exhaust me with your foolishness and reward my efforts with nothing but pain, do you understand me?"

32   The world opened up, and it was with great joy that I responded, "I know the thing what you speak exact now. Talk me more, plus, please, plus."

2000

37 Who Saw Murder Didn't Call the Police

Martin Gansberg

1 For more than half an hour 38 respectable, law-abiding citizens in Queens watched a killer stalk and stab a woman in three separate attacks in Kew Gardens.

2   Twice the sound of their voices and the sudden glow of their bedroom lights interrupted him and frightened him off. Each time he returned, sought her out and stabbed her again. Not one person telephoned the police during the assault; one witness called after the woman was dead.

3   That was two weeks ago today. But Assistant Chief Inspector Frederick M. Lussen, in charge of the borough's detectives

and a veteran of 25 years of homicide investigations, is still shocked.

He can give a matter-of-fact recitation of many murders. But 4 the Kew Gardens slaying baffles him—not because it is a murder, but because the "good people" failed to call the police.

"As we have reconstructed the crime," he said, "the assailant 5 had three chances to kill this woman during a 35-minute period. He returned twice to complete the job. If we had been called when he first attacked, the woman might not be dead now."

This is what the police say happened beginning at 3:20 A.M. in 6 the staid, middle-class, tree-lined Austin Street area:

Twenty-eight-year-old Catherine Genovese, who was called 7 Kitty by almost everyone in the neighborhood, was returning home from her job as manager of a bar in Hollis. She parked her red Fiat in a lot adjacent to the Kew Gardens Long Island Rail Road Station, facing Mowbray Place. Like many residents of the neighborhood, she had parked there day after day since her arrival from Connecticut a year ago, although the railroad frowns on the practice.

She turned off the lights to her car, locked the door and 8 started to walk the 100 feet to the entrance of her apartment at 82-70 Austin Street, which is in a Tudor building, with stores on the first floor and apartments on the second.

The entrance to the apartment is in the rear of the building 9 because the front is rented to retail stores. At night the quiet neighborhood is shrouded in the slumbering darkness that marks most residential areas.

Miss Genovese noticed a man at the far end of the lot, near a 10 seven-story apartment house at 82-40 Austin Street. She halted. Then, nervously, she headed up Austin Street toward Leffers Boulevard, where there is a call box to the 102d Police Precinct in nearby Richmond Hill.

She got as far as a street light in front of a bookstore before the 11 man grabbed her. She screamed. Lights went on in the 10-story apartment house at 82-67 Austin Street, which faces the book-store. Windows slid open, and voices punctured the early-morning stillness.

Miss Genovese screamed: "Oh, my God, he stabbed me! 12 Please help me! Please help me!"

13   From one of the upper windows in the apartment house, a man called down: "Let that girl alone!"

14   The assailant looked up at him, shrugged and walked down Austin Street toward a white sedan parked a short distance away. Miss Genovese struggled to her feet.

15   Lights went out. The killer returned to Miss Genovese, now trying to make her way around the side of the building by the parking lot to get to her apartment. The assailant stabbed her again.

16   "I'm dying!" she shrieked. "I'm dying!"

17   Windows were opened again, and lights went on in many apartments. The assailant got into his car and drove away. Miss Genovese staggered to her feet. A city bus, Q-10, the Lefferts Boulevard line to Kennedy International Airport, passed. It was 3:35 A.M.

18   The assailant returned. By then, Miss Genovese had crawled to the back of the building, where the freshly painted brown doors to the apartment house held out hope of safety. The killer tried the first door; she wasn't there. At the second door, 82-62 Austin Street, he saw her slumped on the floor at the foot of the stairs. He stabbed her a third time—fatally.

19   It was 3:50 by the time the police received their first call, from a man who was a neighbor of Miss Genovese. In two minutes they were at the scene. The neighbor, a 70-year-old woman and another woman were the only persons on the street. Nobody else came forward.

20   The man explained that he had called the police after much deliberation. He had phoned a friend in Nassau County for advice and then he had crossed the roof of the building to the apartment of the elderly woman to get her to make the call.

21   "I didn't want to get involved," he sheepishly told the police.

22   Six days later, the police arrested Winston Moseley, a 29-year-old business-machine operator, and charged him with the homicide. Moseley had no previous record. He is married, has two children and owns a home at 133-19 Sutter Avenue, South Ozone Park, Queens. On Wednesday, a court committed him to Kings County Hospital for psychiatric observation.

23   When questioned by the police, Moseley also said that he had slain Mrs. Annie Mae Johnson, 24, of 146-12 133d Avenue,

Jamaica, on Feb. 29 and Barbara Kralik, 15, of 174-17 140th Avenue, Springfield Gardens, last July. In the Kralik case the police are holding Alvin L. Mitchell, who is said to have confessed to that slaying.

The police stressed how simple it would have been to have gotten in touch with them. "A phone call," said one of the detectives, "would have done it." The police may be reached by dialing "O" for operator or SPring 7-3100. 24

The question of whether the witnesses can be held legally responsible in any way for the failure to report the crime was put to the Police Department's legal bureau. There, a spokesman said: 25

"There is no legal responsibility, with few exceptions, for any citizen to report a crime." 26

Under the statutes of the city, he said, a witness to a suspicious or violent death must report it to the medical examiner. Under the state law, a witness cannot withhold information in a kidnapping. 27

Today witnesses from the neighborhood, which is made up of one-family homes in the $35,000 to $60,000 range with the exception of the two apartment houses near the railroad station, find it difficult to explain why they didn't call the police. 28

Lieut. Bernard Jacobs, who handled the investigation by the detectives, said: 29

"It is one of the better neighborhoods. There are few reports of crimes. You only get the usual complaints about boys playing or garbage cans being turned over." 30

The police said most persons had told them they had been afraid to call but had given meaningless answers when asked what they had feared. 31

"We can understand the reticence of people to become involved in an area of violence," Lieutenant Jacobs said, "but when they are in their homes, near phones, why should they be afraid to call the police?" 32

He said his men were able to piece together what happened—and capture the suspect—because the residents furnished all the information when detectives rang doorbells during the days following the slaying. 33

"But why didn't someone call us that night?" he asked unbelievingly. 34

35   Witnesses—some of them unable to believe what they had allowed to happen—told a reporter why.

36   A housewife, knowingly if quite casual, said, "We thought it was a lover's quarrel." A husband and wife both said, "Frankly, we were afraid." They seemed aware of the fact that events might have been different. A distraught woman, wiping her hands in her apron, said, "I didn't want my husband to get involved."

37   One couple, now willing to talk about that night, said they heard the first screams. The husband looked thoughtfully at the bookstore where the killer first grabbed Miss Genovese.

38   "We went to the window to see what was happening," he said, "But the light from our bedroom made it difficult to see the street." The wife, still apprehensive, added: "I put out the light, and we were able to see better."

39   Asked why they hadn't called the police, she shrugged and replied: "I don't know."

40   A man peeked out from a slight opening in the doorway to his apartment and rattled off an account of the killer's second attack. Why hadn't he called the police at the time? "I was tired," he said without emotion. "I went back to bed."

41   It was 4:25 A.M. when the ambulance arrived for the body of Miss Genovese. It drove off. "Then," a solemn police detective said, "the people came out."

1964

2

Description

Fifth Avenue, Uptown

James Baldwin

There is a housing project standing now where the house in   1
which we grew up once stood, and one of those stunted city trees
is snarling where our doorway used to be. This is on the rehabilitated side of the avenue. The other side of the avenue—for
progress takes time—has not been rehabilitated yet and it looks
exactly as it looked in the days when we sat with our noses
pressed against the windowpane, longing to be allowed to go
"across the street." The grocery store which gave us credit is still
there, and there can be no doubt that it is still giving credit. The
people in the project certainly need it—far more, indeed, than
they ever needed the project. The last time I passed by, the Jewish
proprietor was still standing among his shelves, looking sadder
and heavier but scarcely any older. Farther down the block stands
the shoe-repair store in which our shoes were repaired until reparation became impossible and in which, then, we bought all our
"new" ones. The Negro proprietor is still in the window, head
down, working at the leather.

These two, I imagine, could tell a long tale if they would (per-   2
haps they would be glad to if they could), having watched so
many, for so long, struggling in the fishhooks, the barbed wire, of
this avenue.

The avenue is elsewhere the renowned and elegant Fifth.   3
The area I am describing, which, in today's gang parlance, would
be called "the turf," is bounded by Lenox Avenue on the west, the

29

Harlem River on the east, 135th Street on the north, and 130th
Street on the south. We never lived beyond these boundaries; this
is where we grew up. Walking along 145th Street—for example—
familiar as it is, and similar, does not have the same impact
because I do not know any of the people on the block. But when I
turn east on 131st Street and Lenox Avenue, there is first a soda-
pop joint, then a shoeshine "parlor," then a grocery store, then a
dry cleaners', then the houses. All along the street there are people
who watched me grow up, people who grew up with me, people
I watched grow up along with my brothers and sisters; and,
sometimes in my arms, sometimes underfoot, sometimes at my
shoulder—or on it—their children, a riot, a forest of children, who
include my nieces and nephews.

4   When we reach the end of this long block, we find ourselves on
wide, filthy, hostile Fifth Avenue, facing that project which hangs
over the avenue like a monument to the folly, and the cowardice, of
good intentions. All along the block, for anyone who knows it, are
immense human gaps, like craters. These gaps are not created
merely by those who have moved away, inevitably into some other
ghetto; or by those who have risen, almost always into a greater
capacity for self-loathing and self-delusion; or yet by those who, by
whatever means—World War II, the Korean war, a policeman's
gun or billy, a gang war, a brawl, madness, an overdose of heroin,
or, simply, unnatural exhaustion—are dead. I am talking about
those who are left, and I am talking principally about the young.
What are they doing? Well, some, a minority, are fanatical church-
goers, members of the more extreme of the Holy Roller sects. Many,
many more are "moslems," by affiliation or sympathy, that is to say
that they are united by nothing more—and nothing less—than a
hatred of the white world and all its works. They are present, for
example, at every Buy Black street-corner meeting—meetings in
which the speaker urges his hearers to cease trading with white
men and establish a separate economy. Neither the speaker nor his
hearers can possibly do this, of course, since Negroes do not own
General Motors or RCA or the A & P, nor, indeed, do they own
more than a wholly insufficient fraction of anything else in Harlem
(those who *do* own anything are more interested in their profits
than in their fellows). But these meetings nevertheless keep alive
in the participators a certain pride of bitterness without which,

however futile this bitterness may be, they could scarcely remain alive at all. Many have given up. They stay home and watch the TV screen, living on the earnings of their parents, cousins, brothers, or uncles, and only leave the house to go to the movies or to the nearest bar. "How're you making it?" one may ask, running into them along the block, or in the bar. "Oh, I'm TV-ing it"; with the saddest, sweetest, most shamefaced of smiles, and from a great distance. This distance one is compelled to respect; anyone who has traveled so far will not easily be dragged again into the world. There are further retreats, of course, than the TV screen or the bar. There are those who are simply sitting on their stoops, "stoned," animated for a moment only, and hideously, by the approach of someone who may lend them the money for a "fix." Or by the approach of someone from whom they can purchase it, one of the shrewd ones, on the way to prison or just coming out.

And the others, who have avoided all of these deaths, get up in the morning and go downtown to meet "the man." They work in the white man's world all day and come home in the evening to this fetid block. They struggle to instill in their children some private sense of honor or dignity which will help the child to survive. This means, of course, that they must struggle, stolidly, incessantly, to keep this sense alive in themselves, in spite of the insults, the indifference, and the cruelty they are certain to encounter in their working day. They patiently browbeat the landlord into fixing the heat, the plaster, the plumbing; this demands prodigious patience; nor is patience usually enough. In trying to make their hovels habitable, they are perpetually throwing good money after bad. Such frustration, so long endured, is driving many strong, admirable men and women whose only crime is color to the very gates of paranoia. ⁵

One remembers them from another time—playing handball ⁶ in the playground, going to church, wondering if they were going to be promoted at school. One remembers them going off to war—gladly, to escape this block. One remembers their return. Perhaps one remembers their wedding day. And one sees where the girl is now—vainly looking for salvation from some other embittered, trussed, and struggling boy—and sees the all-but-abandoned children in the streets.

1948

Once More to the Lake

E. B. White

AUGUST 1941

1   One summer, along about 1904, my father rented a camp on a lake in Maine and took us all there for the month of August. We all got ringworm from some kittens and had to rub Pond's Extract on our arms and legs night and morning, and my father rolled over in a canoe with all his clothes on; but outside of that the vacation was a success and from then on none of us ever thought there was any place in the world like that lake in Maine. We returned summer after summer—always on August 1 for one month. I have since become a salt-water man, but sometimes in summer there are days when the restlessness of the tides and the fearful cold of the sea water and the incessant wind that blows across the afternoon and into the evening make me wish for the placidity of a lake in the woods. A few weeks ago this feeling got so strong I bought myself a couple of bass hooks and a spinner and returned to the lake where we used to go, for a week's fishing and to revisit old haunts.

2   I took along my son, who had never had any fresh water up his nose and who had seen lily pads only from train windows. On the journey over to the lake I began to wonder what it would be like. I wondered how time would have marred this unique, this holy spot—the coves and streams, the hills that the sun set behind, the camps and the paths behind the camps. I was sure that the tarred road would have found it out, and I wondered in what other ways it would be desolated. It is strange how much you can remember about places like that once you allow your mind to return into the grooves that lead back. You remember one thing, and that suddenly reminds you of another thing. I guess I remembered clearest of all the early mornings, when the lake was cool and motionless, remembered how the bedroom smelled of the lumber it was made of and of the wet woods whose scent entered through the screen. The partitions in the camp were thin and did not extend clear to the top of the rooms,

and as I was always the first up I would dress softly so as not to
wake the others, and sneak out into the sweet outdoors and start
out in the canoe, keeping close along the shore in the long shadows of the pines. I remembered being very careful never to rub
my paddle against the gunwale for fear of disturbing the stillness
of the cathedral.

The lake had never been what you would call a wild lake.
There were cottages sprinkled around the shores, and it was in
farming country although the shores of the lake were quite
heavily wooded. Some of the cottages were owned by nearby
farmers, and you would live at the shore and eat your meals at
the farmhouse. That's what our family did. But although it wasn't
wild, it was a fairly large and undisturbed lake and there were
places in it that, to a child at least, seemed infinitely remote and
primeval.

I was right about the tar: it led to within half a mile of the
shore. But when I got back there, with my boy, and we settled
into a camp near a farmhouse and into the kind of summertime
I had known, I could tell that it was going to be pretty much the
same as it had been before—I knew it, lying in bed the first
morning smelling the bedroom and hearing the boy sneak quietly out and go off along the shore in a boat. I began to sustain
the illusion that he was I, and therefore, by simple transposition,
that I was my father. This sensation persisted, kept cropping up
all the time we were there. It was not an entirely new feeling, but
in this setting it grew much stronger. I seemed to be living a dual
existence. I would be in the middle of some simple act, I would
be picking up a bait box or laying down a table fork, or I would
be saying something and suddenly it would be not I but my
father who was saying the words or making the gesture. It gave
me a creepy sensation.

We went fishing the first morning. I felt the same damp moss
covering the worms in the bait can, and saw the dragonfly alight
on the tip of my rod as it hovered a few inches from the surface
of the water. It was the arrival of this fly that convinced me
beyond any doubt that everything was as it always had been, that
the years were a mirage and that there had been no years. The
small waves were the same, chucking the rowboat under the chin

as we fished at anchor, and the boat was the same boat, the same color green and the ribs broken in the same places, and under the floorboards the same fresh water leavings and debris—the dead hellgrammite, the wisps of moss, the rusty discarded fishhook, the dried blood from yesterday's catch. We stared silently at the tips of our rods, at the dragonflies that came and went. I lowered the tip of mine into the water, tentatively, pensively dislodging the fly, which darted two feet away, poised, darted two feet back, and came to rest again a little farther up the rod. There had been no years between the ducking of this dragonfly and the other one—the one that was part of memory. I looked at the boy, who was silently watching his fly, and it was my hands that held his rod, my eyes watching. I felt dizzy and didn't know which rod I was at the end of.

6   We caught two bass, hauling them in briskly as though they were mackerel, pulling them over the side of the boat in a businesslike manner without any landing net, and stunning them with a blow on the back of the head. When we got back for a swim before lunch, the lake was exactly where we had left it, the same number of inches from the dock, and there was only the merest suggestion of a breeze. This seemed an utterly enchanted sea, this lake you could leave to its own devices for a few hours and come back to, and find that it had not stirred, this constant and trustworthy body of water. In the shallows, the dark, water-soaked sticks and twigs, smooth and old, were undulating in clusters on the bottom against the clean ribbed sand, and the track of the mussel was plain. A school of minnows swam by, each minnow with its small individual shadow, doubling the attendance, so clear and sharp in the sunlight. Some of the other campers were in swimming, along the shore, one of them with a cake of soap, and the water felt thin and clear and unsubstantial. Over the years there had been this person with the cake of soap, this cultist, and here he was. There had been no years.

7   Up to the farmhouse to dinner through the teeming dusty field, the road under our sneakers was only a two-track road. The middle track was missing, the one with the marks of the hooves and the splotches of dried, flaky manure. There had always been three tracks to choose from in choosing which track

to walk in; now the choice was narrowed down to two. For a moment I missed terribly the middle alternative. But the way led past the tennis court, and something about the way it lay there in the sun reassured me; the tape had loosened along the backline, the alleys were green with plantains and other weeds, and the net (installed in June and removed in September) sagged in the dry noon, and the whole place steamed with midday heat and hunger and emptiness. There was a choice of pie for dessert, and one was blueberry and one was apple, and the waitresses were the same country girls, there having been no passage of time, only the illusion of it as in a dropped curtain—the waitresses were still fifteen; their hair had been washed, that was the only difference—they had been to the movies and seen the pretty girls with the clean hair.

Summertime, oh, summertime, pattern of life indelible with 8 fade-proof lake, the wood unshatterable, the pasture with the sweetfern and the juniper forever and ever, summer without end; this was the background, and the life along the shore was the design, the cottages with their innocent and tranquil design, their tiny docks with the flagpole and the American flag floating against the white clouds in the blue sky, and little paths over the roots of the trees leading from camp to camp and the paths leading back to the outhouses and the can of lime for sprinkling, and at the souvenir counters at the store the miniature birch-bark canoes and the post-cards that showed things looking a little better than they looked. This was the American family at play, escaping the city heat, wondering whether the newcomers in the camp at the head of the cove were "common" or "nice," wondering whether it was true that the people who drove up for Sunday dinner at the farmhouse were turned away because there wasn't enough chicken.

It seemed to me, as I kept remembering all this, that those 9 times and those summers had been infinitely precious and worth saving. There had been jollity and peace and goodness. The arriving (at the beginning of August) had been so big a business in itself, at the railway station the farm wagon drawn up, the first smell of the pine-laden air, the first glimpse of the smiling farmer, and the great importance of the trunks and your father's enormous authority in such matters, and the feel of the wagon under

you for the long ten-mile haul, and at the top of the last long hill
catching the first view of the lake after eleven months of not seeing this cherished body of water. The shouts and cries of the other
campers when they saw you, and the trunks to be unpacked, to
give up their rich burden. (Arriving was less exciting nowadays,
when you sneaked up in your car and parked it under a tree near
the camp and took out the bags and in five minutes it was all over,
no fuss, no loud wonderful fuss about trunks.)

10   Peace and goodness and jollity. The only thing that was
wrong now, really, was the sound of the place, an unfamiliar
nervous sound of the outboard motors. This was the note that
jarred, the one thing that would sometimes break the illusion and
set the years moving. In those other summertimes all motors
were inboard; and when they were at a little distance, the noise
they made was a sedative, an ingredient of summer sleep. They
were one-cylinder and two-cylinder engines, and some were
make-and-break and some were jump-spark, but they all made a
sleepy sound across the lake. The one-lungers throbbed and flut-
tered, and the twin-cylinder ones purred and purred, and that
was a quiet sound, too. But now the campers all had outboards.
In the daytime, in the hot mornings, these motors made a petu-
lant, irritable sound; at night in the still evening when the after-
glow lit the water, they whined about one's ears like mosquitoes.
My boy loved our rented outboard, and his great desire was to
achieve single-handed mastery over it, and authority, and he soon
learned the trick of choking it a little (but not too much), and the
adjustment of the needle valve. Watching him I would remember
the things you could do with the old one-cylinder engine with the
heavy flywheel, how you could have it eating out of your hand if
you got really close to it spiritually. Motorboats in those days didn't
have clutches, and you would make a landing by shutting off the
motor at the proper time and coasting in with a dead rudder. But
there was a way of reversing them, if you learned the trick, by
cutting the switch and putting it on again exactly on the final
dying revolution of the flywheel, so that it would kick back
against compression and begin reversing. Approaching a dock in
a strong following breeze, it was difficult to slow up sufficiently
by the ordinary coasting method, and if a boy felt he had complete

mastery over his motor, he was tempted to keep it running beyond its time and then reverse it a few feet from the dock. It took a cool nerve, because if you threw the switch a twentieth of a second too soon you would catch the flywheel when it still had speed enough to go up past center, and the boat would leap ahead, charging bull-fashion at the dock.

We had a good week at the camp. The bass were biting well 11 and the sun shone endlessly, day after day. We would be tired at night and lie down in the accumulated heat of the little bedrooms after the long hot day and the breeze would stir almost imperceptibly outside and the smell of the swamp drifted in through the rusty screens. Sleep would come easily and in the morning the red squirrel would be on the roof, tapping out his gay routine. I kept remembering everything, lying in bed in the mornings—the small steamboat that had a long rounded stern like the lip of a Ubangi, and how quietly she ran on the moonlight sails, when the older boys played their mandolins and the girls sang and we ate doughnuts dipped in sugar, and how sweet the music was on the water in the shining night, and what it had felt like to think about girls then. After breakfast we would go up to the store and the things were in the same place—the minnows in a bottle, the plugs and spinners disarranged and pawed over by the youngsters from the boys' camp, the Fig Newtons and the Beeman's gum. Outside, the road was tarred and cars stood in front of the store. Inside, all was just as it had always been, except there was more Coca-Cola and not so much Moxie and root beer and birch beer and sarsaparilla. We would walk out with the bottle of pop apiece and sometimes the pop would backfire up our noses and hurt. We explored the streams, quietly, where the turtles slid off the sunny logs and dug their way into the soft bottom; and we lay on the town wharf and fed worms to the tame bass. Everywhere we went I had trouble making out which was I, the one walking at my side, the one walking in my pants.

One afternoon while we were at that lake, a thunderstorm 12 came up. It was like the revival of an old melodrama that I had seen long ago with childish awe. The second-act climax of the drama of the electrical disturbance over a lake in America had not

Everything changes, you can never go back, time moves on. [handwritten]

Swimming in Rain [handwritten, left margin]

changed in any important respect. This was the big scene, still the big scene. The whole thing was so familiar, the first feeling of oppression and heat and a general air around camp of not wanting to go very far away. In mid-afternoon (it was all the same) a curious darkening of the sky, and a lull in everything that had made life tick; and then the way the boats suddenly swung the other way at their moorings with the coming of a breeze out of the new quarter, and the premonitory rumble. Then the kettle drum, then the snare, then the bass drum and cymbals, then crackling light against the dark, and the gods grinning and licking their chops in the hills. Afterward the calm, the rain steadily rustling in the calm lake, the return of light and hope and spirits, and the campers running out in joy and relief to go swimming in the rain, their bright cries perpetuating the deathless joke about how they were getting simply drenched, and the children screaming with delight at the new sensation of bathing in the rain, and the joke about getting drenched linking the generations in a strong indestructible chain. And the comedian who waded in carrying an umbrella.

13   When the others went swimming my son said he was going in, too. He pulled his dripping trunks from the line where they had hung all through the shower and wrung them out. Languidly, and with no thought of going in, I watched him, his hard little body, skinny and bare, saw him wince slightly as he pulled up around his vitals the small, soggy, icy garment. As he buckled the swollen belt, suddenly my groin felt the chill of death.

Realization of his own mortality [handwritten]

1939

He is replaying his childhood as he watches his son. [handwritten]

Marrying Absurd

Joan Didion

1 To be married in Las Vegas, Clark County, Nevada, a bride must swear that she is eighteen or has parental permission and a bridegroom that he is twenty-one or has parental permission. Someone must put up five dollars for the license. (On Sundays

and holidays, fifteen dollars. The Clark County Courthouse issues marriage licenses at any time of the day or night except between noon and one in the afternoon, between eight and nine in the evening, and between four and five in the morning.) Nothing else is required. The State of Nevada, alone among these United States, demands neither a premarital blood test nor a waiting period before or after the issuance of a marriage license. Driving in across the Mojave from Los Angeles, one sees the signs way out on the desert, looming up from that moonscape of rattlesnakes and mesquite, even before the Las Vegas lights appear like a mirage on the horizon: "GETTING MARRIED? Free License Information First Strip Exit." Perhaps the Las Vegas wedding industry achieved its peak operational efficiency between 9:00 P.M. and midnight of August 26, 1965, an otherwise unremarkable Thursday which happened to be, by Presidential order, the last day on which anyone could improve his draft status merely by getting married. One hundred and seventy-one couples were pronounced man and wife in the name of Clark County and the State of Nevada that night, sixty-seven of them by a single justice of the peace, Mr. James A. Brennan. Mr. Brennan did one wedding at the Dunes and the other sixty-six in his office, and charged each couple eight dollars. One bride lent her veil to six others. "I got it down from five to three minutes," Mr. Brennan said later of his feat. "I could've married them *en masse*, but they're people, not cattle. People expect more when they get married."

What people who get married in Las Vegas actually do ₂ expect—what, in the largest sense, their "expectations" are— strikes one as a curious and self-contradictory business. Las Vegas is the most extreme and allegorical of American settlements, bizarre and beautiful in its venality and in its devotion to immediate gratification, a place the tone of which is set by mobsters and call girls and ladies' room attendants with amyl nitrite poppers in their uniform pockets. Almost everyone notes that there is no "time" in Las Vegas, no night and no day and no past and no future (no Las Vegas casino, however, has taken the obliteration of the ordinary time sense quite so far as Harold's Club in Reno, which for a while issued, at odd intervals in the day and night,

mimeographed "bulletins" carrying news from the world outside); neither is there any logical sense of where one is. One is
standing on a highway in the middle of a vast hostile desert looking at an eighty-foot sign which blinks "STARDUST" or "CAESAR'S
PALACE." Yes, but what does that explain? This geographical
implausibility reinforces the sense that what happens there has
no connection with "real" life; Nevada cities like Reno and
Carson City are ranch towns, Western towns, places behind
which there is some historical imperative. But Las Vegas seems to
exist only in the eye of the beholder. All of which makes it an
extraordinarily stimulating and interesting place, but an odd one
in which to want to wear a candlelight satin Priscilla of Boston
wedding dress with Chantilly lace insets, tapered sleeves and a
detachable modified train.

3   And yet the Las Vegas wedding business seems to appeal to
precisely that impulse. "Sincere and Dignified Since 1954," one
wedding chapel advertises. There are nineteen such wedding
chapels in Las Vegas, intensely competitive, each offering better,
faster, and, by implication, more sincere services than the next: Our
Photos Best Anywhere, Your Wedding on A Phonograph Record,
Candlelight with Your Ceremony, Honeymoon Accommodations,
Free Transportation from Your Motel to Courthouse to Chapel and
Return to Motel, Religious or Civil Ceremonies, Dressing Rooms,
Flowers, Rings, Announcements, Witnesses Available, and Ample
Parking. All of these services, like most others in Las Vegas (sauna
baths, payroll-check cashing, chinchilla coats for sale or rent) are
offered twenty-four hours a day, seven days a week, presumably
on the premise that marriage, like craps, is a game to be played
when the table seems hot.

4   But what strikes one most about the Strip chapels, with
their wishing wells and stained-glass paper windows and their
artificial bouvardia, is that so much of their business is by no
means a matter of simple convenience, of late-night liaisons
between show girls and baby Crosbys. Of course there is some
of that. (One night about eleven o'clock in Las Vegas I watched
a bride in an orange minidress and masses of flame-colored
hair stumble from a Strip chapel on the arm of her bridegroom,
who looked the part of the expendable nephew in the movies

like *Miami Syndicate.* "I gotta get the kids," the bride whimpered. "I gotta pick up the sitter, I gotta get to the midnight show." "What you gotta get," the bridegroom said, opening the door of a Cadillac Coupe de Ville and watching her crumple on the seat, "is sober.") But Las Vegas seems to offer something other than "convenience"; it is merchandising "niceness," the facsimile of proper ritual, to children who do not know how else to find it, how to make the arrangements, how to do it "right." All day and evening long on the Strip, one sees actual wedding parties, waiting under the harsh lights at a crosswalk, standing uneasily in the parking lot of the Frontier while the photographer hired by The Little Church of the West ("Wedding Place of the Stars") certifies the occasion, takes the picture: the bride in a veil and white satin pumps, the bridegroom usually in a white dinner jacket, and even an attendant or two, a sister or a best friend in hot-pink *peau de soie,* a flirtation veil, a carnation nosegay. "When I Fall in Love It Will Be Forever," the organist plays, and then a few bars of Lohengrin. The mother cries; the stepfather, awkward in his role, invites the chapel hostess to join them for a drink at the Sands. The hostess declines with a professional smile; she has already transferred her interest to the group waiting outside. One bride out, another in, and again the sign goes up on the chapel door: "One moment please—Wedding."

I sat next to one such wedding party in a Strip restaurant the ₅ last time I was in Las Vegas. The marriage had just taken place; the bride still wore her dress, the mother her corsage. A bored waiter poured out a few swallows of pink champagne ("on the house") for everyone but the bride, who was too young to be served. "You'll need something with more kick than that," the bride's father said with heavy jocularity to his new son-in-law; the ritual jokes about the wedding night had a certain Panglossian character, since the bride was clearly several months pregnant. Another round of pink champagne, this time not on the house, and the bride began to cry. "It was just as nice," she sobbed, "as I hoped and dreamed it would be."

                                                                1967

A Partial Remembrance
of a Puerto Rican Childhood

Judith Ortiz Cofer

1   At three or four o'clock in the afternoon, the hour of *café con leche*,
the women of my family gathered in Mamá's living room to
speak of important things and retell familiar stories meant to be
overheard by us young girls, their daughters. In Mamá's house
(everyone called my grandmother Mamá) was a large parlor
built by my grandfather to his wife's exact specifications so that
it was always cool, facing away from the sun. The doorway was
on the side of the house so no one could walk directly into her
living room. First they had to take a little stroll through and
around her beautiful garden where prize-winning orchids grew
in the trunk of an ancient tree she had hollowed out for that purpose. This room was furnished with several mahogany rocking
chairs, acquired at the births of her children, and one intricately
carved rocker that had passed down to Mamá at the death of her
own mother.

2   It was on these rockers that my mother, her sisters, and my
grandmother sat on these afternoons of my childhood to tell their
stories, teaching each other, and my cousin and me, what it was
like to be a woman, more specifically, a Puerto Rican woman.
They talked about life on the island, and life in *Los Nueva Yores*,
their way of referring to the United States from New York City to
California: the other place, not home, all the same. They told real-
life stories though, as I later learned, always embellishing them
with a little or a lot of dramatic detail. And they told *cuentos*, the
morality and cautionary tales told by the women in our family for
generations: stories that became a part of my subconscious as I
grew up in two worlds, the tropical island and the cold city, and
that would later surface in my dreams and in my poetry.

3   One of these tales was about the woman who was left at the
altar. Mamá liked to tell that one with histrionic intensity. I
remember the rise and fall of her voice, the sighs, and her constantly gesturing hands, like two birds swooping through her

words. This particular story usually would come up in a conversation as a result of someone mentioning a forthcoming engagement or wedding. The first time I remember hearing it, I was sitting on the floor at Mamá's feet, pretending to read a comic book. I may have been eleven or twelve years old, at that difficult age when a girl was no longer a child who could be ordered to leave the room if the women wanted freedom to take their talk into forbidden zones, nor really old enough to be considered a part of their conclave. I could only sit quietly, pretending to be in another world, while absorbing it all in a sort of unspoken agreement of my status as silent auditor. On this day, Mamá had taken my long, tangled mane of hair into her ever-busy hands. Without looking down at me and with no interruption of her flow of words, she began braiding my hair, working at it with the quickness and determination that characterized all her actions. My mother was watching us impassively from her rocker across the room. On her lips played a little ironic smile. I would never sit still for *her* ministrations, but even then, I instinctively knew that she did not possess Mamá's matriarchal power to command and keep everyone's attention. This was never more evident than in the spell she cast when telling a story.

"It is not like it used to be when I was a girl," Mamá 4
announced. "Then a man could leave a girl standing at the church altar with a bouquet of fresh flowers in her hands and disappear off the face of the earth. No way to track him down if he was from another town. He could be a married man, with maybe even two or three families all over the island. There was no way to know. And there were men who did this. Hombres with the devil in their flesh who would come to a pueblo, like this one, take a job at one of the haciendas, never meaning to stay, only to have a good time and to seduce the women."

The whole time she was speaking, Mamá would be weaving 5
my hair into a flat plait that required pulling apart the two sections of hair with little jerks that made my eyes water; but knowing how grandmother detested whining and *boba* (sissy) tears, as she called them, I just sat up as straight and stiff as I did at La Escuela San José, where the nuns enforced good posture with a flexible plastic ruler they bounced off of slumped shoulders and

heads. As Mamá's story progressed, I noticed how my young Aunt Laura lowered her eyes, refusing to meet Mamá's meaningful gaze. Laura was seventeen, in her last year of high school, and already engaged to a boy from another town who had staked his claim with a tiny diamond ring, then left for Los Nueva Yores to make his fortune. They were planning to get married in a year. Mamá had expressed serious doubts that the wedding would ever take place. In Mamá's eyes, a man set free without a legal contract was a man lost. She believed that marriage was not something men desired, but simply the price they had to pay for the privilege of children and, of course, for what no decent (synonymous with "smart") woman would give away for free.

6   "María La Loca was only seventeen when *it* happened to her." I listened closely at the mention of this name. María was a town character, a fat middle-aged woman who lived with her old mother on the outskirts of town. She was to be seen around the pueblo delivering the meat pies the two women made for a living. The most peculiar thing about María, in my eyes, was that she walked and moved like a little girl though she had the thick body and wrinkled face of an old woman. She would swing her hips in an exaggerated, clownish way, and sometimes even hop and skip up to someone's house. She spoke to no one. Even if you asked her a question, she would just look at you and smile, showing her yellow teeth. But I had heard that if you got close enough, you could hear her humming a tune without words. The kids yelled out nasty things to her, calling her *La Loca,* and the men who hung out at the bodega playing dominoes sometimes whistled mockingly as she passed by with her funny, outlandish walk. But María seemed impervious to it all, carrying her basket of *pasteles* like a grotesque Little Red Riding Hood through the forest.

7   María La Loca interested me, as did all the eccentrics and crazies of our pueblo. Their weirdness was a measuring stick I used in my serious quest for a definition of normal. As a Navy brat shuttling between New Jersey and the pueblo, I was constantly made to feel like an oddball by my peers, who made fun of my two-way accent: a Spanish accent when I spoke English, and when I spoke Spanish I was told that I sounded like a *Gringa.* Being the outsider had already turned my brother and me into

cultural chameleons. We developed early on the ability to blend into a crowd, to sit and read quietly in a fifth story apartment building for days and days when it was too bitterly cold to play outside, or, set free, to run wild in Mamá's realm, where she took charge of our lives, releasing Mother for a while from the intense fear for our safety that our father's absences instilled in her. In order to keep us from harm when Father was away, Mother kept us under strict surveillance. She even walked us to and from Public School No. 11, which we attended during the months we lived in Paterson, New Jersey, our home base in the states. Mamá freed all three of us like pigeons from a cage. I saw her as my liberator and my model. Her stories were parables from which to glean the *Truth*.

"María La Loca was once a beautiful girl. Everyone thought 8 she would marry the Méndez boy." As everyone knew, Rogelio Méndez was the richest man in town. "But," Mamá continued, knitting my hair with the same intensity she was putting into her story, "this *macho* made a fool out of her and ruined her life." She paused for the effect of her use of the word *macho*, which at that time had not yet become a popular epithet for an unliberated man. This word had for us the crude and comical connotation of "male of the species," stud; a *macho* was what you put in a pen to increase your stock.

I peeked over my comic book at my mother. She too was under 9 Mamá's spell, smiling conspiratorially at this little swipe at men. She was safe from Mamá's contempt in this area. Married at an early age, an unspotted lamb, she had been accepted by a good family of strict Spaniards whose name was old and respected, though their fortune had been lost long before my birth. In a rocker Papá had painted sky blue sat Mamá's oldest child, Aunt Nena. Mother of three children, step-mother of two more, she was a quiet woman who liked books but had married an ignorant and abusive widower whose main interest in life was accumulating wealth. He too was in the mainland working on his dream of returning home rich and triumphant to buy the *finca* of his dreams. She was waiting for him to send for her. She would leave her children with Mamá for several years while the two of them slaved away in factories. He would one day be a rich man, and she a sadder woman.

Even now her life-light was dimming. She spoke little, an aberration in Mamá's house, and she read avidly, as if storing up spiritual food for the long winters that awaited her in Los Nueva Yores without her family. But even Aunt Nena came alive to Mamá's words, rocking gently, her hands over a thick book in her lap.

10   Her daughter, my cousin Sara, played jacks by herself on the tile porch outside the room where we sat. She was a year older than I. We shared a bed and all our family's secrets. Collaborators in search of answers, Sara and I discussed everything we heard the women say, trying to fit it all together like a puzzle that, once assembled, would reveal life's mysteries to us. Though she and I still enjoyed taking part in boys' games—chase, volleyball and even *vaqueros,* the island version of cowboys and Indians involving capgun battles and violent shoot-outs under the mango tree in Mamá's backyard—we loved best the quiet hours in the afternoon when the men were still at work and the boys had gone to play serious baseball at the park. Then Mamá's house belonged only to us women. The aroma of coffee perking in the kitchen, the mesmerizing creaks and groans of the rockers, and the women telling their lives in *cuentos* are forever woven into the fabric of my imagination, braided like my hair that day I felt my grandmother's hands teaching me about strength, her voice convincing me of the power of storytelling.

11   That day Mamá told how the beautiful María had fallen prey to a man whose name was never the same in subsequent versions of the story; it was Juan one time, José, Rafael, Diego, another. We understood that neither the name nor any of the *facts* were important, only that a woman had allowed love to defeat her. Mamá put each of us in María's place by describing her wedding dress in loving detail: how she looked like a princess in her lace as she waited at the altar. Then, as Mamá approached the tragic denouement of her story, I was distracted by the sound of my Aunt Laura's violent rocking. She seemed on the verge of tears. She knew the fable was intended for her. That week she was going to have her wedding gown fitted, though no firm date had been set for the marriage. Mamá ignored Laura's obvious discomfort, digging out a ribbon from the sewing basket she kept by her rocker while describing María's long illness, "a fever that would not

break for days." She spoke of a mother's despair: "that woman climbed the church steps on her knees every morning, wore only black as a *promesa* to the Holy Virgin in exchange for her daughter's health." By the time María returned from her honeymoon with death, she was ravished, no longer young or sane. "As you can see, she is almost as old as her mother already," Mamá lamented while tying the ribbon to the ends of my hair, pulling it back with such force that I just knew I would never be able to close my eyes completely again.

"That María is getting crazier every day." Mamá's voice 12 would take a lighter tone now, expressing satisfaction, either for the perfection of my braid, or for a story well told—it was hard to tell. "You know that tune María is always humming?" Carried away by her enthusiasm, I tried to nod, but Mamá still had me pinned between her knees.

"Well, that's the wedding march." Surprising us all, Mamá 13 sang out, "Da, da, dara . . . da, da, dara." Then lifting me off the floor by my skinny shoulders, she would lead me around the room in an impromptu waltz—another session ending with the laughter of women, all of us caught up in the infectious joke of our lives.

1990

Revisiting Sacred Ground

N. Scott Momaday

There is great good in returning to a landscape that has had 1 extraordinary meaning in one's life. It happens that we return to such places in our minds irresistibly. There are certain villages and towns, mountains and plains that, having seen them, walked in them, lived in them, even for a day, we keep forever in the mind's eye. They become indispensable to our well-being; they define us, and we say, I am who I am because I have been there, or there. There is good, too, in actual, physical return.

Comparing adventures

2   Some years ago I made a pilgrimage into the heart of North America. I began the journey proper in western Montana. From there I traveled across the high plains of Wyoming into the Black Hills, then southward to the southern plains, to a cemetery at Rainy Mountain, in Oklahoma. It was a journey made by my Kiowa ancestors long before. In the course of their migration they became a people of the Great Plains, and theirs was the last culture to evolve in North America. They had been for untold generations a mountain tribe of hunters. Their ancient nomadism, which had determined their way of life even before they set foot on this continent, perhaps thirty thousand years ago, was raised to its highest level of expression when they entered upon the Great Plains and acquired horses. Their migration brought them to a golden age. At the beginning of their journey they were a people of hard circumstances, often hungry and cold, fighting always for sheer survival. At its end, and for a hundred years, they were the lords of the land, a daring race of centaurs and buffalo hunters whose love of freedom and space was profound.

3   Recently I returned to the old migration route of the Kiowas. I had in me a need to behold again some of the principal landmarks of that long, prehistoric quest, to descend again from the mountain to the plain.

4   With my close friend Chuck I drove north to the Montana–Wyoming border. I wanted to intersect the Kiowa migration route at the Bighorn Medicine Wheel, high in the Bighorn Mountains. We gradually ascended to eight thousand feet on a well-maintained but winding highway. Then we climbed sharply, bearing upon timberline. It was early October, and although the plain below had been comfortable, even warm at midday, the mountain air was cold, and much of the ground was covered with snow. We turned off the pavement, on a dirt road that led three miles to the Medicine Wheel. The road was forbidding; it was narrow and winding, and the grades were steep and slippery; here and there the shoulders fell away into deep ravines. But at the same time something wonderful happened: we crossed the line between civilization and wilderness. Suddenly the earth persisted in its original being. Directly in front of us a huge white-tailed buck crossed our path, ambling without haste into a thicket

Quest

of pines. As we drove over his tracks we saw four does above on the opposite bank, looking down at us, their great black eyes bright and benign, curious. There seemed no wariness, nothing of fear or alienation. Their presence was a good omen, we thought; somehow in their attitude they bade us welcome to their sphere of wildness.   *Descending highway*

There was a fork in the road, and we took the wrong branch. [5] At a steep, hairpin curve we got out of the car and climbed to the top of a peak. An icy wind whipped at us; we were among the bald summits of the Bighorns. Great flumes of sunlit snow erupted on the ridges and dissolved in spangles on the sky. Across a deep saddle we caught sight of the Medicine Wheel. It was perhaps two miles away.

When we returned to the car we saw another vehicle [6] approaching. It was a very old Volkswagen bus, in much need of repair, cosmetic repair at least. Out stepped a thin, bearded young man in thick glasses. He wore a wool cap, a down parka, jeans, and well-worn hiking boots. "I am looking for Medicine Wheel," *accomplishment* he said, having nodded to us. He spoke softly, with a pronounced accent. His name was Jurg, and he was from Switzerland; he had been traveling for some months in Canada and the United States. Chuck and I shook his hand and told him to follow us, and we drove down into the saddle. From there we climbed on foot to the Medicine Wheel.

The Medicine Wheel is a ring of stones, some fifty feet in [7] diameter. Stone spokes radiate from the center to the circumference. Cairns are placed at certain points on the circumference, one in the center, and one just outside the ring to the southwest. We do not know as a matter of fact who made the wheel or to what *Medicine Wheel* purpose. It has been proposed that it is an astronomical observatory, a solar calendar, and the ground design of a Kiowa Sun Dance lodge. What we know without doubt is that it is a sacred expression, an equation of man's relation to the cosmos.

There was a great calm upon that place. The hard, snow- [8] bearing wind that had burned our eyes and skin only minutes before had died away altogether. The sun was warm and bright, and there was a profound silence. On the wire fence which had been erected to enclose and protect the wheel were fixed offerings,

reflection

small prayer bundles. Chuck and Jurg and I walked about slowly, standing for long moments here and there, looking into the wheel or out across the great distances. We did not say much; there was little to be said. But we were deeply moved by the spirit of that place. The silence was such that it must be observed. To the north we could see down to timberline, to the snowfields and draws that marked the black planes of forest among the peaks of the Bighorns. To the south and west the mountains fell abruptly to the plains. We could see thousands of feet down and a hundred miles across the dim expanse.

9   When we were about to leave, I took from my pocket an eagle-bone whistle that my father had given me, and I blew it in the four directions. The sound was very high and shrill, and it did not break the essential silence. As we were walking down we saw far below, crossing our path, a coyote sauntering across the snow into a wall of trees. It was just there, a wild being to catch sight of, and then it was gone. The wilderness, which had admitted us with benediction, with benediction let us go.

10   When we came within a stone's throw of the highway, Chuck and I said goodbye to Jurg, but not before he had got out his camp stove and boiled water for tea. There in the dusk we enjoyed a small ceremonial feast of tea and crackers. The three of us had become friends. Only later did I begin to understand the extraordinary character of that friendship. It was the friendship of those who come together in recognition of the sacred. If we never meet again. I thought, we shall not forget this day.

11   On the plains the fences and roads and windmills and houses seemed almost negligible, all but overwhelmed by the earth and sky. It is a landscape of great clarity; its vastness is that of the ocean. It is the near revelation of infinity. Antelope were everywhere in the grassy folds, grazing side by side with horses and cattle. Hawks sailed above, and crows scattered before us. The place names were American—Tensleep, Buffalo, Dull Knife, Crazy Woman, Spotted Horse.

12   The Black Hills are an isolated and ancient group of mountains in South Dakota and Wyoming. They lie very close to both the geographic center of the United States, if you include Alaska and Hawaii, and the geographic center of the North American

continent. They form an island, an elliptical area of nearly six thousand square miles, in the vast sea of grasses that is the northern Great Plains. The Black Hills are a calendar of geologic time that is truly remarkable. Their foundation rocks are much older than the sedimentary layers of which the Americas are primarily formed. An analysis of this foundation, made in 1964, indicates an age of between two and three billion years.

back ground

A documented record of exploration in this region is found 13 in the Lewis and Clark journals, 1804–1806. The first white party known definitely to have entered the Black Hills proper was led by Jedidiah Smith in 1823. The diary of this expedition, kept by one James Clyman, is notable. Clyman reports a confrontation between Jedidiah Smith and a grizzly bear, in which Smith lost one of his ears. There is also reported the discovery of a petrified ("putrified," as Clyman has it) forest in which petrified birds sing petrified songs.

Pgst

The Lakotas, or Teton Sioux, called these mountains *Paha* 14 *Sapa*, "hills that are black." Other tribes, besides the Kiowas and the Sioux, thought of the Black Hills as sacred ground, a place that is crucial in their past. The Arapahos lived here. So did the Cheyennes. Bear Butte, near Sturgis, South Dakota, on the northeast edge of the Black Hills, is the Cheyennes' sacred mountain. It remains, like the Medicine Wheel, a place of the greatest spiritual intensity. So great was thought to be the power inherent in the Black Hills that the Indians did not camp there. It was a place of rendezvous, a hunting ground, but above all an inviolate, sacred ground. It was a place of thunder and lightning, a dwelling place of the gods.

Indian lore

On the edge of the Black Hills nearest the Bighorn Mountains 15 is Devil's Tower, the first of our national monuments. The Lakotas called it *Mateo Tepee*, "Grizzly Bear Lodge." The Kiowas called it *Tsoai*, "Rock Tree." Devil's Tower is a great monolith that rises high above the timber of the Black Hills. In conformation it closely resembles the stump of a tree. It is a cluster of rock columns of phonolite porphyry 1,000 feet across at the base and 275 feet across at the top. It rises 865 feet above the high ground upon which it stands and 1,280 feet above the Belle Fourche River, which runs in the valley below.

Devils Tower

16   It has to be seen to be believed. "There are things in nature that engender an awful quiet in the hart of man; Devil's Tower is one of them." I wrote these words almost twenty years ago. They remain true to my experience. Each time I behold this *Tsoai* anew I am more than ever in awe of it.

17   Two hundred years ago, more or less, the Kiowas came upon this place. They were moved to tell a story about it:

> Eight children were there at play, seven sisters and their brother. Suddenly the boy was struck dumb; he trembled and began to run upon his hands and feet. His fingers became claws, and his body was covered with fur. Directly there was a bear where the boy had been. The sisters were terrified; they ran, and the bear after them. They came to the stump of a great tree, and the tree spoke to them. It bade them climb upon it, and as they did so it began to rise into the air. The bear came to kill them, but they were just beyond its reach. It reared against the tree and scored the bark all around with its claws. The seven sisters were borne into the sky, and they became the stars of the Big Dipper.

This story, which I have known from the time I could first understand language, exemplifies the sacred for me. The storyteller, that anonymous, man who told the story for the first time, succeeded in raising the human condition to the level of universal significance. Not only did he account for the existence of the rock tree, but in the process he related his people to the stars.

18   When Chuck and I had journeyed over this ground together, when we were about to go our separate ways, I reminded him of our friend Jurg, knowing well enough that I needn't have; Jurg was on our minds. I can't account for it. He had touched us deeply with his trust, not unlike that of the wild animals we had seen, and with his generosity of spirit, his concern to see beneath the surface of things, his attitude of free, clear, direct, disinterested kindness.

19   "Did he tell us what he does?" I asked. "Does he have a profession?"

20   "I don't think he said," Chuck replied. "I think he's a pilgrim."

21   "Yes."

22   "Yes."

1997

Monuments to Our Better Nature

Michael Byers

Growing up in the seventies in Bethesda, Maryland, a suburb of   1
Washington, D.C., I had the good fortune to be taken regularly to
the National Mall by my mother. She was a scientist, and in the
aftermath of the Vietnam War she found much to be disheartened
by. The immense Smithsonian museums on the Mall acted, for
her, as repositories of truth and exactitude in an age of cupidity,
paranoia, and evasion; they were her solace.

   In the National Museum of Natural History, the gargantuan   2
blue whale hanging above us with its great grooved throat was a
fact about the world that could not be denied. The stuffed African
elephant on its circular dais in the rotunda was composed of billions of skin cells and tiny cilia, and its ivory tusks wore an un-
falsifiable brown patina of age. The chambered skull of the
brontosaurus, the irrefutable chain of his vertebrae, his ponderous thighbones, and his sculpted metatarsals—each the size
and heft of an anchor—had been painstakingly recovered from
a stony Canadian grave, cleaned, and finally pieced together
again, eons after the original owner had ceased to have any use
for them.

   Certain truths, the museums assured us, were undeniable.   3
The meteorites upstairs had roamed the vacuum of space for billions of years until at last, following the Keplerian laws of orbit
and velocity, they had collided with Earth, their nickel cores
becoming polished by the final scalding plunge through the
atmosphere. What a wonder it all was, and how true. And how
could anyone not grasp that these truths were, in so many cases,
utterly beautiful? This was the sort of thing my young mother
wanted to be reassured of in those days, and it was an idea she
wanted me to appreciate, too.

   But my secret love was not the museums themselves but their   4
grand exteriors and their placement among the other monuments
and memorials. Looking ghostly in the distance, these stone
structures spoke of a grandeur whose reach and glory had no
measure. While for my mother these temples were tainted by

chauvinism—in them she saw the young, rough-edged country trying to polish its image—for me they were transcendent. Even as a very young boy I knew they had the power to draw me across the grass, and they still do.

5   Washington, particularly the vast, open Mall, is the place where I first felt like a *citizen*. Standing in front of this monument or that memorial, I understood what it meant to belong to a country so populous as this one. This is the first purpose of these places, it seems to me: to inform citizens of the nation's collective character. They are massive, and beside them we are tiny. So it is politically. Alone, each of us is almost without value, but in the aggregate we are the point of the whole improbable enterprise. One is lost in the multitude, but the multitude itself is essential. It is no mistake that the White House—often the scene of great reputations made and lost—is on the back of the twenty-dollar bill, while Lincoln and his memorial find themselves on the penny. You are only a penny, the monuments tell us, but you are dearly counted.

6   And in life, while the White House may resemble an over-built embassy, the Lincoln Memorial is sublime. What American can approach Henry Bacon's temple to the humble son of Illinois and not feel his own soul beginning to rise eerily through the top of his head? What a glory to mount the broad stairs; what a thrilling incantation to count the thirty-six Doric columns, one for every state of the Union in 1864. And what a pleasure it is to call out the rank of states whose names, inscribed here above the entrance—VIRGINIA TENNESSEE GEORGIA—bring to mind not demagogic governors or backward pockets of creation science but ideal, benign subrepublics run by citizens much like ourselves. All around us, as we climb the stairs, fellow Americans are dressed in logo-covered T-shirts and careless blue jeans, and many are young, and loud. But there they are beside us anyhow, and at the top of the stairs we all stop and turn—we cannot help ourselves—to see where we have come from. And how far indeed it is that we, as a people, have traveled. Below us lie the steps where in Easter of 1939 the contralto Marian Anderson, black daughter of a coal dealer, sang "America" and "Nobody Knows the Trouble I've Seen," as seventy-five thousand looked

on in the April cold. On these steps, Martin Luther King, Jr., shrugged himself away from his prepared text and in that extemporaneous moment produced a supreme example of American oratory—his long Whitmanesque lines echoing with the names of the states carved high on the temple's walls behind him: "Let freedom ring from the snowcapped Rockies of Colorado! Let freedom ring from the curvaceous peaks of California! But not only that; let freedom ring from Stone Mountain of Georgia! Let freedom ring from Lookout Mountain of Tennessee! Let freedom ring from every hill and every mole-hill of Mississippi!"

What a glory it is to stand where Anderson sang and King ₇ spoke—and what a glory to have been permitted to climb these steps unwatched, unquestioned, without a ticket of admission, and at last to arrive at the portico, where the simple Indiana limestone pillars are much larger than they appeared from below, and where the Tennessee pink marble floor is scuffed with millions of our footsteps, and where, as we pass inside, the Alabama marble ceiling—soaked in paraffin to make it translucent—casts a pale light. Hushed, we stop. There he is, Lincoln, on his throne, looking down at us all, while at the other end of the Mall the messy business of the Capitol goes on under his tireless, admonitory gaze.

Americans are not known for good behavior in public, but ₈ here we become subdued, reflective. It is a long way to the ceiling, and our voices fade. Who is not moved by the sentences carved into the walls? "With malice toward none; with charity for all; with firmness in the right . . . Let us strive on to finish the work we are in; to bind up the nation's wounds . . . to do all which may achieve and cherish a just and lasting peace, among ourselves, and with all nations." At this, who does not feel grateful, and feel a lump in the throat? And even those few of us who are ignorant, or disdainful, who choose to snap gum or answer cell phones—well, we are Americans, and this is our monument, and whatever we do here is by definition permissible because it is ours.

Everyone goes to the Lincoln Memorial. Not everyone goes to ₉ the Jefferson. You can drive there and park, but from the Lincoln

Memorial you must walk along the Tidal Basin and cross a busy bridge. The monument faces the water, so you must approach it obliquely, or from the back. Jefferson stands, bronze, his coattails flared, his proud calves on display, his handsome head erect. Under the dome, pigeons flutter from place to place like thoughts moving in a great curved brain. The building, designed by John Russell Pope, is modeled after the Pantheon in Rome, but where is the dramatic soaring reach of the ceiling? Jefferson seems too large for his temple.

10   Disappointment may come from our feelings about Jefferson himself: we appreciate the need for him, but still we do not much like him. Surely we take him too much for granted. He is remote, a rationalist. And what are we to make of the arcane inscriptions? "I am not an advocate for frequent changes in laws and constitution, but laws and institutions go hand in hand with the progress of the human mind. . . . We might as well require a man to wear the same coat that fitted him when he was a boy." All right, but where is the poetry? We have left it over there across the water, in the big rough hands of Lincoln.

11   We approach the third great presidential monument, Robert Mills's stark tribute to George Washington, without much excitement. It is the Mall's least lovely structure, and its most primitive. Thirty-seven years in the making, and what do we have? An obelisk, which seems to the eye not quite vertical as it rises above the city. But maybe it is fitting that this most distant figure of the American pantheon should have this least expressive tower built in his name: the first president as Zoroaster, a demigod whose name we have heard but whom we do not know personally. This monument seems Egyptian, and as such out of place here on the green among the more welcoming Greek and Roman temples. But this is fitting too. Washington, we know, was himself somewhat uncomfortable in civilian life, by turns noble, humble, and clumsy. Like some of the other lifelong military men who would later find themselves in the presidency, he was never quite sure where he stood. At the top of his monument, people shove their way to the windows. If we swoon at the drop and step back from the glass, our place is quickly taken.

There is no shoving at the Vietnam Veterans Memorial. 12
Behavior here is impeccable, and we have its intuitive, minimalist
design by Maya Lin to thank. This monument is public architecture at its finest: open, instructive, and moving. The ambivalent
descent, deeper and deeper, along a sinister black wall, exactly
mimics the national experience of the war: the early trickle of bad
news, the growing sense of obligation, the gradual realization that
we are in over our heads, and at its nadir, the dark hopelessness
from which there seems no escaping. We catch our breath as we
descend. We are silent, knowing that some of the visitors here will
have lost a brother, son, father, friend.

Adults climb out of this hole sadder and wiser. But do the 13
twelve-year-olds also behave well here only because of the crying
man in the army fatigues? Or do they, like their parents, feel that
something terrible has happened, and been preserved somehow
in black marble? And will their children feel the same way, or will
they need to learn the lessons of Vietnam again?

At the top of the ramp we are released again onto the green. 14
We walk to the Korean War Veterans Memorial but leave with a
bad taste. It tries too hard to move us, and it fails. And so we look
suspiciously at the construction under way at the foot of the
Reflecting Pool where the World War II Memorial is at last taking
shape. We are willing to suspend judgment, but we are concerned
about the loss of open space.

Because ultimately the defined space of the Mall is its great- 15
est asset. It is one of America's most venerable and trafficked
pedestrian public spaces, where you can fly a kite alone or
stand among a hundred thousand and hear a speech being
given half a mile away by a barely discernible figure. It is the
distance between monuments that I find myself appreciating
every time I visit. The buildings appear on the horizon and
resolve, slowly, as you approach them on foot across the grass.
In this way the Mall itself functions like an enormous, museum,
and these imperfect places are what we have so far in our
national display case, laid out on the green velvet of the enormous lawn.

As adults, we eventually learn that the brontosaurus is 16
now called apatosaurus, and half of its bones are informed

reconstructions. We discover there were ten million African elephants in 1930, and that now there are only thirty-five thousand. We see that government is bought and paid for, no matter what party is in power. But still: Who can stand on the top step of the Lincoln Memorial and not think *I am a participant in a world civilization, I have history entrusted to me, we are all in this together*—and feel it, for a minute or two, as the simple, honest truth?

2003

Process Analysis

Why Leaves Turn Color in the Fall

Diane Ackerman

The stealth of autumn catches one unaware. Was that a 1
goldfinch perching in the early September woods, or just the
first turning leaf? A red-winged blackbird or a sugar maple clos-
ing up shop for the winter? Keen-eyed as leopards, we stand
still and squint hard, looking for signs of movement. Early
morning frost sits heavily on the grass, and turns barbed wire
into a string of stars. On a distant hill, a small square of yellow
appears to be a lighted stage. At last the truth dawns on us: Fall
is staggering in, right on schedule, with its baggage of chilly
nights, macabre holidays, and spectacular, heart-stoppingly
beautiful leaves. Soon the leaves will start cringing on the trees,
and roll up in clenched fists before they actually fall off. Dry
seedpods will rattle like tiny gourds. But first there will be
weeks of gushing color so bright, so pastel, so confettilike, that
people will travel up and down the East Coast just to stare at
it—a whole season of leaves.

Where do the colors come from? Sunlight rules most living 2
things with its golden edicts. When the days begin to shorten,
soon after the summer solstice on June 21, a tree reconsiders its
leaves. All summer it feeds them so they can process sunlight, but
in the dog days of summer the tree begins pulling nutrients back
into its trunk and roots, pares down, and gradually chokes off its
leaves. A corky layer of cells forms at the leaves' slender petioles,
then scars over. Undernourished, the leaves stop producing the

59

pigment chlorophyll, and photosynthesis ceases. Animals can migrate, hibernate, or store food to prepare for winter. But where can a tree go? It survives by dropping its leaves, and by the end of autumn only a few fragile threads of fluid-carrying xylem hold leaves to their stems.

3   A turning leaf stays partly green at first, then reveals splotches of yellow and red as the chlorophyll gradually breaks down. Dark green seems to stay longest in the veins, outlining and defining them. During the summer, chlorophyll dissolves in the heat and light, but it is also being steadily replaced. In the fall, on the other hand, no new pigment is produced, and so we notice the other colors that were always there, right in the leaf, although chlorophyll's shocking green hid them from view. With their camouflage gone, we see these colors for the first time all year, and marvel, but they were always there, hidden like a vivid secret beneath the hot glowing greens of summer.

4   The most spectacular range of fall foliage occurs in the northeastern United States and in eastern China, where the leaves are robustly colored, thanks in part to a rich climate. European maples don't achieve the same flaming reds as their American relatives, which thrive on cold nights and sunny days. In Europe, the warm, humid weather turns the leaves brown or mildly yellow. Anthocyanin, the pigment that gives apples their red and turns leaves red or red-violet, is produced by sugars that remain in the leaf after the supply of nutrients dwindles. Unlike the carotenoids, which color carrots, squash, and corn, and turn leaves orange and yellow, anthocyanin varies from year to year, depending on the temperature and amount of sunlight. The fiercest colors occur in years when the fall sunlight is strongest and the nights are cool and dry (a state of grace scientists find vexing to forecast). This is also why leaves appear dizzyingly bright and clear on a sunny fall day: The anthocyanin flashes like a marquee.

5   Not all leaves turn the same colors. Elms, weeping willows, and the ancient ginkgo all grow radiant yellow, along with hickories, aspens, bottlebrush buckeyes, cottonweeds, and tall, keening poplars. Basswood turns bronze, birches bright gold. Water-loving maples put on a symphonic display of scarlets. Sumacs turn red,

too, as do flowering dogwoods, black gums, and sweet gums. Though some oaks yellow, most turn a pinkish brown. The farmlands also change color, as tepees of cornstalks and bales of shredded-wheat-textured hay stand drying in the fields. In some spots, one slope of a hill may be green and the other already in bright color, because the hillside facing south gets more sun and heat than the northern one.

An odd feature of the colors is that they don't seem to have 6 any special purpose. We are predisposed to respond to their beauty, of course. They shimmer with the colors of sunset, spring flowers, the tawny buff of a colt's pretty rump, the shuddering pink of a blush. Animals and flowers color for a reason—adaptation to their environment—but there is no adaptive reason for leaves to color so beautifully in the fall any more than there is for the sky or ocean to be blue. It's just one of the haphazard marvels the planet bestows every year. We find the sizzling colors thrilling, and in a sense they dupe us. Colored like living things, they signal death and disintegration. In time, they will become fragile and, like the body, return to dust. They are as we hope our own fate will be when we die: Not to vanish, just to sublime from one beautiful state into another. Though leaves lose their green life, they bloom with urgent colors, as the woods grow mummified day by day, and Nature becomes more carnal, mute, and radiant.

We call the season "fall," from the Old English *feallan*, to fall, 7 which leads back through time to the Indo-European *phol*, which also means to fall. So the word and the idea are both extremely ancient, and haven't really changed since the first of our kind needed a name for fall's leafy abundance. As we say the word, we're reminded of that other Fall, in the garden of Eden, when fig leaves never withered and scales fell from our eyes. Fall is the time when leaves fall from the trees, just as spring is when flowers spring up, summer is when we simmer, and winter is when we whine from the cold.

Children love to play in piles of leaves, hurling them into the 8 air like confetti, leaping into soft unruly mattresses of them. For children, leaf fall is just one of the odder figments of Nature, like hailstones or snowflakes. Walk down a lane overhung with trees in the never-never land of autumn, and you will forget about time and death, lost in the sheer delicious spill of color. Adam and Eve concealed their nakedness with leaves, remember? Leaves have always hidden our awkward secrets.

9   But how do the colored leaves fall? As a leaf ages, the growth hormone, auxin, fades, and cells at the base of the petiole divide. Two or three rows of small cells, lying at right angles to the axis of the petiole, react with water, then come apart, leaving the petioles hanging on by only a few threads of xylem. A light breeze, and the leaves are airborne. They glide and swoop, rocking in invisible cradles. They are all wing and may flutter from yard to yard on small whirlwinds or updrafts, swiveling as they go. Firmly tethered to earth, we love to see things rise up and fly—soap bubbles, balloons, birds, fall leaves. They remind us that the end of a season is capricious, as is the end of life. We especially like the way leaves rock, careen, and swoop as they fall. Everyone knows the motion. Pilots sometimes do a maneuver called a "falling leaf," in which the plane loses altitude quickly and on purpose, by slipping first to the right, then to the left. The machine weighs a ton or more, but in one pilot's mind it is a weightless thing, a falling leaf. She has seen the motion before, in the Vermont woods where she played as a child. Below her the trees radiate gold, copper, and red. Leaves are falling, although she can't see them fall, as she falls, swooping down for a closer view.

10   At last the leaves leave. But first they turn color and thrill us for weeks on end. Then they crunch and crackle underfoot. They *shush*, as children drag their small feet through leaves heaped along the curb. Dark, slimy mats of leaves cling to one's heels after a rain. A damp, stuccolike mortar of semidecayed leaves protects the tender shoots with a roof until spring, and makes a rich humus. An occasional bulge or ripple in the leafy mounds signals a shrew or a field mouse tunneling out of sight. Sometimes one finds in fossil stones the imprint of a leaf, long since disintegrated whose outlines remind us how detailed, vibrant, and alive are the things of this earth that perish.

1990

Behind the Formaldehyde Curtain

Jessica Mitford

The drama begins to unfold with the arrival of the corpse at the   1
mortuary.

   Alas, poor Yorick! How surprised he would be to see how his   2
counterpart of today is whisked off to a funeral parlor and is in
short order sprayed, sliced, pierced, pickled, trussed, trimmed,
creamed, waxed, painted, rouged and neatly dressed—transformed
from a common corpse into a Beautiful Memory Picture. This
process is known in the trade as embalming and restorative art,
and is so universally employed in the United States and Canada
that the funeral director does it routinely, without consulting
corpse or kin. He regards as eccentric those few who are hardy
enough to suggest that it might be dispensed with. Yet no law
requires embalming, no religious doctrine commends it, nor is it
dictated by considerations of health, sanitation, or even of personal daintiness. In no part of the world but in Northern America
is it widely used. The purpose of embalming is to make the corpse
presentable for viewing in a suitably costly container; and here too
the funeral director routinely, without first consulting the family,
prepares the body for public display.

   Is all this legal? The processes to which a dead body may be   3
subjected are after all to some extent circumscribed by law. In
most states, for instance, the signature of next of kin must be
obtained before an autopsy may be performed, before the
deceased may be cremated, before the body may be turned over
to a medical school for research purposes; or such provision must
be made in the decedent's will. In the case of embalming, no such
permission is required nor is it ever sought. A textbook, *The
Principles and Practices of Embalming,* comments on this: "There is
some question regarding the legality of much that is done within
the preparation room." The author points out that it would be most
unusual for a responsible member of a bereaved family to instruct
the mortician, in so many words, to *"embalm"* the body of a
deceased relative. The very term "embalming" is so seldom used
that the mortician must rely upon custom in the matter. The author

concludes that unless the family specifies otherwise, the act of entrusting the body to the care of a funeral establishment carries with it an implied permission to go ahead and embalm.

4   Embalming is indeed a most extraordinary procedure, and one must wonder at the docility of Americans who each year pay hundreds of millions of dollars for its perpetuation, blissfully ignorant of what it is all about, what is done, how it is done. Not one in ten thousand has any idea of what actually takes place. Books on the subject are extremely hard to come by. They are not to be found in most libraries or bookshops.

5   In an era when huge television audiences watch surgical operations in the comfort of their living rooms, when, thanks to the animated cartoon, the geography of the digestive system has become familiar territory even to the nursery school set, in a land where the satisfaction of curiosity about almost all matters is a national pastime, the secrecy surrounding embalming can, surely, hardly be attributed to the inherent gruesomeness of the subject. Custom in this regard has within this century suffered a complete reversal. In the early days of American embalming, when it was performed in the home of the deceased, it was almost mandatory for some relative to stay by the embalmer's side and witness the procedure. Today, family members who might wish to be in attendance would certainly be dissuaded by the funeral director. All others, except apprentices, are excluded by law from the preparation room.

6   A close look at what does actually take place may explain in large measure the undertaker's intractable reticence concerning a procedure that has become his major *raison d'être*. Is it possible he fears that public information about embalming might lead patrons to wonder if they really want this service? If the funeral men are loath to discuss the subject outside the trade, the reader may, understandably, be equally loath to go on reading at this point. For those who have the stomach for it, let us part the formaldehyde curtain. . . .

7   The body is first laid out in the undertaker's morgue—or rather, Mr. Jones is reposing in the preparation room—to be readied to bid the world farewell.

8   The preparation room in any of the better funeral establishments has the tiled and sterile look of a surgery, and indeed the

embalmer-restorative artist who does his chores there is beginning to adopt the term "dermasurgeon" (appropriately corrupted
by some mortician-writers as "demi-surgeon") to describe his
calling. His equipment, consisting of scalpels, scissors, augers,
forceps, clamps, needles, pumps, tubes, bowls, and basins, is
crudely imitative of the surgeon's, as is his technique, acquired in
a nine- or twelve-month post-high school course in an embalming
school. He is supplied by an advanced chemical industry with a
bewildering array of fluids, sprays, pastes, oils, powders, creams,
to fix or soften tissue, shrink or distend it as needed, dry it here,
restore the moisture there. There are cosmetics, waxes and paints
to fill and cover features, even plaster of Paris to replace entire
limbs. There are ingenious aids to prop and stabilize the cadaver:
A Vari-Pose Head Rest, the Edwards Arm and Hand Positioner,
the Repose Block (to support the shoulders during the embalming), and the Throop Foot Positioner, which resembles an old-
fashioned stock.

Mr. John H. Eckels, president of the Eckels College of 9
Mortuary Science, thus describes the first part of the embalming
procedure: "In the hands of a skilled practitioner, this work may
be done in a comparatively short time and without mutilating the
body other than by slight incision—so slight that it scarcely
would cause serious inconvenience if made upon a living person.
It is necessary to remove the blood, and doing this not only helps
in the disinfecting, but removes the principal cause of disfigurements due to discoloration."

Another textbook discusses the all-important time element: 10
"The earlier this is done, the better, for every hour that elapses
between death and embalming will add to the problems and com-
plications encountered. . . ." Just how soon should one get going
on the embalming? The author tells us, "On the basis of such
scanty information made available to this profession through its
rudimentary and haphazard system of technical research, we
must conclude that the best results are to be obtained if the subject
is embalmed before life is completely extinct—that is, before
cellular death has occurred. In the average case, this would mean
within an hour after somatic death." For those who feel that there
is something a little rudimentary, not to say haphazard, about

this advice, a comforting thought is offered by another writer. Speaking of fears entertained in early days of premature burial, he points out, "One of the effects of embalming by chemical injection, however, has been to dispel fears of live burial." How true; once the blood is removed, chances of live burial are indeed remote.

11   To return to Mr. Jones, the blood is drained out through the veins and replaced by embalming fluid pumped in through the arteries. As noted in *The Principles and Practices of Embalming*, "every operator has a favorite injection and drainage point—a fact which becomes a handicap only if he fails or refuses to forsake his favorites when conditions demand it." Typical favorites are the carotid artery, femoral artery, jugular vein, subclavian vein. There are various choices of embalming fluid. If Flextone is used, it will produce a "mild, flexible rigidity. The skin retains a velvety softness, the tissues are rubbery and pliable. Ideal for women and children." It may be blended with B. and G. Products Company's Lyf-Lyk tint, which is guaranteed to reproduce "nature's own skin texture . . . the velvety appearance of living tissue." Suntone comes in three separate tints: Suntan; Special Cosmetic Tint, a pink shade "especially indicated for female subjects"; and Regular Cosmetic Tint, moderately pink.

12   About three to six gallons of a dyed and perfumed solution of formaldehyde, glycerin, borax, phenol, alcohol and water is soon circulating through Mr. Jones, whose mouth has been sewn together with a "needle directed upward between the upper lip and gum and brought out through the left nostril," with the corners raised slightly "for a more pleasant expression." If he should be bucktoothed, his teeth are cleaned with Bon Ami and coated with colorless nail polish. His eyes, meanwhile, are closed with flesh-tinted eye caps and eye cement.

13   The next step is to have at Mr. Jones with a thing called a trocar. This is a long, hollow needle attached to a tube. It is jabbed into the abdomen, poked around the entrails and chest cavity, the contents of which are pumped out and replaced with "cavity fluid." This done, and the hole in the abdomen sewn up, Mr. Jones's face is heavily creamed (to protect the skin from burns which may be caused by leakage of the chemicals), and he is covered with a sheet and left unmolested for a while. But not for long—there is more,

much more, in store for him. He has been embalmed, but not yet
restored, and the best time to start the restorative work is eight
to ten hours after embalming, when the tissues have become
firm and dry.

The object of all this attention to the corpse, it must be 14
remembered, is to make it presentable for viewing in an attitude
of healthy repose. "Our customs require the presentation of our
dead in the semblance of normality . . . unmarred by the ravages
of illness, disease or mutilation," says Mr. J. Sheridan Mayer in his
Restorative Art. This is rather a large order since few people die in
the full bloom of health, unravaged by illness and unmarked by
some disfigurement. The funeral industry is equal to the challenge: "In some cases the gruesome appearance of a mutilated or
disease-ridden subject may be quite discouraging. The task of
restoration may seem impossible and shake the confidence of the
embalmer. This is the time for intestinal fortitude and determination. Once the formative work is begun and affected tissues are
cleaned or removed, all doubts of success vanish. It is surprising
and gratifying to discover the results which may be obtained."

The embalmer, having allowed an appropriate interval to 15
elapse, returns to the attack, but now he brings into play the skill
and equipment of sculptor and cosmetician. Is a hand missing?
Casting one in plaster of Paris is a simple matter. "For replacement purposes, only a cast of the back of the hand is necessary;
this is within the ability of the average operator and is quite adequate." If a lip or two, a nose or an ear should be missing, the
embalmer has at hand a variety of restorative waxes with which
to model replacements. Pores and skin texture are simulated by
stippling with a little brush, and over this cosmetics are laid
on. Head off? Decapitation cases are rather routinely handled.
Ragged edges are trimmed, and head joined to torso with a series
of splints, wires and sutures. It is a good idea to have a little
something at the neck—a scarf or a high collar—when time for
viewing comes. Swollen mouth? Cut out tissue as needed from
inside the lips. If too much is removed, the surface contour can
easily be restored by padding with cotton. Swollen necks and
cheeks are reduced by removing tissue through vertical incisions
made down each side of the neck. "When the deceased is casketed,

the pillow will hide the suture incisions . . . as an extra precaution against leakage, the suture may be painted with liquid sealer."

16   The opposite condition is more likely to present itself—that of emaciation. His hypodermic syringe now loaded with massage cream, the embalmer seeks out and fills the hollowed and sunken areas by injection. In this procedure the backs of the hands and fingers and the under-chin area should not be neglected.

17   Positioning the lips is a problem that recurrently challenges the ingenuity of the embalmer. Closed too tightly, they tend to give a stern, even disapproving expression. Ideally, embalmers feel, the lips should give the impression of being ever so slightly parted, the upper lip protruding slightly for a more youthful appearance. This takes some engineering, however, as the lips tend to drift apart. Lip drift can sometimes be remedied by pushing one or two straight pins through the inner margin of the lower lip and then inserting them between the two front upper teeth. If Mr. Jones happens to have no teeth, the pins can just as easily be anchored in his Armstrong Face Former and Denture Replacer. Another method to maintain lip closure is to dislocate the lower jaw, which is then held in its new position by a wire run through holes which have been drilled through the upper and lower jaws at the midline. As the French are fond of saying, *il faut souffrir pour être belle.*

18   If Mr. Jones has died of jaundice, the embalming fluid will very likely turn him green. Does this deter the embalmer? Not if he has intestinal fortitude. Masking pastes and cosmetics are heavily laid on, burial garments and casket interiors are color-correlated with particular care, and Jones is displayed beneath rose-colored lights. Friends will say "How *well* he looks." Death by carbon monoxide, on the other hand, can be rather a good thing from the embalmer's viewpoint: "One advantage is the fact that this type of discoloration is an exaggerated form of a natural pink coloration." This is nice because the healthy glow is already present and needs but little attention.

19   The patching and filling completed, Mr. Jones is now shaved, washed and dressed. Cream-based cosmetic, available in pink, flesh, suntan, brunette and blond, is applied to his hands and face, his hair is shampooed and combed (and, in the case of

Mrs. Jones, set), his hands manicured. For the horny-handed son of toil special care must be taken; cream should be applied to remove ingrained grime, and the nails cleaned. "If he were not in the habit of having them manicured in life, trimming and shaping is advised for better appearance—never questioned by kin."

Jones is now ready for casketing (this is the present participle 20 of the verb "to casket"). In this operation his right shoulder should be depressed slightly "to turn the body a bit to the right and soften the appearance of lying flat on the back." Positioning the hands is a matter of importance, and special rubber position- ing blocks may be used. The hands should be cupped slightly for a more life-like, relaxed appearance. Proper placement of the body requires a delicate sense of balance. It should lie as high as possible in the casket, yet not so high that the lid, when lowered, will hit the nose. On the other hand, we are cautioned, placing the body too low "creates the impression that the body is in a box."

Jones is next wheeled into the appointed slumber room 21 where a few last touches may be added—his favorite pipe placed in his hand or, if he was a great reader, a book propped into posi- tion. (In the case of little Master Jones a Teddy bear may be clutched.) Here he will hold open house for a few days, visiting hours 10 A.M. To 9 P.M.

All now being in readiness, the funeral director calls a staff 22 conference to make sure that each assistant knows his precise duties. Mr. Wilber Kriege writes: "This makes your staff feel that they are a part of the team, with a definite assignment that must be properly carried out if the whole plan is to succeed. You never heard of a football coach who failed to talk to his entire team before they go on the field. They have drilled on the plays they are to exe- cute for hours and days, and yet the successful coach knows the importance of making even the bench-warming third-string sub- stitute feel that he is important if the game is to be won." The win- ning of *this* game is predicated upon glass-smooth handling of the logistics. The funeral director has notified the pallbearers whose names were furnished by the family, has arranged for the presence of clergyman, organist, and soloist, has provided transportation for everybody, has organized and listed the flowers sent by friends. In *Psychology of Funeral Service* Mr. Edward A. Martin points out:

"He may not always do as much as the family thinks he is doing, but it is his helpful guidance that they appreciate in knowing they are proceeding as they should. . . . The important thing is how well his services can be used to make the family believe they are giving unlimited expression to their own sentiment."

23   The religious service may be held in a church or in the chapel of the funeral home; the funeral director vastly prefers the latter arrangement, for not only is it more convenient for him but it affords him the opportunity to show off his beautiful facilities to the gathered mourners. After the clergyman has had his say, the mourners queue up to file past the casket for a last look at the deceased. The family is *never* asked whether they want an open-casket ceremony; in the absence of their instruction to the contrary, this is taken for granted. Consequently, well over 90 percent of all American funerals feature the open casket—a custom unknown in other parts of the world. Foreigners are astonished by it. An English woman living in San Francisco described her reaction in a letter to the writer:

> I myself have attended only one funeral here—that of an elderly fellow worker of mine. After the service I could not understand why everyone was walking towards the coffin (sorry, I mean casket), but thought I had better follow the crowd. It shook me rigid to get there and find the casket open and poor old Oscar lying there in his brown tweed suit, wearing a suntan makeup and just the wrong shade of lipstick. If I had not been extremely fond of the old boy, I have a horrible feeling that I might have giggled. Then and there I decided that I could never face another American funeral—even dead.

24   The casket (which has been resting throughout the service on a Classic Beauty Ultra Metal Casket Bier) is now transferred by a hydraulically operated device called Porto-Lift to a balloon-tired, Glide Easy casket carriage which will wheel it to yet another conveyance, the Cadillac Funeral Coach. This may be lavender, cream, light green—anything but black. Interiors, of course, are color-correlated, "for the man who cannot stop short of perfection."

25   At graveside, the casket is lowered into the earth. This office, once the prerogative of friends of the deceased, is now performed by a patented mechanical lowering device. A "Lifetime Green" artificial grass mat is at the ready to conceal the sere earth, and overhead, to conceal the sky, is a portable Steril Chapel Tent ("resists the intense

heat and humidity of summer and the terrific storms of winter . . . available in Silver Grey, Rose or Evergreen"). Now is the time for the ritual scattering of earth over the coffin, as the solemn words "earth to earth, ashes to ashes, dust to dust" are pronounced by the offici- ating cleric. This can today be accomplished "with a mere flick of the wrist with the Gordon Leak-Proof Earth Dispenser. No grasping of a handful of dirt, no soiled fingers. Simple, dignified, beautiful, rever- ent! The modern way!" The Gordon Earth Dispenser (at $5) is of nickel-plated brass construction. It is not only "attractive to the eye and long wearing"; it is also "one of the 'tools' for building better public relations" if presented as "an appropriate non-commercial gift" to the clergyman. It is shaped something like a saltshaker.

Untouched by human hand, the coffin and the earth are now 26 united.

It is in the function of directing the participants through this 27 maze of gadgetry that the funeral director has assigned to himself his relatively new role of "grief therapist." He has relieved the family of every detail, he has revamped the corpse to look like a living doll, he has arranged for it to nap for a few days in a slum- ber room, he has put on a well-oiled performance in which the concept of *death* has played no part whatsoever—unless it was inconsiderately mentioned by the clergyman who conducted the religious service. He has done everything in his power to make the funeral a real pleasure for everybody concerned. He and his team have given their all to score an upset victory over death.

1963

Writing Drafts

Richard Marius

Finally the moment comes when you sit down to begin your first 1 draft. It is always a good idea at the start to list the points you want to cover. A list is not as elaborate as a formal outline. In writing your first list, don't bother to set items down in the order of importance. List your main points and trust your mind to organize them. You will probably make one list, study it, make another, study it, and perhaps make another. You can organize each list more completely than the last. This preliminary process may save you hours of starting and stopping.

2   Write with your list outline in front of you. Once you begin to write, commit yourself to the task at hand. Do not get up until you have written for an hour. Write your thoughts quickly. Let one sentence give you an idea to develop in the next. Organization, grammar, spelling, and even clarity of sentences are not nearly as important as getting the first draft together. No matter how desperate you feel, keep going.

3   Always keep your mind open to new ideas that pop into your head as you write. Let your list outline help you, but don't become a slave to it. Writers often start an essay with one topic in mind only to discover that another pushes the first one aside as they work. Ideas you had not even thought of before you began to write may pile onto your paper, and five or six pages into your first draft you may realize that you are going to write about something you did not imagine when you started.

4   If such a revelation comes, be grateful and accept it. But don't immediately tear up or erase your draft and start all over again. Make yourself keep on writing, developing these new ideas as they come. If you suddenly start all over again, you may break the train of thought that has given you the new topic. Let your thoughts follow your new thesis, sailing on that tack until the wind changes.

5   When you have said everything you can say in this draft, print it out if you are working on a computer. Get up from your desk and go sit in a chair somewhere else to read it without correcting anything. Then put it aside, preferably overnight. If possible, read your rough draft just before you go to sleep. Many psychological tests have shown that our minds organize and create while we sleep if we pack them full before bedtime. Study a draft just before sleep, and you may discover new ideas in the morning.

6   Be willing to make radical changes in your second draft. If your thesis changed while you were writing your first draft, you will base your second draft on this new subject. Even if your

thesis has not changed, you may need to shift paragraphs around, eliminate paragraphs, or add new ones. Inexperienced writers often suppose that revising a paper means changing only a word or two or adding a sentence or two. This kind of editing is part of the writing process, but it is not the most important part. The most important part of rewriting is a willingness to turn the paper upside down, to shake out of it those ideas that interest you most, to set them in a form where they will interest the reader, too.

I mentioned earlier that some writers cut up their first drafts 7 with a pair of scissors. They toss some paragraphs into the trash; others they paste up with rubber cement in the order that seems most logical and coherent. Afterward they type the whole thing through again, smoothing out the transitions, adding new material, getting new ideas as they work. The translation of the first draft into the second nearly always involves radical cutting and shifting around. Now and then you may firmly fix the order of your thoughts in your first draft, but I find that the order of my essays is seldom established until the second draft.

With the advent of computers the shifting around of parts of 8 the essays has become easy. We can cut and paste electronically with a few strokes of the keyboard. We can also make back-up copies of our earlier drafts so we can go back to them if we wish. But as I said earlier, computers do not remove from us the necessity to think hard about revising.

Always be firm enough with yourself to cut out thoughts or 9 stories that have nothing to do with your thesis, even if they are interesting. Cutting is the supreme test of a writer. You may create a smashing paragraph or sentence only to discover later that it does not help you make your point. You may develop six or seven examples to illustrate a point and discover you need only one.

Now and then you may digress a little. If you digress too often 10 or too far, readers will not follow you unless your facts, your thoughts, and your style are so compelling that they are somehow driven to follow you. Not many writers can pull such digressions off, and most editors will cut out the digressions even when they are interesting. In our hurried and harried time, most readers get impatient with the rambling scenic route. They want to take the most direct way to their destination. To appeal to most of them, you must cut things that do not apply to your main argument.

11   In your third draft, you can sharpen sentences, add information here and there, cut some things, and attend to other details to heighten the force of your writing. In the third draft, writing becomes a lot of fun (for most of us). By then you have usually decided what you want to say. You can now play a bit, finding just the right word, choosing just the right sentence form, compressing here, expanding there.

12   I find it helpful to put a printed draft down beside my keyboard and type the whole thing through again as a final draft, letting all the words run through my mind and fingers one more time rather than merely deleting and inserting on the computer screen. I wrote four drafts of the first edition of this book; I have preserved the final draft of that edition on computer diskettes. But I am writing this draft by propping the first edition up here beside me and typing it all over again. By comparing the first draft and the second draft, one can see how many changes I have made, most of them unforeseen until I sat down here to work.

13   I have outlined here my own writing process. It works for me. You must find the process that works for you. It may be different from mine. A friend tells me that his writing process consists of writing a sentence, agonizing over it, walking around the room, thinking, sitting down, and writing the next sentence. He does not revise very much. I think it unnecessarily painful to bleed out prose that way, but he bleeds out enough to write what he needs to write. Several of my friends tell me they cannot compose at a typewriter; they must first write with a pencil on a yellow pad. These are the people most likely to cut up their drafts with scissors and paste them together in a different form. They also tend to be older. Most young writers are learning to compose at a keyboard, and they cannot imagine another way to write. Neither can I—though on occasion yet I go back to my pencil for pages at a time.

14   The main thing is to keep at it. B. F. Skinner has pointed out that if you write only fifty words a night, you will produce a good-sized book every two or three years. That's not a bad record

for any writer. William Faulkner outlined the plot of his Nobel Prize–winning novel *A Fable* on a wall inside his house near Oxford, Mississippi. You can see it there to this day. Once he got the outline on the wall, he sat down with his typewriter and wrote, following the outline to the end. If writing an outline on a kitchen wall does the trick for you, do it. You can always repaint the wall if you must.

Think of writing as a process making its way toward a product—sometimes painfully. Don't imagine you must know everything you are going to say before you begin. Don't demean yourself and insult your readers by letting your first draft be your final draft. Don't imagine that writing is easy or that you can do it without spending time on it. And don't let anything stand in your way of doing it. Let your house get messy. Leave your magazines unread and your mail unanswered. Put off getting up for a drink of water or a cup of tea. (Never mix alcohol with your writing; true, lots of writers have become alcoholics, but it has not helped their writing.) Don't make a telephone call. Don't straighten up your desk. Sit down and write. And write, and write, and write.

1988

Alone on the Hilltop

John (Fire) Lame Deer and Richard Erdoes

I was all alone on the hilltop. I sat there in the vision pit, a hole dug into the hill, my arms hugging my knees as I watched old man Chest, the medicine man who had brought me there, disappear far down in the valley. He was just a moving black dot among the pines, and soon he was gone altogether.

Now I was all by myself, left on the hilltop for four days and nights without food or water until he came back for me. You know, we Indians are not like some white folks—a man and a wife, two children, and one baby sitter who watches the TV set while the parents are out visiting somewhere.

3   Indian children are never alone. They are always surrounded by grandparents, uncles, cousins, relatives of all kinds, who fondle the kids, sing to them, tell them stories. If the parents go someplace, the kids go along.

4   But here I was, crouched in my vision pit, left alone by myself for the first time in my life. I was sixteen then, still had my boy's name and, let me tell you, I was scared. I was shivering and not only from the cold. The nearest human being was many miles away, and four days and nights is a long, long time. Of course, when it was all over, I would no longer be a boy, but a man. I would have had my vision. I would be given a man's name.

5   Sioux men are not afraid to endure hunger, thirst and loneliness, and I was only ninety-six hours away from being a man. The thought was comforting. Comforting, too, was the warmth of the star blanket which old man Chest had wrapped around me to cover my nakedness. My grandmother had made it especially for this, my first *hanblechia*, my first vision-seeking. It was a beautifully designed quilt, white with a large morning star made of many pieces of brightly colored cloth. That star was so big it covered most of the blanket. If Waken Tanka, the Great Spirit, would give me the vision and the power, I would become a medicine man and perform many ceremonies wrapped in that quilt. I am an old man now and many times a grandfather, but I still have that star blanket my grandmother made for me. I treasure it; some day I shall be buried in it.

6   The medicine man had also left a peace pipe with me, together with a bag of *kinnickinnick*—our kind of tobacco made of red willow bark. This pipe was even more of a friend to me than my star blanket. To us the pipe is like an open Bible. White people need a church house, a preacher and a pipe organ to get into a praying mood. There are so many things to distract you: who else is in the church, whether the other people notice that you have come, the pictures on the wall, the sermon, how much money you should give and did you bring it with you. We think you can't have a vision that way.

For us Indians there is just the pipe, the earth we sit on and ₇ the open sky. The spirit is everywhere. Sometimes it shows itself through an animal, a bird or some trees and hills. Sometimes it speaks from the Badlands, a stone, or even from the water. That smoke from the peace pipe, it goes straight up to the spirit world. But this is a two-way thing. Power flows down to us through that smoke, through the pipe stem. You feel that power as you hold your pipe; it moves from the pipe right into your body. It makes your hair stand up. That pipe is not just a thing; it is alive. Smoking this pipe would make me feel good and help me to get rid of my fears.

As I ran my fingers along its bowl of smooth red pipestone, ₈ red like the blood of my people, I no longer felt scared. That pipe had belonged to my father and to his father before him. It would someday pass to my son and, through him, to my grandchildren. As long as we had the pipe there would be a Sioux nation. As I fingered the pipe, touched it, felt its smoothness that came from long use, I sensed that my forefathers who had once smoked this pipe were with me on the hill, right in the vision pit. I was no longer alone.

Besides the pipe the medicine man had also given me a ₉ gourd. In it were forty small squares of flesh which my grand-mother had cut from her arm with a razor blade. I had seen her do it. Blood had been streaming down from her shoulder to her elbow as she carefully put down each piece of skin on a handker-chief, anxious not to lose a single one. It would have made those anthropologists mad. Imagine, performing such an ancient cere-mony with a razor blade instead of a flint knife! To me it did not matter. Someone dear to me had undergone pain, given me some-thing of herself, part of her body, to help me pray and make me stronghearted. How could I be afraid with so many people—living and dead—helping me?

One thing still worried me. I wanted to become a medicine ₁₀ man, a *yuwipi,* a healer carrying on the ancient ways of the Sioux nation. But you cannot learn to be a medicine man like a white man going to medical school. An old holy man can teach you about herbs and the right ways to perform a ceremony where everything must be in its proper place, where every move, every word has its own, special meaning. These things you can learn—like spelling, like training a horse. But by themselves these things mean nothing. Without the vision and the power this learning will do no good. It would not make me a medicine man.

11   What if I failed, if I had no vision? Or if I dreamed of the Thunder Beings, or lightning struck the hill? That would make me at once into a *heyoka*, a contrarywise, an upside-down man, a clown. "You'll know it, if you get the power," my Uncle Chest had told me. "If you are not given it, you won't lie about it, you won't pretend. That would kill you, or kill somebody close to you, somebody you love."

12   Night was coming on. I was still lightheaded and dizzy from my first sweat bath in which I had purified myself before going up the hill. I had never been in a sweat lodge before. I had sat in the little beehive-shaped hut made of bent willow branches and covered with blankets to keep the heat in. Old Chest and three other medicine men had been in the lodge with me. I had my back against the wall, edging as far away as I could from the red-hot stones glowing in the center. As Chest poured water over the rocks, hissing white steam enveloped me and filled my lungs. I thought the heat would kill me, burn the eyelids off my face! But right in the middle of all this swirling steam I heard Chest singing. So it couldn't be all that bad. I did not cry out "All my relatives!"—which would have made him open the flap of the sweat lodge to let in some cool air—and I was proud of this. I heard him praying for me: "Oh, holy rocks, we receive your white breath, the steam. It is the breath of life. Let this young boy inhale it. Make him strong."

13   The sweat bath had prepared me for my vision-seeking. Even now, an hour later, my skin still tingled. But it seemed to have made my brains empty. Maybe that was good, plenty of room for new insights.

14   Darkness had fallen upon the hill. I knew that *hanhepiwi* had risen, the night sun, which is what we call the moon. Huddled in my narrow cave, I did not see it. Blackness was wrapped around me like a velvet cloth. It seemed to cut me off from the outside world, even from my own body. It made me listen to the voices within me. I thought of my forefathers who had crouched on this

hill before me, because the medicine men in my family had chosen this spot for a place of meditation and vision-seeking ever
since the day they had crossed the Missouri to hunt for buffalo in
the White River country some two hundred years ago. I thought
that I could sense their presence right through the earth I was
leaning against. I could feel them entering my body, feel them
stirring in my mind and heart.

Sounds came to me through the darkness: the cries of the   15
wind, the whisper of the trees, the voices of nature, animal
sounds, the hooting of an owl. Suddenly I felt an overwhelming
presence. Down there with me in my cramped hole was a big
bird. The pit was only as wide as myself, and I was a skinny boy,
but that huge bird was flying around me as if he had the whole
sky to himself. I could hear his cries, sometimes near and sometimes far, far away. I felt feathers or a wing touching my back and
head. This feeling was so overwhelming that it was just too much
for me. I trembled and my bones turned to ice. I grasped the rattle with the forty pieces of my grandmother's flesh. It also had
many little stones in it, tiny fossils picked up from an ant heap.
Ants collect them. Nobody knows why. These little stones are
supposed to have a power in them. I shook the rattle and it made
a soothing sound, like rain falling on rock. It was talking to me,
but it did not calm my fears. I took the sacred pipe in my other
hand and began to sing and pray: "Tunkashila, grandfather spirit,
help me." But this did not help. I don't know what got into me, but
I was no longer myself. I started to cry. Crying, even my voice was
different. I sounded like an older man, I couldn't even recognize
this strange voice. I used long-ago words in my prayer, words no
longer used nowadays. I tried to wipe away my tears, but they
wouldn't stop. In the end I just pulled that quilt over me, rolled
myself up in it. Still I felt the bird wings touching me.

Slowly I perceived that a voice was trying to tell me some-   16
thing. It was a bird cry, but I tell you, I began to understand some
of it. That happens sometimes. I know a lady who had a butterfly
sitting on her shoulder. That butterfly told her things. This made
her become a great medicine woman.

I heard a human voice too, strange and high-pitched, a   17
voice which could not come from an ordinary, living being.

All at once I was way up there with the birds. The hill with the vision pit was way above everything. I could look down even on the stars, and the moon was close to my left side. It seemed as though the earth and the stars were moving below me. A voice said, "You are sacrificing yourself here to be a medicine man. In time you will be one. You will teach other medicine men. We are the fowl people, the winged ones, the eagles and the owls. We are a nation and you shall be our brother. You will never kill or harm any one of us. You are going to understand us whenever you come to seek a vision here on this hill. You will learn about herbs and roots, and you will heal people. You will ask them for nothing in return. A man's life is short. Make yours a worthy one."

18   I felt that these voices were good, and slowly my fear left me. I had lost all sense of time. I did not know whether it was day or night. I was asleep, yet wide awake. Then I saw a shape before me. It rose from the darkness and the swirling fog which penetrated my earth hole. I saw that this was my great-grandfather, Tahca Ushte, Lame Deer, old man chief of the Minneconjou. I could see the blood dripping from my great-grandfather's chest where a white soldier had shot him. I understood that my great-grandfather wished me to take his name. This made me glad beyond words.

19   We Sioux believe that there is something within us that controls us, something like a second person almost. We call it *nagi*, what other people might call soul, spirit or essence. One can't see it, feel it or taste it, but that time on the hill—and only that once—I knew it was there inside of me. Then I felt the power surge through me like a flood. I cannot describe it, but it filled all of me. Now I knew for sure that I would become a *wicasa wakan*, a medicine man. Again I wept, this time with happiness.

20   I didn't know how long I had been up there on that hill—one minute or a lifetime. I felt a hand on my shoulder gently shaking me. It was old man Chest, who had come for me. He told me that I had been in the vision pit four days and four nights and that it was time to come down. He would give me something to eat and water to drink and then I was to tell him everything that had happened to me during my *hanblechia*. He would interpret my visions

for me. He told me that the vision pit had changed me in a way that I would not be able to understand at that time. He told me also that I was no longer a boy, that I was a man now. I was Lame Deer.

1972

The Serpents of Paradise

Edward Abbey

The April mornings are bright, clear and calm. Not until the after- 1
noon does the wind begin to blow, raising dust and sand in fun-
nelshaped twisters that spin across the desert briefly, like dancers,
and then collapse—whirlwinds from which issue no voice or
word except the forlorn moan of the elements under stress. After
the reconnoitering dust-devils comes the real, the serious wind,
the voice of the desert rising to a demented howl and blotting out
sky and sun behind yellow clouds of dust, sand, confusion,
embattled birds, last year's scrub-oak leaves, pollen, the husks of
locusts, bark of juniper. . . .

Time of the red eye, the sore and bloody nostril, the sand- 2
pitted windshield, if one is foolish enough to drive his car into
such a storm. Time to sit indoors and continue that letter which is
never finished—while the fine dust forms neat little windrows
under the edge of the door and on the windowsills. Yet the
springtime winds are as much a part of the canyon country as the
silence and the glamorous distances; you learn, after a number of
years, to love them also.

The mornings therefore, as I started to say and meant to say, 3
are all the sweeter in the knowledge of what the afternoon is
likely to bring. Before beginning the morning chores I like to sit
on the sill of my doorway, bare feet planted on the bare ground
and a mug of hot coffee in hand, facing the sunrise. The air is
gelid, not far above freezing, but the butane heater inside the
trailer keeps my back warm, the rising sun warms the front, and
the coffee warms the interior.

4   Perhaps this is the loveliest hour of the day, though it's hard to choose. Much depends on the season. In midsummer the sweetest hour begins at sundown, after the awful heat of the afternoon. But now, in April, we'll take the opposite, that hour beginning with the sunrise. The birds, returning from wherever they go in winter, seem inclined to agree. The pinyon jays are whirling in garrulous, gregarious flocks from one stunted tree to the next and back again, erratic exuberant games without any apparent practical function. A few big ravens hang around and croak harsh clanking statements of smug satisfaction from the rimrock, lifting their greasy wings now and then to probe for lice. I can hear but seldom see the canyon wrens singing their distinctive song from somewhere up on the cliffs: a flutelike descent—never ascent—of the whole-tone scale. Staking out new nesting claims, I understand. Also invisible but invariably present at some indefinable distance are the mourning doves whose plaintive call suggests irresistibly a kind of seeking-out, the attempt by separated souls to restore a lost communion:

5   *Hello . . . they seem to cry, who . . . are . . . you?*

6   And the reply from a different quarter. *Hello . . .* (pause) *where . . . are . . . you?*

7   No doubt this line of analogy must be rejected. It's foolish and unfair to impute to the doves, with serious concerns of their own, an interest in questions more appropriate to their human-kin. Yet their song, if not a mating call or a warning, must be what it sounds like, a brooding meditation on space, on solitude. The game.

8   Other birds, silent, which I have not yet learned to identify, are also lurking in the vicinity, watching me. What the ornithologist terms l.g.b.'s—little gray birds—they flit about from point to point on noiseless wings, their origins obscure.

9   As mentioned before, I share the housetrailer with a number of mice. I don't know how many but apparently only a few, perhaps a single family. They don't disturb me and are welcome to my crumbs and leavings. Where they came from, how they got into the trailer, how they survived before my arrival (for the trailer had been locked up for six months), these are puzzling matters I am not prepared to resolve. My only reservation concerning the mice is that they do attract rattlesnakes.

I'm sitting on my doorstep early one morning, facing the 10 sun as usual, drinking coffee, when I happen to look down and see almost between my bare feet, only a couple of inches to the rear of my heels, the very thing I had in mind. No mistaking that wedgelike head, that tip of horny segmented tail peeping out of the coils. He's under the doorstep and in the shade where the ground and air remain very cold. In his sluggish condition he's not likely to strike unless I rouse him by some careless move of my own.

There's a revolver inside the trailer, a huge British Webley .45, 11 loaded, but it's out of reach. Even if I had it in my hands I'd hesitate to blast a fellow creature at such close range, shooting between my own legs at a living target flat on solid rock thirty inches away. It would be like murder; and where would I set my coffee? My cherry-wood, walking stick leans against the trailerhouse wall only a few feet away but I'm afraid that in leaning over for it I might stir up the rattler or spill some hot coffee on his scales.

Other considerations come to mind. Arches National Monu- 12 ment is meant to be among other things a sanctuary for wildlife— for all forms of wildlife. It is my duty as a park ranger to protect, preserve and defend all living things within the park boundaries, making no exceptions. Even if this were not the case I have personal convictions to uphold. Ideals, you might say. I prefer not to kill animals. I'm a humanist; I'd rather kill a *man* than a snake.

What to do. I drink some more coffee and study the dormant 13 reptile at my heels. It is not after all the mighty diamondback, *Crotalus atrox*, I'm confronted with but a smaller species known locally as the horny rattler or more precisely as the Faded Midget. An insulting name for a rattlesnake, which may explain the Faded Midget's alleged bad temper. But the name is apt: he is small and dusty-looking, with a little knob above each eye—the horns. His bite, though temporarily disabling, would not likely kill a full-grown man in normal health. Even so I don't really want him around. Am I to be compelled to put on boots or shoes every time I wish to step outside? The scorpions, tarantulas, centipedes, and black widows are nuisance enough.

I finish my coffee, lean back and swing my feet up and inside 14 the doorway of the trailer. At once there is a buzzing sound from below and the rattler lifts his head from his coils, eyes brightening, and extends his narrow black tongue to test the air.

15   After thawing out my boots over the gas flame I pull them on and come back to the doorway. My visitor is still waiting beneath the doorstep, basking in the sun, fully alert. The trailerhouse has two doors. I leave by the other and get a long-handled spade out of the bed of the government pickup. With this tool I scoop the snake into the open. He strikes; I can hear the click of the fangs against steel, see the strain of venom. He wants to stand and fight, but I am patient; I insist on herding him well away from the trailer. On guard, head aloft—that evil slit-eyed weaving head shaped like the ace of spades—tail whirring, the rattler slithers sideways, retreating slowly before me until he reaches the shelter of a sandstone slab. He backs under it.

16   You better stay there, cousin, I warn him; if I catch you around the trailer again I'll chop your head off.

17   A week later he comes back. If not him, his twin brother. I spot him one morning under the trailer near the kitchen drain, waiting for a mouse. I have to keep my promise.

18   This won't do. If there are midget rattlers in the area there may be diamondbacks too—five, six or seven feet long, thick as a man's wrist, dangerous. I don't want *them* camping under my home. It looks as though I'll have to trap the mice.

19   However, before being forced to take that step I am lucky enough to capture a gopher snake. Burning garbage one morning at the park dump, I see a long slender yellow-brown snake emerge from a mound of old tin cans and plastic picnic plates and take off down the sandy bed of a gulch. There is a burlap sack in the cab of the truck which I carry when plucking Kleenex flowers from the brush and cactus along the road; I grab that and my stick, run after the snake and corner it beneath the exposed roots of a bush. Making sure it's a gopher snake and not something less useful, I open the neck of the sack and with a great deal of coaxing and prodding get the snake into it. The gopher snake, *Drymarchon corais couperi*, or bull snake, has a reputation as the enemy of rattlesnakes, destroying or driving them away whenever encountered.

20   Hoping to domesticate this sleek, handsome and docile reptile, I release him inside the trailerhouse and keep him there for

several days. Should I attempt to feed him? I decide against it—
let him eat mice. What little water he may need can also be
extracted from the flesh of his prey.

The gopher snake and I get along nicely. During the day he curls 21
up like a cat in the warm corner behind the heater and at night he
goes about his business. The mice, singularly quiet for a change,
make themselves scarce. The snake is passive, apparently contented,
and makes no resistance when I pick him up with my hands and
drape him over an arm or around my neck. When I take him outside
into the wind and sunshine his favorite place seems to be inside my
shirt, where he wraps himself around my waist and rests on my belt.
In this position he sometimes sticks his head out between shirt buttons for a survey of the weather, astonishing and delighting any
tourists who may happen to be with me at the time. The scales of a
snake are dry and smooth, quite pleasant to the touch. Being a cold-
blooded creature, of course, he takes his temperature from that of
the immediate environment—in this case my body.

We are compatible. From my point of view, friends. After a 22
week of close association I turn him loose on the warm sandstone
at my doorstep and leave for patrol of the park. At noon when I
return he is gone. I search everywhere beneath, nearby and inside
the trailerhouse, but my companion has disappeared. Has he left
the area entirely or is he hiding somewhere close by? At any rate
I am troubled no more by rattlesnakes under the door.

The snake story is not yet ended. 23

In the middle of May, about a month after the gopher snake's 24
disappearance, in the evening of a very hot day, with all the rosy
desert cooling like a griddle with the fire turned off, he reappears.
This time with a mate.

I'm in the stifling heat of the trailer opening a can of beer, bare- 25
footed, about to go outside and relax after a hard day watching
cloud formations. I happen to glance out the little window near
the refrigerator and see two gopher snakes on my verandah
engaged in what seems to be a kind of ritual dance. Like a living
caduceus they wind and unwind about each other in undulant,
graceful, perpetual motion, moving slowly across a dome of
sandstone. Invisible but tangible as music is the passion which
joins them—sexual? combative? both? A shameless *voyeur*, I stare

at the lovers, and then to get a closer view run outside and around the trailer to the back. There I get down on hands and knees and creep toward the dancing snakes, not wanting to frighten or disturb them. I crawl to within six feet of them and stop, flat on my belly, watching from the snake's-eye level. Obsessed with their ballet, the serpents seem unaware of my presence.

26   The two gopher snakes are nearly identical in length and coloring; I cannot be certain that either is actually my former household pet. I cannot even be sure that they are male and female, though their performance resembles so strongly a *pas de deux* by formal lovers. They intertwine and separate, glide side by side in perfect congruence, turn like mirror images of each other and glide back again, wind and unwind again. This is the basic pattern but there is a variation: at regular intervals the snakes elevate their heads, facing one another, as high as they can go, as if each is trying to outreach or overawe the other. Their heads and bodies rise, higher and higher, then topple together and the rite goes on.

27   I crawl after them, determined to see the whole thing. Suddenly and simultaneously they discover me, prone on my belly a few feet away. The dance stops. After a moment's pause the two snakes come straight toward me, still in flawless unison, straight toward my face, the forked tongues flickering, their intense wild yellow eyes staring directly into my eyes. For an instant I am paralyzed by wonder; then, stung by a fear too ancient and powerful to overcome I scramble back, rising to my knees. The snakes veer and turn and race away from me in parallel motion, their lean elegant bodies making a soft hissing noise as they slide over the sand and stone. I follow them for a short distance, still plagued by curiosity, before remembering my place and the requirements of common courtesy. For godsake let them go in peace, I tell myself. Wish them luck and (if lovers) innumerable offspring, a life of happily ever after. Not for their sake alone but for your own.

28   In the long hot days and cool evenings to come I will not see the gopher snakes again. Nevertheless I will feel their presence watching over me like totemic deities, keeping the rattlesnakes far back in the brush where I like them best, cropping off the surplus mouse population, maintaining useful connections with the primeval Sympathy, mutual aid, symbiosis, continuity.

How can I descend to such anthropomorphism? Easily—but ₂₉
is it, in this case, entirely false? Perhaps not. I am not attributing
human motives to my snake and bird acquaintances. I recognize
that when and where they serve purposes of mine they do so for
beautifully selfish reasons of their own. Which is exactly the way
it should be. I suggest, however, that it's a foolish, simple-minded
rationalism which denies any form of emotion to all animals but
man and his dog. This is no more justified than the Moslems are
in denying souls to women. It seems to me possible, even probable, that many of the nonhuman undomesticated animals experience emotions unknown to us. What do the coyotes mean when
they yodel at the moon? What are the dolphins trying so patiently
to tell us? Precisely what did those two enraptured gopher snakes
have in mind when they came gliding toward my eyes over the
naked sandstone? If I had been as capable of trust as I am susceptible to fear I might have learned something new or some
truth so very old we have all forgotten it.

> They do not sweat and whine about their condition,
> They do not lie awake in the dark and weep for their sins. . . .

All men are brothers, we like to say, half-wishing sometimes ₃₀
in secret it were not true. But perhaps it is true. And is the evolu-
tionary line from protozoan to Spinoza any less certain? That also
may be true. We are obliged, therefore, to spread the news,
painful and bitter though it may be for some to hear, that all living things on earth are kindred.

1968

Smile

Alan Lightman

It is a Saturday in March. The man wakes up slowly, reaches over ₁
and feels the windowpane, and decides it is warm enough to skip
his thermal underwear. He yawns and dresses and goes out for
his morning jog. When he comes back, he showers, cooks himself

a scrambled egg, and settles down on the sofa with *The Essays of E. B. White.* Around noon, he rides his bike to the bookstore. He spends a couple of hours there, just poking around the books. Then he pedals back through the little town, past his house, and to the lake.

2   When the woman woke up this morning, she got out of bed and went immediately to her easel, where she picked up her pastels and set to work on her painting. After an hour, she is satisfied with the light effect and quits to have breakfast. She dresses quickly and walks to a nearby store to buy shutters for her bathroom. At the store, she meets friends and has lunch with them. Afterward, she wants to be alone and drives to the lake.

3   Now, the man and the woman stand on the wooden dock, gazing at the lake and the waves on the water. They haven't noticed each other.

4   The man turns. And so begins the sequence of events informing him of her. Light reflected from her body instantly enters the pupils of his eyes, at the rate of ten trillion particles of light per second. Once through the pupil of each eye, the light travels through an oval-shaped lens, then through a transparent, jellylike substance filling up the eyeball, and lands on the retina. Here it is gathered by one hundred million rod and cone cells.

5   Cells in the path of the reflected highlights receive a great deal of light; cells falling in the shadows of the reflected scene receive very little. The woman's lips, for example, are just now glistening in the sunlight, reflecting light of high intensity onto a tiny patch of cells slightly northeast of back center of the man's retina. The edges around her mouth, on the other hand, are rather dark, so that cells neighboring the northeast path receive much less light.

6   Each particle of light ends its journey in the eye upon meeting a retinene molecule, consisting of 20 carbon atoms, 28 hydrogen atoms, and 1 oxygen atom. In its dormant condition, each retinene molecule is attached to a protein molecule and has a twist between the eleventh and fifteenth carbon atoms. But when light strikes it, as is now happening in about 30,000 trillion retinene molecules every second, the molecule straightens out and separates from its protein. After several intermediate steps, it

wraps into a twist again, awaiting arrival of a new particle of light. Far less than a thousandth of a second has elapsed since the man saw the woman.

Triggered by the dance of the retinene molecules, the nerve 7 cells, or neurons, respond. First in the eye and then in the brain. One neuron, for instance, has just gone into action. Protein molecules on its surface suddenly change their shape, blocking the flow of positively charged sodium atoms from the surrounding body fluid. This change in flow of electrically charged atoms produces a change in voltage that shudders through the cell. After a distance of a fraction of an inch, the electrical signal reaches the end of the neuron, altering the release of specific molecules, which migrate a distance of a hundred-thousandth of an inch until they reach the next neuron, passing along the news.

The woman, in fact, holds her hands by her sides and tilts her 8 head at an angle of five and a half degrees. Her hair falls just to her shoulders. This information and much, much more is exactingly encoded by the electrical pulses in the various neurons of the man's eyes.

In another few thousandths of a second, the electrical signals 9 reach the ganglion neurons, which bunch together in the optic nerve at the back of the eye and carry their data to the brain. Here, the impulses race to the primary visual cortex, a highly folded layer of tissue about a tenth of an inch thick and two square inches in area, containing one hundred million neurons in half a dozen layers. The fourth layer receives the input first, does a preliminary analysis, and transfers the information to neurons in other layers. At every stage, each neuron may receive signals from a thousand other neurons, combine the signals—some of which cancel each other out—and dispatch the computed result to a thousand-odd other neurons.

After about thirty seconds—after several hundred trillion 10 particles of reflected light have entered the man's eyes and been processed—the woman says hello. Immediately, molecules of air are pushed together, then apart, then together, beginning in her vocal cords and traveling in a spring like motion to the man's ears. The sound makes the trip from her to him (twenty feet) in a fiftieth of a second.

11   Within each of his ears, the vibrating air quickly covers the distance to the eardrum. The eardrum, an oval membrane about .3 inch in diameter and tilted fifty-five degrees from the floor of the auditory canal, itself begins trembling and transmits its motion to three tiny bones. From there, the vibrations shake the fluid in the cochlea, which spirals snail-like two and a half turns around.

12   Inside the cochlea the tones are deciphered. Here, a very thin membrane undulates in step with the sloshing fluid, and through this basilar membrane run tiny filaments of varying thickness, like strings on a harp. The woman's voice, from afar, is playing this harp. Her hello begins in the low registers and rises in pitch toward the end. In precise response, the thick filaments in the basilar membrane vibrate first, followed by the thinner ones. Finally, tens of thousands of rod-shaped bodies perched on the basilar membrane convey their particular quiverings to the auditory nerve.

13   News of the woman's hello, in electrical form, races along the neurons of the auditory nerve and enters the man's brain, through the thalamus, to a specialized region of the cerebral cortex for further processing. Eventually, a large fraction of the trillion neurons in the man's brain become involved with computing the visual and auditory data just acquired. Sodium and potassium gates open and close. Electrical currents speed along neuron fibers. Molecules flow from one nerve ending to the next.

14   All of this is known. What is not known is why, after about a minute, the man walks over to the woman and smiles.

1996

Definition

Women's Beauty:
Put Down or Power Source?

Susan Sontag

For the Greeks, beauty was a virtue: A kind of excellence. Persons 1
then were assumed to be what we now have to call—lamely,
enviously—*whole* persons. If it did occur to the Greeks to distinguish between a person's "inside" and "outside," they still expected
that inner beauty would be matched by beauty of the other kind.
The well-born young Athenians who gathered around Socrates
found it quite paradoxical that their hero was so intelligent, so
brave, so honorable, so seductive—and so ugly. One of Socrates'
main pedagogical acts was to be ugly—and teach those innocent,
no doubt splendid-looking disciples of his how full of paradoxes
life really was.

They may have resisted Socrates' lesson. We do not. Several 2
thousand years later, we are more wary of the enchantments of
beauty. We not only split off—with the greatest facility—the
"inside" (character, intellect) from the "outside" (looks); but we
are actually surprised when someone who is beautiful is also
intelligent, talented, good.

It was principally the influence of Christianity that deprived 3
beauty of the central place it had in classical ideals of human
excellence. By limiting excellence (*virtus* in Latin) to *moral* virtue
only, Christianity set beauty adrift—as an alienated, arbitrary,
superficial enchantment. And beauty has continued to lose

prestige. For close to two centuries it has become a convention to attribute beauty to only one of the two sexes: The sex which, however Fair, is always Second. Associating beauty with women has put beauty even further on the defensive, morally.

4   A beautiful woman, we say in English. But a handsome man. "Handsome" is the masculine equivalent of—and refusal of— a compliment which has accumulated certain demeaning overtones, by being reserved for women only. That one can call a man "beautiful" in French and in Italian suggests that Catholic countries—unlike those countries shaped by the Protestant version of Christianity—still retain some vestiges of the pagan admiration for beauty. But the difference, if one exists, is of degree only. In every modern country that is Christian or post-Christian, women *are* the beautiful sex—to the detriment of the notion of beauty as well as of women.

5   To be called beautiful is thought to name something essential to women's character and concerns. (In contrast to men—whose essence is to be strong, or effective, or competent.) It does not take someone in the throes of advanced feminist awareness to perceive that the way women are taught to be involved with beauty encourages narcissism, reinforces dependence and immaturity. Everybody (women and men) knows that. For it is "everybody," a whole society, that has identified being feminine with caring about how one *looks*. (In contrast to being masculine—which is identified with caring about what one *is* and *does* and only secondarily, if at all, about how one looks.) Given these stereotypes, it is no wonder that beauty enjoys, at best, a rather mixed reputation.

6   It is not, of course, the desire to be beautiful that is wrong but the obligation to be—or to try. What is accepted by most women as a flattering idealization of their sex is a way of making women feel inferior to what they actually are—or normally grow to be. For the ideal of beauty is administered as a form of self-oppression. Women are taught to see their bodies in *parts,* and to evaluate each part separately. Breasts, feet, hips, waistline, neck, eyes, nose, complexion, hair, and so on—each in turn is submitted to an anxious, fretful, often despairing scrutiny. Even if some pass muster, some will always be found wanting. Nothing less than perfection will do.

In men, good looks is a whole, something taken in at a   7
glance. It does not need to be confirmed by giving measurements of different regions of the body, nobody encourages a man to dissect his appearance, feature by feature. As for perfection, that is considered trivial—almost unmanly. Indeed, in the ideally good-looking man a small imperfection or blemish is considered positively desirable. According to one movie critic (a woman) who is a declared Robert Redford fan, it is having that cluster of skin-colored moles on one cheek that saves Redford from being merely a "pretty face." Think of the depreciation of women—as well as of beauty—that is implied in that judgment.

"The privileges of beauty are immense," said Cocteau. To be   8
sure, beauty is a form of power. And deservedly so. What is lamentable is that it is the only form of power that most women are encouraged to seek. This power is always conceived in relation to men; it is not the power to do but the power to attract. It is a power that negates itself. For this power is not one that can be chosen freely—at least, not by women—or renounced without social censure.

To preen, for a woman, can never be just a pleasure. It is   9
also a duty. It is her work. If a woman does real work—and even if she has clambered up to a leading position in politics, law, medicine, business, or whatever—she is always under pressure to confess that she still works at being attractive. But insofar as she is keeping up as one of the Fair Sex, she brings under suspicion her very capacity to be objective, professional, authoritative, thoughtful. Damned if they do—women are. And damned if they don't.

One could hardly ask for more important evidence of the   10
dangers of considering persons as split between what is "inside" and what is "outside" than that interminable half-comic, half-tragic tale, the oppression of women. How easy it is to start off by defining women as caretakers of their surfaces, and then to disparage them (or find them adorable) for being "superficial." It is a crude trap, and it has worked for too long. But to get out of the trap requires that women get some critical distance from that excellence and privilege which is beauty, enough distance to see

how much beauty itself has been abridged in order to prop up the mythology of the "feminine." There should be a way of saving beauty *from* women—and *for* them.

1975

What Is Poverty?

Jo Goodwin Parker

1 You ask me what is poverty? Listen to me. Here I am, dirty, smelly, and with no "proper" underwear on and with the stench of my rotting teeth near you. I will tell you. Listen to me. Listen without pity. I cannot use your pity. Listen with understanding. Put yourself in my dirty, worn out, ill-fitting shoes, and hear me.

2   Poverty is getting up every morning from a dirt- and illness-stained mattress. The sheets have long since been used for diapers. Poverty is living in a smell that never leaves. This is a smell of urine, sour milk, and spoiling food sometimes joined with the strong smell of long-cooked onions. Onions are cheap. If you have smelled this smell, you did not know how it came. It is the smell of the outdoor privy. It is the smell of young children who cannot walk the long dark way in the night. It is the smell of the mattresses where years of "accidents" have happened. It is the smell of the milk which has gone sour because the refrigerator long has not worked, and it costs money to get it fixed. It is the smell of rotting garbage. I could bury it, but where is the shovel? Shovels cost money.

3   Poverty is being tired. I have always been tired. They told me at the hospital when the last baby came that I had chronic anemia caused from poor diet, a bad case of worms, and that I needed a corrective operation. I listened politely—the poor are always polite. The poor always listen. They don't say that there is no money for iron pills, or better food, or worm medicine. The idea of an operation is frightening and costs so much that, if I had dared, I would

have laughed. Who takes care of my children? Recovery from an operation takes a long time. I have three children. When I left them with "Granny" the last time I had a job, I came home to find the baby covered with fly specks, and a diaper that had not been changed since I left. When the dried diaper came off, bits of my baby's flesh came with it. My other child was playing with a sharp bit of broken glass, and my oldest was playing alone at the edge of a lake. I made twenty-two dollars a week, and a good nursery school costs twenty dollars a week for three children. I quit my job.

Poverty is dirt. You can say in your clean clothes coming from 4 your clean house, "Anybody can be clean." Let me explain about housekeeping with no money. For breakfast I give my children grits with no oleo or cornbread without eggs and oleo. This does not use up many dishes. What dishes there are, I wash in cold water and with no soap. Even the cheapest soap has to be saved for the baby's diapers. Look at my hands, so cracked and red. Once I saved for two months to buy a jar of Vaseline for my hands and the baby's diaper rash. When I had saved enough, I went to buy it and the price had gone up two cents. The baby and I suffered on. I have to decide every day if I can bear to put my cracked sore hands into the cold water and strong soap. But you ask, why not hot water? Fuel costs money. If you have a wood fire it costs money. If you burn electricity, it costs money. Hot water is a luxury. I do not have luxuries. I know you will be surprised when I tell you how young I am. I look so much older. My back has been bent over the wash tubs every day for so long. I cannot remember when I ever did anything else. Every night I wash every stitch my school age child has on and just hope her clothes will be dry by morning.

Poverty is staying up all night on cold nights to watch the fire 5 knowing one spark on the newspaper covering the walls means your sleeping child dies in flames. In summer, poverty is watching gnats and flies devour your baby's tears when he cries. The screens are torn and you pay so little rent you know they will never be fixed. Poverty means insects in your food, in your nose, in your eyes, and crawling over you when you sleep. Poverty is hoping it never rains because diapers won't dry when it rains and soon you are using newspapers. Poverty is seeing your children forever with runny noses. Paper handkerchiefs cost money and all your rags you need for other things. Even more costly are antihistamines. Poverty is cooking without food and cleaning without soap.

6   Poverty is asking for help. Have you ever had to ask for help, knowing your children will suffer unless you get it? Think about asking for a loan from a relative, if this is the only way you can imagine asking for help. I will tell you how it feels. You find out where the office is that you are supposed to visit. You circle that block four or five times. Thinking of your children, you go in. Everyone is very busy. Finally, someone comes out and you tell her that you need help. That never is the person you need to see. You go see another person, and after spilling the whole shame of your poverty all over the desk between you, you find that this isn't the right office after all—you must repeat the whole process, and it never is any easier at the next place.

7   You have asked for help, and after all it has a cost. You are again told to wait. You are told why, but you don't really hear because of the red cloud of shame and the rising cloud of despair.

8   Poverty is remembering. It is remembering quitting school in junior high because "nice" children had been so cruel about my clothes and my smell. The attendance officer came. My mother told him I was pregnant. I wasn't, but she thought that I could get a job and help out. I had jobs off and on, but never long enough to learn anything. Mostly I remember being married. I was so young then. I am still young. For a time, we had all the things you have. There was a little house in another town, with hot water and everything. Then my husband lost his job. There was unemployment insurance for a while and what few jobs I could get. Soon, all our nice things were repossessed and we moved back here. I was pregnant then. This house didn't look so bad when we first moved in. Every week it gets worse. Nothing is ever fixed. We now had no money. There were a few odd jobs for my husband, but everything went for food then, as it does now. I don't know how we lived through three years and three babies, but we did. I'll tell you something, after the last baby I destroyed my marriage. It had been a good one, but could you keep on bringing children in this dirt? Did you ever think how much it costs for any kind of birth control? I knew my husband was leaving the day he left, but there were no

goodbys between us. I hope he has been able to climb out of this mess somewhere. He never could hope with us to drag him down.

That's when I asked for help. When I got it, you know how much it was? It was, and is, seventy-eight dollars a month for the four of us; that is all I ever can get. Now you know why there is no soap, no needles and thread, no hot water, no aspirin, no worm medicine, no hand cream, no shampoo. None of these things forever and ever and ever. So that you can see clearly, I pay twenty dollars a month rent, and most of the rest goes for food. For grits and cornmeal, and rice and milk and beans. I try my best to use only the minimum electricity. If I use more, there is that much less for food. 9

Poverty is looking into a black future. Your children won't play with my boys. They will turn to other boys who steal to get what they want. I can already see them behind the bars of their prison instead of behind the bars of my poverty. Or they will turn to the freedom of alcohol or drugs, and find themselves enslaved. And my daughter? At best, there is for her a life like mine. 10

But you say to me, there are schools. Yes, there are schools. My children have no extra books, no magazines, no extra pencils, or crayons, or paper and most important of all, they do not have health. They have worms, they have infections, they have pinkeye all summer. They do not sleep well on the floor, or with me in my one bed. They do not suffer from hunger, my seventy-eight dollars keeps us alive, but they do suffer from malnutrition. Oh yes, I do remember what I was taught about health in school. It doesn't do much good. In some places there is a surplus commodities program. Not here. The county said it cost too much. There is a school lunch program. But I have two children who will already be damaged by the time they get to school. 11

But, you say to me, there are health clinics. Yes, there are health clinics and they are in the towns. I live out here eight miles from town. I can walk that far (even if it is sixteen miles both ways), but can my little children? My neighbor will take me when he goes; but he expects to get paid, *one way or another*. I bet you know my neighbor. He is that large man who spends his time at the gas station, the barbershop, and the corner store complaining about the government spending money on the immoral mothers of illegitimate children. 12

13   Poverty is an acid that drips on pride until all pride is worn away. Poverty is a chisel that chips on honor until honor is worn away. Some of you say that you would do *something* in my situation, and maybe you would, for the first week or the first month, but for year after year after year?

14   Even the poor can dream. A dream of a time when there is money. Money for the right kinds of food, for worm medicine, for iron pills, for toothbrushes, for hand cream, for a hammer and nails and a bit of screening, for a shovel, for a bit of paint, for some sheeting, for needles and thread. Money to pay *in money* for a trip to town. And, oh, money for hot water and money for soap. A dream of when asking for help does not eat away the last bit of pride. When the office you visit is as nice as the offices of other governmental agencies, when there are enough workers to help you quickly, when workers do not quit in defeat and despair. When you have to tell your story to only one person, and that person can send you for other help and you don't have to prove your poverty over and over and over again.

15   I have come out of my despair to tell you this. Remember I did not come from another place or another time. Others like me are all around you. Look at us with an angry heart, anger that will help you help me. Anger that will let you tell of me. The poor are always silent. Can you be silent too?

1971

The Company Man

Ellen Goodman

1   He worked himself to death, finally and precisely, at 3:00 A.M. Sunday morning.

2   The obituary didn't say that, of course. It said that he died of a coronary thrombosis—I think that was it—but everyone among his friends and acquaintances knew it instantly. He was a perfect Type A, a workaholic, a classic, they said to each other

and shook their heads—and thought for five or ten minutes about the way they lived.

This man who worked himself to death finally and precisely   3
at 3:00 A.M. Sunday morning—on his day off—was fifty-one years old and a vice-president. He was, however, one of six vice-presidents, and one of three who might conceivably—if the president died or retired soon enough—have moved to the top spot. Phil knew that.

He worked six days a week, five of them until eight or nine at   4
night, during a time when his own company had begun the four-day week for everyone but the executives. He worked like the Important People. He had no outside "extracurricular interests," unless, of course, you think about a monthly golf game that way. To Phil, it was work. He always ate egg salad sandwiches at his desk. He was, of course, overweight, by 20 or 25 pounds. He thought it was okay, though, because he didn't smoke.

On Saturdays, Phil wore a sports jacket to the office instead of   5
a suit, because it was the weekend.

He had a lot of people working for him, maybe sixty, and   6
most of them liked him most of the time. Three of them will be seriously considered for his job. The obituary didn't mention that.

But it did list his "survivors" quite accurately. He is survived   7
by his wife, Helen, forty-eight years old, a good woman of no par-ticular marketable skills, who worked in an office before marry-ing and mothering. She had, according to her daughter, given up trying to compete with his work years ago, when the children were small. A company friend said, "I know how much you will miss him." And she answered, "I already have."

"Missing him all these years," she must have given up part of   8
herself which had cared too much for the man. She would be "well taken care of."

His "dearly beloved" eldest of the "dearly beloved" children   9
is a hard-working executive in a manufacturing firm down South. In the day and a half before the funeral, he went around the neighborhood researching his father, asking the neighbors what he was like. They were embarrassed.

His second child is a girl, who is twenty-four and newly   10
married. She lives near her mother and they are close, but whenever

she was alone with her father, in a car driving somewhere, they had nothing to say to each other.

11   The youngest is twenty, a boy, a high-school graduate who has spent the last couple of years, like a lot of his friends, doing enough odd jobs to stay in grass and food. He was the one who tried to grab at his father, and tried to mean enough to him to keep the man at home. He was his father's favorite. Over the last two years, Phil stayed up nights worrying about the boy.

12   The boy once said, "My father and I only board here." At the funeral, the sixty-year-old company president told the forty-eight-year-old widow that the fifty-one-year-old deceased had meant much to the company and would be missed and would be hard to replace. The widow didn't look him in the eye. She was afraid he would read her bitterness and, after all, she would need him to straighten out the finances—the stock options and all that.

13   Phil was overweight and nervous and worked too hard. If he wasn't at the office, he was worried about it. Phil was a Type A, a heart-attack natural. You could have picked him out in a minute from a lineup.

14   So when he finally worked himself to death, at precisely 3:00 A.M. Sunday morning, no one was really surprised.

15   By 5:00 P.M. the afternoon of the funeral, the company president had begun, discreetly of course, with care and taste, to make inquiries about his replacement. One of three men. He asked around: "Who's been working the hardest?"

1981

Meanings of a Word

Gloria Naylor

1   Language is the subject. It is the written form with which I've managed to keep the wolf away from the door and, in diaries, to keep my sanity. In spite of this, I consider the written word inferior to the spoken, and much of the frustration experienced by novelists is the awareness that whatever we manage to capture in even the

most transcendent passages falls far short of the richness of life. Dialogue achieves its power in the dynamics of a fleeting moment of sight, sound, smell and touch.

I'm not going to enter the debate here about whether it is lan- 2 guage that shapes reality or vice versa. That battle is doomed to be waged whenever we seek intermittent reprieve from the chicken and egg dispute. I will simply take the position that the spoken word, like the written word, amounts to a nonsensical arrangement of sounds or letters without a consensus that assigns "meaning." And building from the meanings of what we hear, we order reality. Words themselves are innocuous; it is the consensus that gives them true power.

I remember the first time I heard the word nigger. In my 3 third-grade class, our math tests were being passed down the rows, and as I handed the papers to a little boy in back of me, I remarked that once again he had received a much lower mark than I did. He snatched his test from me and spit out that word. Had he called me a nymphomaniac or a necrophiliac, I couldn't have been more puzzled. I didn't know what a nigger was, but I knew that whatever it meant, it was something he shouldn't have called me. This was verified when I raised my hand, and in a loud voice repeated what he had said and watched the teacher scold him for using a "bad" word. I was later to go home and ask the inevitable question that every black parent must face—"Mommy, what does 'nigger' mean?"

And what exactly did it mean? Thinking back, I realize that 4 this could not have been the first time the word was used in my presence. I was part of a large extended family that had migrated from the rural South after World War II and formed a close-knit network that gravitated around my maternal grandparents. Their ground-floor apartment in one of the buildings they owned in Harlem was a weekend mecca for my immediate family, along with countless aunts, uncles and cousins who brought along assorted friends. It was a bustling and open house with assorted neighbors and tenants popping in and out to exchange bits of gossip, pick up an old quarrel or referee the ongoing checkers game in which my grandmother cheated shamelessly. They were all there to let down their hair and put up their feet after a week of labor in the factories, laundries and shipyards of New York.

⁵ Amid the clamor, which could reach deafening proportions—two or three conversations going on simultaneously, punctuated by the sound of a baby's crying somewhere in the back rooms or out on the street—there was still a rigid set of rules about what was said and how. Older children were sent out of the living room when it was time to get into the juicy details about "you-know-who" up on the third floor who had gone and gotten herself "p-r-e-g-n-a-n-t!" But my parents, knowing that I could spell well beyond my years, always demanded that I follow the others out to play. Beyond sexual misconduct and death, everything else was considered harmless for our young ears. And so among the anecdotes of the triumphs and disappointments in the various workings of their lives, the word nigger was used in my presence, but it was set within contexts and inflections that caused it to register in my mind as something else.

⁶ In the singular, the word was always applied to a man who had distinguished himself in some situation that brought their approval for his strength, intelligence or drive:

⁷ "Did Johnny really do that?"

⁸ "I'm telling you, that nigger pulled in $6,000 of overtime last year. Said he got enough for a down payment on a house."

⁹ When used with a possessive adjective by a woman—"my nigger"—it became a term of endearment for husband or boyfriend. But it could be more than just a term applied to a man. In their mouths it became the pure essence of manhood—a disembodied force that channeled their past history of struggle and present survival against the odds into a victorious statement of being: "Yeah, that old foreman found out quick enough—you don't mess with a nigger."

¹⁰ In the plural, it became a description of some group within the community that had overstepped the bounds of decency as my family defined it: Parents who neglected their children, a drunken couple who fought in public, people who simply refused to look for work, those with excessively dirty mouths or unkempt households were all "trifling niggers." This particular circle could forgive hard times, unemployment, the occasional bout of depression—they had gone through all of that themselves—but the unforgivable sin was lack of self-respect.

A woman could never be a "nigger" in the singular, with its   11
connotation of confirming worth. The noun "girl" was its closest
equivalent in that sense, but only when used in direct address
and regardless of the gender doing the addressing. "Girl" was a
token of respect for a woman. The one-syllable word was drawn
out to sound like three in recognition of the extra ounce of wit,
nerve or daring that the woman had shown in the situation under
discussion.

"G-i-r-l, stop. You mean you said that to his face?"   12

But if the word was used in a third-person reference or short-   13
ened so that it almost snapped out of the mouth, it always involved
some element of communal disapproval. And age became an
important factor in these exchanges. It was only between individuals of the same generation, or from an older person to a younger
(but never the other way around), that "girl" would be considered
a compliment.

I don't agree with the argument that use of the word nigger   14
at this social stratum of the black community was an internal-
ization of racism. The dynamics were the exact opposite: the
people in my grandmother's living room took a word that
whites used to signify worthlessness or degradation and ren-
dered it impotent. Gathering there together, they transformed
"nigger" to signify the varied and complex human beings they
knew themselves to be. If the word was to disappear totally from
the mouths of even the most racist of white society, no one in that
room was naïve enough to believe it would disappear from
white minds. Meeting the word head on, they proved it had
absolutely nothing to do with the way they were determined to
live their lives.

So there must have been dozens of times that the word "nigger"   15
was spoken in front of me before I reached the third grade. But I
didn't "hear" it until it was said by a small pair of lips that had
already learned it could be a way to humiliate me. That was the
word I went home and asked my mother about. And since she
knew that I had to grow up in America, she took me in her lap
and explained.

1986

Facing Famine

Tom Haines

1 Burtukan Abe braces against the hard mud wall as Osman, her 2-year-old son, wails and wobbles on stick legs.

2 Are there others? I ask.

3 Yes, one, she says. A boy, 1 month old. He is inside.

4 There is no turning back. Through the low, narrow doorway, in the darkness that guards cool by day, heat by night, lies little Nurhusein.

5 May I see him?

6 This journey began weeks earlier, when yet another report described widespread drought and the threat of famine across much of Africa.

7 What can that life be like?

8 Travel often approaches boundaries of wealth and health. But what does it feel like to cross those boundaries and enter a place that is, everywhere, collapsing? What comes from knowing people who, with an empty grain basket or a thinning goat, edge closer to death?

9 The route led first to Addis Ababa, a highland capital, then east and south, down into rolling stretches of the Great Rift Valley. In the tattered town of Ogolcho, Berhanu Muse, a local irrigation specialist, agreed to serve as translator and guide.

10 A narrow road of rock headed south, through one village, then another, for one hour, then two.

11 In late afternoon, before evening wind lifted dirt from north to south, east to west, we stopped and parked near a hilltop. A man and woman collected grain from a tall stick bin on the corner of their rectangular plot of land.

12 Gebi Egato offered his hand from his perch inside the bin. Halima, his wife, smiled warmly, then carried a half-filled sack toward the family's low, round hut. Abdo, a 3-year-old with determined eyes, barreled out the door.

13 I asked if we could stay.

14 "Welcome," Gebi said.

For four nights, a photographer and I would sleep here, 15
beneath open sky, then wake to wander this village of 1,000 people.
We would step into a schoolhouse, a clinic, and other thatch-roofed
huts, including the one that held Nurhusein.

But that first afternoon, the village came to us. They were 16
mostly old, all men, a group of perhaps two dozen. Many held
walking sticks, one a long spear. One man said he would like to
show us something: a hole, not too far, that used to hold water. The
hole was shallow and wide, perhaps the size of a Boston backyard.
It was empty, nothing but hard earth.

The men calmly debated how many months it had been since 17
water filled the hole. Flies buzzed and jumped from eyelids to lips.

A young schoolteacher, a specialist in math and science, sat at 18
my side, his legs crossed, hands in his lap.

"Thirst is thirst, hunger is hunger," he said. 19

Hours later, I awoke to a setting moon and could imagine this 20
land as it long had been: Beneath my cot, wheat, barley, and teff shot
from the ground. Birds swarmed tree branches, trading throaty,
bubbling calls. Water pooled in ditches and holes. Thick green
hedges framed the farmyard.

Gebi would describe to me what this can feel like. The land 21
offers so much bounty, so much comfort, he said, that even when
the sun is high and hot, you want to lie down on the earth, close
your eyes, and sleep.

In the hut's outer room, there is a low, wooden bench, but little 22
else. The food, furniture, even a grandmother and three uncles
have gone.

Now, five people remain: Burtukan, the mother, age 19; 23
Abdurkedir Beriso, her husband, 27; Abduraman Beriso, his
brother, 16. And the children, Osman and Nurhusein.

They have no animals, no money. Neighbors share hard bread 24
and flour.

"I have nowhere to go," Abdurkedir told me. "I will die 25
here."

From behind a curtain, in the hut's back room, I hear the rustle 26
of blankets, a whimper, a soothing voice: sounds of a mother
gathering a baby in her arms.

27 On our first morning, as nighttime hilltop sounds—a howling hyena, a barking dog, a farting donkey—gave way to those of dawn, we were outsiders, in the cool air, listening.

28   Beneath Gebi and Halima's thatch roof, Abdo squealed and pouted. Bontu, barely a year old, cried for breakfast.

29   Soon, with the fire made, the children fed, Halima strapped plastic canisters on the back of the family donkey and began to walk. Gebi followed with the ox.

30   Halima sauntered gracefully, as though out for a stroll. She crossed a parched soccer field to a footpath lined with huts. She greeted a woman walking toward her. They held hands and talked.

31   Farther along, in an empty cradle of land set back from the trail, a stack of branches and twigs covered a hole, roughly 12 inches in diameter. Three times, the government had tried to dig a well in this village, which sits far from any river. The last time, a powerful machine made the narrow hole and bore in search of water. Villagers gathered and watched as earth spit upward. Then the drill bit broke, 820 feet underground. It was there, still.

32   Halima walked on, for more than an hour, then stopped in a spot of shade. She untied the canisters and knelt by a wide pond of muddy water. The pond teemed with salmonella, the root of typhoid fever, and parasites that thrive in intestines, infecting 70 percent of Adere Lepho's children.

33   Another young woman leaned at the pond's edge and filled every last ounce of space in her canister. She stuffed the spout with a plug of withered grass.

34   Hundreds of people came each day to this pond, the only water source for Adere Lepho and two neighboring villages, and carted home water to quench the thirst of thousands.

35   A month earlier, this pond, too, had been nearly empty. Then two days of heavy February rain filled it. How long would it last? Even village elders, men and women 40, 45, and 50 years old, had never seen this kind of drought.

36   Two years earlier, and two years before that, meager rains had fallen. Families had to sell animals, eat thinner harvests, and spend precious savings just to survive. But this was worse: The February downpour was the first time it had rained in nearly a year.

Late the next afternoon, rain fell. As the drops landed thick 37
and heavy, men, women, and children took shelter in the low,
open building that houses the village's grain mill. After three,
maybe four minutes, the rain stopped.

Women heaved sacks of grain, some of them holding well- 38
rationed harvests from years past, others gifts from farmland
half a world away, onto a scale. Across the room, the mill owner
sat alongside a conveyor belt spun by a howling generator, the
only power in the village. The owner opened sacks into the
mouth of a grinder that turned kernel to flour. Dust filled the air,
sticking to hair and eyelashes.

Outside, dozens of men gathered beneath the branches of a 39
wide tree.

Gebi Tola, elected leader of a local farmer's group, explained 40
that the government had offered land for 10 volunteers to move
to another region. The government owns all land in Ethiopia. This
resettlement program provided a rare chance.

The men, sitting on the ground in orderly rows, faced Tola. 41
He explained that some plots of land were north, in a neighboring district. Most would be farther, 300 miles to the west.

Voices rose. How can we know this land is good, one man 42
asked. How can we trust that life will be better there?

Kedir Husein, a young father who had stood to ask many ques- 43
tions, stepped away from the group. He told me he had decided not
to volunteer to leave.

"I am afraid," he said. 44

Nurhusein emerges, his head resting in the crook of his mother's 45
left elbow.

A soft cotton blanket opens to shocks of slick, curly hair. Tiny 46
fingers spread in the air. I touch Nurhusein's forehead, cool and
smooth.

"He is beautiful," I say. 47

Nurhusein bleats softly. His lips often latch on to a dry breast. 48
He has a small stomachache, Burtukan tells me.

The bleating rises then falls, just beyond the blanket's edge. 49
Nurhusein is already too wise. It is as if he knows.

50   Morning inside Gebi Egato's hut: Glowing coals. Boisterous children. Hearty porridge. A calf, head low, softly chewed its cud.

51   Shilla, the oldest at 5, licked her fingers and pondered her favorite foods as Abdo crammed both hands full of porridge.

52   "Milk," she said. She raised her head and smiled. "And sugar."

53   Finished, Shilla and Abdo scrambled to waiting friends. Gebi and Halima took turns digging a wooden scoop deep into a jug decorated with shells.

54   Each bite brought more peril.

55   Gebi's tired cow and thirsty goats were giving little milk. The porridge was made from wheat that had been meant as seed for planting if the spring rains came. Neighbors with less were already selling cows and goats, driving prices down.

56   As the coals darkened, I asked how long the family could last. Gebi told me that in two weeks the family's wheat would be gone. He would then sell his goats, then the cow. Then the ox and, finally, the donkey. He paused.

57   "Five months," he said.

58   Gebi, like most villagers a Muslim, said he was confident rain would come. Then, he could partner his ox with that of a neighbor and together they could churn the dark, moist earth.

59   "We have seen so much hardship already, God will not add more," Gebi said. "I hope."

60   After breakfast, Gebi took the donkey and walked beneath the high sun for three hours. He crested three low ridges and crossed three shallow valleys. The first was carpeted in six inches of dust. The second traced the steep gorge of a dry creek. The third, staggered with acacia trees, opened widely toward the village of Cheffe Jilla.

61   A group of men, women, children, and donkeys swayed in the village's main square. White sacks of grain sat in lopsided piles. Gebi joined the hopeful and registered his name in a government office.

62   I saw Gebi Tola, the leader of Adere Lepho's farmer's association, standing beneath a tree. He told me families from his village would take home 500 sacks of grain. But they could use 1,000. How do you judge the needy when a whole village is staggering?

He spoke quickly. A crowd of dozens, young, old, pressed in 63
around us.

I asked Gebi how he felt. 64

"I feel sorry," he said. 65

I had grown used to stoicism. But sorry? I stepped aside with 66
Berhanu, our translator. "Sorry" does not feel like the right word,
I said.

In English, I explained, "sorry" often has a light sense. Sorry 67
I stepped on your toe. Sorry I'm late for dinner. It is not something felt by someone watching his friends and neighbors beginning to starve.

Berhanu is a compassionate, intimate man. He raised his 68
hand to his chin.

He told me that, in that case, "sorry" was not the word he 69
meant.

The crowd moved in again and curious eyes followed our 70
exchange.

I asked Berhanu to choose another English word that more 71
closely matched the Oromigna word Tola had used. He could not
find an exact translation. I asked him to describe the feeling.

"Well," Berhanu said, "it is the feeling you have when some- 72
thing bad happens. Say, for example, when you lose your lovely
brother. Is there a word in English for that?"

Misery? 73

Yes, Berhanu said calmly, that is part of it. 74

Emptiness? Yes, he said, that too. 75

Anguish, despair? 76

His eyes sparked at the connection. 77

Anger? Yes. 78

Frustration? Yes. 79

Fear? No. 80

Fear, Berhanu said, like sorry, was too light a word. 81

Terror? 82

Yes, Berhanu said, "terror" is a good word. 83

I stand before Nurhusein and start to cry. 84

Is it empathy? I have a 10-month-old son, a spirited boy with 85
muscles across his back and a quick laugh.

86   Or am I crying from fear?

87   In the hot sun, looking from hut to hut, from face to face, the problem was always too vast.

88   I stare at Nurhusein. I cannot look again into his mother's eyes.

2004

The Green-Eyed Monster:
Envy Is Nothing to Be Jealous Of
Joseph Epstein

1 Of the seven deadly sins, only envy is no fun at all. Sloth may not seem that enjoyable, nor anger either, but giving way to deep laziness has its pleasures, and the expression of anger entails a release that is not without its small delights. In recompense, envy may be the subtlest—perhaps I should say the most insidious—of the seven deadly sins. Surely it is the one that people are least likely to want to own up to, for to do so is to admit that one is probably ungenerous, mean, small-hearted. It may also be the most endemic. Apart from Socrates, Jesus, Marcus Aurelius, Saint Francis, Mother Teresa, and only a few others, at one time or another, we have all felt flashes of envy, even if in varying intensities, from its minor pricks to its deep, soul-destroying, lacerating stabs. So widespread is it—a word for envy, I have read, exists in all known languages—that one is ready to believe it is the sin for which the best argument can be made that it is part of human nature.

2   In politics, envy, or at any rate the hope of eliminating it, is said to be the reigning principle of socialism, as greed is said to be that of capitalism (though modern capitalist advertising is about few things more than the regular stimulation of envy). On the international scene, many if not most wars have been fought because of one nation's envy of another's territory and all they derive from it, or out of jealously guarded riches that a nation

feels are endangered by those less rich who are likely to be envious of their superior position. In this connection, it is difficult not
to feel that, at least in part, much of the anti-American feeling that
arose after September 11, 2001, had envy, some of it fairly ran-
corous, at its heart. In the magazine *Granta*, the Indian writer
Ramachandra Guha wrote that "historically, anti-Americanism in
India was shaped by an aesthetic distaste for America's greatest
gift—the making of money." But can "aesthetic distaste" here be
any more than a not-very-well-disguised code word for envy?

Is envy a "feeling," an "emotion," a "sin," a "temperamental ₃
disposition," or a "world-view"? Might it also be a Rorschach
test: Tell what you envy, and you reveal a great deal about yourself. It can be all of these things—and more. No one would doubt
that, whatever else it is, envy is certainly a charged, indeed a
supercharged, word: One of the few words left in the English language that retains the power to scandalize. Most of us could still
sleep decently if accused of any of the other six deadly sins; but
to be accused of envy would be seriously distressing, so clearly
does such an accusation go directly to character. The other deadly
sins, though all have the disapproval of religion, do not so thoroughly, so deeply demean, diminish, and disqualify a person. Not
the least of its stigmata is the pettiness implicit in envy.

The *Webster's* definition of the word won't quite do: "(1) *Obs.* ₄
malice; (2) painful or resentful awareness of the advantage
enjoyed by another joined with a desire to possess the same
advantage." The *Oxford English Dictionary* is rather better: It
defines envy first as "malignant or hostile feeling; ill-will, malice,
enmity," and then as "active evil, harm, mischief," both definitions accounted *Obscure*. But the great *OED* only gets down to
serious business in its third definition, where it defines envy as
"the feeling of mortification and ill-will occasioned by the contemplation of superior advantages possessed by another," in
which usage the word envy first pops up around 1500. It adds a
fourth definition, one in which the word is used without "notions
of malevolence," and has to do with the (a) "desire to equal
another in achievement, or excellence; emulation," and (b) speaks
to "a longing for the advantages enjoyed by another person."
Aristotle, in *The Rhetoric*, writes of emulation as good envy, or

envy ending in admiration and thus in the attempt to imitate the qualities one began by envying. Yet it must be added that envy doesn't generally work this way. Little is good about envy, except shaking it off, which, as any of us who have felt it deeply knows, is not so easily done.

5   Both the *OED* and *Webster's* definitions are inattentive to the crucial distinction between envy and jealousy. Most people, failing to pick up the useful distinction, mistakenly use the two words interchangeably. I suspect people did not always do so. H. W. Fowler, in his splendid *Modern English Usage* of 1926, carries no entry on either word, suggesting that formerly there was no confusion. Bryan A. Garner, in his 1998 *Dictionary of Modern American Usage*, says that "the careful writer distinguishes between these terms," but does not himself do so sufficiently. He writes that "*jealousy* is properly restricted to contexts involving affairs of the heart, *envy* is used more broadly of resentful contemplation of a more fortunate person."

6   With the deep pedantic delight one takes in trumping a recognized usage expert, it pleases me to say, "Not quite so." The real distinction is that *one is jealous of what one has, envious of what other people have.* Jealousy is not always pejorative; one can after all be jealous of one's dignity, civil rights, honor. Envy, except when used in the emulative sense mentioned by Aristotle, is always pejorative. If jealousy is, in cliché parlance, spoken of as the "green-eyed monster," envy is cross-, squinty-, and blearily red-eyed. Never, to put it very gently, a handsome or good thing, envy. Although between jealousy and envy, jealousy is often the more intensely felt of the two, it can also be the more realistic: One is, after all, sometimes correct to feel jealousy. And not all jealousy plays the familiar role of sexual jealousy. One may be jealous—again, rightly—of one's reputation, integrity, and other good things. One is almost never right to feel envy: To be envious is to be, *ipso facto*, wrong.

7   Apart from emulative envy, the only aspect of envy that does not seem to me pejorative is a form of envy I have myself felt, as I suspect have others who are reading this article: the envy that I think of as faith envy. This is the envy one feels for those who have the true and deep and intelligent religious faith that sees

them through the darkest of crises, death among them. If one is oneself without faith and wishes to feel this emotion, I cannot recommend a better place to find it than in the letters of Flannery O'Connor. There one will discover a woman still in her thirties, who, after coming into her radiant talent, knows she is going to die well before her time and, fortified by her Catholicism, faces her end without voicing complaint or fear. I not long ago heard, in Vienna, what seemed to me a perfect rendering of Beethoven's *Ninth Symphony*, and was hugely moved by it, but how much more would I have been moved, I could not help wonder, if I were in a state of full religious belief, since the *Ninth Symphony* seems to me in many ways a religious work. Faith envy is envy, alas, about which one can do nothing but quietly harbor it.

Envy must also be distinguished from general yearning. One sees people at great social ease and wishes to be more like them; or feels keenly how good it would be once more to be young; or longs to be wealthier; or pines to be taller, thinner, more muscular, less awkward, more beautiful generally. All this is yearning. Envy is never general, but always very particular—at least envy of the kind one feels strongly. 8

The envious tend to be injustice collectors. "Envy, among other ingredients, has a love of justice in it," William Hazlitt wrote. "We are more angry at undeserved than at deserved good fortune." Something to it, but, my sense is, not all that much. Much more often than not, envy expresses feelings more personal than the love of justice. In another useful distinction, Kierkegaard in *The Sickness Unto Death* wrote that "admiration is happy self-surrender; envy is unhappy self-satisfaction." Envy asks one leading question: What about me? Why does he or she have beauty, talent, wealth, power, the world's love, and other gifts, or at any rate a larger share of them than I? Why not me? Dorothy Sayers, in a little book on the seven deadly sins, writes: "Envy is the great leveler: if it cannot level things up, it will level them down. . . . At its best, envy is a climber and a snob; at its worst it is a destroyer—rather than have anyone happier than itself, it will see us all miserable together." A self-poisoning of the mind, envy is usually less about what one lacks than about what other people have. A strong element of the begrudging resides in envy, thus 9 making the envious, as Immanuel Kant remarked in *The Metaphysics of Morals,* "intent on the destruction of the happiness of others."

10   One might call someone or something—another's family life, health, good fortune—"enviable" without intending rancor. In the same way, one might say, "I envy you your two-month holiday in the south of France," without, in one's mind, plotting how to do the person out of it. Or one might say, "I don't envy him the responsibilities of his job," by which one merely means that one is pleased not to have another's worries. There probably ought to be a word falling between envy and admiration, as there ought to be a word that falls between talent and genius. Yet there isn't. The language is inept. Nor ought envy to be confused with open conflict. Someone has something that one feels one wants—customers, a high ranking or rating, government office, a position of power—and one contends for it, none or less aggressively, but out in the open. The openness changes the nature of the game. Envy is almost never out in the open; it is secretive, plotting, behind the scenes. Helmut Schoeck, who in *Envy: A Theory of Social Behavior* has written the most comprehensive book on the subject, notes that it "is a silent, secretive process and not always verifiable." Envy, to qualify as envy, has to have a strong touch—sometimes more than a touch—of malice behind it. Malice that cannot speak its name, cold-blooded but secret hostility, impotent desire, hidden rancor, and spite all cluster at the center of envy. La Rochefoucauld opened the subject of envy nicely with a silver stiletto, when he wrote: "In the misfortune of our best friends, we always find something that is not displeasing to us." Yes, really not displeasing at all. Dear old envy.

2003

Chapter

Classification and Division

5

Predictable Crises of Adulthood

Gail Sheehy

We are not unlike a particularly hardy crustacean. The lobster 1
grows by developing and shedding a series of hard, protective
shells. Each time it expands from within, the confining shell must
be sloughed off. It is left exposed and vulnerable until, in time, a
new covering grows to replace the old.

With each passage from one stage of human growth to the next 2
we, too, must shed a protective structure. We are left exposed and
vulnerable—but also yeasty and embryonic again, capable of
stretching in ways we hadn't known before. These sheddings may
take several years or more. Coming out of each passage, though, we
enter a longer and more stable period in which we can expect relative tranquility and a sense of equilibrium regained. . . .

As we shall see, each person engages the steps of develop- 3
ment in his or her own characteristic *step-style*. Some people never
complete the whole sequence. And none of us "solves" with one
step—by jumping out of the parental home into a job or marriage,
for example—the problems in separating from the caregivers of
childhood. Nor do we "achieve" autonomy once and for all by
converting our dreams into concrete goals, even when we attain
those goals. The central issues or tasks of one period are never
fully completed, tied up, and cast aside. But when they lose their
primacy and the current life structure has served its purpose, we
are ready to move on to the next period.

Can one catch up? What might look to others like listlessness, 4
contrariness, a maddening refusal to face up to an obvious task

115

may be a person's own unique detour that will bring him out later on the other side. Developmental gains won can later be lost—and rewon. It's plausible, though it can't be proven, that the mastery of one set of tasks fortifies us for the next period and the next set of challenges. But it's important not to think too mechanistically. Machines work by units. The bureaucracy (supposedly) works step by step. Human beings, thank God, have an individual inner dynamic that can never be precisely coded.

5 Although I have indicated the ages when Americans are likely to go through each stage, and the differences between men and women where they are striking, do not take the ages too seriously. The stages are the thing, and most particularly the sequence.

6 Here is the briefest outline of the developmental ladder.

PULLING UP ROOTS

7 Before 18, the motto is loud and clear: "I have to get away from my parents." But the words are seldom connected to action. Generally still safely part of our families, even if away at school, we feel our autonomy to be subject to erosion from moment to moment.

8 After 18, we begin Pulling Up Roots in earnest. College, military service, and short-term travels are all customary vehicles our society provides for the first round-trips between family and a base of one's own. In the attempt to separate our view of the world from our family's view, despite vigorous protestations to the contrary—"I know exactly what I want!"—we cast about for any beliefs we can call our own. And in the process of testing those beliefs we are often drawn to fads, preferably those most mysterious and inaccessible to our parents.

9 Whatever tentative memberships we try out in the world, the fear haunts us that we are really kids who cannot take care of ourselves. We cover that fear with acts of defiance and mimicked confidence. For allies to replace our parents, we turn to our contemporaries. They become conspirators. So long as their perspective meshes with our own, they are able to substitute for the sanctuary of the family. But that doesn't last very long. And the

instant they diverge from the shaky ideals of "our group," they are seen as betrayers. Rebounds to the family are common between the ages of 18 and 22.

The tasks of this passage are to locate ourselves in a peer group role, a sex role, an anticipated occupation, an ideology or world view. As a result, we gather the impetus to leave home physically and the identity to *begin* leaving home emotionally.

Even as one part of us seeks to be an individual, another part longs to restore the safety and comfort of merging with another. Thus one of the most popular myths of this passage is: We can piggyback our development by attaching to a Stronger One. But people who marry during this time often prolong financial and emotional ties to the family and relatives that impede them from becoming self-sufficient.

A stormy passage through the Pulling Up Roots years will probably facilitate the normal progression of the adult life cycle. If one doesn't have an identity crisis at this point, it will erupt during a later transition, when the penalties may be harder to bear.

THE TRYING TWENTIES

The Trying Twenties confront us with the question of how to take hold in the adult world. Our focus shifts from the interior turmoils of late adolescence—"Who am I?" "What is truth?"—and we become almost totally preoccupied with working out the externals. "How do I put my aspirations into effect?" "What is the best way to start?" "Where do I go?" "Who can help me?" "How did *you* do it?"

In this period, which is longer and more stable compared with the passage that leads to it, the tasks are as enormous as they are exhilarating: To shape a Dream, that vision of ourselves which will generate energy, aliveness, and hope. To prepare for a life-work. To find a mentor if possible. And to form the capacity for intimacy without losing in the process whatever consistency of self we have thus far mustered. The first test structure must be erected around the life we choose to try.

Doing what we "should" is the most pervasive theme of the twenties. The "shoulds" are largely defined by family models, the press of the culture, or the prejudices of our peers. If the prevailing cultural instructions are that one should get married and settle down behind one's own door, a nuclear family is born. If instead the peers insist that one should do one's own thing, the 25-year-old is likely to harness himself onto a Harley-Davidson and burn up Route 66 in the commitment to have no commitments.

16   One of the terrifying aspects of the twenties is the inner conviction that the choices we make are irrevocable. It is largely a false fear. Change is quite possible, and some alteration of our original choices is probably inevitable.

17   Two impulses, as always, are at work. One is to build a firm, safe structure for the future by making strong commitments, to "be set." Yet people who slip into a ready-made form without much self-examination are likely to find themselves *locked* in.

18   The other urge is to explore and experiment, keeping any structure tentative and therefore easily reversible. Taken to the extreme, these are people who skip from one trial job and one limited personal encounter to another, spending their twenties in the *transient* state.

19   Although the choices of our twenties are not irrevocable, they do set in motion a Life Pattern. Some of us follow the lock-in pattern, others the transient pattern; the wunderkind pattern, the caregiver pattern, and there are a number of others. Such patterns strongly influence the particular questions raised for each person during each passage. . . .

20   Buoyed by powerful illusions and belief in the power of the will, we commonly insist in our twenties that what we have chosen to do is the one true course in life. Our backs go up at the merest hint that we are like our parents, that two decades of parental training might be reflected in our current actions and attitudes.

21   "Not me," is the motto, "I'm different."

CATCH-30

22   Impatient with devoting ourselves to the "shoulds," a new vitality springs from within as we approach 30. Men and women alike speak of feeling too narrow and restricted. They blame all sorts of

things, but what the restrictions boil down to are the outgrowth of career and personal choices of the twenties. They may have been choices perfectly suited to that stage. But now the fit feels different. Some inner aspect that was left out is striving to be taken into account. Important new choices must be made, and commitments altered or deepened. The work involves great change, turmoil, and often crisis—a simultaneous feeling of rock bottom and the urge to bust out.

One common response is the tearing up of the life we spent 23 most of our twenties putting together. It may mean striking out on a secondary road toward a new vision or converting a dream of "running for president" into a more realistic goal. The single person feels a push to find a partner. The woman who was previously content at home with children chafes to venture into the world. The childless couple reconsiders children. And almost everyone who is married, especially those married for seven years, feels a discontent.

If the discontent doesn't lead to a divorce, it will, or should, 24 call for a serious review of the marriage and of each partner's aspirations in their Catch-30 condition. The gist of that condition was expressed by a 29-year-old associate with a Wall Street law firm:

"I'm considering leaving the firm. I've been there four years 25 now; I'm getting good feedback, but I have no clients of my own. I feel weak. If I wait much longer, it will be too late, too close to that fateful time of decision on whether or not to become a partner. I'm success-oriented. But the concept of being 55 years old and stuck in a monotonous job drives me wild. It drives me crazy now, just a little bit. I'd say that 85 percent of the time I thoroughly enjoy my work. But when I get a screwball case, I come away from court saying, 'What am I doing here?' It's a *visceral* reaction that I'm wasting my time. I'm trying to find some way to make a social contribution or a slot in city government. I keep saying, 'There's something more.'"

Besides the push to broaden himself professionally, there is a 26 wish to expand his personal life. He wants two or three more children. "The concept of a home has become very meaningful to me, a place to get away from troubles and relax. I love my son in a way I could not have anticipated. I never could live alone."

27   Consumed with the work of making his own critical life-steering decisions, he demonstrates the essential shift at this age: An absolute requirement to be more self-concerned. The self has new value now that his competency has been proved.

28   His wife is struggling with her own age-30 priorities. She wants to go to law school, but he wants more children. If she is going to stay home, she wants him to make more time for the family instead of taking on even wider professional commitments. His view of the bind, of what he would most like from his wife, is this:

29   "I'd like not to be bothered. It sounds cruel, but I'd like not to have to worry about what she's going to do next week. Which is why I've told her several times that I think she should do something. Go back to school and get a degree in social work or geography or whatever. Hopefully that would fulfill her, and then I wouldn't have to worry about her line of problems. I want her to be decisive about herself."

30   The trouble with his advice to his wife is that it comes out of concern with *his* convenience, rather than with *her* development. She quickly picks up on this lack of goodwill: He is trying to dispose of her. At the same time, he refuses her the same latitude to be "selfish" in making an independent decision to broaden her horizons. Both perceive a lack of mutuality. And that is what Catch-30 is all about for the couple.

ROOTING AND EXTENDING

31 Life becomes less provisional, more rational and orderly in the early thirties. We begin to settle down in the full sense. Most of us begin putting down roots and sending out new shoots. People buy houses and become very earnest about climbing career ladders. Men in particular concern themselves with "making it." Satisfaction with marriage generally goes downhill in the thirties (for those who have remained together) compared with the highly valued, vision-supporting marriage of the twenties. This coincides with the couple's reduced social life outside the family and the inturned focus on raising their children.

THE DEADLINE DECADE

In the middle of the thirties we come upon a crossroads. We have 32 reached the halfway mark. Yet even as we are reaching our prime, we begin to see there is a place where it finishes. Time starts to squeeze.

The loss of youth, the faltering of physical powers we have 33 always taken for granted, the fading purpose of stereotyped roles by which we have thus far identified ourselves, the spiritual dilemma of having no absolute answers—any or all of these shocks can give this passage the character of crisis. Such thoughts usher in a decade between 35 and 45 that can be called the Deadline Decade. It is a time of both danger and opportunity. All of us have the chance to rework the narrow identity by which we defined ourselves in the first half of life. And those of us who make the most of the opportunity will have a full-out authenticity crisis.

To come through this authenticity crisis, we must reexamine 34 our purposes and reevaluate how to spend our resources from now on. "Why am I doing all this? What do I really believe in?" No matter what we have been doing, there will be parts of ourselves that have been suppressed and now need to find expression. "Bad" feelings will demand acknowledgment along with the good.

It is frightening to step off onto the treacherous footbridge 35 leading to the second half of life. We can't take everything with us on this journey through uncertainty. Along the way, we discover that we are alone. We no longer have to ask permission because we are the providers of our own safety. We must learn to give ourselves permission. We stumble upon feminine or masculine aspects of our natures that up to this time have usually been masked. There is grieving to be done because an old self is dying. By taking in our suppressed and even our unwanted parts, we prepare at the gut level for the reintegration of an identity that is ours and ours alone—not some artificial form put together to please the culture or our mates. It is a dark passage at the beginning. But by disassembling ourselves, we can glimpse the light and gather our parts into a renewal.

Women sense this inner crossroads earlier than men do. The 36 time pinch often prompts a woman to stop and take an all-points survey at age 35. Whatever options she has already played out, she feels a "my last chance" urgency to review those options she has set aside and those that aging and biology will close off in the now *foreseeable* future. For all her qualms and confusion about where to start looking for a new future, she usually enjoys an exhilaration of release. Assertiveness begins rising. There are so many firsts ahead.

37   Men, too, feel the time push in the mid-thirties. Most men respond by pressing down harder on the career accelerator. It's "my last chance" to pull away from the pack. It is no longer enough to be the loyal junior executive, the promising young novelist, the lawyer who does a little *pro bono* work on the side. He wants now to become part of top management, to be recognized as an established writer, or an active politician with his own legislative program. With some chagrin, he discovers that he has been too anxious to please and too vulnerable to criticism. He wants to put together his own ship.

38   During this period of intense concentration on external advancement, it is common for men to be unaware of the more difficult, gut issues that are propelling them forward. The survey that was neglected at 35 becomes a crucible at 40. Whatever rung of achievement he has reached, the man of 40 usually feels stale, restless, burdened, and unappreciated. He worries about his health. He wonders, "Is this all there is?" He may make a series of departures from well-established lifelong base lines, including marriage. More and more men are seeking second careers in midlife. Some become self-destructive. And many men in their forties experience a major shift of emphasis away from pouring all their energies into their own advancement. A more tender, feeling side comes into play. They become interested in developing an ethical self.

RENEWAL OR RESIGNATION

39 Somewhere in the mid-forties, equilibrium is regained. A new stability is achieved, which may be more or less satisfying.

40   If one has refused to budge through the midlife transition, the sense of staleness will calcify into resignation. One by one,

the safety and supports will be withdrawn from the person who is standing still. Parents will become children; children will become strangers; a mate will grow away or go away; the career will become just a job—and each of these events will be felt as an abandonment. The crisis will probably emerge again around 50. And although its wallop will be greater, the jolt may be just what is needed to prod the resigned middle-ager toward seeking revitalization.

On the other hand . . .   41

If we have confronted ourselves in the middle passage and   42
found a renewal of purpose around which we are eager to build a more authentic life structure, these may well be the best years. Personal happiness takes a sharp turn upward for partners who can now accept the fact: "I cannot expect *anyone* to fully understand me." Parents can be forgiven for the burdens of our childhood. Children can be let go without leaving us in collapsed silence. At 50, there is a new warmth and mellowing. Friends become more important than ever, but so does privacy. Since it is so often proclaimed by people past midlife, the motto of this stage might be "No more bullshit."

1976

Four Kinds of Reading

Donald Hall

Everywhere one meets the idea that reading is an activity desir-   1
able in itself. It is understandable that publishers and librarians—and even writers—should promote this assumption, but it is strange that the idea should have general currency. People surround the idea of reading with piety, and do not take into account the purpose of reading or the value of what is being read. Teachers and parents praise the child who reads, and praise themselves, whether the text be *The Reader's Digest* or *Moby Dick.* The advent of TV has increased the false values ascribed to reading,

since TV provides a vulgar alternative. But this piety is silly; and most reading is no more cultural nor intellectual nor imaginative than shooting pool or watching *What's My Line.*

2   It is worth asking how the act of reading became something to value in itself, as opposed for instance to the act of conversation or the act of taking a walk. Mass literacy is a recent phenomenon, and I suggest that the aura which decorates reading is a relic of the importance of reading to our great-great-grandparents. Literacy used to be a mark of social distinction, separating a small portion of humanity from the rest. The farm laborer who was ambitious for his children did not daydream that they would become schoolteachers or doctors; he daydreamed that they would learn to read, and that a world would therefore open up to them in which they did not have to labor in the fields fourteen hours a day for six days a week in order to buy salt and cotton. On the next rank of society, ample time for reading meant that the reader was free from the necessity to spend most of his waking hours making a living. This sort of attitude shades into the contemporary man's boast of his wife's cultural activities. When he says that his wife is interested in books and music and pictures, he is not only enclosing the arts in a female world, he is saying that he is rich enough to provide her with the leisure to do nothing. Reading is an inactivity, and therefore a badge of social class. Of course, these reasons for the piety attached to reading are never acknowledged. They show themselves in the shape of our attitudes toward books; reading gives off an air of gentility.

3   It seems to me possible to name four kinds of reading, each with a characteristic manner and purpose. The first is reading for information—reading to learn about a trade, or politics, or how to accomplish something. We read a newspaper this way, or most textbooks, or directions on how to assemble a bicycle. With most of this material, the reader can learn to scan the page quickly, coming up with what he needs and ignoring what is irrelevant to him, like the rhythm of the sentence, or the play of metaphor. Courses in speed reading can help us read for this purpose, training the eye to jump quickly across the page. If we read the *New York Times* with the attention we should give a novel or a poem, we will have time for nothing else, and our mind will be cluttered

with clichés and dead metaphor. Quick eye-reading is a necessity to anyone who wants to keep up with what's happening, or learn much of what has happened in the past. The amount of reflection, which interrupts and slows down the reading, depends on the material.

But it is not the same activity as reading literature. There ought to be another word. If we read a work of literature properly, we read slowly, and we *hear* all the words. If our lips do not actually move, it's only laziness. The muscles in our throat move, and come together when we see the word "squeeze." We hear the sounds so accurately that if a syllable is missing in a line of poetry we hear the lack, though we may not know what we are lacking. In prose we accept the rhythms, and hear the adjacent sounds. We also register a track of feeling through the metaphors and associations of words. Careless writing prevents this sort of attention, and becomes offensive. But the great writers reward it. Only by the full exercise of our powers to receive language can we absorb their intelligence and their imagination. This kind of reading goes through the ear—though the eye takes in the print, and decodes it into sound—to the throat and the understanding, and it can never be quick. It is slow and sensual, a deep pleasure that begins with touch and ends with the sort of comprehension that we associate with dream.

Too many intellectuals read in order to reduce images to abstractions. One reads philosophy slowly, as if it were literature, but much time must be spent with the eyes turned away from the page, reflecting on the text. To read literature this way is to turn it into something it is not—to concepts clothed in character, or philosophy sugar-coated. I think that most literary intellectuals read this way, including brighter professors of English, with the result that they miss literature completely, and concern themselves with a minor discipline called the history of ideas. I remember a course in Chaucer at my university in which the final exam required the identification of a hundred or more fragments of Chaucer, none as long as a line. If you like poetry, and read Chaucer through a couple of times slowly, you found yourself knowing them all. If you were a literary intellectual, well-informed about the great chain of being, chances are you had a difficult time. To read literature is to be intimately involved with the words on the page, and never to think of them as the embodiments of ideas which can be expressed in other terms. On the other hand, intellectual writing—closer to mathematics on a continuum that has at its opposite pole lyric poetry—requires intellectual reading, which is slow because it is reflective and because the reader must pause to evaluate concepts.

6   But most of the reading which is praised for itself is neither literary nor intellectual. It is narcotic. Novels, stories, and biographies—historical sagas, monthly regurgitations of book clubs, four- and five-thousand word daydreams of the magazines—these are the opium of the suburbs. The drug is not harmful except to the addict himself, and is no more injurious to him than Johnny Carson or a bridge club, but it is nothing to be proud of. This reading is the automated daydream, the mild trip of the housewife and the tired businessman, interested not in experience and feeling but in turning off the possibilities of experience and feeling. Great literature, if we read it well, opens us up to the world, and makes us more sensitive to it, as if we acquired eyes that could see through walls and ears that could hear the smallest sounds. But by narcotic reading, one can reduce great literature to the level of *The Valley of the Dolls*. One can read *Anna Karenina* passively and inattentively, and float down the river of lethargy as if one were reading a confession magazine: "I Spurned My Husband for a Count."

7   I think that everyone reads for narcosis occasionally, and perhaps most consistently in late adolescence, when great readers are born. I remember reading to shut the world out, away at a school where I did not want to be; I invented a word for my disease: "Bibliolepsy," on the analogy of narcolepsy. But after a while the books became a window on the world, and not a screen against it. This change doesn't always happen. I think that late adolescent narcotic reading accounts for some of the badness of English departments. As a college student, the boy loves reading and majors in English because he would be reading anyway. Deciding on a career, he takes up English teaching for the same reason. Then in graduate school he is trained to be a scholar, which is painful and irrelevant, and finds he must write papers and publish

them to be a Professor—and at about this time he no longer requires reading for narcosis, and he is left with nothing but a Ph.D. and the prospect of fifty years of teaching literature; and he does not even like literature.

Narcotic reading survives the impact of television, because this type of reading has even less reality than melodrama; that is, the reader is in control: Once the characters reach into the reader's feelings, he is able to stop reading, or glance away, or superimpose his own daydream. The trouble with television is that it embodies its own daydream. Literature is often valued precisely because of its distance from the tangible. Some readers prefer looking into the text of a play to seeing it performed. Reading a play, it is possible to stage it oneself by an imaginative act; but it is also possible to remove it from real people. Here is Virginia Woolf, who was lavish in her praise of the act of reading, talking about reading a play rather than seeing it: "Certainly there is a good deal to be said for reading *Twelfth Night* in the book if the book can be read in a garden, with no sound but the thud of an apple falling to the earth, or of the wind ruffling the branches of the trees." She sets her own stage; the play is called *Virginia Woolf Reads Twelfth Night in a Garden.* Piety moves into narcissism, and the high metaphors of Shakespeare's lines dwindle into the flowers of an English garden; actors in ruffles wither, while the wind ruffles branches.

1968

Growing Up Asian in America
Kesaya E. Noda

Sometimes when I was growing up, my identity seemed to hurtle toward me and paste itself right to my face. I felt that way, encountering the stereotypes of my race perpetuated by non-Japanese people (primarily white) who may or may not have had contact with other Japanese in America. "You don't like cheese, do you?" someone would ask. "I know your people don't like cheese." Sometimes questions came making allusions to history. That was another aspect of the identity. Events that had happened quite apart from the me who stood silent in that moment connected my face with an incomprehensible past. "Your parents were in California? Were they in those camps during the war?" And sometimes there were phrases or nicknames: "Lotus Blossom." I was sometimes addressed or referred to as racially Japanese, sometimes as Japanese-American, and sometimes as an Asian woman. Confusions and distortions abounded.

2   How is one to know and define oneself? From the inside—within a context that is self-defined, from a grounding in community and a connection with culture and history that are comfortably accepted? Or from the outside—within terms or messages received from the media and people who are often ignorant? Even as an adult I can still see two sides of my face and past. I can see from the inside out, in freedom. And I can see from the outside in, driven by the old voices of childhood and lost in anger and fear.

I AM RACIALLY JAPANESE

3 A voice from my childhood says: "You are other. You are less than. You are unalterably alien." This voice has its own history. We have indeed been seen as other and alien since the early years of our arrival in the United States. The very first immigrants were welcomed and sought as laborers to replace the dwindling numbers of Chinese, whose influx had been cut off by the Chinese Exclusion Act of 1882. The Japanese fell natural heir to the same anti-Asian prejudice that had arisen against the Chinese. As soon as they began striking for better wages, they were no longer welcomed.

4   I can see myself today as a person historically defined by law and custom as being forever alien. Being neither "free white," nor "African," our people in California were deemed "aliens, ineligible for citizenship," no matter how long they intended to stay here. Aliens ineligible for citizenship were prohibited from owning, buying, or leasing land. They did not and could not belong

here. The voice in me remembers that I am always a *Japanese*-American in the eyes of many. A third-generation German-American is an American. A third-generation Japanese-American is a Japanese-American. Being Japanese means being a danger to the country during the war and knowing how to use chopsticks. I wear this history on my face.

I move to the other side. I see a different light and claim a dif- 5 ferent context. My race is a line that stretches across ocean and time to link me to the shrine where my grandmother was raised. Two high, white banners lift in the wind at the top of the stone steps leading to the shrine. It is time for the summer festival. Black characters are written against the sky as boldly as the clouds, as lightly as kites, as sharply as the big black crows I used to see above the fields in New Hampshire. At festival time there is liquor and food, ritual, discipline, and abandonment. There is music and drunkenness and invocation. There is hope. Another season has come. Another season has gone.

I am racially Japanese. I have a certain claim to this crazy 6 place where the prayers intoned by a neighboring Shinto priest (standing in for my grandmother's nephew who is sick) are drowned out by the rehearsals for the pop singing contest in which most of the villagers will compete later that night. The village elders, the priest, and I stand respectfully upon the immaculate, shining wooden floor of the outer shrine, bowing our heads before the hidden powers. During the patchy intervals when I can hear him, I notice the priest has a stutter. His voice flutters up to my ears only occasionally because two men and a woman are singing gustily into a microphone in the compound, testing the sound system. A pre-recorded tape of guitars, samisens, and drums accompanies them. Rock music and Shinto prayers. That night, to loud applause and cheers, a young man is given the award for the most *netsuretsu*—passionate, burning—rendition of a song. We roar our approval of the reward. Never mind that his voice had wandered and slid, now slightly above, now slightly below the given line of the melody. Netsuretsu. Netsuretsu.

In the morning, my grandmother's sister kneels at the foot of 7 the stone stairs to offer her morning prayers. She is too crippled to climb the stairs, so each morning she kneels here upon the path. She shuts her eyes for a few seconds, her motions as matter of fact as when she washes rice. I linger longer than she does, so reluctant to leave, savoring the connection I feel with my grandmother in America, the past, and the power that lives and shines in the morning sun.

8   Our family has served this shrine for generations. The family's need to protect this claim to identity and place outweighs any individual claim to any individual hope. I am Japanese.

I AM A JAPANESE-AMERICAN

9   "Weak." I hear the voice from my childhood years. "Passive," I hear. Our parents and grandparents were the ones who were put into those camps. They went without resistance; they offered cooperation as proof of loyalty to America. "Victim," I hear. And, "Silent."

10   Our parents are painted as hard workers who were socially uncomfortable and had difficulty expressing even the smallest opinion. Clean, quiet, motivated, and determined to match the American way; that is us, and that is the story of our time here.

11   "Why did you go into those camps?" I raged at my parents, frightened by my own inner silence and timidity. "Why didn't you do anything to resist? Why didn't you name it the injustice it was?" Couldn't our parents even think? Couldn't they? Why were we so passive?

12   I shift my vision and my stance. I am in California. My uncle is in the midst of the sweet potato harvest. He is pressed, trying to get the harvesting crews onto the field as quickly as possible, worried about the flow of equipment and people. His big pickup is pulled off to the side, motor running, door ajar. I see two tractors in the yard in front of an old shed; the flatbed harvesting platform on which the workers will stand has already been brought over from the other field. It's early morning. The workers stand loosely grouped and at ease, but my uncle looks as harried and tense as a police officer trying to unsnarl a New York City traffic jam. Driving toward the shed, I pull my car off the road to make way for an approaching tractor. The front wheels of the car sink luxuriously

into the soft, white sand by the roadside and the car slides to a
dreamy halt, tail still on the road. I try to move forward. I try to
move back. The front bites contentedly into the sand, the back lifts
itself at a jaunty angle. My uncle sees me and storms down the
road, running. He is shouting before he is even near me.

"What's the matter with you?" he screams. "What the hell are   13
you doing?" In his frenzy, he grabs his hat off his head and
slashes it through the air across his knee. He is beside himself.
"Don't you know how to drive in sand? What's the matter with
you? You've blocked the whole roadway. How am I supposed to
get my tractors out of here? Can't you use your head? You've cut
off the whole roadway, and we've got to get out of here."

I stand on the road before him helplessly thinking. "No, I   14
don't know how to drive in sand. I've never driven in sand."

"I'm sorry, uncle," I say, burying a smile beneath a look of   15
sincere apology. I notice my deep amusement and my affection
for him with great curiosity. I am usually devastated by anger.
Not this time.

During the several years that follow I learn about the people   16
and the place, and much more about what has happened in this
California village where my parents grew up. The issei, our
grandparents, made this settlement in the desert. Their first crops
were eaten by rabbits and ravaged by insects. The land was so barren that men walking from house to house sometimes got lost.
Women came here too. They bore children in 114-degree heat, then
carried the babies with them into the fields to nurse when they
reached the end of each row of grapes or other truck-farm crops.

I had had no idea what it meant to buy this kind of land and   17
make it grow green. Or how, when the war came, there was no
space at all for the subtlety of being who we were—Japanese-
Americans. Either/or was the way. I hadn't understood that people were literally afraid for their lives then, that their money had
been frozen in banks; that there was a five-mile travel limit; that
when the early evening curfew came and they were inside their
houses, some of them watched helplessly as people they knew
went into their barns to steal their belongings. The police were
patrolling the road, interested only in violators of curfew. There
was no help for them in the face of thievery. I had not been able to

imagine before what it must have felt like to be an American—to know absolutely that one is an American—and yet to have almost everyone else deny it. Not only deny it, but challenge that identity with machine guns and troops of white American soldiers. In those circumstances it was difficult to say, "I'm a Japanese-American." "American" had to do.

18   But now I can say that I am a Japanese-American. It means I have a place here in this country, too. I have a place here on the East Coast, where our neighbor is so much a part of our family that my mother never passes her house at night without glancing at the lights to see if she is home and safe; where my parents have hauled hundreds of pounds of rocks from fields and arduously planted Christmas trees and blueberries, lilacs, asparagus, and crab apples; where my father still dreams of angling a stream to a new bed so that he can dig a pond in the field and fill it with water and fish. "The neighbors already came for their Christmas tree?" he asks in December. "Did they like it? Did they like it?"

19   I have a place on the West Coast where my relatives still farm, where I heard the stories of feuds and backbiting, and where I saw that people survived and flourished because fundamentally they trusted and relied upon one another. A death in the family is not just a death in a family; it is a death in the community. I saw people help each other with money, materials, labor, attention, and time. I saw men gather once a year, without fail, to clean the grounds of a ninety-year-old woman who had helped the community before, during, and after the war. I saw her remembering them with birthday cards sent to each of their children.

20   I come from a people with a long memory and a distinctive grace. We live our thanks. And we are Americans. Japanese-Americans.

I AM A JAPANESE-AMERICAN WOMAN

21 Woman. The last piece of my identity. It has been easier by far for me to know myself in Japan and to see my place in America than it has been to accept my line of connection with my own mother. She was my dark self, a figure in whom I thought I saw all that I

feared most in myself. Growing into womanhood and looking for some model of strength, I turned away from her. Of course, I could not find what I sought. I was looking for a black feminist or a white feminist. My mother is neither white nor black.

My mother is a woman who speaks with her life as much as 22 with her tongue. I think of her with her own mother. Grandmother had Parkinson's disease and it had frozen her gait and set her fingers, tongue, and feet jerking and trembling in a terrible dance. My aunts and uncles wanted her to be able to live in her own home. They fed her, bathed her, dressed her, awoke at midnight to take her for one last trip to the bathroom. My aunts (her daughters-in-law) did most of the care, but my mother went from New Hampshire to California each summer to spend a month living with Grandmother, because she wanted to and because she wanted to give my aunts at least a small rest. During those hot summer days, mother lay on the couch watching the television or reading, cooking foods that Grandmother liked, and speaking little. Grandmother thrived under her care.

The time finally came when it was too dangerous for 23 Grandmother to live alone. My relatives kept finding her on the floor beside her bed when they went to wake her in the mornings. My mother flew to California to help clean the house and make arrangements for Grandmother to enter a local nursing home. On her last day at home, while Grandmother was sitting in her big, overstuffed armchair, hair combed and wearing a green summer dress, my mother went to her and knelt at her feet. "Here, Mamma," she said. "I've polished your shoes." She lifted Grandmother's legs and helped her into the shiny black shoes. My Grandmother looked down and smiled slightly. She left her house walking, supported by her children, carrying her pocketbook, and wearing her polished black shoes. "Look, Mamma," my mom had said, kneeling. "I've polished your shoes."

Just the other day, my mother came to Boston to visit. She 24 had recently lost a lot of weight and was pleased with her new shape and her feeling of good health. "Look at me, Kes," she exclaimed, turning toward me, front and back, as naked as the day she was born. I saw her small breasts and the wide, brown scar, belly button to pubic hair, that marked her because my brother and I were both born by Caesarean section. Her hips were small. I was not a large baby, but there was so little room for me in her that when she was carrying me she could not even begin to bend over toward the floor. She hated it, she said.

25   "Don't I look good? Don't you think I look good?"

26   I looked at my mother, smiling and as happy as she, thinking of all the times I have seen her naked. I have seen both my parents naked throughout my life, as they have seen me. From childhood through adulthood we've had our naked moments, sharing baths, idle conversations picked up as we moved between showers and closets, hurried moments at the beginning of days, quiet moments at the end of days.

27   I know this to be Japanese, this ease with the physical, and it makes me think of an old Japanese folk song. A young nursemaid, a fifteen-year-old girl, is singing a lullaby to a baby who is strapped to her back. The nursemaid has been sent as a servant to a place far from her own home. "We're the beggars," she says, "and they are the nice people. Nice people wear fine sashes. Nice clothes."

> If I should drop dead,
> bury me by the roadside!
> I'll give a flower to
> everyone who passes.
>
> What kind of flower?
> The cam-cam-camellia [tsun-tsun-tsubaki]
> watered by Heaven:
> alms water.

28   The nursemaid is the intersection of heaven and earth, the intersection of the human, the natural world, the body, and the soul. In this song, with clear eyes, she looks steadily at life, which is sometimes so very terrible and sad. I think of her while looking at my mother, who is standing on the red and purple carpet before me, laughing, without any clothes.

29   I am my mother's daughter. And I am myself.

30   I am a Japanese-American woman.

EPILOGUE

I recently heard a man from West Africa share some memories of 31 his childhood. He was raised Muslim, but when he was a young man, he found himself deeply drawn to Christianity. He struggled against his inner impulse for years, trying to avoid the church yet feeling pushed to return to it again and again. "I would have done anything to avoid the change," he said. At last, he became Christian. Afterwards he was afraid to go home, fearing that he would not be accepted. The fear was groundless, he discovered, when at last he returned—he had separated himself, but his family and friends (all Muslim) had not separated themselves from him.

The man, who is now a professor of religion, said that in the 32 Africa he knew as a child and a young man, pluralism was embraced rather than feared. There was "a kind of tolerance that did not deny your particularity," he said. He alluded to zestful, spontaneous debates that would sometimes loudly erupt between Muslims and Christians in the village's public spaces. His memories of an atheist who harangued the villagers when he came to visit them once a week moved me deeply. Perhaps the man was an agricultural advisor or inspector. He harassed the women. He would say: "Don't go to the fields! Don't even bother to go to the fields. Let God take care of you. He'll send you the food. If you believe in God, why do you need to work? You don't need to work! Let God put the seeds in the ground. Stay home."

The professor said, "The women laughed, you know? They 33 just laughed. Their attitude was, 'Here is a child of God. When will he come home?'"

The storyteller, the professor of religion, smiled a most fan- 34 tastic tender smile as he told this story. "In my country, there is a deep affirmation of the oneness of God," he said. "The atheist and the women were having quite different experiences in their encounter, though the atheist did not know this. He saw himself as quite separate from the women. But the women did not see themselves as being separate from him. 'Here is a child of God,' they said. 'When will he come home?'"

1989

The Truth about Lying

Judith Viorst

1   I've been wanting to write on a subject that intrigues and challenges me: The subject of lying. I've found it very difficult to do.
Everyone I've talked to has a quite intense and personal but often
rather intolerant point of view about what we can—and can
never *never*—tell lies about. I've finally reached the conclusion
that I can't present any ultimate conclusions, for too many people
would promptly disagree. Instead, I'd like to present a series of
moral puzzles, all concerned with lying. I'll tell you what I think
about them. Do you agree?

SOCIAL LIES

2   Most of the people I've talked with say that they find social lying
acceptable and necessary. They think it's the civilized way for folks
to behave. Without these little white lies, they say, our relationships
would be short and brutish and nasty. It's arrogant, they say, to
insist on being so incorruptible and so brave that you cause other
people unnecessary embarrassment or pain by compulsively assail-
ing them with your honesty. I basically agree. What about you?

3   Will you say to people, when it simply isn't true, "I like your
new hairdo," "You're looking much better," "It's so nice to see
you," "I had a wonderful time"?

4   Will you praise hideous presents and homely kids?

5   Will you decline invitations with "We're busy that night—so
sorry we can't come," when the truth is you'd rather stay home
than dine with the So-and-sos?

6   And even though, as I do, you may prefer the polite evasion
of "You really cooked up a storm" instead of "The soup"—which
tastes like warmed-over coffee—"is wonderful," will you, if you
must, proclaim it wonderful?

7   There's one man I know who absolutely refuses to tell social
lies. "I can't play that game," he says; "I'm simply not made that
way." And his answer to the argument that saying nice things to

someone doesn't cost anything is, "Yes, it does—it destroys your credibility." Now, he won't, unsolicited, offer his views on the painting you just bought, but you don't ask his frank opinion unless you want *frank,* and his silence at those moments when the rest of us liars are muttering, "Isn't it lovely?" is, for the most part, eloquent enough. My friend does not indulge in what he calls "flattery, false praise and mellifluous comments." When others tell fibs he will not go along. He says that social lying is lying, that little white lies are still lies. And he feels that telling lies is morally wrong. What about you?

PEACE-KEEPING LIES

Many people tell peace-keeping lies; lies designed to avoid irrita- 8 tion or argument; lies designed to shelter the liar from possible blame or pain; lies (or so it is rationalized) designed to keep trouble at bay without hurting anyone.

I tell these lies at times, and yet I always feel they're wrong. I 9 understand why we tell them, but still they feel wrong. And whenever I lie so that someone won't disapprove of me or think less of me or holler at me, I feel I'm a bit of a coward, I feel I'm dodging responsibility, I feel . . . guilty. What about you?

Do you, when you're late for a date because you overslept, 10 say that you're late because you got caught in a traffic jam?

Do you, when you forget to call a friend, say that you called 11 several times but the line was busy?

Do you, when you didn't remember that it was your father's 12 birthday, say that his present must be delayed in the mail?

And when you're planning a weekend in New York City and 13 you're not in the mood to visit your mother, who lives there, do you conceal—with a lie, if you must—the fact that you'll be in New York? Or do you have the courage—or is it the cruelty?—to say, "I'll be in New York, but sorry—I don't plan on seeing you"?

(Dave and his wife Elaine have two quite different points of 14 view on this very subject. He calls her a coward. She says she's being wise. He says she must assert her right to visit New York sometimes and not see her mother. To which she always patiently replies: "Why should we have useless fights? My mother's too old to change. We get along much better when I lie to her.")

15   Finally, do you keep the peace by telling your husband lies on the subject of money? Do you reduce what you really paid for your shoes? And in general do you find yourself ready, willing and able to lie to him when you make absurd mistakes or lose or break things?

16   "I used to have a romantic idea that part of intimacy was confessing every dumb thing that you did to your husband. But after a couple of years of that," says Laura, "have I changed my mind!"

17   And having changed her mind, she finds herself telling peace-keeping lies. And yes, I tell them too. What about you?

PROTECTIVE LIES

18   Protective lies are lies folks tell—often quite serious lies—because they're convinced that the truth would be too damaging. They lie because they feel there are certain human values that supersede the wrong of having lied. They lie, not for personal gain, but because they believe it's for the good of the person they're lying to. They lie to those they love, to those who trust them most of all, on the grounds that breaking this trust is justified.

19   They may lie to their children on money or marital matters.

20   They may lie to the dying about the state of their health.

21   They may lie about adultery, and not—or so they insist—to save their own hide, but to save the heart and the pride of the men they are married to.

22   They may lie to their closest friend because the truth about her talents or son or psyche would be—or so they insist—utterly devastating.

23   I sometimes tell such lies, but I'm aware that it's quite presumptuous to claim I know what's best for others to know. That's called playing God. That's called manipulation and control. And we never can be sure, once we start to juggle lies, just where they'll land, exactly where they'll roll.

24   And furthermore, we may find ourselves lying in order to back up the lies that are backing up the lie we initially told.

And furthermore—let's be honest—if conditions were 25
reversed, we certainly wouldn't want anyone lying to us.

Yet, having said all that, I still believe that there are times 26
when protective lies must nonetheless be told. What about you?

If your Dad had a very bad heart and you had to tell him 27
some bad family news, which would you choose: To tell him the
truth or to lie?

If your former husband failed to send his monthly child sup- 28
port check and in other ways behaved like a total rat, would you
allow your children—who believed he was simply wonderful—
to continue to believe that he was wonderful?

If your dearly beloved brother selected a wife whom you 29
deeply disliked, would you reveal your feelings or would you
fake it?

And if you were asked, after making love, "And how was 30
that for you?" would you reply, if it wasn't too good, "Not too
good"?

Now, some would call a sex lie unimportant, little more than 31
social lying, a simple act of courtesy that makes all human intercourse run smoothly. And some would say all sex lies are bad
news and unacceptably protective. Because, says Ruth, "a man
with an ego that fragile doesn't need your lies—he needs a psychiatrist." Still others feel that sex lies are indeed protective lies,
more serious than simple social lying, and yet at times they tell
them on the grounds that when it comes to matters sexual, everybody's ego is somewhat fragile.

"If most of the time things go well in sex," says Sue, "I think 32
you're allowed to dissemble when they don't. I can't believe it's
good to say, 'Last night was four stars, darling, but tonight's performance rates only a half.'"

I'm inclined to agree with Sue. What about you?   33

TRUST-KEEPING LIES

Another group of lies are trust-keeping lies, lies that involve tri- 34
angulation, with *A* (that's you) telling lies to *B* on behalf of *C*
(whose trust you'd promised to keep). Most people concede that

once you've agreed not to betray a friend's confidence, you can't betray it, even if you must lie. But I've talked with people who don't want you telling them anything that they might be called on to lie about.

35   "I don't tell lies for myself," says Fran, "and I don't want to have to tell them for other people." Which means, she agrees, that if her best friend is having an affair, she absolutely doesn't want to know about it.

36   "Are you saying," her best friend asks, "that if I went off with a lover and I asked you to tell my husband I'd been with you, that you wouldn't lie for me, that you'd betray me?"

37   Fran is very pained but very adamant. "I wouldn't want to betray you, so . . . don't ask me."

38   Fran's best friend is shocked. What about you?

39   Do you believe you can have close friends if you're not prepared to receive their deepest secrets?

40   Do you believe you must always lie for your friends?

41   Do you believe, if your friend tells a secret that turns out to be quite immoral or illegal, that once you've promised to keep it, you must keep it?

42   And what if your friend were your boss—if you were perhaps one of the President's men—would you betray or lie for him over, say, Watergate?

43   As you can see, these issues get terribly sticky.

44   It's my belief that once we've promised to keep a trust, we must tell lies to keep it. I also believe that we can't tell Watergate lies. And if these two statements strike you as quite contradictory, you're right—they're quite contradictory. But for now they're the best I can do. What about you?

45   Some say that truth will out and thus you might as well tell the truth. Some say you can't regain the trust that lies lose. Some say that even though the truth may never be revealed, our lies pervert and damage our relationships. Some say . . . well, here's what some of them have to say.

46   "I'm a coward," says Grace, "about telling close people important, difficult truths. I find that I'm unable to carry it off. And so if something is bothering me, it keeps building up inside till I end up just not seeing them any more."

"I lie to my husband on sexual things, but I'm furious," says   47
Joyce, "that he's too insensitive to know I'm lying."

"I suffer most from the misconception that children can't take   48
the truth," says Emily. "But I'm starting to see that what's harder
and more damaging for them is being told lies, is *not* being told
the truth."

"I'm afraid," says Joan, "that we often wind up feeling a bit   49
of contempt for the people we lie to."

And then there are those who have no talent for lying.   50

"Over the years, I tried to lie," a friend of mine explained,   51
"but I always got found out and I always got punished. I guess I
gave myself away because I feel guilty about any kind of lying. It
looks as if I'm stuck with telling the truth."

For those of us, however, who are good at telling lies, for   52
those of us who lie and don't get caught, the question of whether
or not to lie can be a hard and serious moral problem. I liked the
remark of a friend of mine who said, "I'm willing to lie. But just
as a last resort—the truth's always better."

"Because," he explained, "though others may completely   53
accept the lie I'm telling, I don't."

I tend to feel that way too.   54

What about you?   55

1981

Doublespeak

William Lutz

There are no potholes in the streets of Tucson, Arizona, just "pave-   1
ment deficiencies." The Reagan Administration didn't propose any
new taxes, just "revenue enhancement" through new "user's fees."
Those aren't bums on the street, just "non-goal-oriented members
of society." There are no more poor people, just "fiscal under-
achievers." There was no robbery of an automatic teller machine,
just an "unauthorized withdrawal." The patient didn't die because

of medical malpractice, it was just a "diagnostic misadventure of a high magnitude." The U.S. Army doesn't kill the enemy anymore, it just "services the target." And the doublespeak goes on.

2   Doublespeak is language that pretends to communicate but really doesn't. It is language that makes the bad seem good, the negative appear positive, the unpleasant appear attractive or at least tolerable. Doublespeak is language that avoids or shifts responsibility, language that is at variance with its real or purported meaning. It is language that conceals or prevents thought; rather than extending thought, doublespeak limits it. . . .

HOW TO SPOT DOUBLESPEAK

3   How can you spot doublespeak? Most of the time you will recognize doublespeak when you see or hear it. But, if you have any doubts, you can identify doublespeak just by answering these questions: Who is saying what to whom, under what conditions and circumstances, with what intent, and with what results? Answering these questions will usually help you identify as doublespeak language that appears to be legitimate or that at first glance doesn't even appear to be doublespeak.

First Kind of Doublespeak

4   There are at least four kinds of doublespeak. The first is the euphemism, an inoffensive or positive word or phrase used to avoid a harsh, unpleasant, or distasteful reality. But a euphemism can also be a tactful word or phrase which avoids directly mentioning a painful reality, or it can be an expression used out of concern for the feelings of someone else, or to avoid directly discussing a topic subject to a social or cultural taboo.

5   When you use a euphemism because of your sensitivity for someone's feelings or out of concern for a recognized social or cultural taboo, it is not doublespeak. For example, you express your condolences that someone has "passed away" because you do not want to say to a grieving person, "I'm sorry your father is dead." When you use the euphemism "passed away," no one is misled. Moreover, the euphemism functions here not just to protect the

feelings of another person, but to communicate also your concern for that person's feelings during a period of mourning. When you excuse yourself to go to the "restroom," or you mention that someone is "sleeping with" or "involved with" someone else, you do not mislead anyone about your meaning, but you do respect the social taboos about discussing bodily functions and sex in direct terms. You also indicate your sensitivity to the feelings of your audience, which is usually considered a mark of courtesy and good manners.

However, when a euphemism is used to mislead or deceive, 6 it becomes doublespeak. For example, in 1984 the U.S. State Department announced that it would no longer use the word "killing" in its annual report on the status of human rights in countries around the world. Instead, it would use the phrase "unlawful or arbitrary deprivation of life," which the department claimed was more accurate. Its real purpose for using this phrase was simply to avoid discussing the embarrassing situation of government-sanctioned killings in countries that are supported by the United States and have been certified by the United States as respecting the human rights of their citizens. This use of a euphemism constitutes doublespeak, since it is designed to mislead, to cover up the unpleasant. Its real intent is at variance with its apparent intent. It is language designed to alter our perception of reality.

The Pentagon, too, avoids discussing unpleasant realities 7 when it refers to bombs and artillery shells that fall on civilian targets as "incontinent ordnance." And in 1977 the Pentagon tried to slip funding for the neutron bomb unnoticed into an appropriations bill by calling it a "radiation enhancement device."

Second Kind of Doublespeak

A second kind of doublespeak is jargon, the specialized language 8 of a trade, profession, or similar group, such as that used by doctors, lawyers, engineers, educators, or car mechanics. Jargon can serve an important and useful function. Within a group, jargon functions as a kind of verbal shorthand that allows members of the group to communicate with each other clearly, efficiently, and quickly. Indeed, it is a mark of membership in the group to be able to use and understand the group's jargon.

9   But jargon, like the euphemism, can also be doublespeak. It can be—and often is—pretentious, obscure, and esoteric terminology used to give an air of profundity, authority, and prestige to speakers and their subject matter. Jargon as doublespeak often makes the simple appear complex, the ordinary profound, the obvious insightful. In this sense it is used not to express but impress. With such doublespeak, the act of smelling something becomes "organoleptic analysis," glass becomes "fused silicate," a crack in a metal support beam becomes a "discontinuity," conservative economic policies become "distributionally conservative notions."

10   Lawyers, for example, speak of an "involuntary conversion" of property when discussing the loss or destruction of property through theft, accident, or condemnation. If your house burns down or if your car is stolen, you have suffered an involuntary conversion of your property. When used by lawyers in a legal situation, such jargon is a legitimate use of language, since lawyers can be expected to understand the term.

11   However, when a member of a specialized group uses its jargon to communicate with a person outside the group, and uses it knowing that the nonmember does not understand such language, then there is doublespeak. For example, on May 9, 1978, a National Airlines 727 airplane crashed while attempting to land at the Pensacola, Florida, airport. Three of the fifty-two passengers aboard the airplane were killed. As a result of the crash, National made an after-tax insurance benefit of $1.7 million, or an extra 18¢ a share dividend for its stockholders. Now National Airlines had two problems: It did not want to talk about one of its airplanes crashing, and it had to account for the $1.7 million when it issued its annual report to its stockholders. National solved the problem by inserting a footnote in its annual report which explained that the $1.7 million income was due to "the involuntary conversion of a 727." National thus acknowledged the crash of its airplane and the subsequent profit it made from the crash, without once mentioning the accident or the deaths. However, because airline officials knew that most stockholders in the company, and indeed most of the

general public, were not familiar with legal jargon, the use of such jargon constituted doublespeak.

Third Kind of Doublespeak

A third kind of doublespeak is gobbledygook or bureaucratese. 12 Basically, such doublespeak is simply a matter of piling on words, of overwhelming the audience with words, the bigger the words and the longer the sentences the better. Alan Greenspan, then chair of President Nixon's Council of Economic Advisors, was quoted in *The Philadelphia Inquirer* in 1974 as having testified before a Senate committee that "It is a tricky problem to find the particular calibration in timing that would be appropriate to stem the acceleration in risk premiums created by falling incomes without prematurely aborting the decline in the inflation-generated risk premiums."

Nor has Mr. Greenspan's language changed since then. 13 Speaking to the meeting of the Economic Club of New York in 1988, Mr. Greenspan, now Federal Reserve chair, said, "I guess I should warn you, if I turn out to be particularly clear, you've probably misunderstood what I've said." Mr. Greenspan's doublespeak doesn't seem to have held back his career.

Sometimes gobbledygook may sound impressive, but when 14 the quote is later examined in print it doesn't even make sense. During the 1988 presidential campaign, vice-presidential candidate Senator Dan Quayle explained the need for a strategic defense initiative by saying, "Why wouldn't an enhanced deterrent, a more stable peace, a better prospect to denying the ones who enter conflict in the first place to have a reduction of offensive systems and an introduction to defense capability? I believe this is the route the country will eventually go."

The investigation into the *Challenger* disaster in 1986 revealed 15 the doublespeak of gobbledygook and bureaucratese used by too many involved in the shuttle program. When Jesse Moore, NASA's associate administrator, was asked if the performance of the shuttle program had improved with each launch or if it had remained the same, he answered, "I think our performance in terms of the liftoff performance and in terms of the orbital performance, we knew more about the envelope we were operating under, and we have been pretty accurately staying in that. And so I would say the performance has not by design drastically improved. I think we have been able to characterize the performance more as a function of our launch experience as opposed to it improving as a function of time." While this language may appear to be jargon, a close look will reveal that it is really just gobbledygook laced with jargon. But you really have to wonder if Mr. Moore had any idea what he was saying.

Fourth Kind of Doublespeak

16 The fourth kind of doublespeak is inflated language that is designed to make the ordinary seem extraordinary; to make everyday things seem impressive; to give an air of importance to people, situations, or things that would not normally be considered important; to make the simple seem complex. Often this kind of doublespeak isn't hard to spot, and it is usually pretty funny. While car mechanics may be called "automotive internists," elevator operators members of the "vertical transportation corps," used cars "pre-owned" or "experienced cars," and black-and-white television sets described as having "non-multicolor capability," you really aren't misled all that much by such language.

17 However, you may have trouble figuring out that, when Chrysler "initiates a career alternative enhancement program," it is really laying off five thousand workers; or that "negative patient care outcome" means the patient died; or that "rapid oxidation" means a fire in a nuclear power plant.

18 The doublespeak of inflated language can have serious consequences. In Pentagon doublespeak, "pre-emptive counterattack" means that American forces attacked first; "engaged the enemy on all sides" means American troops were ambushed; "backloading of augmentation personnel" means a retreat by American troops. In the doublespeak of the military, the 1983 invasion of Grenada was conducted not by the U.S. Army, Navy, Air Force, and Marines, but by the "Caribbean Peace Keeping Forces." But then, according to the Pentagon, it wasn't an invasion, it was a "predawn vertical insertion." . . .

THE DANGERS OF DOUBLESPEAK

These . . . examples of doublespeak should make it clear that dou- 19
blespeak is not the product of carelessness or sloppy thinking.
Indeed, most doublespeak is the product of clear thinking and is
carefully designed and constructed to appear to communicate when
in fact it doesn't. It is language designed not to lead but mislead. It
is language designed to distort reality and corrupt thought. . . . When
a fire in a nuclear reactor building is called "rapid oxidation," an
explosion in a nuclear power plant is called an "energetic disas-
sembly," the illegal overthrow of a legitimate government is termed
"destabilizing a government," and lies are seen as "inoperative
statements," we are hearing doublespeak that attempts to avoid
responsibility and make the bad seem good, the negative appear
positive, something unpleasant appear attractive; and which seems
to communicate but doesn't. It is language designed to alter our
perception of reality and corrupt our thinking. Such language does
not provide us with the tools we need to develop, advance, and
preserve our culture and our civilization. Such language breeds
suspicion, cynicism, distrust, and, ultimately, hostility.

1989

9 Failures of the Imagination

Jonathan Lethem

ONE

It began for me here, in the same room where I sit now, in Boerum 1
Hill. It began as a non sequitur crackle of sunlight thunder, on a
gorgeous morning after an evening of thunderstorms. I ignored the
sound, took a shower instead, wondering about the sports page:
had Roger Clemens won his 20th? The phone rang, and a friend
asked: "Did you see it?" So I went to the window, and saw. In this
part of Brooklyn the towers are the nearest bit of Manhattan, easily

visible from upper stories or rooftops. Neighbors commute—
excuse me, commuted—to them by walking across the Brooklyn
Bridge. Both planes had arrived by the time I looked out the window. My denial slid from the fact of it—they're on fire, wow—to
tangential irritations, stuff I had to get done this week. I'd re-enact
this denial again and again in the next hours: the mind's raw dis-
inclination to grant this new actuality, cognitive dissonance run
riot. I'd entered—we'd all entered—a world containing a fresh category of phenomena: the unimaginable fact.

TWO

2 For the first 40 hours of this war all I've done is shuttle between
my apartment on Bergen Street, the homes of a few nearby
friends and the front-row seat provided by the Brooklyn Heights
Promenade, a rim of park that looks out over the tip of Manhattan
Island. All I've done, really, is try again and again to grasp the
unimaginable fact. I've stared across the river at the raw, unmedi-
ated plume, now black, now white, now gray, now black again.
I've stared and stared and felt my mind slide from it again and
again: unimaginable fact, confirmed by senses and testimony,
confirmed by the procession of ash-bathed faces shambling through
the neighborhood after crossing the bridge, confirmed by the television and yet granted no status by reeling, refusing mind. No
status whatsoever. Turning from the plume to the television. I try
again: maybe CNN can sell it to me with its video loop, plane slic-
ing cake of tower forever, the footage more ferociously lush and
inevitable every time. I'll understand this fact soon, yes? No. No.
Back to the promenade, then, to contemplation of my lovely
plume, Manhattan's inverted Fuji of roiling particles. And now
back to the television.

THREE

3 Am I willing? Can I bear to narrate this into normality, 40 hours
after they crumbled and fell? To craft a story: and then, and
then, and then? Will the words I'm spilling here seem fatuous or

hysterical or naïve by the time they're read? Likely so. I'm failing and relieved to fail. I'm disgusted with myself for consent-
ing to try. Speculation feels obscene. So does this self-indulgent
self-castigation. Except, there may be some slim value in offering to a rapidly toughening future some hint of the white noise
of one human imagination failing, on what they're calling the
Day After, to yet meet the task at hand. The channel surf of
denial and incomprehension: an extremely local report.

FOUR

When I was a kid in this neighborhood it was a regular thing to 4
walk to the promenade to see the harbor and skyline. I'd go with
my grandmother, and she'd point out the statue, the ferry, Ellis,
Governor's. Later we stared from that perch as they assembled
these erector-set-looking things, these twinned towers. Even
then I was a New York purist. I preferred old things, and I
resented the dull Saltiné boxes for dwarfing the Empire State. But
they were mine anyway. I couldn't help it. Big Apple, Abe Beame,
Bicentennial, World Trade Center, my cheesy 70s New York. A
decade later, when I first married, I dragged a California bride to
my city, and we elevated to the roof of one of the buildings to
exhilarate in the chill, dizzying wind of outer space. Yesterday,
the erector set reappeared, just for a moment. Yesterday the same
west-to-east wind that once nearly whisked newlyweds from the
rooftop blew pulverized tower across the river and into my
mouth. I've eaten my towers.

FIVE

Back to the promenade, back. I've abandoned the television 5
five, six times now to walk to the edge and widen my recalcitrant eyes and mind again at the plume. On the way up Henry
Street I gather one of the crisped papers twinkling everywhere to
the ground. A printout on old-style, tabbed computer paper.
7WTC 034: World Trade Center, Building 7, 34th floor, I guess.
Kirshenbaum, Joan. "For any report change complete this section

and return to ops support, data centre." Joan Kirshenbaum, if you're reading this, I've got your scrap of paper.

SIX

6 Dear reader, two Sundays in the future: you know vastly more than I do about what I mean when I say war. Do you envy me, living in this before, this last shred of relative innocence? I hope not. I hope I ought to envy you, the wild sweet peace you enjoy, the simultaneous epiphany of universal human amity and accord, the melting of all world guns into memorial sculpture which took place on, say, Sept. 16, the miracle that occurred in place of the carnage I'm dreading today. Oh, I hope I ought to envy you; I hope I'm a moron.

SEVEN

7 Reality check. As I write, sirens wheeling past my window. My apartment is two blocks from Atlantic Avenue and the city's largest Arabic neighborhood, which the cops have cordoned from traffic, anticipating and protecting against retaliatory chuckleheadedness. The radio's telling of another building that has fallen—you know, just another large, unmemorable office building in Lower Manhattan crumbling to dust, not a big deal these days, it happens sometimes, relax—it's not as if the twin towers fell down! The many, many things they're not telling us on the radio fall into two categories: things they're not telling us that we can pretty easily riddle out for ourselves, like we're picking up ears, we're picking up toes, God have mercy, we're picking up penises and vaginas, and things they're not telling us that we really can't fathom, like for instance what the hell all these presently rushing sirens are rushing toward.

EIGHT

8 The promenade yesterday was full of people, more than I've seen since the tall ships were in the harbor, and yet all absolutely still and silent. Each one of us came and stood, rooted at the spot

where we first got the plume in full view. Every third or fourth mouth covered with a surgical mask; those without masks feeling just that tiny bit sorrier for ourselves, but then again not really caring. That vast communal silence. This language is useless. I was doing better there, standing with others, rightly gathered into a commonality, a field of eyes, with mouths emitting, if anything, only slight, undramatized moans.

NINE

At the promenade, in the gathered silence and stillness of many minds looking through haze at an altered city, one woman, seated on a bench, elbows on knees, calmly, effortlessly tilted her head and vomited. A splash heard in the silence. The head tilted just enough to avoid chin-dribble. Eyes never breaking from the task of gazing, gathering the new information.

2001

6

Comparison and Contrast

Grant and Lee: A Study in Contrasts

Bruce Catton

1   When Ulysses S. Grant and Robert E. Lee met in the parlor of a modest house at Appomattox Court House, Virginia, on April 9, 1865, to work out the terms for the surrender of Lee's Army of Northern Virginia, a great chapter in American life came to a close, and a great new chapter began.

2   These men were bringing the Civil War to its virtual finish. To be sure, other armies had yet to surrender, and for a few days the fugitive Confederate government would struggle desperately and vainly, trying to find some way to go on living now that its chief support was gone. But in effect it was all over when Grant and Lee signed the papers. And the little room where they wrote out the terms was the scene of one of the poignant, dramatic contrasts in American history.

3   They were two strong men, these oddly different generals, and they represented the strengths of two conflicting currents that, through them, had come into final collision.

4   Back of Robert E. Lee was the notion that the old aristocratic concept might somehow survive and be dominant in American life.

5   Lee was tidewater Virginia, and in his background were family, culture, and tradition . . . the age of chivalry transplanted to a New World which was making its own legends and its own myths. He embodied a way of life that had come down through the age of knighthood and the English country squire. America was a land that was beginning all over again,

dedicated to nothing much more complicated than the rather hazy belief that all men had equal rights, and should have an equal chance in the world. In such a land Lee stood for the feeling that it was somehow of advantage to human society to have a pronounced inequality in the social structure. There should be a leisure class, backed by ownership of land; in turn, society itself should be keyed to the land as the chief source of wealth and influence. It would bring forth (according to this ideal) a class of men with a strong sense of obligation to the community; men who lived not to gain advantage for themselves, but to meet the solemn obligations which had been laid on them by the very fact that they were privileged. From them the country would get its leadership; to them it could look for the higher values—of thought, of conduct, of personal deportment—to give it strength and virtue.

Lee embodied the noblest elements of this aristocratic ideal. 6 Through him, the landed nobility justified itself. For four years, the Southern states had fought a desperate war to uphold the ideals for which Lee stood. In the end, it almost seemed as if the Confederacy fought for Lee; as if he himself was the Confederacy . . . the best thing that the way of life for which the Confederacy stood could ever have to offer. He had passed into legend before Appomattox. Thousands of tired, underfed, poorly clothed Confederate soldiers, long-since past the simple enthusiasm of the early days of the struggle, somehow considered Lee the symbol of everything for which they had been willing to die. But they could not quite put this feeling into words. If the Lost Cause, sanctified by so much heroism and so many deaths, had a living justification, its justification was General Lee.

Grant, the son of a tanner on the Western frontier, was every- 7 thing Lee was not. He had come up the hard way, and embodied nothing in particular except the eternal toughness and sinewy fiber of the men who grew up beyond the mountains. He was one of a body of men who owed reverence and obeisance to no one, who were self-reliant to a fault, who cared hardly anything for the past but who had a sharp eye for the future.

8   These frontier men were the precise opposites of the tidewater aristocrats. Back of them, in the great surge that had taken people over the Alleghenies and into the opening Western country, there was a deep, implicit dissatisfaction with a past that had settled into grooves. They stood for democracy, not from any reasoned conclusion about the proper ordering of human society, but simply because they had grown up in the middle of democracy and knew how it worked. Their society might have privileges, but they would be privileges each man had won for himself. Forms and patterns meant nothing. No man was born to anything, except perhaps to a chance to show how far he could rise. Life was competition.

9   Yet along with this feeling had come a deep sense of belonging to a national community. The Westerner who developed a farm, opened a shop or set up in business as a trader, could hope to prosper only as his own community prospered—and his community ran from the Atlantic to the Pacific and from Canada down to Mexico. If the land was settled, with towns and highways and accessible markets, he could better himself. He saw his fate in terms of the nation's own destiny. As its horizons expanded, so did his. He had, in other words, an acute dollars-and-cents stake in the continued growth and development of his country.

10   And that, perhaps, is where the contrast between Grant and Lee becomes most striking. The Virginia aristocrat, inevitably, saw himself in relation to his own region. He lived in a static society which could endure almost anything except change. Instinctively, his first loyalty would go to the locality in which that society existed. He would fight to the limit of endurance to defend it, because in defending it he was defending everything that gave his own life its deepest meaning.

11   The Westerner, on the other hand, would fight with an equal tenacity for the broader concept of society. He fought so because everything he lived by was tied to growth, expansion, and a constantly widening horizon. What he lived by would survive or fall with the nation itself. He could not possibly stand by unmoved in the face of an attempt to destroy the Union. He would combat it with everything he had, because

he could only see it as an effort to cut the ground out from under his feet.

So Grant and Lee were in complete contrast, representing two 12 diametrically opposed elements in American life. Grant was the modern man emerging; beyond him, ready to come on the stage, was the great age of steel and machinery, of crowded cities and a restless, burgeoning vitality. Lee might have ridden down from the old age of chivalry, lance in hand, silken banner fluttering over his head. Each man was the perfect champion of his cause, drawing both his strengths and his weaknesses from the people he led.

Yet it was not all contrast, after all. Different as they were—in 13 background, in personality, in underlying aspiration—these two great soldiers had much in common. Under everything else, they were marvelous fighters. Furthermore, their fighting qualities were really very much alike.

Each man had, to begin with, the great virtue of utter tenac- 14 ity and fidelity. Grant fought his way down the Mississippi Valley in spite of acute personal discouragement and profound military handicaps. Lee hung on in the trenches at Petersburg after hope itself had died. In each man there was an indomitable quality . . . the born fighter's refusal to give up as long as he can still remain on his feet and lift his two fists.

Daring and resourcefulness they had, too; the ability to think 15 faster and move faster than the enemy. These were the qualities which gave Lee the dazzling campaigns of Second Manassas and Chancellorsville and won Vicksburg for Grant.

Lastly, and perhaps greatest of all, there was the ability, at the 16 end, to turn quickly from war to peace once the fighting was over. Out of the way these two men behaved at Appomattox came the possibility of a peace of reconciliation. It was a possi- bility not wholly realized, in the years to come, but which did, in the end, help the two sections to become one nation again . . . after a war whose bitterness might have seemed to make such a reunion wholly impossible. No part of either man's life became him more than the part he played in their brief meeting in the McLean house at Appomattox. Their behavior there put all suc- ceeding generations of Americans in their debt. Two great Americans, Grant and Lee—very different, yet under everything very much alike. Their encounter at Appomattox was one of the great moments of American history.

1958

Talk in the Intimate Relationship: His and Hers

Deborah Tannen

1   Male-female conversation is cross-cultural communication. Culture is simply a network of habits and patterns gleaned from past experience, and women and men have different past experiences. From the time they're born, they're treated differently, talked to differently, and talk differently as a result. Boys and girls grow up in different worlds, even if they grow up in the same house. And as adults they travel in different worlds, reinforcing patterns established in childhood. These cultural differences include different expectations about the role of talk in relationships and how it fulfills that role.

2   Everyone knows that as a relationship becomes long-term, its terms change. But women and men often differ in how they expect them to change. Many women feel, "After all this time, you should know what I want without my telling you." Many men feel, "After all this time, we should be able to tell each other what we want."

3   These incongruent expectations capture one of the key differences between men and women. Communication is always a matter of balancing conflicting needs for involvement and independence. Though everyone has both these needs, women often have a relatively greater need for involvement, and men a relatively greater need for independence. Being understood without saying what you mean gives a payoff in involvement, and that is why women value it so highly.

4   If you want to be understood without saying what you mean explicitly in words, you must convey meaning somewhere else—in

how words are spoken, or by metamessages. Thus it stands to reason that women are often more attuned than men to the metamessages of talk. When women surmise meaning in this way, it seems mysterious to men, who call it "women's intuition" (if they think it's right) or "reading things in" (if they think it's wrong). Indeed, it could be wrong, since metamessages are not on record. And even if it is right, there is still the question of scale: How significant are the metamessages that are there?

Metamessages are a form of indirectness. Women are more 5 likely to be indirect, and to try to reach agreement by negotiation. Another way to understand this preference is that negotiation allows a display of solidarity, which women prefer to the display of power (even though the aim may be the same—getting what you want). Unfortunately, power and solidarity are bought with the same currency: Ways of talking intended to create solidarity have the simultaneous effect of framing power differences. When they think they're being nice, women often end up appearing deferential and unsure of themselves or of what they want.

When styles differ, misunderstandings are always rife. As 6 their differing styles create misunderstandings, women and men try to clear them up by talking things out. These pitfalls are compounded in talks between men and women because they have different ways of going about talking things out, and different assumptions about the significance of going about it.

Sylvia and Harry celebrated their fiftieth wedding anniver- 7 sary at a mountain resort. Some of the guests were at the resort for the whole weekend, others just for the evening of the celebration: A cocktail party followed by a sit-down dinner. The manager of the dining room approached Sylvia during dinner. "Since there's so much food tonight," he said, "and the hotel prepared a fancy dessert and everyone already ate at the cocktail party anyway, how about cutting and serving the anniversary cake at lunch tomorrow?" Sylvia asked the advice of the others at her table. All the men agreed: "Sure, that makes sense. Save the cake for tomorrow." All the women disagreed: "No, the party is tonight. Serve the cake tonight." The men were focusing on the message: The cake as food. The women were thinking of the metamessage: Serving a special cake frames an occasion as a celebration.

8   Why are women more attuned to metamessages? Because they are more focused on involvement, that is, on relationships among people, and it is through metamessages that relationships among people are established and maintained. If you want to take the temperature and check the vital signs of a relationship, the barometers to check are its metamessages: What is said and how.

9   Everyone can see these signals, but whether or not we pay attention to them is another matter—a matter of being sensitized. Once you are sensitized, you can't roll your antennae back in; they're stuck in the extended position.

10   When interpreting meaning, it is possible to pick up signals that weren't intentionally sent out, like an innocent flock of birds on a radar screen. The birds are there—and the signals women pick up are there—but they may not mean what the interpreter thinks they mean. For example, Maryellen looks at Larry and asks, "What's wrong?" because his brow is furrowed. Since he was only thinking about lunch, her expression of concern makes him feel under scrutiny.

11   The difference in focus on messages and metamessages can give men and women different points of view on almost any comment. Harriet complains to Morton, "Why don't you ask me how my day was?" He replies, "If you have something to tell me, tell me. Why do you have to be invited?" The reason is that she wants the metamessage of interest: Evidence that he cares how her day was, regardless of whether or not she has something to tell.

12   A lot of trouble is caused between women and men by, of all things, pronouns. Women often feel hurt when their partners use "I" or "me" in a situation in which they would use "we" or "us." When Morton announces, "I think I'll go for a walk," Harriet feels specifically uninvited, though Morton later claims she would have been welcome to join him. She felt locked out by his use of "I" and his omission of an invitation: "Would you like to come?" Metamessages can be seen in what is not said as well as what is said.

13   It's difficult to straighten out such misunderstandings because each one feels convinced of the logic of his or her position and the illogic—or irresponsibility—of the other's. Harriet knows that she always asks Morton how his day was, and that she'd never announce, "I'm going for a walk," without inviting

him to join her. If he talks differently to her, it must be that he feels differently. But Morton wouldn't feel unloved if Harriet didn't ask about his day, and he would feel free to ask, "Can I come along?" if she announced she was taking a walk. So he can't believe she is justified in feeling responses he knows he wouldn't have.

These processes are dramatized with chilling yet absurdly 14 amusing authenticity in Jules Feiffer's play *Grown Ups*. To get a closer look at what happens when men and women focus on different levels of talk in talking things out, let's look at what happens in this play.

Jake criticizes Louise for not responding when their daughter, 15 Edie, called her. His comment leads to a fight even though they're both aware that this one incident is not in itself important.

JAKE: Look, I don't care if it's important or not, when a kid calls its
  mother the mother should answer.
LOUISE: Now I'm a bad mother.
JAKE: I didn't say that.
LOUISE: It's in your stare.
JAKE: Is that another thing you know? My stare?

Louise ignores Jake's message—the question of whether or not she responded when Edie called—and goes for the metamessage: His implication that she's a bad mother, which Jake insistently disclaims. When Louise explains the signals she's reacting to, Jake not only discounts them but is angered at being held accountable not for what he said but for how he looked—his stare.

As the play goes on, Jake and Louise replay and intensify 16 these patterns:

LOUISE: If I'm such a terrible mother, do you want a divorce?
JAKE: I do not think you're a terrible mother and no, thank you, I
  do not want a divorce. Why is it that whenever I bring up any
  difference between us you ask me if I want a divorce?

The more he denies any meaning beyond the message, the more she blows it up, the more adamantly he denies it, and so on:

JAKE: I have brought up one thing that you do with Edie that I
  don't think you notice that I have noticed for some time but

which I have deliberately not brought up before because I had hoped you would notice it for yourself and stop doing it and also—frankly, baby, I have to say this—I knew if I brought it up we'd get into exactly the kind of circular argument we're in right now. And I wanted to avoid it. But I haven't and we're in it, so now, with your permission, I'd like to talk about it.

LOUISE: You don't see how that puts me down?

JAKE: What?

LOUISE: If you think I'm so stupid why do you go on living with me?

JAKE: *Dammit! Why can't anything ever be simple around here?!*

It can't be simple because Louise and Jake are responding to different levels of communication. As in Bateson's example of the dual-control electric blanket with crossed wires, each one intensifies the energy going to a different aspect of the problem. Jake tries to clarify his point by over-elaborating it, which gives Louise further evidence that he's condescending to her, making it even less likely that she will address his point rather than his condescension.

17   What pushes Jake and Louise beyond anger to rage is their different perspectives on metamessages. His refusal to admit that his statements have implications and overtones denies her authority over her own feelings. Her attempts to interpret what he didn't say and put the metamessage into the message makes him feel she's putting words into his mouth—denying his authority over his own meaning.

18   The same thing happens when Louise tells Jake that he is being manipulated by Edie:

LOUISE: Why don't you ever make her come to see you? Why do you always go to her?

JAKE: You want me to play power games with a nine year old? I want her to know I'm interested in her. Someone around here has to show interest in her.

LOUISE: You love her more than I do.

JAKE: I didn't say that.

LOUISE: Yes, you did.

JAKE: You don't know how to listen. You have never learned how to listen. It's as if listening to you is a foreign language.

Again, Louise responds to his implication—this time, that he loves Edie more because he runs when she calls. And yet again, Jake cries literal meaning, denying he meant any more than he said.

Throughout their argument, the point to Louise is her feelings— 19 that Jake makes her feel put down—but to him the point is her actions—that she doesn't always respond when Edie calls:

LOUISE: You talk about what I do to Edie, what do you think you do to me?
JAKE: This is not the time to go into what we do to each other.

Since she will talk only about the metamessage, and he will 20 talk only about the message, neither can get satisfaction from their talk, and they end up where they started—only angrier:

JAKE: That's not the point!
LOUISE: It's my point!
JAKE: It's hopeless!
LOUISE: Then get a divorce.

American conventional wisdom (and many of our parents and English teachers) tell us that meaning is conveyed by words, so men who tend to be literal about words are supported by conventional wisdom. They may not simply deny but actually miss the cues that are sent by how words are spoken. If they sense something about it, they may nonetheless discount what they sense. After all, it wasn't said. Sometimes that's a dodge—a plausible defense rather than a gut feeling. But sometimes it is a sincere conviction. Women are also likely to doubt the reality of what they sense. If they don't doubt it in their guts, they nonetheless may lack the arguments to support their position and thus are reduced to repeating, "You said it. You did so." Knowing that metamessages are a real and fundamental part of communication makes it easier to understand and justify what they feel.

An article in a popular newspaper reports that one of the five 21 most common complaints of wives about their husbands is "He doesn't listen to me anymore." Another is "He doesn't talk to me anymore." Political scientist Andrew Hacker noted that lack of communication, while high on women's lists of reasons for divorce, is much less often mentioned by men. Since couples are parties to the same conversations, why are women more dissatisfied with them than men? Because what they expect is different, as well as what they see as the significance of talk itself.

22   First, let's consider the complaint "He doesn't talk to me."

23   One of the most common stereotypes of American men is the strong silent type. Jack Kroll, writing about Henry Fonda on the occasion of his death, used the phrases "quiet power," "abashed silences," "combustible catatonia," and "sense of power held in check." He explained that Fonda's goal was not to let anyone see "the wheels go around," not to let the "machinery" show. According to Kroll, the resulting silence was effective on stage but devastating to Fonda's family.

24   The image of a silent father is common and is often the model for the lover or husband. But what attracts us can become flypaper to which we are unhappily stuck. Many women find the strong silent type to be a lure as a lover but a lug as a husband. Nancy Schoenberger begins a poem with the lines "It was your silence that hooked me, / so like my father's." Adrienne Rich refers in a poem to the "husband who is frustratingly mute." Despite the initial attraction of such quintessentially male silence, it may begin to feel, to a woman in a long-term relationship, like a brick wall against which she is banging her head.

25   In addition to these images of male and female behavior— both the result and the cause of them—are differences in how women and men view the role of talk in relationships as well as how talk accomplishes its purpose. These differences have their roots in the settings in which men and women learn to have conversations among their peers, growing up.

26   Children whose parents have foreign accents don't speak with accents. They learn to talk like their peers. Little girls and little boys learn how to have conversations as they learn how to pronounce words from their playmates. Between the ages of five and fifteen, when children are learning to have conversations, they play mostly with friends of their own sex. So it's not surprising that they learn different ways of having and using conversations.

27   Anthropologists Daniel Maltz and Ruth Borker point out that boys and girls socialize differently. Little girls tend to play in

small groups or, even more common, in pairs. Their social life usually centers around a best friend, and friendships are made, maintained, and broken by talk—especially "secrets." If a little girl tells her friend's secret to another little girl, she may find herself with a new best friend. The secrets themselves may or may not be important, but the fact of telling them is all-important. It's hard for newcomers to get into these tight groups, but anyone who is admitted is treated as an equal. Girls like to play cooperatively; if they can't cooperate, the group breaks up.

Little boys tend to play in larger groups, often outdoors, and they spend more time doing things than talking. It's easy for boys to get into the group, but not everyone is accepted as an equal. Once in the group, boys must jockey for their status in it. One of the most important ways they do this is through talk: Verbal display such as telling stories and jokes, challenging and sidetracking the verbal displays of other boys, and withstanding other boys' challenges in order to maintain their own story—and status. Their talk is often competitive talk about who is best at what. 28

Feiffer's play is ironically named *Grown Ups* because adult men and women struggling to communicate often sound like children: "You said so!" "I did not!" The reason is that when they grow up, women and men keep the divergent attitudes and habits they learned as children—which they don't recognize as attitudes and habits but simply take for granted as ways of talking. 29

Women want their partners to be a new and improved version of a best friend. This gives them a soft spot for men who tell them secrets. As Jack Nicholson once advised a guy in a movie: "Tell her about your troubled childhood—that always gets 'em." Men expect to do things together and don't feel anything is missing if they don't have heart-to-heart talks all the time. 30

If they do have heart-to-heart talks, the meaning of those talks may be opposite for men and women. To many women, the relationship is working as long as they can talk things out. To many men, the relationship isn't working out if they have to keep working it over. If she keeps trying to get talks going to save the relationship, and he keeps trying to avoid them because he sees them as weakening it, then each one's efforts to preserve the relationship appear to the other as reckless endangerment. 31

32   If talks (of any kind) do get going, men's and women's ideas about how to conduct them may be very different. For example, Dora is feeling comfortable and close to Tom. She settles into a chair after dinner and begins to tell him about a problem at work. She expects him to ask questions to show he's interested; reassure her that he understands and that what she feels is normal; and return the intimacy by telling her a problem of his. Instead, Tom sidetracks her story, cracks jokes about it, questions her interpretation of the problem, and gives her advice about how to solve it and avoid such problems in the future.

33   All of these responses, natural to men, are unexpected to women, who interpret them in terms of their own habits—negatively. When Tom comments on side issues or cracks jokes, Dora thinks he doesn't care about what she's saying and isn't really listening. If he challenges her reading of what went on, she feels he is criticizing her and telling her she's crazy, when what she wants is to be reassured that she's not. If he tells her how to solve the problem, it makes her feel as if she's the patient to his doctor—a metamessage of condescension, echoing male one-upmanship compared to the female etiquette of equality. Because he doesn't volunteer information about his problems, she feels he's implying he doesn't have any.

34   His way of responding to her bid for intimacy makes her feel distant from him. She tries harder to regain intimacy the only way she knows how—by revealing more and more about herself. He tries harder by giving more insistent advice. The more problems she exposes, the more incompetent she feels, until they both see her as emotionally draining and problem-ridden. When his efforts to help aren't appreciated, he wonders why she asks for his advice if she doesn't want to take it . . .

35   When women talk about what seems obviously interesting to them, their conversations often include reports of conversations. Tone of voice, timing, intonation, and wording are all re-created in the telling in order to explain—dramatize, really—the experience that is being reported. If men tell about an incident and give a brief summary instead of re-creating what was said and how, the women often feel that the essence of the experience is being omitted. If the woman asks, "What exactly did he say?,"

and "How did he say it?," the man probably can't remember. If she continues to press him, he may feel as if he's being grilled.

All these different habits have repercussions when the man 36 and the woman are talking about their relationship. He feels out of his element, even one down. She claims to recall exactly what he said, and what she said, and in what sequence, and she wants him to account for what he said. He can hardly account for it since he has forgotten exactly what was said—if not the whole conversation. She secretly suspects he's only pretending not to remember, and he secretly suspects that she's making up the details.

One woman reported such a problem as being a matter of her 37 boyfriend's poor memory. It is unlikely, however, that his problem was poor memory in general. The question is what types of material each person remembers or forgets.

Frances was sitting at her kitchen table talking to Edward, 38 when the toaster did something funny. Edward began to explain why it did it. Frances tried to pay attention, but very early in his explanation, she realized she was completely lost. She felt very stupid. And indications were that he thought so too.

Later that day they were taking a walk. He was telling her 39 about a difficult situation in his office that involved a complex network of interrelationships among a large number of people. Suddenly he stopped and said, "I'm sure you can't keep track of all these people." "Of course I can," she said, and she retraced his story with all the characters in place, all the details right. He was genuinely impressed. She felt very smart.

How could Frances be both smart and stupid? Did she have a 40 good memory or a bad one? Frances's and Edward's abilities to follow, remember, and recount depended on the subject—and paralleled her parents' abilities to follow and remember. Whenever Frances told her parents about people in her life, her mother could follow with no problem, but her father got lost as soon as she introduced a second character. "Now who was that?" he'd ask. "Your boss?" "No, my boss is Susan. This was my friend." Often he'd still be in the previous story. But whenever she told them about her work, it was her mother who would get lost as soon as she mentioned a second step: "That was your tech report?" "No, I handed my tech report in last month. This was a special project."

41   Frances's mother and father, like many men and women, had honed their listening and remembering skills in different arenas. Their experience talking to other men and other women gave them practice in following different kinds of talk.

42   Knowing whether and how we are likely to report events later influences whether and how we pay attention when they happen. As women listen to and take part in conversations, knowing they may talk about them later makes them more likely to pay attention to exactly what is said and how. Since most men aren't in the habit of making such reports, they are less likely to pay much attention at the time. On the other hand, many women aren't in the habit of paying attention to scientific explanations and facts because they don't expect to have to perform in public by reciting them—just as those who aren't in the habit of entertaining others by telling jokes "can't" remember jokes they've heard, even though they listened carefully enough to enjoy them.

43   So women's conversations with their women friends keep them in training for talking about their relationships with men, but many men come to such conversations with no training at all—and an uncomfortable sense that this really isn't their event.

44   Most of us place enormous emphasis on the importance of a primary relationship. We regard the ability to maintain such relationships as a sign of mental health—our contemporary metaphor for being a good person.

45   Yet our expectations of such relationships are nearly—maybe in fact—impossible. When primary relationships are between women and men, male-female differences contribute to the impossibility. We expect partners to be both romantic interests and best friends. Though women and men may have fairly similar expectations for romantic interests, obscuring their differences when relationships begin, they have very different ideas about how to be friends, and these are the differences that mount over time.

46   In conversations between friends who are not lovers, small misunderstandings can be passed over or diffused by breaks in contact. But in the context of a primary relationship, differences can't be ignored, and the pressure cooker of continued contact keeps both people stewing in the juice of accumulated minor misunderstandings. And stylistic differences are sure to cause

misunderstandings—not, ironically, in matters such as sharing values and interests or understanding each other's philosophies of life. These large and significant yet palpable issues can be talked about and agreed on. It is far harder to achieve congruence—and much more surprising and troubling that it is hard—in the simple day-to-day matters of the automatic rhythms and nuances of talk. Nothing in our backgrounds or in the media (the present-day counterpart to religion or grandparents' teachings) prepares us for this failure. If two people share so much in terms of point of view and basic values, how can they continually get into fights about insignificant matters?

If you find yourself in such a situation and you don't know 47 about differences in conversational style, you assume something's wrong with your partner, or you for having chosen your partner. At best, if you are forward thinking and generous minded, you may absolve individuals and blame the relationship. But if you know about differences in conversational style, you can accept that there are differences in habits and assumptions about how to have conversation, show interest, be considerate, and so on. You may not always correctly interpret your partner's intentions, but you will know that if you get a negative impression, it may not be what was intended—and neither are your responses unfounded. If he says he really is interested even though he doesn't seem to be, maybe you should believe what he says and not what you sense.

Sometimes explaining assumptions can help. If a man starts 48 to tell a woman what to do to solve her problem, she may say, "Thanks for the advice but I really don't want to be told what to do. I just want you to listen and say you understand." A man might want to explain, "If I challenge you, it's not to prove you wrong; it's just my way of paying attention to what you're telling me." Both may try either or both to modify their ways of talking and to try to accept what the other does. The important thing is to know that what seem like bad intentions may really be good intentions expressed in a different conversational style. We have to give up our conviction that, as Robin Lakoff put it, "Love means never having to say 'What do you mean?'"

1986

Two Views of the Mississippi

Mark Twain

1 Now when I had mastered the language of this water, and had come to know every trifling feature that bordered the great river as familiarly as I knew the letters of the alphabet, I had made a valuable acquisition. But I had lost something, too. I had lost something which could never be restored to me while I lived. All the grace, the beauty, the poetry, had gone out of the majestic river! I still keep in mind a certain wonderful sunset which I witnessed when steamboating was new to me. A broad expanse of the river was turned to blood; in the middle distance the red hue brightened into gold, through which a solitary log came floating black and conspicuous; in one place a long, slanting mark lay sparkling upon the water; in another the surface was broken by boiling, tumbling rings, that were as many-tinted as an opal; where the ruddy flush was faintest, was a smooth spot that was covered with graceful circles and radiating lines, ever so delicately traced; the shore on our left was densely wooded, and the somber shadow that fell from this forest was broken in one place by a long, ruffled trail that shone like silver; and high above the forest wall a cleanstemmed dead tree waved a single leafy bough that glowed like a flame in the unobstructed splendor that was flowing from the sun. There were graceful curves, reflected images, woody heights, soft distances; and over the whole scene, far and near, the dissolving lights drifted steadily, enriching it every passing moment with new marvels of coloring.

2 I stood like one bewitched. I drank it in, in a speechless rapture. The world was new to me, and I had never seen anything like this at home. But as I have said, a day came when I began to cease from noting the glories and the charms which the moon and the sun and the twilight wrought upon the river's face; another day came when I ceased altogether to note them. Then, if that sunset scene had been repeated, I should have looked upon it without rapture, and should have commented upon it, inwardly, after this fashion: "This sun means that we are going to have wind tomorrow; that floating log means that the river is rising, small thanks to it; that

slanting mark on the water refers to a bluff reef which is going to kill somebody's steamboat one of these nights, if it keeps on stretching out like that; those tumbling 'boils' show a dissolving bar and a changing channel there; the lines and circles in the slick water over yonder are a warning that that troublesome place is shoaling up dangerously; that silver streak in the shadow of the forest is the 'break' from a new snag, and he has located himself in the very best place he could have found to fish for steamboats; that tall dead tree, with a single living branch, is not going to last long, and then how is a body ever going to get through this blind place at night without the friendly old landmark?"

No, the romance and beauty were all gone from the river. All 3 the value any feature of it had for me now was the amount of usefulness it could furnish toward compassing the safe piloting of a steamboat. Since those days, I have pitied doctors from my heart. What does the lovely flush in a beauty's cheek mean to a doctor but a "break" that ripples above some deadly disease? Are not all her visible charms sown thick with what are to him the signs and symbols of hidden decay? Does he ever see her beauty at all, or doesn't he simply view her professionally, and comment upon her unwholesome condition all to himself? And doesn't he sometimes wonder whether he has gained most or lost most by learning his trade?

1883

The Men We Carry in Our Minds

Scott Russell Sanders

The first men, besides my father, I remember seeing were black 1 convicts and white guards, in the cottonfield across the road from our farm on the outskirts of Memphis. I must have been three or four. The prisoners wore dingy gray-and-black zebra suits, heavy as canvas, sodden with sweat. Hatless, stooped, they chopped weeds in the fierce heat, row after row, breathing the acrid dust of boll-weevil poison. The overseers wore dazzling white shirts and broad shadowy hats. The oiled barrels of their shotguns flashed in the sunlight. Their faces in memory are utterly blank. Of course those men, white and black, have become for me an emblem of racial hatred. But they have also come to stand for the twin poles of my early vision of manhood—the brute toiling animal and the boss.

2   When I was a boy, the men I knew labored with their bodies. They were marginal farmers, just scraping by, or welders, steel workers, carpenters; they swept floors, dug ditches, mined coal, or drove trucks, their forearms ropy with muscle; they trained horses, stoked furnaces, built tires, stood on assembly lines wrestling parts onto cars and refrigerators. They got up before light, worked all day long whatever the weather, and when they came home at night they looked as though somebody had been whipping them. In the evenings and on weekends they worked on their own places, tilling gardens that were lumpy with clay, fixing broken-down cars, hammering on houses that were always too drafty, too leaky, too small.

3   The bodies of the men I knew were twisted and maimed in ways visible and invisible. The nails of their hands were black and split, the hands tattooed with scars. Some had lost fingers. Heavy lifting had given many of them finicky backs and guts weak from hernias. Racing against conveyor belts had given them ulcers. Their ankles and knees ached from years of standing on concrete. Anyone who had worked for long around machines was hard of hearing. They squinted, and the skin of their faces was creased like the leather of old work gloves. There were times, studying them, when I dreaded growing up. Most of them coughed, from dust or cigarettes, and most of them drank cheap wine or whiskey, so their eyes looked bloodshot and bruised. The fathers of my friends always seemed older than the mothers. Men wore out sooner. Only women lived into old age.

4   As a boy I also knew another sort of men, who did not sweat and break down like mules. They were soldiers, and so far as I could tell they scarcely worked at all. During my early school years we lived on a military base, an arsenal in Ohio, and every day I saw GIs in the guardshacks, on the stoops of barracks, at the

wheels of olive drab Chevrolets. The chief fact of their lives was boredom. Long after I left the Arsenal I came to recognize the sour smell the soldiers gave off as that of souls in limbo. They were all waiting—for wars, for transfers, for leaves, for promotions, for the end of their hitch—like so many braves waiting for the hunt to begin. Unlike the warriors of older tribes, however, they would have no say about when the battle would start or how it would be waged. Their waiting was broken only when they practiced for war. They fired guns at targets, drove tanks across the churned-up fields of the military reservation, set off bombs in the wrecks of old fighter planes. I knew this was all play. But I also felt certain that when the hour for killing arrived, they would kill. When the real shooting started, many of them would die. This was what soldiers were *for*, just as a hammer was for driving nails.

Warriors and toilers: those seemed, in my boyhood vision, to 5 be the chief destinies for men. They weren't the only destinies, as I learned from having a few male teachers, from reading books, and from watching television. But the men on television—the politicians, the astronauts, the generals, the savvy lawyers, the philosophical doctors, the bosses who gave orders to both soldiers and laborers— seemed as remote and unreal to me as the figures in tapestries. I could no more imagine growing up to become one of these cool, potent creatures than I could imagine becoming a prince.

A nearer and more hopeful example was that of my father, 6 who had escaped from a red-dirt farm to a tire factory, and from the assembly line to the front office. Eventually he dressed in a white shirt and tie. He carried himself as if he had been born to work with his mind. But his body, remembering the earlier years of slogging work, began to give out on him in his fifties, and it quit on him entirely before he turned sixty-five. Even such partial escape from man's fate as he had accomplished did not seem possible for most of the boys I knew. They joined the Army, stood in line for jobs in the smoky plants, helped build highways. They were bound to work as their fathers had worked, killing themselves or preparing to kill others.

A scholarship enabled me not only to attend college, a rare 7 enough feat in my circle, but even to study in a university meant for the children of the rich. Here I met for the first time young men who had assumed from birth that they would lead lives of comfort and power. And for the first time I met women who told me that men were guilty of having kept all the joys and privileges of the earth for themselves. I was baffled. What privileges? What joys? I thought about the maimed, dismal lives of most of the men back home. What had they stolen from their wives and daughters? The right to go five days a week, twelve months a year, for thirty or forty years to a steel mill or a coal mine? The right to drop bombs and die in war? The right to feel every leak in the roof, every gap in the fence, every cough in the engine, as a wound they must mend? The right to feel, when the layoff comes or the plant shuts down, not only afraid but ashamed?

8   I was slow to understand the deep grievances of women. This was because, as a boy, I had envied them. Before college, the only people I had ever known who were interested in art or music or literature, the only ones who read books, the only ones who ever seemed to enjoy a sense of ease and grace were the mothers and daughters. Like the menfolk, they fretted about money, they scrimped and made-do. But, when the pay stopped coming in, they were not the ones who had failed. Nor did they have to go to war, and that seemed to me a blessed fact. By comparison with the narrow, ironclad days of fathers, there was an expansiveness, I thought, in the days of mothers. They went to see neighbors, to shop in town, to run errands at school, at the library, at church. No doubt, had I looked harder at their lives, I would have envied them less. It was not my fate to become a woman, so it was easier for me to see the graces. Few of them held jobs outside the home, and those who did filled thankless roles as clerks and waitresses. I didn't see, then, what a prison a house could be, since houses seemed to me brighter, handsomer places than any factory. I did not realize—because such things were never spoken of—how often women suffered from men's bullying. I did learn about the wretchedness of abandoned wives, single mothers, widows; but I also learned about the wretchedness of lone men. Even then I could see how exhausting it was for a mother to cater all day to the needs of young children. But if I had been asked, as a boy, to

choose between tending a baby and tending a machine, I think I would have chosen the baby. (Having now tended both, I know I would choose the baby.)

So I was baffled when the women at college accused me and 9 my sex of having cornered the world's pleasures. I think something like my bafflement has been felt by other boys (and by girls as well) who grew up in dirt-poor farm country, in mining country, in black ghettos, in Hispanic barrios, in the shadows of factories, in Third World nations—any place where the fate of men is as grim and bleak as the fate of women. Toilers and warriors. I realize now how ancient these identities are, how deep the tug they exert on men, the undertow of a thousand generations. The miseries I saw, as a boy, in the lives of nearly all men I continue to see in the lives of many—the body-breaking toil, the tedium, the call to be tough, the humiliating powerlessness, the battle for a living and for territory.

When the women I met at college thought about the joys and 10 privileges of men, they did not carry in their minds the sort of men I had known in my childhood. They thought of their fathers, who were bankers, physicians, architects, stockbrokers, the big wheels of the big cities. These fathers rode the train to work or drove cars that cost more than any of my childhood houses. They were attended from morning to night by female helpers, wives and nurses and secretaries. They were never laid off, never short of cash at month's end, never lined up for welfare. These fathers made decisions that mattered. They ran the world.

The daughters of such men wanted to share in this power, 11 this glory. So did I. They yearned for a say over their future, for jobs worthy of their abilities, for the right to live at peace, unmolested, whole. Yes, I thought, yes yes. The difference between me and these daughters was that they saw me, because of my sex, as destined from birth to become like their fathers, and therefore as an enemy to their desires. But I knew better. I wasn't an enemy, in fact or in feeling. I was an ally. If I had known, then, how to tell them so, would they have believed me? Would they now?

1984

Neat People vs. Sloppy People

Suzanne Britt

1   I've finally figured out the difference between neat people and sloppy people. The distinction is, as always, moral. Neat people are lazier and meaner than sloppy people.

2   Sloppy people, you see, are not really sloppy. Their sloppiness is merely the unfortunate consequence of their extreme moral rectitude. Sloppy people carry in their mind's eye a heavenly vision, a precise plan, that is so stupendous, so perfect, it can't be achieved in this world or the next.

3   Sloppy people live in Never-Never Land. Someday is their métier. Someday they are planning to alphabetize all their books and set up home catalogs. Someday they will go through their wardrobes and mark certain items for tentative mending and certain items for passing on to relatives of similar shape and size. Someday sloppy people will make family scrapbooks into which they will put newspaper clippings, postcards, locks of hair, and the dried corsage from their senior prom. Someday they will file everything on the surface of their desks, including the cash receipts from coffee purchases at the snack shop. Someday they will sit down and read all the back issues of the *New Yorker*.

4   For all these noble reasons and more, sloppy people never get neat. They aim too high and wide. They save everything, planning someday to file, order, and straighten out the world. But while these ambitious plans take clearer and clearer shape in their heads, the books spill from the shelves onto the floor, the clothes pile up in the hamper and closet, the family mementos accumulate in every drawer, the surface of the desk is buried under mounds of paper and the unread magazines threaten to reach the ceiling.

5   Sloppy people can't bear to part with anything. They give loving attention to every detail. When sloppy people say they're going to tackle the surface of the desk, they really mean it. Not a paper will go unturned; not a rubber band will go unboxed. Four hours or two weeks into the excavation, the desk looks exactly the same, primarily because the sloppy person is meticulously creating new piles of papers with new headings and scrupulously

stopping to read all the old book catalogs before he throws them away. A neat person would just bulldoze the desk.

Neat people are bums and clods at heart. They have cavalier attitudes toward possessions, including family heirlooms. Everything is just another dustcatcher to them. If anything collects dust, it's got to go and that's that. Neat people will toy with the idea of throwing the children out of the house just to cut down on the clutter. 6

Neat people don't care about process. They like results. What they want to do is get the whole thing over with so they can sit down and watch the rasslin' on TV. Neat people operate on two unvarying principles: Never handle any item twice, and throw everything away. 7

The only thing messy in a neat person's house is the trash can. The minute something comes to a neat person's hand, he will look at it, try to decide if it has immediate use and, finding none, throw it in the trash. 8

Neat people are especially vicious with mail. They never go through their mail unless they are standing directly over a trash can. If the trash can is beside the mailbox, even better. All ads, catalogs, pleas for charitable contributions, church bulletins and money-saving coupons go straight into the trash can without being opened. All letters from home, postcards from Europe, bills and paychecks are opened, immediately responded to, then dropped in the trash can. Neat people keep their receipts only for tax purposes. That's it. No sentimental salvaging of birthday cards or the last letter a dying relative ever wrote. Into the trash it goes. 9

Neat people place neatness above everything, even economics. They are incredibly wasteful. Neat people throw away several toys every time they walk through the den. I knew a neat person once who threw away a perfectly good dish drainer because it had mold on it. The drainer was too much trouble to wash. And neat people sell their furniture when they move. They will sell a La-Z-Boy recliner while you are reclining in it. 10

Neat people are no good to borrow from. Neat people buy everything in expensive little single portions. They get their flour and sugar in two-pound bags. They wouldn't consider clipping a coupon, saving a leftover, reusing plastic nondairy whipped 11 cream containers or rinsing off tin foil and draping it over the unmoldy dish drainer. You can never borrow a neat person's newspaper to see what's playing at the movies. Neat people have the paper all wadded up and in the trash by 7:05 A.M.

12   Neat people cut a clean swath through the organic as well as the inorganic world. People, animals, and things are all one to them. They are so insensitive. After they've finished with the pantry, the medicine cabinet, and the attic, they will throw out the red geranium (too many leaves), sell the dog (too many fleas), and send the children off to boarding school (too many scuff-marks on the hardwood floors).

1983

Shakespeare's Sister

Virginia Woolf

1   For it is a perennial puzzle why no woman wrote a word of that extraordinary literature when every other man, it seemed, was capable of song or sonnet. What were the conditions in which women lived, I asked myself; for fiction, imaginative work that is, is not dropped like a pebble upon the ground, as science may be; fiction is like a spider's web, attached ever so lightly perhaps, but still attached to life at all four corners. Often the attachment is scarcely perceptible; Shakespeare's plays, for instance, seem to hang there complete by themselves. But when the web is pulled askew, hooked up at the edge, torn in the middle, one remembers that these webs are not spun in midair by incorporeal creatures, but are the work of suffering human beings, and are attached to grossly material things, like health and money and the houses we live in.

2   I went, therefore, to the shelf where the histories stand and took down one of the latest, Professor Trevelyan's *History of England.* Once more I looked up Women, found "position of," and turned to the pages indicated. "Wife-beating," I read, "was a recognized right of man, and was practiced without shame by high as

well as low. . . . Similarly," the historian goes on, "the daughter who refused to marry the gentleman of her parents' choice was liable to be locked up, beaten and flung about the room, without any shock being inflicted on public opinion. Marriage was not an affair of personal affection, but of family avarice, particularly in the 'chivalrous' upper classes. . . . Betrothal often took place while one or both of the parties was in the cradle, and marriage when they were scarcely out of the nurses' charge." That was about 1470, soon after Chaucer's time. The next reference to the position of women is some two hundred years later, in the time of the Stuarts. "It was still the exception for women of the upper and middle class to choose their own husbands, and when the husband had been assigned, he was lord and master, so far at least as law and custom could make him. Yet even so," Professor Trevelyan concludes, "neither Shakespeare's women nor those of authentic seventeenth-century memoirs . . . seem wanting in personality and character.". . . Indeed, if woman had no existence save in the fiction written by men, one would imagine her a person of the utmost importance; very various; heroic and mean; splendid and sordid; infinitely beautiful and hideous in the extreme; as great as a man, some think even greater. But this is woman in fiction. In fact, as Professor Trevelyan points out, she was locked up, beaten and flung about the room.

A very queer, composite being thus emerges. Imaginatively ₃ she is of the highest importance; practically she is completely insignificant. She pervades poetry from cover to cover; she is all but absent from history. She dominates the lives of kings and conquerors in fiction; in fact she was the slave of any boy whose parents forced a ring upon her finger. Some of the most inspired words, some of the most profound thoughts in literature fall from her lips; in real life she could hardly read, could scarcely spell, and was the property of her husband.

It was certainly an odd monster that one made up by reading ₄ the historians first and the poets afterwards—a worm winged like an eagle; the spirit of life and beauty in a kitchen chopping up suet. But these monsters, however amusing to the imagination, have no existence in fact. What one must do to bring her to life was to think poetically and prosaically at one and the same moment, thus keeping in touch with fact—that she is Mrs. Martin, aged thirty-six, dressed in blue, wearing a black hat and brown shoes; but not losing sight of fiction either—that she is a vessel in which all sorts of spirits and forces are coursing and flashing perpetually. The moment, however, that one tries this method with the Elizabethan woman, one branch of illumination fails; one is held up by the scarcity of facts. One knows nothing detailed, nothing perfectly true and substantial about her. History scarcely mentions her. . . .

5   . . . Occasionally an individual woman is mentioned, an Elizabeth or a Mary; a queen or a great lady. But by no possible means could middle-class women with nothing but brains and character at their command have taken part in any one of the great movements which, brought together, constitute the historian's view of the past. Nor shall we find her in any collection of anecdotes. Aubrey hardly mentions her. She never writes her own life and scarcely keeps a diary; there are only a handful of her letters in existence. She left no plays or poems by which we can judge her. What one wants, I thought—and why does not some brilliant student at Newnham or Girton supply it?—is a mass of information; at what age did she marry; how many children had she as a rule; what was her house like; had she a room to herself; did she do the cooking; would she be likely to have a servant? All these facts lie somewhere, presumably, in parish registers and account books; the life of the average Elizabethan woman must be scattered about somewhere, could one collect it and make a book of it. It would be ambitious beyond my daring, I thought, looking about the shelves for books that were not there, to suggest to the students of those famous colleges that they should re-write history, though I own that it often seems a little queer as it is, unreal, lop-sided; but why should they not add a supplement to history? Calling it, of course, by some inconspicuous name so that women might figure there without impropriety? For one often catches a glimpse of them in the lives of the great, whisking away into the background, concealing, I sometimes think, a wink, a laugh, perhaps a tear. . . . But what I find deplorable, . . . is that nothing is known about women before the eighteenth century. I have no model in my mind to turn about this way and that. Here am I asking why women did not write poetry in the Elizabethan age, and

I am not sure how they were educated; whether they were taught to write; whether they had sitting-rooms to themselves; how many women had children before they were twenty-one; what, in short, they did from eight in the morning till eight at night. They had no money evidently; according to Professor Trevelyan they were married whether they liked it or not before they were out of the nursery, at fifteen or sixteen very likely. It would have been extremely odd, even upon this showing, had one of them suddenly written the plays of Shakespeare, I concluded, and I thought of that old gentleman, who is dead now, but was a bishop, I think, who declared that it was impossible for any woman, past, present, or to come, to have the genius of Shakespeare. He wrote to the papers about it. He also told a lady who applied to him for information that cats do not as a matter of fact go to heaven, though they have, he added, souls of a sort. How much thinking those old gentlemen used to save one! How the borders of ignorance shrank back at their approach! Cats do not go to heaven. Women cannot write the plays of Shakespeare.

Be that as it may, I could not help thinking, as I looked at the works of Shakespeare on the shelf, that the bishop was right at least in this; it would have been impossible, completely and entirely, for any woman to have written the plays of Shakespeare in the age of Shakespeare. Let me imagine, since the facts are so hard to come by, what would have happened had Shakespeare had a wonderfully gifted sister, called Judith, let us say. Shakespeare himself went, very probably—his mother was an heiress—to the grammar school, where he may have learnt Latin—Ovid, Virgil and Horace—and the elements of grammar and logic. He was, it is well known, a wild boy who poached rabbits, perhaps shot a deer, and had, rather sooner than he should have done, to marry a woman in the neighbourhood, who bore him a child rather quicker than was right. That escapade sent him to seek his fortune in London. He had, it seemed, a taste for the theatre; he began by holding horses at the stage door. Very soon he got work in the theatre, became a successful actor, and lived at the hub of the universe, meeting everybody, knowing everybody, practicing his art on the boards, exercising his wits in the streets, and even getting access to the palace of the queen. Meanwhile his extraordinarily gifted sister, let us suppose, remained at home. She was as adventurous, as imaginative, as agog to see the world as he was. But she was not sent to school. She had no chance of learning grammar and logic, let alone of reading Horace and Virgil. She picked up a book now and then, one of her brother's perhaps, and read a few pages. But then her parents came in and told her to mend the stockings or mind the stew and not moon about with books and papers. They would have spoken sharply but kindly, for they were substantial people who knew the conditions of life for a woman and loved their daughter—indeed, more likely than not she was the apple of her father's eye. Perhaps she scribbled some pages up in an apple loft on the sly, but was careful to hide them or set fire to them. Soon, however, before she was out of her teens, she was to be betrothed to the son of a neighbouring wool-stapler. She cried out that marriage was hateful to her, and for that she was severely beaten by her father. Then he ceased to scold her. He begged her instead not to hurt him, not to shame him in this matter of her marriage. He would give her a chain of beads or a fine petticoat, he said; and there were tears in his eyes. How could she disobey him? How could she break his heart? The force of her own gift alone drove her to it. She made up a small parcel of her belongings, let herself down by a rope one summer's night and took the road to London. She was not seventeen. The birds that sang in the hedge were not more musical than she was. She had the quickest fancy, a gift like her brother's, for the tune of words. Like him, she had a taste for the theatre. She stood at the stage door; she wanted to act, she said. Men laughed in her face. The manager—a fat, loose-lipped man— guffawed. He bellowed something about poodles dancing and women acting—no woman, he said, could possibly be an actress. He hinted—you can imagine what. She could get no training in her craft. Could she even seek her dinner in a tavern or roam the streets at midnight? Yet her genius was for fiction and lusted to feed abundantly upon the lives of men and women and the study of their ways. At last—for she was very young, oddly like Shakespeare the poet in her face, with the same grey eyes and rounded brows—at last Nick Greene the actor-manager took pity on her; she found herself with child by that gentleman and so—who shall measure the heat and violence of the poet's heart when caught and tangled

in a woman's body?—killed herself one winter's night and lies
buried at some crossroads where the omnibuses now stop outside
the Elephant and Castle.

That, more or less, is how the story would run, I think, if a 7
woman in Shakespeare's day had had Shakespeare's genius.
But for my part, I agree with the deceased bishop, if such he
was—it is unthinkable that any woman in Shakespeare's day
should have had Shakespeare's genius. For genius like Shakespeare's is not born among labouring, uneducated, servile people. It was not born in England among the Saxons and the
Britons. It is not born today among the working classes. How,
then, could it have been born among women whose work
began, according to Professor Trevelyan, almost before they
were out of the nursery, who were forced to it by their parents
and held to it by all the power of law and custom? Yet genius of
a sort must have existed among women as it must have existed
among the working classes.

1929

Two Ways to Belong in America
Bharati Mukherjee

This is a tale of two sisters from Calcutta, Mira and Bharati, 1
who have lived in the United States for some 35 years, but who
find themselves on different sides in the current debate over the
status of immigrants. I am an American citizen and she is not. I
am moved that thousands of long-term residents are finally taking the oath of citizenship. She is not.

Mira arrived in Detroit in 1960 to study child psychology and 2
pre-school education. I followed her a year later to study creative
writing at the University of Iowa. When we left India, we were
almost identical in appearance and attitude. We dressed alike, in
saris; we expressed identical views on politics, social issues, love
and marriage in the same Calcutta convent-school accent. We

would endure our two years in America, secure our degrees, then return to India to marry the grooms of our father's choosing.

3   Instead, Mira married an Indian student in 1962 who was getting his business administration degree at Wayne State University. They soon acquired the labor certifications necessary for the green card of hassle-free residence and employment.

4   Mira still lives in Detroit, works in the Southfield, Mich., school system, and has become nationally recognized for her contributions in the fields of pre-school education and parent-teacher relationships. After 36 years as a legal immigrant in this country, she clings passionately to her Indian citizenship and hopes to go home to India when she retires.

5   In Iowa City in 1963, I married a fellow student, an American of Canadian parentage. Because of the accident of his North Dakota birth, I bypassed labor-certification requirements and the race-related "quota" system that favored the applicant's country of origin over his or her merit. I was prepared for (and even welcomed) the emotional strain that came with marrying outside my ethnic community. In 33 years of marriage, we have lived in every part of North America. By choosing a husband who was not my father's selection, I was opting for fluidity, self-invention, blue jeans and T-shirts, and renouncing 3,000 years (at least) of caste-observant, "pure culture" marriage in the Mukherjee family. My books have often been read as unapologetic (and in some quarters overenthusiastic) texts for cultural and psychological "mongrelization." It's a word I celebrate.

6   Mira and I have stayed sisterly close by phone. In our regular Sunday morning conversations, we are unguardedly affectionate. I am her only blood relative on this continent. We expect to see each other through the looming crises of aging and ill health without being asked. Long before Vice President Gore's "Citizenship U.S.A." drive, we'd had our polite arguments over the ethics of retaining an overseas citizenship while expecting the permanent protection and economic benefits that come with living and working in America.

7   Like well-raised sisters, we never said what was really on our minds, but we probably pitied one another. She, for the lack of structure in my life, the erasure of Indianness, the absence of an

unvarying daily core. I, for the narrowness of her perspective, her uninvolvement with the mythic depths or the superficial pop culture of this society. But, now, with the scapegoating of "aliens" (documented or illegal) on the increase, and the targeting of long-term legal immigrants like Mira for new scrutiny and new self-consciousness, she and I find ourselves unable to maintain the same polite discretion. We were always unacknowledged adversaries, and we are now, more than ever, sisters.

"I feel used," Mira raged on the phone the other night. "I feel 8 manipulated and discarded. This is such an unfair way to treat a person who was invited to stay and work here because of her talent. My employer went to the I.N.S. and petitioned for the labor certification. For over 30 years, I've invested my creativity and professional skills into the improvement of *this* country's pre-school system. I've obeyed all the rules, I've paid my taxes, I love my work, I love my students, I love the friends I've made. How dare America now change its rules in midstream? If America wants to make new rules curtailing benefits of legal immigrants, they should apply only to immigrants who arrive after those rules are already in place."

To my ears, it sounded like the description of a long-enduring, 9 comfortable yet loveless marriage, without risk or recklessness. Have we the right to demand, and to expect, that we be loved? (That, to me, is the subtext of the arguments by immigration advocates.) My sister is an expatriate, professionally generous and creative, socially courteous and gracious, and that's as far as her Americanization can go. She is here to maintain an identity, not to transform it.

I asked her if she would follow the example of others who 10 have decided to become citizens because of the anti-immigration bills in Congress. And here, she surprised me. "If America wants to play the manipulative game, I'll play it too," she snapped. "I'll become a U.S. citizen for now, then change back to Indian when I'm ready to go home. I feel some kind of irrational attachment to India that I don't to America. Until all this hysteria against legal immigrants, I was totally happy. Having my green card meant I could visit any place in the world I wanted to and then come back to a job that's satisfying and that I do very well."

11   In one family, from two sisters alike as peas in a pod, there could not be a wider divergence of immigrant experience. America spoke to me—I married it—I embraced the demotion from expatriate aristocrat to immigrant nobody, surrendering those thousands of years of "pure culture," the saris, the delightfully accented English. She retained them all. Which of us is the freak?

12   Mira's voice, I realize, is the voice not just of the immigrant South Asian community but of an immigrant community of the millions who have stayed rooted in one job, one city, one house, one ancestral culture, one cuisine, for the entirety of their productive years. She speaks for greater numbers than I possibly can. Only the fluency of her English and the anger, rather than fear, born of confidence from her education, differentiate her from the seamstresses, the domestics, the technicians, the shop owners, the millions of hard-working but effectively silenced documented immigrants as well as their less fortunate "illegal" brothers and sisters.

13   Nearly 20 years ago, when I was living in my husband's ancestral homeland of Canada, I was always well-employed but never allowed to feel part of the local Quebec or larger Canadian society. Then, through a Green Paper that invited a national referendum on the unwanted side effects of "nontraditional" immigration, the Government officially turned against its immigrant communities, particularly those from South Asia.

14   I felt then the same sense of betrayal that Mira feels now. I will never forget the pain of that sudden turning, and the casual racist outbursts the Green Paper elicited. That sense of betrayal had its desired effect and drove me, and thousands like me, from the country.

15   Mira and I differ, however, in the ways in which we hope to interact with the country that we have chosen to live in. She is happier to live in America as expatriate Indian than as an immigrant American. I need to feel like a part of the community I have adopted (as I tried to feel in Canada as well). I need to put roots down, to vote and make the difference that I can. The price that the immigrant willingly pays, and that the exile avoids, is the trauma of self-transformation.

1996

Chapter 7

Example and Illustration

A Few Kind Words for Superstition

Robertson Davies

In grave discussions of "the renaissance of the irrational" in our 1
time, superstition does not figure largely as a serious challenge to
reason or science. Parapsychology, UFOs, miracle cures, transcen-
dental meditation and all the paths to instant enlightenment are
condemned, but superstition is merely deplored. Is it because it
has an unacknowledged hold on so many of us?

Few people will admit to being superstitious; it implies 2
naïveté or ignorance. But I live in the middle of a large university,
and I see superstition in its four manifestations, alive and flour-
ishing among people who are indisputably rational and learned.

You did not know that superstition takes four forms? 3
Theologians assure us that it does. First is what they call Vain
Observances, such as not walking under a ladder, and that kind
of thing. Yet I saw a deeply learned professor of anthropology,
who had spilled some salt, throwing a pinch of it over his left
shoulder; when I asked him why, he replied, with a wink, that it
was "to hit the Devil in the eye." I did not question him further
about his belief in the Devil: but I noticed that he did not smile
until I asked him what he was doing.

The second form is Divination, or consulting oracles. Another 4
learned professor I know, who would scorn to settle a problem by
tossing a coin (which is a humble appeal to Fate to declare itself),
told me quite seriously that he had resolved a matter related to
university affairs by consulting the I Ching. And why not? There

are thousands of people on this continent who appeal to the I Ching, and their general level of education seems to absolve them of superstition. Almost, but not quite. The I Ching, to the embarrassment of rationalists, often gives excellent advice.

5   The third form is Idolatry, and universities can show plenty of that. If you have ever supervised a large examination room, you know how many jujus, lucky coins and other bringers of luck are placed on the desks of the candidates. Modest idolatry, but what else can you call it?

6   The fourth form is Improper Worship of the True God. A while ago, I learned that every day, for several days, a $2 bill (in Canada we have $2 bills, regarded by some people as unlucky) had been tucked under a candlestick on the altar of a college chapel. Investigation revealed that an engineering student, worried about a girl, thought that bribery of the Deity might help. When I talked with him, he did not think he was pricing God cheap, because he could afford no more. A reasonable argument, but perhaps God was proud that week, for the scientific oracle went against him.

7   Superstition seems to run, a submerged river of crude religion, below the surface of human consciousness. It has done so for as long as we have any chronicle of human behavior, and although I cannot prove it, I doubt if it is more prevalent today than it has always been. Superstition, the theologians tell us, comes from the Latin *supersisto,* meaning to stand in terror of the Deity. Most people keep their terror within bounds, but they cannot root it out, nor do they seem to want to do so.

8   The more the teaching of formal religion declines, or takes a sociological form, the less God appears to great numbers of people as a God of Love, resuming his older form of a watchful, minatory power, to be placated and cajoled. Superstition makes its appearance, apparently unbidden, very early in life, when children fear that stepping on cracks in the sidewalk will bring ill fortune. It may persist even among the greatly learned and devout, as in the case of Dr. Samuel Johnson, who felt it necessary to touch posts that he passed in the street. The psychoanalysts have their explanation, but calling a superstition a compulsion neurosis does not banish it.

Many superstitions are so widespread and so old that they ₉ must have risen from a depth of the human mind that is indifferent to race or creed. Orthodox Jews place a charm on their doorposts; so do (or did) the Chinese. Some peoples of Middle Europe believe that when a man sneezes, his soul, for that moment, is absent from his body, and they hasten to bless him, lest the soul be seized by the Devil. How did the Melanesians come by the same idea? Superstition seems to have a link with some body of belief that far antedates the religions we know—religions which have no place for such comforting little ceremonies and charities.

People who like disagreeable historical comparisons recall ₁₀ that when Rome was in decline, superstition proliferated wildly, and that something of the same sort is happening in our Western world today. They point to the popularity of astrology, and it is true that sober newspapers that would scorn to deal in love philters carry astrology columns and the fashion magazines count them among their most popular features. But when has astrology not been popular? No use saying science discredits it. When has the heart of man given a damn for science?

Superstition in general is linked to man's yearning to know ₁₁ his fate, and to have some hand in deciding it. When my mother was a child, she innocently joined her Roman Catholic friends in killing spiders on July 11, until she learned that this was done to ensure heavy rain the day following, the anniversary of the Battle of Boyne, when the Orangemen would hold their parade. I knew an Italian, a good scientist, who watched every morning before leaving his house, so that the first person he met would not be a priest or a nun, as this would certainly bring bad luck.

I am not one to stand aloof from the rest of humanity in this ₁₂ matter, for when I was a university student, a gypsy woman with a child in her arms used to appear every year at examination time, and ask a shilling of anyone who touched the Lucky Baby; that swarthy infant cost me four shillings altogether, and I never failed an examination. Of course, I did it merely for the joke—or so I thought then. Now, I am humbler.

1978

The Anthropology of Manners

Edward T. Hall

> The Goops they lick their fingers
>   and the Goops they lick their knives;
> They spill their broth on the table cloth—
>   Oh, they lead disgusting lives.
> The Goops they talk while eating,
>   and loud and fast they chew;
> And that is why I'm glad that I
>   am not a Goop—are you?

1   In Gelett Burgess's classic on the Goops we have an example of what anthropologists call "an enculturating device"—a means of conditioning the young to life in our society. Having been taught the lesson of the goops from childhood (with or without the aid of Mr. Burgess) Americans are shocked when they go abroad and discover whole groups of people behaving like goops—eating with their fingers, making noises and talking while eating. When this happens, we may (1) remark on the barbarousness or quaintness of the "natives" (a term cordially disliked all over the world) or (2) try to discover the nature and meaning of the differences in behavior. One rather quickly discovers that what is good manners in one context may be bad in the next. It is to this point that I would like to address myself.

2   The subject of manners is complex; if it were not, there would not be so many injured feelings and so much misunderstanding in international circles everywhere. In any society the code of manners tends to sum up the culture—to be a frame of reference for all behavior. Emily Post goes so far as to say: "There is not a single thing that we do, or say, or choose, or use, or even think, that does not follow or break one of the exactions of taste, or tact, or ethics of good manners, or etiquette—call it what you will." Unfortunately many of the most important standards of acceptable behavior in different cultures are elusive: They are intangible, undefined and unwritten.

3   An Arab diplomat who recently arrived in the U.S. from the Middle East attended a banquet which lasted several hours.

When it was over, he met a fellow countryman outside and suggested they go get something to eat, as he was starving. His friend, who had been in this country for some time, laughed and said: "But, Habib, didn't you know that if you say, 'No, thank you,' they think you really don't want any?" In an Arab country etiquette dictates that the person being served must refuse the proffered dish several times, while his host urges him repeatedly to partake. The other side of the coin is that Americans in the Middle East, until they learn better, stagger away from banquets having eaten more than they want or is good for them.

When a public-health movie of a baby being bathed in a bathinette was shown in India recently, the Indian women who saw it were visibly offended. They wondered how people could be so inhuman as to bathe a child in stagnant (not running) water. Americans in Iran soon learn not to indulge themselves in their penchant for chucking infants under the chin and remarking on the color of their eyes, for the mother has to pay to have the "evil eye" removed. We also learn that in the Middle East you don't hand people things with your left hand, because it is unclean. In India we learn not to touch another person, and in Southeast Asia we learn that the head is sacred.

In the interest of intercultural understanding various U.S. Government agencies have hired anthropologists from time to time as technical experts. The State Department especially has pioneered in the attempt to bring science to bear on this difficult and complex problem. It began by offering at the Foreign Service Institute an intensive four-week course for Point 4 technicians. Later these facilities were expanded to include other foreign service personnel.

The anthropologist's job here is not merely to call attention to obvious taboos or to coach people about types of thoughtless behavior that have very little to do with culture. One should not need an anthropologist to point out, for instance, that it is insulting to ask a foreigner: "How much is this in real money?" Where technical advice is most needed is in the interpretation of the unconscious aspects of a culture—the things people do automatically without being aware of the full implications of what they have done. For example, an ambassador who has been kept waiting for more than half an hour by a foreign visitor needs to understand that if his visitor "just mutters an apology" this is not necessarily an insult. The time system in the foreign country may be composed of different basic units, so that the visitor is not as late as he may appear to us. You must know the time system of the country to know at what point apologies are really due.

7   Twenty years of experience in working with Americans in foreign lands convinces me that the real problem in preparing them to work overseas is not with taboos, which they catch on to rather quickly, but rather with whole congeries of habits and attitudes which anthropologists have only recently begun to describe systematically.

8   Can you remember tying your shoes this morning? Could you give the rules for when it is proper to call another person by his first name? Could you describe the gestures you make in conversation? These examples illustrate how much of our behavior is "out of awareness," and how easy it is to get into trouble in another culture.

9   Nobody is continually aware of the quality of his own voice, the subtleties of stress and intonation that color the meaning of his words or the posture and distance he assumes in talking to another person. Yet all these are taken as cues to the real nature of an utterance, regardless of what the words say. A simple illustration is the meaning in the tone of voice. In the U.S. we raise our voices not only when we are angry but also when we want to emphasize a point, when we are more than a certain distance from another person, when we are concluding a meeting and so on. But to the Chinese, for instance, overloudness of the voice is most characteristically associated with anger and loss of self-control. Whenever we become really interested in something, they are apt to have the feeling we are angry, in spite of many years' experience with us. Very likely most of their interviews with us, however cordial, seem to end on a sour note when we exclaim heartily: "WELL, I'M CERTAINLY GLAD YOU DROPPED IN, MR. WONG."

10   The Latin Americans, who as a rule take business seriously, do not understand our mixing business with informality and

recreation. We like to put our feet up on the desk. If a stranger enters the office, we take our feet down. If it turns out that the stranger and we have a lot in common, up go the feet again—a cue to the other fellow that we feel at ease. If the office boy enters, the feet stay up; if the boss enters and our relationship with him is a little strained at the moment, they go down. To a Latin American this whole behavior is shocking. All he sees in it is insult or just plain rudeness.

Differences in attitudes toward space—what would be ter- 11 ritoriality in lower forms of life—raise a number of other interesting points. U.S. women who go to live in Latin America all complain about the "waste" of space in the houses. On the other hand, U.S. visitors to the Middle East complain about crowding, in the houses and on the streetcars and buses. Everywhere we go space seems to be distorted. When we see a gardener in the mountains of Italy planting a single row on each of six separate terraces, we wonder why he spreads out his crop so that he has to spend half his time climbing up and down. We overlook the complex chain of communication that would be broken if he didn't cultivate alongside his brothers and his cousin and if he didn't pass his neighbors and talk to them as he moves from one terrace to the next.

A colleague of mine was caught in a snowstorm while trav- 12 eling with companions in the mountains of Lebanon. They stopped at the next house and asked to be put up for the night. The house had only one room. Instead of distributing the guests around the room, their host placed them next to the pallet where he slept with his wife—so close that they almost touched the couple. To have done otherwise in that country would have been unnatural and unfriendly. In the U.S. we distribute ourselves more evenly than many other people. We have strong feelings about touching and being crowded; in a streetcar, bus or elevator we draw ourselves in. Toward a person who relaxes and lets himself come into full contact with others in a crowded place we usually feel reactions that could not be printed on this page. It takes years for us to train our children not to crowd and lean on us. We tell them to stand up, that it is rude to slouch, not to sit so close or not to "breathe down our necks." After a while they get the point. By the time we Americans are in our teens we can tell what relationship exists between a man and woman by how they walk or sit together.

13   In Latin America, where touching is more common and the basic units of space seem to be smaller, the wide automobiles made in the U.S. pose problems. People don't know where to sit. North Americans are disturbed by how close the Latin Americans stand when they converse. "Why do they have to get so close when they talk to you?" "They're so pushy." "I don't know what it is, but it's something in the way they stand next to you." And so on. The Latin Americans, for their part, complain that people in the U.S. are distant and cold—*retraídos* (withdrawing and uncommunicative).

14   An analysis of the handling of space during conversations shows the following: A U.S. male brought up in the Northeast stands 18 to 20 inches away when talking face to face to a man he does not know very well; talking to a woman under similar circumstances, he increases the distance about four inches. A distance of only eight to 13 inches between males is considered either very aggressive or indicative of a closeness of a type we do not ordinarily want to think about. Yet in many parts of Latin America and the Middle East distances which are almost sexual in connotation are the only ones at which people can talk comfortably. In Cuba, for instance, there is nothing suggestive in a man's talking to an educated woman at a distance of 13 inches. If you are a Latin American, talking to a North American at the distance he insists on maintaining is like trying to talk across a room.

15   To get a more vivid idea of this problem of the comfortable distance, try starting a conversation with a person eight or 10 feet away or one separated from you by a wide obstruction in a store or other public place. Any normally enculturated person can't help trying to close up the space, even to the extent of climbing over benches or walking around tables to arrive within comfortable distance. U.S. businessmen working in Latin America try to prevent people from getting uncomfortably close by barricading themselves behind desks, typewriters or the like, but their Latin American office visitors will often

climb up on desks or over chairs and put up with loss of dignity in order to establish a spatial context in which interaction can take place for them.

The interesting thing is that neither party is specifically aware 16 of what is wrong when the distance is not right. They merely have vague feelings of discomfort or anxiety. As the Latin American approaches and the North American backs away, both parties take offense without knowing why. When a North American, having had the problem pointed out to him, permits the Latin American to get close enough, he will immediately notice that the latter seems much more at ease.

My own studies of space and time have engendered consider- 17 able cooperation and interest on the part of friends and colleagues. One case recently reported to me had to do with a group of seven-year-olds in a crowded Sunday-school classroom. The children kept fighting. Without knowing quite what was involved, the teacher had them moved to a larger room. The fighting stopped. It is interesting to speculate as to what would have happened had the children been moved to a smaller room.

The embarrassment about intimacy in space applies also to the 18 matter of addressing people by name. Finding the proper distance in the use of names is even more difficult than in space, because the rules for first-naming are unbelievably complex. As a rule we tend to stay on the "mister" level too long with Latins and some others, but very often we swing into first naming too quickly, which amounts to talking down to them. Whereas in the U.S. we use Mr. with the surname, in Latin America the first and last names are used together and señor (Sr.) is a title. Thus when one says, "My name is Sr. So-and-So," it is interpreted to mean, "I am the Honorable, his Excellency So-and-So." It is no wonder that when we stand away, barricade ourselves behind our desks (usually a reflection of status) and call ourselves mister, our friends to the south wonder about our so-called "good neighbor" policy and think of us as either high-hat or unbelievably rude. Fortunately most North Americans learn some of these things after living in Latin America for a while, but the aversion to being touched and to touching sometimes persists after 15 or more years of residence and even under such conditions as intermarriage.

19   The difference in sense of time is another thing of which we are not aware. An Iranian, for instance, is not taught that it is rude to be late in the same way that we in the U.S. are. In a general way we are conscious of this, but we fail to realize that their time system is structured differently from ours. The different cultures simply place different values on the time units.

20   Thus let us take as a typical case of the North European time system (which has regional variations) the situation in the urban eastern U.S. A middle-class businessman meeting another of equivalent rank will ordinarily be aware of being two minutes early or late. If he is three minutes late, it will be noted as significant but usually neither will say anything. If four minutes late, he will mutter something by way of apology; at five minutes he will utter a full sentence of apology. In other words, the major unit is a five-minute block. Fifteen minutes is the smallest significant period for all sorts of arrangements and it is used very commonly. A half hour of course is very significant, and if you spend three quarters of an hour or an hour, either the business you transact or the relationship must be important. Normally it is an insult to keep a public figure or a person of significantly higher status than yourself waiting even two or three minutes, though the person of higher position can keep you waiting or even break an appointment.

21   Now among urban Arabs in the Eastern Mediterranean, to take an illustrative case of another time system, the unit that corresponds to our five-minute period is 15 minutes. Thus when an Arab arrives nearly 30 minutes after the set time, by his reckoning he isn't even "10 minutes" late yet (in our time units). Stated differently, the Arab's tardiness will not amount to one significant period (15 minutes in our system). An American normally will wait no longer than 30 minutes (two significant periods) for another person to turn up in the middle of the day. Thereby he often unwittingly insults people in the Middle East who want to be his friends.

22   How long is one expected to stay when making a duty call at a friend's house in the U.S.? While there are regional variations, I have observed that the minimum is very close to 45 minutes, even in the face of pressing commitments elsewhere, such as a roast in

the oven. We may think we can get away in 30 minutes by saying something about only stopping for "a minute," but usually we discover that we don't feel comfortable about leaving until 45 minutes have elapsed. I am referring to afternoon social calls; evening calls last much longer and operate according to a different system. In Arab countries an American paying a duty call at the house of a desert sheik causes consternation if he gets up to leave after half a day. There a duty call lasts three days—the first day to prepare the feast, the second for the feast itself and the third to taper off and say farewell. In the first half day the sheik has barely had time to slaughter the sheep for the feast. The guest's departure would leave the host frustrated.

There is a well-known story of a tribesman who came to 23 Kabul, the capital of Afghanistan, to meet his brother. Failing to find him, he asked the merchants in the marketplace to tell his brother where he could be found if the brother showed up. A year later the tribesman returned and looked again. It developed that he and his brother had agreed to meet in Kabul but had failed to specify what year! If the Afghan time system were structured similarly to our own, which it apparently is not, the brother would not offer a full sentence of apology until he was five years late.

Informal units of time such as "just a minute," "a while," 24 "later," "a long time," "a spell," "a long, long time," "years" and so on provide us with the culturological equivalent of Evil-Eye Fleegle's "double-whammy" (in *Li'l Abner*). Yet these expressions are not as imprecise as they seem. Any American who has worked in an office with someone else for six months can usually tell within five minutes when that person will be back if he says, "I'll be gone for a while." It is simply a matter of learning from experience the individual's system of time indicators. A reader who is interested in communications theory can fruitfully speculate for a while on the very wonderful way in which culture provides the means whereby the receiver puts back all the redundant material that was stripped from such a message. Spelled out, the message might go somewhat as follows: "I am going downtown to see So-and-So about the Such-and-Such contract, but I don't know what the traffic conditions will be like or how long it will take me to get a place to park nor do I know what shape So-and-So will be in today, but taking all this into account I think I will be out of the office about an hour but don't like to commit myself, so if anyone calls you can say I'm not sure how long I will be; in any event I expect to be back before 4 o'clock."

25   Few of us realize how much we rely on built-in patterns to interpret messages of this sort. An Iranian friend of mine who came to live in the U.S. was hurt and puzzled for the first few years. The new friends he met and liked would say on parting: "Well, I'll see you later." He mournfully complained: "I kept expecting to see them, but the 'later' never came." Strangely enough we ourselves are exasperated when a Mexican can't tell us precisely what he means when he uses the expression *mañana*.

26   The role of the anthropologist in preparing people for service overseas is to open their eyes and sensitize them to the subtle qualities of behavior—tone of voice, gestures, space and time relationships—that so often build up feelings of frustration and hostility in other people with a different culture. Whether we are going to live in a particular foreign country or travel in many, we need a frame of reference that will enable us to observe and learn the significance of differences in manners. Progress is being made in this anthropological study, but it is also showing us how little is known about human behavior.

1955

Black Men and Public Space

Brent Staples

1   My first victim was a woman—white, well dressed, probably in her late twenties. I came upon her late one evening on a deserted street in Hyde Park, a relatively affluent neighborhood in an otherwise mean, impoverished section of Chicago. As I swung onto the avenue behind her, there seemed to be a discreet, uninflammatory distance between us. Not so. She cast back a worried glance. To her, the youngish black man—a broad six feet two inches with a beard

and billowing hair, both hands shoved into the pockets of a bulky military jacket—seemed menacingly close. After a few more quick glimpses, she picked up her pace and was soon running in earnest. Within seconds, she disappeared into a cross street.

That was more than a decade ago. I was twenty-two years 2 old, a graduate student newly arrived at the University of Chicago. It was in the echo of that terrified woman's footfalls that I first began to know the unwieldy inheritance I'd come into—the ability to alter public space in ugly ways. It was clear that she thought herself the quarry of a mugger, a rapist, or worse. Suffering a bout of insomnia, however, I was stalking sleep, not defenseless wayfarers. As a softy who is scarcely able to take a knife to a raw chicken—let alone hold one to a person's throat—I was surprised, embarrassed, and dismayed all at once. Her flight made me feel like an accomplice in tyranny. It also made it clear that I was indistinguishable from the muggers who occasionally seeped into the area from the surrounding ghetto. That first encounter, and those that followed, signified that a vast, unnerving gulf lay between nighttime pedestrians—particularly women—and me. And I soon gathered that being perceived as dangerous is a hazard in itself. I only needed to turn a corner into a dicey situation, or crowd some frightened, armed person in a foyer somewhere, or make an errant move after being pulled over by a policeman. Where fear and weapons meet—and they often do in urban America—there is always the possibility of death.

In that first year, my first away from my hometown, I was to 3 become thoroughly familiar with the language of fear. At dark, shadowy intersections, I could cross in front of a car stopped at a traffic light and elicit the *thunk,* thunk, thunk, thunk of the driver—black, white, male, or female—hammering down the door locks. On less traveled streets after dark, I grew accustomed to but never comfortable with people crossing to the other side of the street rather than pass me. Then there were the standard unpleasantries with policemen, doormen, bouncers, cabdrivers, and others whose business it is to screen out troublesome individuals *before* there is any nastiness.

I moved to New York nearly two years ago and I have remained 4 an avid night walker. In central Manhattan, the near-constant crowd cover minimizes tense one-on-one street encounters. Elsewhere—in SoHo, for example, where sidewalks are narrow and tightly spaced buildings shut out the sky—things can get very taut indeed.

5   After dark, on the warrenlike streets of Brooklyn where I live, I often see women who fear the worst from me. They seem to have set their faces on neutral, and with their purse straps strung across their chests bandolier-style, they forge ahead as though bracing themselves against being tackled. I understand, of course, that the danger they perceive is not a hallucination. Women are particularly vulnerable to street violence, and young black males are drastically overrepresented among the perpetrators of that violence. Yet these truths are no solace against the kind of alienation that comes of being ever the suspect, a fearsome entity with whom pedestrians avoid making eye contact.

6   It is not altogether clear to me how I reached the ripe old age of twenty-two without being conscious of the lethality nighttime pedestrians attributed to me. Perhaps it was because in Chester, Pennsylvania, the small, angry industrial town where I came of age in the 1960s, I was scarcely noticeable against a backdrop of gang warfare, street knifings, and murders. I grew up one of the good boys, had perhaps a half-dozen fistfights. In retrospect, my shyness of combat has clear sources.

7   As a boy, I saw countless tough guys locked away; I have since buried several, too. They were babies, really—a teenage cousin, a brother of twenty-two, a childhood friend in his mid-twenties—all gone down in episodes of bravado played out in the streets. I came to doubt the virtues of intimidation early on. I chose, perhaps unconsciously, to remain a shadow—timid, but a survivor.

8   The fearsomeness mistakenly attributed to me in public places often has a perilous flavor. The most frightening of these confusions occurred in the late 1970s and early 1980s, when I worked as a journalist in Chicago. One day, rushing into the office of a magazine I was writing for with a deadline story in hand, I was mistaken for a burglar. The office manager called security and, with an ad hoc posse, pursued me through the labyrinthine halls, nearly to my editor's door. I had no way of proving who I was. I could only move briskly toward the company of someone who knew me.

Another time I was on assignment for a local paper and ₉
killing time before an interview. I entered a jewelry store on the
city's affluent Near North Side. The proprietor excused herself
and returned with an enormous red Doberman pinscher straining
at the end of a leash. She stood, the dog extended toward me,
silent to my questions, her eyes bulging nearly out of her head. I
took a cursory look around, nodded, and bade her good night.

Relatively speaking, however, I never fared as badly as ₁₀
another black male journalist. He went to nearby Waukegan,
Illinois, a couple of summers ago to work on a story about a mur-
derer who was born there. Mistaking the reporter for the killer,
police officers hauled him from his car at gunpoint and but for
his press credentials would probably have tried to book him.
Such episodes are not uncommon. Black men trade tales like this
all the time.

Over the years, I learned to smother the rage I felt at so ₁₁
often being taken for a criminal. Not to do so would surely
have led to madness. I now take precautions to make myself
less threatening. I move about with care, particularly late in
the evening. I give a wide berth to nervous people on subway
platforms during the wee hours, particularly when I have
exchanged business clothes for jeans. If I happen to be entering
a building behind some people who appear skittish, I may walk
by, letting them clear the lobby before I return, so as not to seem
to be following them. I have been calm and extremely congenial
on those rare occasions when I've been pulled over by the
police.

And on late-evening constitutionals I employ what has ₁₂
proved to be an excellent tension-reducing measure: I whistle
melodies from Beethoven and Vivaldi and the more popular classical composers. Even steely New Yorkers hunching toward
nighttime destinations seem to relax, and occasionally they even
join in the tune. Virtually everybody seems to sense that a mugger wouldn't be warbling bright, sunny selections from Vivaldi's
Four Seasons. It is my equivalent of the cowbell that hikers wear
when they know they are in bear country.

1986

Letter to His Father

Franz Kafka

Dearest Father:

1   You asked me recently why I maintain that I am afraid of you. As usual, I was unable to think of any answer to your question, partly for the very reason that I am afraid of you, and partly because an explanation of the grounds for this fear would mean going into far more details than I could even approximately keep in mind while talking. And if I now try to give you an answer in writing, it will still be very incomplete, because even in writing this fear and its consequences hamper me in relation to you and because [anyway] the magnitude of the subject goes far beyond the scope of my memory and power of reasoning.

2   Oddly enough you have some sort of notion of what I mean. For instance, a short time ago you said to me: "I have always been fond of you, even though outwardly I didn't act towards you as other fathers generally do, and this precisely because I can't pretend as other people can." Now, Father, on the whole I have never doubted your goodness towards me, but this remark is one I consider wrong. You can't pretend, that's fact, but merely for that reason to maintain that other fathers pretend is either mere opinionatedness, and as such beyond discussion, or on the other hand—and this in my view is what it really is—a veiled expression of the fact that something is wrong in our relationship and that you have played your part in causing it to be so, but without its being your fault. If you really mean that, then we are in agreement.

3   Compare the two of us: I, to put it in a very much abbreviated form, a Löwy with a certain basis of Kafka, which, however, is not set in motion by the Kafka will to life, business, and conquest, but by a Löwyish spur that urges more secretly, more diffidently, and in another direction, and which often fails to work entirely. You, on the other hand, a true Kafka in strength, health, appetite, loudness of voice, eloquence, self-satisfaction, worldly dominance, endurance, presence of mind, knowledge of human nature, a certain way of doing things on a grand

scale, of course also with all the defects and weaknesses that go with all these advantages and into which your temperament and sometimes your hot temper drive you.

However it was, we were so different and in our difference so 4 dangerous to each other that, if anyone had tried to calculate in advance how I, the slowly developing child, and you, the full-grown man, would stand to each other, he could have assumed that you would simply trample me underfoot so that nothing was left of me. Well, that didn't happen. Nothing alive can be calculated. But perhaps something worse happened. And in saying this I would all the time beg of you not to forget that I never, and not even for a single moment, believe any guilt to be on your side. The effect you had on me was the effect you could not help having. But you should stop considering it some particular malice on my part that I succumbed to that effect.

I was a timid child. For all that, I am sure I was also obstinate, 5 as children are. I am sure that Mother spoilt me too, but I cannot believe I was particularly difficult to manage; I cannot believe that a kindly word, a quiet taking of me by the hand, a friendly look, could not have got me to do anything that was wanted of me. Now you are after all at bottom a kindly and softhearted person (what follows will not be in contradiction to this, I am speaking only of the impression you made on the child), but not every child has the endurance and fearlessness to go on searching until it comes to the kindliness that lies beneath the surface. You can only treat a child in the way you yourself are constituted, with vigor, noise, and hot temper, and in this case this seemed to you, into the bargain, extremely suitable, because you wanted to bring me up to be a strong brave boy. . . .

There is only one episode in the early years of which I have a 6 direct memory. You may remember it, too. Once in the night I kept on whimpering for water, not, I am certain, because I was thirsty, but probably partly to be annoying, partly to amuse myself. After several vigorous threats had failed to have any effect, you took me out of bed, carried me out onto the *pavlatche* and left me there alone for a while in my nightshirt, outside the shut door. I am not going to say that this was wrong—perhaps at that time there was really no other way of getting peace and quiet that night—but I mention it as typical of your methods of bringing up a child and their effect on me. I dare say I was quite obedient afterwards at that period, but it did me inner harm. What was for me a matter of course, that senseless asking for water, and the extraordinary terror of being carried outside were two things that I, my nature being what it was, could never properly connect with each other. Even years afterwards I suffered from the tormenting fancy that the huge man, my father, the ultimate authority, would come almost for no reason at all and take me out of bed in the night and carry me out onto the *pavlatche,* and that therefore I was such a mere nothing for him.

7   That then was only a small beginning, but this sense of nothingness that often dominates me (a feeling that is in another respect, admittedly, also a noble and fruitful one) comes largely from your influence. What I would have needed was a little encouragement, a little friendliness, a little keeping open of my road, instead of which you blocked it for me, though of course with the good intention of making me go another road. But I was not fit for that. . . .

8   At that time, and at that time everywhere, I would have needed encouragement. I was, after all, depressed even by your mere physical presence. I remember, for instance, how we often undressed together in the same bathing hut. There was I, skinny, weakly, slight; you strong, tall, broad. Even inside the hut I felt myself a miserable specimen, and what's more, not only in your eyes but in the eyes of the whole world, for you were for me the measure of all things. But then when we went out of the bathing hut before the people, I with you holding my hand, a little skeleton, unsteady, barefoot on the boards, frightened of the water, incapable of copying your swimming strokes, which you, with the best of intentions, but actually to my profound humiliation, always kept on showing me, then I was frantic with desperation and all my bad experiences in all spheres at such moments fitted magnificently together. What made me feel best was when you sometimes undressed first and I was able to stay behind in the hut alone and put off the disgrace of showing myself in public until at length you came to see what I was doing and drove me

out of the hut. I was grateful to you for not seeming to notice my extremity, and besides, I was proud of my father's body. For the rest, this difference between us remains much the same to this very day.

In keeping with that, furthermore, was your intellectual dom- 9 ination. You had worked your way up so far alone, by your own energies, and as a result you had unbounded confidence in your opinion. For me as a child that was not yet so dazzling as later for the boy growing up. From your armchair you ruled the world. Your opinion was correct, every other was mad, wild, *meshugge*, not normal. With all this your self-confidence was so great that you had no need to be consistent at all and yet never ceased to be in the right. It did sometimes happen that you had no opinion whatsoever about a matter and as a result all opinions that were at all possible with respect to the matter were necessarily wrong, without exception. You were capable, for instance, of running down the Czechs, and then the Germans, and then the Jews, and what is more, not only selectively but in every respect, and finally nobody was left except yourself. For me you took on the enigmatic quality that all tyrants have whose rights are based on their person and not on reason. At least so it seemed to me.

This applied to thoughts as well as to people. It was enough 10 that I should take a little interest in a person—which in any case did not happen often, as a result of my nature—for you, without any consideration for my feelings or respect for my judgment, to butt in with abuse, defamation, and denigration. Innocent, childlike people, such as, for instance, the Yiddish actor Löwy, had to pay for that. Without knowing him you compared him, in a dreadful way that I have now forgotten, to vermin and as was so often the case with people I was fond of you were automatically ready with the proverb of the dog and its fleas. I here particularly recall the actor because at that time I made a note of your pronouncements about him, with the comment: "This is how my father speaks of my friend (whom he does not even know), simply because he is my friend. I shall always be able to bring this up against him whenever he reproaches me with the lack of a child's affection and gratitude." What was always incomprehensible to me was your total lack of feeling for the suffering and shame you could inflict on me with your words and judgments. It was as though you had no notion of your power. I too, I am sure, often hurt you with what I said, but then I always knew, and it pained me, but I could not control myself, could not keep the words back, I was sorry even while I was saying it. But you struck out with your words without more ado, you weren't sorry for anyone, either during or afterwards, one was utterly defenseless against you.

11　　　But that was what your whole method of upbringing was like. You have, I think, a gift for bringing up children; you could, I am sure, have been of use to a human being of your own kind with your methods; such a person would have seen the reasonableness of what you told him, would not have troubled about anything else, and would quietly have done things the way he was told. But for me as a child everything you shouted at me was positively a heavenly commandment, I never forgot it, it remained for me the most important means of forming a judgment of the world, above all of forming a judgment of you yourself, and there you failed entirely. Since as a child I was together with you chiefly at meals, your teaching was to a large extent teaching about proper behavior at table. What was brought to the table had to be eaten up, there could be no discussion of the goodness of the food—but you yourself often found the food uneatable, called it "this swill," said "that brute" (the cook) had ruined it. Because in accordance with your strong appetite and your particular habit you ate everything fast, hot and in big mouthfuls, the child had to hurry, there was a somber silence at table, interrupted by admonitions: "Eat first, talk afterwards," or "faster, faster, faster," or "there you are, you see, I finished ages ago." Bones mustn't be cracked with the teeth, but you could. Vinegar must not be sipped noisily, but you could. The main thing was that the bread should be cut straight. But it didn't matter that you did it with a knife dripping with gravy. One had to take care that no scraps fell on the floor. In the end it was under your chair that there were most scraps. At table one wasn't allowed to do anything but eat, but you cleaned and cut your fingernails, sharpened pencils, cleaned your ears with the toothpick. Please, Father, understand me rightly: these would in themselves have been utterly insignificant details, they only became depressing for me because you, the man who was so tremendously the measure of all things for me, yourself did not keep the commandments you imposed on me. Hence the world was for me divided into three parts: into one in which I, the slave, lived under laws that had been invented only for me and which I could, I did not know why, never completely comply with; then into a second world, which was infinitely remote from mine, in which you lived, concerned with government, with the issuing of orders and with annoyance about their not being obeyed; and finally into a third world where everybody else lived happily and free from orders and from having to obey. . . .

The impossibility of getting on calmly together had one more 12 result, actually a very natural one: I lost the capacity to talk. I dare say I would never have been a very eloquent person in any case, but I would, after all, have had the usual fluency of human language at my command. But at a very early stage you forbade me to talk. Your threat: "Not a word of contradiction!" and the raised hand that accompanied it have gone with me ever since. What I got from you—and you are, as soon as it is a matter of your own affairs, an excellent talker—was a hesitant, stammering mode of speech, and even that was still too much for you, and finally I kept silent, at first perhaps from defiance, and then because I couldn't either think or speak in your presence.

I can't recall your ever having abused me directly and in 13 down right abusive terms. Nor was that necessary; you had so many other methods, and besides, in talk at home and particularly at business the words of abuse went flying around me in such swarms, as they were flung at other people's heads, that as a little boy I was sometimes almost stunned and had no reason not to apply them to myself too, for the people you were abusing were certainly no worse than I was and you were certainly not more displeased with them than with me. And here again, too, was your enigmatic innocence and inviolability; you cursed and swore without the slightest scruple about it; indeed you condemned cursing and swearing in other people and would not have it. . . .

You put special trust in bringing children up by means of 14 irony, and this was most in keeping with your superiority over me.

An admonition from you generally took this form: "Can't you do it in such-and-such a way? That's too hard for you, I suppose. You haven't the time, of course?" and so on. And each such question would be accompanied by malicious laughter and a malicious face. One was so to speak already punished before one even knew that one had done something bad. What was also maddening were those rebukes when one was treated as a third person, in other words accounted not worthy even to be spoken to angrily: that is to say, when you would speak in form to Mother but in fact to me, sitting there at the same time. For instance: "Of course, that's too much to expect of our worthy son" and the like.

15   Fortunately there were, I admit, exceptions to all these things, mostly when you suffered in silence, and affection and kindliness by their own strength overcame all obstacles, and moved me immediately. Admittedly this was rare, but it was wonderful. For instance, when in earlier times, in hot summers, when you were tired after lunch, I saw you having a nap at the office, your elbow on the desk; or when you joined us in the country, in the summer holidays, on Sundays, worn out from work at the office; or the time when Mother was gravely ill and you stood holding on to the bookcase, shaking with sobs; or when, during my last illness, you came tiptoeing to Ottla's room to see me, stopping in the doorway, craning your neck to see me. At such times one would lie back and weep for happiness, and one weeps again now, writing it down. . . .

16   It was true that Mother was illimitably good to me, but all that was for me in relation to you, that is to say, in no good relation. Mother unconsciously played the part of a beater during a hunt. Even if your method of upbringing might in some unlikely case have set me on my own feet by means of producing defiance, dislike, or even hate in me, Mother canceled that out again by kindness, by talking sensibly (in the maze and chaos of my childhood she was the very pattern of good sense and reasonableness), by pleading for me, and I was again driven back into your orbit, which I might perhaps otherwise have broken out of, to your advantage and to my own. Or it was so that no real reconciliation ever came about, that Mother merely shielded me from you in secret, secretly gave me something, or allowed me to do something, and then

where you were concerned I was again the furtive creature, the cheat, the guilty one, who in his worthlessness could only pursue backstairs methods even to get the things he regarded as right. Of course, I then became used to taking such courses also in quest of things to which, even in my own view, I had no right. This again meant an increase in the sense of guilt.

The next eternal result of this whole method of upbringing was that I fled from everything that even remotely reminded me of you. First there was the business. In itself, particularly in my childhood, so long as it was a shop, I ought to have liked it very much, it was so animated, the lights lit at evening, so much to see and hear, being able to help now and then and to distinguish oneself, but above all to admire you for your magnificent commercial talents, the way you sold things, managed people, made jokes, were untiring, knew the right decision to make at once in doubtful cases, and so forth; even the way you wrapped up a parcel or opened a crate was a spectacle worth watching, and all this was certainly not the worst school for a child. But since you gradually began to terrify me on all sides and the business and you became one for me, the business too made me feel uneasy. Things that had at first been a matter of course for me there now began to torment and shame me, particularly the way you treated the staff. . . . 17

If I was to flee from you, I had to flee from the family as well, even from Mother. True, one could always get protection from her, but only in relation to you. She loved you too much and was too devoted and loyal to you to have been able to constitute an independent spiritual force, in the long run, in the child's struggle. It was, incidentally, a true instinct the child had, for with the passing of years Mother became ever more closely allied to you; while, where she herself was concerned, she always kept her independence, within the narrowest limits, delicately and beautifully, and without ever essentially hurting you, still, with the passing of the years she did more and more completely, emotionally rather than intellectually, blindly adopt your judgments and your condemnations with regard to the children. . . . 18

1953

Clutter

William Zinsser

1   Fighting clutter is like fighting weeds—the writer is always slightly behind. New varieties sprout overnight, and by noon they are part of American speech. Consider what President Nixon's aide John Dean accomplished in just one day of testimony on television during the Watergate hearings. The next day everyone in America was saying "at this point in time" instead of "now."

2   Consider all the prepositions that are draped onto verbs that don't need any help. We no longer head committees. We head them up. We don't face problems anymore. We face up to them when we can free up a few minutes. A small detail, you may say—not worth bothering about. It *is* worth bothering about. Writing improves in direct ratio to the number of things we can keep out of it that shouldn't be there. "Up" in "free up" shouldn't be there. Examine every word you put on paper. You'll find a surprising number that don't serve any purpose.

3   Take the adjective "personal," as in "a personal friend of mine," "his personal feeling" or "her personal physician." It's typical of hundreds of words that can be eliminated. The personal friend has come into the language to distinguish him or her from the business friend, thereby debasing both language and friendship. Someone's feeling *is* that person's personal feelings—that's what "his" means. As for the personal physician, that's the man or woman summoned to the dressing room of a stricken actress so she won't have to be treated by the impersonal physician assigned to the theater. Someday I'd like to see that person identified as "her doctor." Physicians are physicians, friends are friends. The rest is clutter.

4   Clutter is the laborious phrase that has pushed out the short word that means the same thing. Even before John Dean, people and businesses had stopped saying "now." They were saying "currently" ("all our operators are currently busy"), or "at the present time," or "presently" (which means "soon"). Yet the idea can always be expressed by "now" to mean the immediate moment

("Now I can see him"), or by "today" to mean the historical present ("Today prices are high"), or simply by the verb "to be" ("It is raining"). There's no need to say, "At the present time we are experiencing precipitation."

"Experiencing" is one of the ultimate clutterers. Even your dentist will ask if you are experiencing any pain. If he had his own kid in the chair he would say, "Does it hurt?" He would, in short, be himself. By using a more pompous phrase in his professional role he not only sounds more important; he blunts the painful edge of truth. It's the language of the flight attendant demonstrating the oxygen mask that will drop down if the plane should run out of air. "In the unlikely possibility that the aircraft should experience such an eventuality," she begins—a phrase so oxygen-depriving in itself that we are prepared for any disaster.

Clutter is the ponderous euphemism that turns a slum into a depressed socioeconomic area, garbage collectors into waste-disposal personnel and the town dump into the volume reduction unit. I think of Bill Mauldin's cartoon of two hoboes riding a freight car. One of them says, "I started as a simple bum, but now I'm hard-core unemployed." Clutter is political correctness gone amok. I saw an ad for a boys' camp designed to provide "individual attention for the minimally exceptional."

Clutter is the official language used by corporations to hide their mistakes. When the Digital Equipment Corporation eliminated 3,000 jobs its statement didn't mention layoffs; those were "involuntary methodologies." When an Air Force missile crashed, it "impacted with the ground prematurely." When General Motors had a plant shutdown, that was a "volume-related production-schedule adjustment." Companies that go belly-up have "a negative cash-flow position."

Clutter is the language of the Pentagon calling an invasion a "reinforced protective reaction strike" and justifying its vast budgets on the need for "counterforce deterrence." As George Orwell pointed out in "Politics and the English Language," an essay written in 1946 but often cited during the Vietnam and Cambodia years of Presidents Johnson and Nixon, "political speech and writing are largely the defense of the indefensible. . . . Thus political language has to consist largely of euphemism, question-begging and sheer cloudy vagueness." Orwell's warning that clutter is not just a nuisance but a deadly tool has come true in the recent decades of American military adventurism in Southwest Asia and other parts of the world.

9   Verbal camouflage reached new heights during General Alexander Haig's tenure as President Reagon's secretary of state. Before Haig nobody had thought of saying "at this juncture of maturization" to mean "now." He told the American people that terrorism could be fought with "meaningful sanctionary teeth" and that intermediate nuclear missiles were "at the vortex of cruciality." As for any worries that the public might harbor, his message was "leave it to Al," though what he actually said was: "We must push this to a lower decibel of public fixation. I don't think there's much of a learning curve to be achieved in this area of content."

10   I could go on quoting examples from various fields—every profession has its growing arsenal of jargon to throw dust in the eyes of the populace. But the list would be tedious. The point of raising it now is to serve notice that clutter is the enemy. Beware, then, of the long word that's no better than the short word: "assistance" (help), "numerous" (many), "facilitate" (ease), "individual" (man or woman), "remainder" (rest), "initial" (first), "implement" (do), "sufficient" (enough), "attempt" (try), "referred to as" (called) and hundreds more. Beware of all the slippery new fad words: paradigm and parameter, prioritize and potentialize. They are all weeds that will smother what you write. Don't dialogue with someone you can talk to. Don't interface with anybody.

11   Just as insidious are all the word clusters with which we explain how we propose to go about our explaining: "I might add," "It should be pointed out," "It is interesting to note." If you might add, add it. If it should be pointed out, point it out. If it is interesting to note, *make* it interesting; are we not all stupefied by what follows when someone says, "This will interest you"? Don't inflate what needs no inflating: "with the possible exception of" (except), "due to the fact that" (because), "he totally lacked the ability to" (he couldn't), "until such time as" (until), "for the purpose of" (for).

Is there any way to recognize clutter at a glance? Here's a 12
device my students at Yale found helpful. I would put brackets
around every component in a piece of writing that wasn't doing
useful work. Often just one word got bracketed: the unnecessary
preposition appended to a verb ("order up"), or the adverb that
carries the same meaning as the verb ("smile happily"), or the
adjective that states a known fact ("tall skyscraper"). Often my
brackets surrounded the little qualifiers that weaken any sentence
they inhabit ("a bit," "sort of"), or phrases like "in a sense," which
don't mean anything. Sometimes my brackets surrounded an
entire sentence—the one that essentially repeats what the previous sentence said, or that says something readers don't need to
know or can figure out for themselves. Most first drafts can be
cut by 50 percent without losing any information or losing the
author's voice.

My reason for bracketing the students' superfluous words, 13
instead of crossing them out, was to avoid violating their sacred
prose. I wanted to leave the sentence intact for them to analyze.
I was saying, "I may be wrong, but I think this can be deleted
and the meaning won't be affected. But *you* decide. Read the
sentence without the bracketed material and see if it works." In
the early weeks of the term I handed back papers that were fes-
tooned with brackets. Entire paragraphs were bracketed. But
soon the students learned to put mental brackets around their
own clutter, and by the end of the term their papers were almost
clean. Today many of those students are professional writers,
and they tell me, "I still see your brackets—they're following me
through life."

You can develop the same eye. Look for the clutter in your 14
writing and prune it ruthlessly. Be grateful for everything you can
throw away. Reexamine each sentence you put on paper. Is every
word doing new work? Can any thought be expressed with more
economy? Is anything pompous or pretentious or faddish? Are
you hanging on to something useless just because you think it's
beautiful?

Simplify, simplify.   15

2001

Forbidden Things

Bailey White

1   I was leaning over the little railing, looking down into the Devil's Millhopper, an interesting geological formation and the focal point of a Florida state park. Waterfalls plunge 120 feet down into a bowl-shaped sinkhole; maidenhair ferns and moss grow in little crevices along the steep, sloping sides of the gorge; and a beautiful mist rises up.

2   I stood there, gazing down, and feeling a reverence for these spectacles of the natural world. I felt the slow sweep of geologic time. I felt the remnants of the spiritual significance this place had had for the Indians who lived here for thousands of years. I felt the wonder and awe of the first European explorers of Florida looking down into this chasm for the first time.

3   Then another feeling crept over me, a deep, almost atavistic longing. It was the urge to throw something down into the Devil's Millhopper. I looked around. A stone or a stick would do, but what I really wanted was a piece of food, the nibbled end of a hotdog bun or a wedge of chocolate cake without the icing. Then I noticed the sign, one of those tastefully unobtrusive state park signs:

DO NOT THROW FOOD OR TRASH IN GORGE

4   It was 4:00 A.M. I was at the Los Angeles, California, bus station, my next-to-last stop on a dreary transcontinental bus trip—three days and three nights on a Greyhound bus. My back ached, my knees ached, my head ached. Ever since El Paso, Texas, my seatmate had been an old man who chain-smoked Marlboro cigarettes and sucked and slobbered over a perpetual ham sandwich that kept oozing out of a greasy crumple of waxed paper.

5   I longed for a bath in my own bathtub, and then a deep sleep in my own bed, stretched out full-length between clean sheets. But, I thought, pushing open the door of the bus station bathroom, if I just wash my feet and my hair I will be all right. I lined up my soap, my washrag, and my little bottle of shampoo on the back of the sink and took off my shoes and socks. Ahh, I thought. Then I saw the sign on the mirror:

DO NOT WASH HAIR OR FEET IN SINK

A few weeks ago I went into our little downtown restaurant 6
and saw that it had replaced its tired old salad bar with a gorgeous saltwater aquarium with sea anemones, chunks of living
coral, and big slow-moving colorful fish with faces I could almost
recognize. I spent my whole lunchtime staring into that tank,
mesmerized by the fish as they gracefully looped and glided,
sending the tentacles of the sea anemones into slow twirls and
fanning out the tall grasses.

When I finished my sandwich I noticed that there were a cou- 7
ple of crumbs left on my plate, just the size to pinch between
thumb and finger. Oh, I thought, to pinch up those crumbs and
dip my fingers down into the water, breaking through the smooth
surface into the coolness and silence of that peaceful world. One
of the fish would make a looping turn, his odd exophthalmic eyes
would rotate slowly in their sockets and fix upon the crumbs in
my fingers. Then he would angle up, and I would feel for just one
exquisite instant those thorny fish lips rasping across my finger-
tips. With rising delight and anticipation, I pinched up a crumb,
two crumbs. I scrabbled across the plastic top of the tank, found
the little door, lifted it open—and then I saw the sign:

DO NOT FEED THE FISH

WE PROHIBIT CLIMBING IN ANY MANNER FROM OR ALONG THE CANYON RIM
DO NOT PICK FLOWERS
NO SMOKING EATING OR DRINKING
NO SWINGING FROM VINES IN TREES
NO PEDESTRIAN TRAFFIC IN WOODS
NO FISHING
NO SWIMMING
NO TRESPASSING

Don't get me wrong; I approve of these prohibitions. 8
Imagine the nasty mess in the bottom of the Devil's Millhopper
if every self-indulgent tourist threw a piece of food into the sinkhole. Imagine the puddles on the floor and the plumbing com-
plications in the Los Angeles bus station if every weary
transcontinental traveler washed her hair and feet in the sink.
Imagine the deadly scum of grease on the surface of that saltwater aquarium if every fish-dazed diner fed the catalufa his last
mayonnaise-coated crumbs.

9   But sometimes I wonder: Who makes up these necessary and useful rules, and how does he know so well the deep and touching urges of human beings to pick flowers, walk in the woods, climb canyon walls, swing from vines, and feed already well-nourished animals? I imagine with distaste a mean, sour, silent little man skulking around in public places, watching us furtively with squinny eyes while scribbling notes on his pad with a gnawed pencil. In national parks he disguises himself as a tourist in reflective sunglasses and plaid Bermuda shorts. "Bryce Canyon," he notes with a smirk, "Urinating on hoodoos and off cliffs." In zoos he wears khaki and lurks in the shadows, hiding behind a bag of peanuts. "Touching giraffe's tongue through fence wire. . . . Feeling camel's hump," he scribbles.

10   At night he goes home, and in his stark white workshop, illuminated with fluorescent lights, he makes those signs. Rounded letters routed out of cypress boards for the parks: "We Prohibit . . . , No . . . , No . . . , and No . . ." Spiky green on white for zoos: "Do Not . . . , . . . Not Allowed, . . . Is Prohibited." *And-we-mean-it* black and white for commercial establishments: "Absolutely NO . . . , . . . Are Required, We Forbid . . ."

11   I imagine, one night, as he works late stacking and bundling signs for the next day's delivery, the tendril of a grapevine creeps in at his window. When his back is turned, its pale nose will gently nudge itself around him.

12   "No Touching!" he will admonish.

13   But with a clutch and a snatch the vine will retract, and he will find himself yanked through the night sky above a central Florida state park.

14   "Do Not Swing from Vines!" he will shriek.

15   And with that, the vine will untwine and drop him into the vortex of a limpid spring.

16   "No Swimming!" he will sputter as the dark, icy water closes over his head. As he sinks, strange, pale-colored fish will swim up and cock their eyes at him. "Do Not Feed the Fish," he will squeak. But, slowly and precisely, the fish will angle up, move in, and then, all over, he will feel the pick pick pick of those prickly lips.

1995

Silk Parachute

John McPhee

When your mother is ninety-nine years old, you have so many 1
memories of her that they tend to overlap, intermingle, and blur.
It is extremely difficult to single out one or two, impossible to
remember any that exemplify the whole.

It has been alleged that when I was in college she heard that 2
I had stayed up all night playing poker and wrote me a letter that
used the word "shame" forty-two times. I do not recall this.

I do not recall being pulled out of my college room and into 3
the church next door.

It has been alleged that on December 24, 1936, when I was 4
five years old, she sent me to my room at or close to 7 P.M. for
using four-letter words while trimming the Christmas tree. I do
not recall that.

The assertion is absolutely false that when I came home from 5
high school with an A-minus she demanded an explanation for
the minus.

It has been alleged that she spoiled me with protectionism, 6
because I was the youngest child and therefore the most vulnerable to attack from overhead—an assertion that I cannot confirm or
confute, except to say that facts don't lie.

We lived only a few blocks from the elementary school and 7
routinely ate lunch at home. It is reported that the following dialogue and ensuing action occurred on January 22, 1941:

"Eat your sandwich."   8
"I don't want to eat my sandwich."   9
"I made that sandwich, and you are going to eat it, Mister 10
Man. You filled yourself up on penny candy on the way home,
and now you're not hungry."

"I'm late. I have to go. I'll eat the sandwich on the way back 11
to school."

"Promise?"   12
"Promise."   13
Allegedly, I went up the street with the sandwich in my 14
hand and buried it in a snowbank in front of Dr. Wright's house.

My mother, holding back the curtain in the window of the side door, was watching. She came out in the bitter cold, wearing only a light dress, ran to the snowbank, dug out the sandwich, chased me up Nassau Street, and rammed the sandwich down my throat, snow and all. I do not recall any detail of that story. I believe it to be a total fabrication.

15   There was the case of the missing Cracker Jack at Lindel's corner store. Flimsy evidence pointed to Mrs. McPhee's smallest child. It has been averred that she laid the guilt on with the following words: "'Like mother like son' is a saying so true, the world will judge largely of mother by you." It has been asserted that she immediately repeated that proverb three times, and also recited it on other occasions too numerous to count. I have absolutely no recollection of her saying that about the Cracker Jack or any other controlled substance.

16   We have now covered everything even faintly unsavory that has been reported about this person in ninety-nine years, and even those items are a collection of rumors, half-truths, prevarications, false allegations, inaccuracies, innuendos, and canards.

17   This is the mother who—when Alfred Knopf wrote her twenty-two-year-old son a letter saying, "The readers' reports in the case of your manuscript would not be very helpful, and I think might discourage you completely"—said, "Don't listen to Alfred Knopf. Who does Alfred Knopf think he is, anyway? Someone should go in there and k-nock his block off." To the best of my recollection, that is what she said.

18   I also recall her taking me, on or about March 8th, my birthday, to the theatre in New York every year, beginning in childhood. I remember those journeys as if they were today. I remember "A Connecticut Yankee." Wednesday, March 8, 1944. Evidently, my father had written for the tickets, because she and I sat in the last row of the second balcony. Mother knew what to do about that. She gave me for my birthday an elegant spyglass, sufficient in power to bring the Connecticut Yankee back from Vermont. I sat there watching the play through my telescope, drawing as many guffaws from the surrounding audience as the comedy on the stage.

On one of those theatre days—when I was eleven or twelve— ₁₉ I asked her if we could start for the city early and go out to LaGuardia Field to see the comings and goings of airplanes. The temperature was well below the freeze point and the March winds were so blustery that the wind-chill factor was forty below zero. Or seemed to be. My mother figured out how to take the subway to a stop in Jackson Heights and a bus from there—a feat I am unable to duplicate to this day. At LaGuardia, she accompanied me to the observation deck and stood there in the icy wind for at least an hour, maybe two, while I, spellbound, watched the DC-3s coming in on final, their wings flapping in the gusts. When we at last left the observation deck, we went downstairs into the terminal, where she bought me what appeared to be a black rubber ball but on closer inspection was a pair of hollow hemispheres hinged on one side and folded together. They contained a silk parachute. Opposite the hinge, each hemisphere had a small nib. A piece of string wrapped round and round the two nibs kept the ball closed. If you threw it high into the air, the string unwound and the parachute blossomed. If you sent it up with a tennis racquet, you could put it into the clouds. Not until the development of the ten-megabyte hard disk would the world ever know such a fabulous toy. Folded just so, the parachute never failed. Always, it floated back to you—silkily, beautifully—to start over and float back again. Even if you abused it, whacked it really hard— gracefully, lightly, it floated back to you.

1997

Cause and Effect

White Guilt

Shelby Steele

1   I don't remember hearing the phrase "white guilt" very much before the mid-1960s. Growing up black in the 1950s, I never had the impression that whites were much disturbed by guilt when it came to blacks. When I would stray into the wrong restaurant in pursuit of a hamburger, it didn't occur to me that the waitress was unduly troubled by guilt when she asked me to leave. I can see now that possibly she was, but then all I saw was her irritability at having to carry out so unpleasant a task. If there was guilt, it was mine for having made an imposition of myself. I can remember feeling a certain sympathy for such people, as if I was victimizing them by drawing them out of an innocent anonymity into the unasked-for role of racial policemen. Occasionally they came right out and asked me to feel sorry for them. A caddymaster at a country club told my brother and me that he was doing us a favor by not letting us caddy at this white club and that we should try to understand his position, "put yourselves in my shoes." Our color had brought this man anguish and, if a part of that anguish was guilt, it was not as immediate to me as my own guilt. I smiled at the man to let him know he shouldn't feel bad and then began my long walk home. Certainly I also judge him a coward, but in that era his cowardice was something I had to absorb.

2   In the 1960s, particularly the black-is-beautiful late 1960s, this absorption of another's cowardice was no longer necessary. The lines of moral power, like plates in the Earth, had shifted. White

218

guilt became so palpable you could see it on people. At the time what it looked like to my eyes was a remarkable loss of authority. And what whites lost in authority, blacks gained. You cannot feel guilty about anyone without giving away power to them. Suddenly, this huge vulnerability had opened up in whites and, as a black, you had the power to step right into it. In fact, black power all but demanded that you do so. What shocked me in the late 1960s, after the helplessness I had felt in the fifties, was that guilt had changed the nature of the white man's burden from the administration of inferiors to the uplift of equals—from the obligations of dominance to the urgencies of repentance.

I think what made the difference between the fifties and sixties, at least as far as white guilt was concerned, was that whites underwent an archetypal Fall. Because of the immense turmoil of the civil rights movement, and later the black-power movement, whites were confronted for more than a decade with their willingness to participate in, or comply with, the oppression of blacks, their indifference to human suffering and denigration, their capacity to abide evil for their own benefit and in the defiance of their own sacred principles. The 1964 Civil Rights Bill that bestowed equality under the law on blacks was also, in a certain sense, an admission of white guilt. Had white society not been wrong, there would have been no need for such a bill. In this bill the nation acknowledged its fallenness, its lack of racial innocence, and confronted the incriminating self-knowledge that it had rationalized for many years a flagrant injustice. Denial is a common way of handling guilt, but in the 1960s there was little will left for denial except in the most recalcitrant whites. With this defense lost there was really only one road back to innocence—through actions and policies that would bring redemption.

In the 1960s the need for white redemption from racial guilt became the most powerful, yet unspoken, element in America's social-policy-making process, first giving rise to the Great Society and then to a series of programs, policies, and laws that sought to make black equality and restitution a national mission. Once America could no longer deny its guilt, it went after redemption, or at least the look of redemption, and did so with a vengeance. Yet today, some twenty years later, study after study tells us that

by many measures the gap between blacks and whites is widening rather than narrowing. A University of Chicago study indicates that segregation is more entrenched in American cities today
than ever imagined. A National Research Council study notes the
"status of blacks relative to whites (in housing and education) has
stagnated or regressed since the early seventies." A follow-up to
the famous Kerner Commission Report warns that blacks are as
much at risk today of becoming a "nation within a nation" as we
were twenty years ago, when the original report was made.

5   I think the white need for redemption has contributed to this
tragic situation by shaping our policies regarding blacks in ways
that may deliver the look of innocence to society and its institutions but that do very little actually to uplift blacks. The specific
effect of this hidden need has been to bend social policy more
toward reparation for black oppression than toward the much
harder and more mundane work of black uplift and development. Rather than facilitate the development of blacks to achieve
parity with whites, these programs and policies—affirmative
action is a good example—have tended to give blacks special
entitlements that in many cases are of no use because blacks lack
the development that would put us in a position to take advantage of them. I think the reason there has been more entitlement
than development is (along with black power) the unacknowledged white need for redemption—not true redemption, which
would have concentrated policy on black development, but the
appearance of redemption, which requires only that society, in
the name of development, seem to be paying back its former
victims with preferences. One of the effects of entitlements, I
believe, has been to encourage in blacks a dependency both on
entitlements and on the white guilt that generates them. Even
when it serves ideal justice, bounty from another man's guilt
weakens. While this is not the only factor in black "stagnation"
and "regression," I believe it is one very potent factor.

6   It is easy enough to say that white guilt too often has the
effect of bending social policies in the wrong direction. But what
exactly is this guilt, and how does it work in American life?

7   I think white guilt, in its broad sense, springs from a knowledge of ill-gotten advantage. More precisely, it comes from the

juxtaposition of this knowledge with the inevitable gratitude one feels for being white rather than black in America. Given the moral instincts of human beings, it is all but impossible to enjoy an ill-gotten advantage, much less to feel at least secretly grateful for it, without consciously or unconsciously experiencing guilt. If, as Kierkegaard writes, "innocence is ignorance," then guilt must always involve knowledge. White Americans *know* that their historical advantage comes from the subjugation of an entire people. So, even for whites today for whom racism is anathema, there is no escape from the knowledge that makes for guilt. Racial guilt simply accompanies the condition of being white in America.

I do not believe that this guilt is a crushing anguish for 8 most whites, but I do believe it constitutes a continuing racial vulnerability—an openness to racial culpability—that is a thread in white life, sometimes felt, sometimes not, but ever present as a potential feeling. In the late 1960s almost any black could charge this vulnerability with enough current for a white person to feel it. I had a friend who had developed this activity into a sort of specialty. I don't think he meant to be mean, though certainly he was mean. I think he was, in that hyperbolic era, exhilarated by the discovery that his race, which had long been a liability, now gave him a certain edge—that white guilt was the true force behind black power. To feel this power he would sometimes set up what he called "race experiments." Once I watched him stop a white businessman in the men's room of a large hotel and convince him to increase his tip to the black attendant from one to twenty dollars.

My friend's tactic was very simple, even corny. Out of the 9 attendant's earshot he asked the man simply to look at the attendant, a frail, elderly, and very dark man in a starched white smock that made the skin on his neck and face look as leathery as a turtle's. He sat listlessly, pathetically, on a straight-backed chair next to a small table on which sat a stack of hand towels and a silver plate for tips. Since the attendant offered no service whatever beyond the handing out of towels, one could only conclude the hotel management offered his lowly presence as flattery to their patrons, as an opportunity for that easy noblesse oblige that could reassure even the harried and weary traveling salesman of his superior station. My friend was quick to make this point to the businessman and to say that no white man would do this job. But when the businessman put the single back in his wallet and took out a five, my friend only sneered. Did he understand the tragedy of a life spent this way, of what it must be like to earn one's paltry living as a symbol of inferiority? And did he realize that his privilege as an affluent white businessman (ironically he had just spent the day trying to sell a printing press to the Black Muslims for their newspaper *Mohammed Speaks*) was connected to the deprivation of this man and others like him?

10   But then my friend made a mistake that ended the game. In the heat of argument, which until then had only been playfully challenging, he inadvertently mentioned his father. This stopped the victim cold and his eyes turned inward. "What about your father?" the businessman asked. My friend replied, "He had a hard life, that's all." "How did he have a hard life?" the businessman asked. Now my friend was on the defensive. I knew he did not get along with his father, a bitter man who worked nights in a factory and demanded that the house be dark and silent all day. My friend blamed his father's bitterness on racism, but I knew he had not meant to exploit his own pain in this silly "experiment." Things had gotten too close to home, but he didn't know how to get out of the situation without losing face. Now, caught in his own trap, he did what he least wanted to do. He gave forth the rage he truly felt to a white stranger in a public men's room. "My father never had a chance," he said with the kind of anger that could easily turn to tears. "He never had a freakin' chance. Your father had all the goddamn chances, and you know he did. You sell printing presses to black people and make thousands and your father probably lives down in Fat City, Florida, all because you're white." On and on he went in this vein, using—against all that was honorable in him—his own profound racial pain to extract a flash of guilt from a white man he didn't even know.

11   He got more than a flash. The businessman was touched. His eyes became mournful, and finally he simply said, "You're right.

Your people got a raw deal." He took a twenty dollar bill from his wallet and walked over and dropped it in the old man's tip plate. When he was gone my friend and I could not look at the old man, nor could we look at each other.

It is obvious that this was a rather shameful encounter for 12 all concerned—my friend and I, as his silent accomplice, trading on our racial pain, tampering with a stranger for no reason, and the stranger then buying his way out of the situation for twenty dollars, a sum that was generous by one count and cheap by another. It was not an encounter of people but of historical grudges and guilts. Yet, when I think about it now twenty years later, I see that it had all the elements of a paradigm that I believe has been very much at the heart of racial policy-making in America since the 1960s.

My friend did two things that made this businessman vul- 13 nerable to his guilt—that brought his guilt into the situation as a force. First he put this man in touch with his own knowledge of his ill-gotten advantage as a white. The effect of this was to disallow the man any pretense of racial innocence, to let him know that, even if he was not the sort of white who used the word *nigger* around the dinner table, he still had reason to feel racial guilt. But, as disarming as this might have been, it was too abstract to do much more than crack open this man's vulnerability, to expose him to the logic of white guilt. This was the five-dollar, intellectual sort of guilt. The twenty dollars required something more visceral. In achieving this, the second thing my friend did was something he had not intended to do, something that ultimately brought him as much shame as he was doling out: He made a display of his own racial pain and anger. (What brought him shame was not the pain and anger, but his trading on them for what turned out to be a mere twenty bucks.) The effect of this display was to reinforce the man's knowledge of ill-gotten advantage, to give credibility and solidity to it by putting a face on it. Here was human testimony, a young black beside himself at the thought of his father's racially constricted life. The pain of one man evidenced the knowledge of the other. When the businessman listened to my friend's pain, his racial guilt—normally only one source of guilt lying dormant among others—was called out like a neglected debt he would finally have to settle. An ill-gotten advantage is not hard to bear—it can be marked up to fate—until it touches the genuine human pain it has brought into the world. This is the pain that hardens guilty knowledge.

14   Such knowledge is a powerful influence when it becomes conscious. What makes it so powerful is the element of fear that guilt always carries, the fear of what the guilty knowledge says about us. Guilt makes us afraid for ourselves, and thus generates as much self-preoccupation as concern for others. The nature of this preoccupation is always the redemption of innocence, the reestablishment of good feeling about oneself.

15   In this sense, the fear for the self that is buried in all guilt is a pressure toward selfishness. It can lead us to put our own need for innocence above our concern for the problem that made us feel guilt in the first place. But this fear for the self does not only inspire selfishness; it also becomes a pressure to *escape* the guilt-inducing situation. When selfishness and escapism are at work, we are no longer interested in the source of our guilt and, therefore, no longer concerned with an authentic redemption from it. Then we only want the look of redemption, the gesture of concern that will give us the appearance of innocence and escape from the situation. Obviously the businessman did not put twenty dollars in the tip plate because he thought it would uplift black Americans. He did it selfishly for the appearance of concern and for the escape it afforded him.

16   This is not to say that guilt is never the right motive for doing good works or showing concern, only that it is a very dangerous one because of its tendency to draw us into self-preoccupation and escapism. Guilt is a civilizing emotion when the fear for the self that it carries is contained—a containment that allows guilt to be more selfless and that makes genuine concern possible. I think this was the kind of guilt that, along with the other forces, made the 1964 Civil Rights Bill possible. But since then I believe too many of our social policies related to race have been shaped by the fearful underside of guilt.

17   Black power evoked white guilt and made it a force in American institutions, very much in the same way as my friend brought it to life in the businessman. Few people volunteer for guilt.

Usually others make us feel it. It was the expression of black anger and pain that hardened the guilty knowledge of white ill-gotten advantage. And black power—whether from militant fringe groups, the civil rights establishment, or big city political campaigns—knew exactly the kind of white guilt it was after. It wanted to trigger the kind of white guilt in which whites fear for their own decency and innocence; it wanted the guilt of white self-preoccupation and escapism. Always at the heart of black power, in whatever form, has been a profound anger at what was done to blacks and an equally profound feeling that there should be reparations. But a sober white guilt (in which fear for the self is still contained) seeks a strict fairness—the 1964 Civil Rights Bill that guaranteed equality under the law. It is of little value when one is after more than fairness. So black power made its mission to have whites fear for their innocence, to feel a visceral guilt from which they would have to seek a more profound redemption. In such redemption was the possibility of black reparation. Black power upped the ante on white guilt.

With black power, all of the elements of the hidden paradigm 18 that shape America's race-related social policy were in place. Knowledge of ill-gotten advantage could now be shown and deep-ened by black power into the sort of guilt from which institutions could only redeem themselves by offering more than fairness—by offering forms of reparation and compensation for past injustice. I believe this bent our policies toward racial entitlements at the expense of racial development. In 1964, one of the assurances Senator Hubert Humphrey and others had to give Congress to get the landmark Civil Rights Bill passed was that the bill would not in any way require employers to use racial preferences to rectify racial imbalances. But this was before the explosion of black power in the late 1960s, before the hidden paradigm was set in motion. After black power, racial preferences became the order of the day.

If this paradigm brought blacks entitlements, it also brought 19 the continuation of the most profound problem in American society, the invisibility of blacks as a people. The white guilt that this paradigm elicits is the kind of guilt that preoccupies whites with their own innocence and pressures them toward escapism—twenty dollars in the plate and out the door. With this guilt, as opposed to the contained guilt of genuine concern, whites tend to see only their own need for quick redemption. Blacks then become a means to this redemption and, as such, they must be seen as generally "less than" others. Their needs are "special," "unique," "different." They are seen exclusively along the dimension of their victimization, so that they become "different" people with whom whites can negotiate entitlements but never fully see as people like themselves. Guilt that preoccupies people with their own innocence blinds them to those who make them feel guilty. This, of course, is not racism, and yet it has the same effect as racism since it makes blacks something of a separate species for whom normal standards and values do not automatically apply.

20   Nowhere is this more evident today than in American universities. At some of America's most elite universities administrators have granted concessions in response to black student demands (black power) that all but sanction racial separatism on campus—black "theme" dorms, black student unions, black yearbooks, homecoming dances, and so forth. I don't believe administrators sincerely believe in these separatist concessions. Most of them are liberals who see racial separatism as wrong. But black student demands pull administrators into the paradigm of self-preoccupied white guilt, whereby they seek a quick redemption by offering special entitlements that go beyond fairness. As a result, black students become all but invisible to them. Though blacks have the lowest grade point average of any racial group in American universities, administrators never sit down with them and "demand" in kind that black students bring their grades up to par. The paradigm of white guilt makes the real problems of black students secondary to the need for white redemption. It also cuts administrators off from their own values, which would most certainly discourage racial separatism and encourage higher academic performance for black students. Lastly, it makes for escapist policies. There is no difference between giving black students a separate lounge and leaving twenty dollars in the tip plate on the way out the door.

1990

Where Have All the Parents Gone?

Barbara Dafoe Whitehead

"Invest in kids," George Bush mused during his 1988 presidential 1
campaign, "I like it." Apparently so do others. A growing number
of corporate CEOs and educators, elected officials and child-welfare
advocates have embraced the same language. "Invest in kids" is the
bumper sticker for an important new cause, aptly tagged the *kids as
capital* argument. It runs as follows:

America's human capital comes in two forms: The active 2
work force and the prospective work force. The bulk of tomorrow's workers are today's children, of course. So children make
up much of the stockpile of America's potential human capital.

If we look at them as tomorrow's workers, we begin to appre- 3
ciate our stake in today's children. They will determine when we
can retire, how well we can live in retirement, how generous our
health insurance will be, how strong our social safety net, how
orderly our society. What's more, today's children will determine how successfully we compete in the global economy. They
will be going head-to-head against Japanese, Korean, and West
German children.

Unfortunately, American children aren't prepared to run the 4
race, let alone win it. Many are illiterate, undernourished,
impaired, unskilled, poor. Consider the children who started first
grade in 1986: 14 percent were illegitimate; 15 percent were physically or emotionally handicapped; 15 percent spoke another
language other than English; 28 percent were poor; and fully
40 percent could be expected to live in a single-parent home
before they reached eighteen. Given falling birth rates, this future
work force is small—all the more reason to worry about its poor
quality. So "invest in kids" is not the cry of the soft-hearted altru-
ist but the call of the hardheaded realist.

Kids as capital has caught on because it responds to a broad set 5
of national concerns. Whether one is worried about the rise of the
underclass, the decline of the family, our standing in the global
economy, the nation's level of educational performance, or intergenerational conflict, kids as capital seems to offer an answer.

6   Further, *kids as capital* offers the rationale for a new coalition for child welfare programs. The argument reaches beyond the community of traditional children's advocates and draws business into the child-saving fold. American corporations clearly have a stake in tomorrow's work force as they don't have in today's children. *Kids as capital* gives the tough-minded, fifty-five-year-old CEO a reason to "care" about the eight-year-old, Hispanic school girl.

7   Nevertheless, the argument left unchallenged could easily become yet another "feel-good" formula that doesn't work. Worse, it could end up betraying those it seeks to save—the nation's children.

8   First, *kids as capital* departs from a classic American vision of the future. Most often, our history has been popularly viewed as progressive, with each generation breaking with and improving on the past. As an immigrant nation, we have always measured our progress through the progress of our children; they have been the bearers of the dream.

9   *Kids as capital* turns this optimistic view on its head. It conjures up a picture of a dark and disorderly future. Essentially, kids as capital is dystopic—closer to the spirit of *Blade Runner* and *Black Rain* than *Wizard of Oz* or *It's a Wonderful Life*. Children, in this view, do not bear the dream. They carry the seeds of our destruction. In short, *kids as capital* plays on our fears, rather than our hopes. It holds out the vision of a troubled future in order to secure a safer and more orderly present.

10   There is something troubling, too, in such an instrumental view of children. To define them narrowly as tomorrow's wonders is to strip them of their full status as humans, as children: Kids can't be kids; they can only be embryonic workers. And treating *kids as capital* makes it easier to measure them solely through IQ tests, class standing, SAT scores, drop-out ratios, physical fitness tests. This leaves no place in the society for the slow starter, the handicapped, the quirky, and the nonconforming.

11   Yet *kids as capital* has an even more serious flaw. It evades the central fact of life for American children: They have parents.

12   As we all know, virtually every child in America grows up in a family with one or more parents. Parents house children. Parents feed children. Parents clothe children. Parents nurture

and protect children. Parents instruct children in everything from using a fork to driving a car. To be sure, there have been vast changes in family life, and, increasingly, parents must depend on teachers, doctors, day-care workers, and technology to help care for and educate their children. Even so, these changes haven't altered one fundamental fact: In American society, parents still bear the primary responsibility for the material and spiritual welfare of children. As our teachers and counselors and politicians keep reminding us, everything begins at home. So, if today's children are in trouble, it's because today's parents are in trouble.

As recently as a dozen years ago, it was the central argument 13 of an ambitious report by the Carnegie Council on Children. The Council put it plainly: "The best way to help children tomorrow is to support parents today." Yet, that view has been lost. The *kids as capital* argument suppresses the connection between parents and children. It imagines that we can improve the standing of children without improving the standing of the parents. In the new rhetoric, it is hard even to find the word "parent." Increasingly, kids are portrayed as standing alone out there somewhere, cosmically parent-free.

As a result, *kids as capital* ignores rather than addresses one of 14 the most important changes in American life: The decline in the power and standing of the nation's parents.

Only a generation ago, parents stood at the center of society. 15 First of all, there were so many of them—fully half the nation's households in 1960 were parent households with one or more children under eighteen. Moreover, parents looked alike—Dad worked and Mom stayed at home. And parents marched through the stages of childbearing and child rearing in virtual lockstep: Most couples who married in the 1940s and 1950s finished having their 3.2 children by the time they were in their late twenties.

Their demographic dominance meant two things: First, it 16 made for broad common ground in child rearing. Parents could do a great deal to support each other in raising the new generation. They could, and did, create a culture hospitable to children. Secondly, it made for political clout. When so many adults were parents and so many parents were part of an expanding consumer economy, private and public interests converged. The concerns of parents—housing, health, education—easily found their way into the national agenda. Locally, too, parents were dominant. In some postwar suburbs like Levittown, Pennsylvania, three-quarters of all residents were either parents or children under ten. Not surprisingly, there was little dissent when it came to building a new junior high or establishing a summer recreation program or installing a new playground. What's more, parents and kids drove the consumer economy. Every time they bought a pair of sneakers or a new bike, they were acting in the nation's best interest.

17   Behind this, of course, lurked a powerful pronatal ideology. Parenthood was the definitive credential of adulthood. More than being married, more than getting a job, it was having a child that baptized you as an adult in postwar America. In survey after survey, postwar parents rated children above marriage itself as the greatest reward of private life. For a generation forced to make personal sacrifices during the Depression and the war, having children and pursuing a private life represented a new kind of freedom.

18   By the 1970s, parents no longer enjoyed so central a place in the society. To baby boom children, postwar family life seemed suffocating and narrow. Women, in particular, wanted room to breathe. The rights movements of the sixties and seventies overturned the pronatal ideology, replacing it with an ideology of choice. Adults were free to choose among many options: Single, married, or divorced; career-primary or career-secondary; parent, stepparent, or child-free.

19   Thus, parenthood lost its singular status. It no longer served as the definitive credential of maturity and adult achievement. In fact, as careers and personal fulfillment beckoned, parenthood seemed just the opposite: A serious limitation on personal growth and success. As Gloria Steinem put it, "I either gave birth to someone else or I gave birth to myself."

20   As the pronatal ideology vanished, so did the close connection between private families and the public interest. Raising children was no longer viewed as a valuable contribution to the society, an activity that boosted the economy, built citizen participation, and increased the nation's confidence in the future. Instead, it became one option among many. No longer a moral imperative, child rearing was just another "lifestyle choice."

Viewed this way, raising children looked like an economic dis- 21
aster. Starting out, parents had to shell out $3,000 for basic prenatal
care and maternity costs; $3,000–$5,000 per child for day care; and
$2,500 for the basic baby basket of goods and services. Crib-to-
college costs for middle-class Americans could run as high as
$135,000 per child. And, increasingly, the period of economic
dependency for children stretched well beyond age eighteen. College
tuitions and start-up subsidies for the new college graduate became
part of the economic burden of parenthood. In an ad campaign,
Manufacturers Hanover Trust gave prospective parents fair warning: "If you want a bundle of joy; you'll need a bundle of money."

Hard-pressed younger Americans responded to these new 22
realities in several ways. Some simply chose not to have children.
Others decided to have one or two, but only after they had a good
job and solid prospects. Gradually, the number of parent households in the nation declined from one-half to one-third, and
America faced a birth dearth.

For those who chose the parent option, there was only one way 23
to face up to the new economic pressures of child rearing: Work
longer and harder outside the home. For all but the extremely well-
off, a second income became essential. But in struggling to pay the
bills, parents seemed to be short-changing their children in another
way. They weren't taking their moral responsibilities seriously
enough. They weren't spending enough time with their kids. They
weren't reading to the children or playing with the kids or super-
vising homework. And, most important, they weren't teaching
good values.

This emerging critique marked a dramatic change in the way 24
society viewed parents. In the postwar period, the stereotypical
parent was self-sacrificing, responsible, caring, attentive—an
impossible standard, to be sure, but one that lent enormous popular support and approval to adults engaged in the messy and difficult work of raising children. Cruel, abusive, self-absorbed
parents might exist, but the popular culture failed to acknowledge
them. It was not until parents began to lose their central place in
the society that this flattering image faded. Then, quite rapidly, the
dominant image of The Good Parent gave way to a new and
equally powerful image—the image of The Bad Parent.

25   The shift occurred in two stages. The first-stage critique emerged in the seventies and focused on an important new figure: The working mother. Working mothers were destroying their children and the family, conservative critics charged. They weren't feeding kids wholesome meals, they weren't taking the kids to church, they weren't serving as moral exemplars. Liberals sided with working mothers, but conceded that they were struggling with some new and difficult issues: Was day care as good as mother care? Was quality time good enough? Were the rewards of twelve-hour workdays great enough to make up for the loss of sleep and leisure-time? Where did the mother of a feverish child belong—at the crib or at her desk?

26   On the whole, the first-stage critique was a sympathetic critique. In its view, parents might be affected by stress and guilt, but they weren't yet afflicted by serious pathology. After all, in the seventies, the nation's most suspect drug was laetrile, not crack or ice. Divorce was still viewed as a healthy alternative to an unhappy family life. But as the eighties began, a darker image of parents appeared. In the second-stage critique, . . . parents became toxic.

27   Day after day, throughout the eighties, Americans confronted an ugly new reality. Parents were hurting and murdering their children. Day after day, the newspapers brought yet another story of a child abandoned or battered. Day after day, the local news told of a child sexually abused by a father or a stepfather or a mother's boyfriend. Week by week, the national media brought us into courtrooms where photographs of battered children were held up to the camera. The sheer volume of stories suggested an epidemic of historic proportion. In even the most staid publications, the news was sensational. *The New York Times* carried bizarre stories usually found only in tabloids: A father who tortured his children for years; a mother who left her baby in a suitcase in a building she then set on fire; parents who abandoned babies dead or alive, in toilets, dumpsters, and alleyways.

28   Drug use among parents was one clear cause of abuse. And, increasingly, child abuse and drug abuse were linked in the most direct way possible. Pregnant women were battering their children in the womb, delivering drugs through their umbilical cords. Nightly images of crack-addicted babies in neonatal units

destroyed any lingering public sympathy for mothers of the under-class. And as the highly publicized Joel Steinberg case made clear, middle-class parents, too, took drugs and killed babies. Even those parents who occasionally indulged were causing their children harm. The Partnership for Drug-Free America ran ads asking: "With millions of parents doing drugs, is it any wonder their kids are too?"

More than drugs, it was divorce that lay at the heart of middle-class parental failure. It wasn't the crackhouse but the courthouse that was the scene of their collapse. Parents engaged in bitter custody battles. Parents kidnapped their own children. Parents used children as weapons against each other or simply walked away from their responsibilities. In an important new study on the long-term effects of divorce, Judith Wallerstein challenged the earlier notion that divorce is healthy for kids. She studied middle-class families for fifteen years after divorce and came up with some startling findings: Almost half of the children in the study entered adulthood as worried, underachieving, self-deprecating, and some-times angry young men and women; one in four experienced a severe and enduring drop in their standard of living; three in five felt rejected by at least one parent. Her study concluded: "Divorce is almost always more devastating for children than for their parents. . . . [W]hile divorce can rescue a parent from an intolerable situation, it can fail to rescue the children." 29

As a group, today's parents have been portrayed as selfish and uncaring: Yuppie parents abandon the children to the au pair; working parents turn their kids over to the mall and the video arcade; single parents hang a key around their kids' necks and a list of emergency numbers on the refrigerator. Even in the health-iest families, parents fail to put their children first. 30

The indictment of parents is pervasive. In a survey by the Carnegie Foundation, 90 percent of a national sample of public school teachers say a lack of parental support is a problem in their classrooms. Librarians gathered at a national convention to draft a new policy to deal with the problem of parents who send unat-tended children to the library after school. Daycare workers com-plain to Ann Landers that all too often parents hand over children with empty stomachs and full diapers. Everywhere, parents are flunking the most basic tests. 31

32   Declining demographically, hard-pressed economically, and disarrayed politically, parents have become part of the problem. For proponents of the *kids as capital* argument, the logic is clear: Why try to help parents—an increasingly marginal and unsympathetic bunch—when you can rescue their children?

33   To blame parents for larger social changes is nothing new. In the past, child-saving movements have depended on building a public consensus that certain parents have failed. Child reformers in the Progressive Era, for example, were able to expand the scope of public sector responsibility for the welfare of children by exploiting mainstream fears about immigrant parents and their child-rearing practices. But what is new is the sense that the majority of parents—up and down the social ladder—are failing. Even middle-class parents, once solid, dependable caretakers of the next generation, don't seem to be up to the job.

34   By leaving parents out of the picture, *kids as capital* conjures up the image of our little workers struggling against the little workers of Germany and the little workers of Japan. But this picture is obviously false. For the little workers of Germany and Japan have parents too. The difference is that their parents are strongly valued and supported by the society for their contributions *as parents.* We won't be facing up to reality until we are ready to pit our parents against their parents, and thus our family policy against theirs.

1990

If Hitler Asked You to Electrocute a Stranger, Would You? Probably

Philip Meyer

1 In the beginning, Stanley Milgram was worried about the Nazi problem. He doesn't worry much about the Nazis anymore. He worries about you and me, and, perhaps, himself a little bit too.

2   Stanley Milgram is a social psychologist, and when he began his career at Yale University in 1960 he had a plan to prove,

scientifically, that Germans are different. The Germans-are-different hypothesis has been used by historians, such as William L. Shirer, to explain the systematic destruction of the Jews by the Third Reich.

The appealing thing about this theory is that it makes those 3 of us who are not Germans feel better about the whole business. Obviously, you and I are not Hitler, and it seems equally obvious that we would never do Hitler's dirty work for him. But now, because of Stanley Milgram, we are compelled to wonder. Milgram developed a laboratory experiment which provided a systematic way to measure obedience. His plan was to try it out in New Haven on Americans and then go to Germany and try it out on Germans. He was strongly motivated by scientific curiosity, but there was also some moral content in his decision to pursue this line of research, which was, in turn, colored by his own Jewish background. If he could show that Germans are more obedient than Americans, he could then vary the conditions of the experiment and try to find out just what it is that makes some people more obedient than others. With this understanding, the world might, conceivably, be just a little bit better.

But he never took his experiment to Germany. He never took 4 it any farther than Bridgeport. The first finding, also the most unexpected and disturbing finding, was that we Americans are an obedient people: Not blindly obedient, and not blissfully obedient, just obedient. "I found so much obedience," says Milgram softly, a little sadly, "I hardly saw the need for taking the experiment to Germany."

There is something of the theatre director in Milgram, and his 5 technique, which he learned from one of the old masters in experimental psychology, Solomon Asch, is to stage a play with every line rehearsed, every prop carefully selected, and everybody an actor except one person. That one person is the subject of the experiment. The subject, of course, does not know he is in a play. He thinks he is in real life.

The experiment worked like this: If you were an innocent 6 subject in Milgram's melodrama, you read an ad in the newspaper or received one in the mail asking for volunteers for an educational experiment. The job would take about an hour and pay $4.50. So you make an appointment and go to an old Romanesque stone structure on High Street with the imposing name of The Yale Interaction Laboratory. It looks something like a broadcasting studio. Inside, you meet a young, crew-cut man in a laboratory coat who says he is Jack Williams, the experimenter. There is another citizen, fiftyish, Irish face, an accountant, a little overweight, and very mild and harmless-looking. This other citizen seems nervous and plays with his hat while the two of you sit in chairs side by side and are told that the $4.50 checks are yours no matter what happens. Then you listen to Jack Williams explain the experiment.

7   It is about learning, says Jack Williams in a quiet, knowledgeable way. Science does not know much about the conditions under which people learn and this experiment is to find out about negative reinforcement. Negative reinforcement is getting punished when you do something wrong, as opposed to positive reinforcement which is getting rewarded when you do something right. The negative reinforcement in this case is electric shock.

8   Then Jack Williams takes two pieces of paper, puts them in a hat, and shakes them up. One piece of paper is supposed to say, "Teacher" and the other, "Learner." Draw one and you will see which you will be. The mild-looking accountant draws one, holds it close to his vest like a poker player, looks at it, and says, "Learner." You look at yours. It says; "Teacher." You do not know that the drawing is rigged, and both slips say "Teacher." The experimenter beckons to the mild-mannered "learner."

9   "Want to step right in here and have a seat, please?" he says. "You can leave your coat on the back of that chair . . . roll up your right sleeve, please. Now what I want to do is strap down your arms to avoid excessive movement on your part during the experiment. This electrode is connected to the shock generator in the next room.

10   "And this electrode paste," he says, squeezing some stuff out of a plastic bottle and putting it on the man's arm, "is to provide a good contact and to avoid a blister or burn. Are there any questions now before we go into the next room?"

11   You don't have any, but the strapped-in "learner" does.

"I do think I should say this," says the learner. "About two 12
years ago, I was at the veterans' hospital . . . they detected a heart
condition. Nothing serious, but as long as I'm having these shocks,
how strong are they—how dangerous are they?"

Williams, the experimenter, shakes his head casually. "Oh, 13
no," he says. "Although they may be painful, they're not dangerous. Anything else?"

Nothing else. And so you play the game. The game is for you 14
to read a series of word pairs: For example, blue-girl, nice-day,
fat-neck. When you finish the list, you read just the first word in
each pair and then a multiple-choice list of four other words,
including the second word of the pair. The learner, from his remote,
strapped-in position, pushes one of four switches to indicate which
of the four answers he thinks is the right one. If he gets it right,
nothing happens and you go on to the next one. If he gets it
wrong, you push a switch that buzzes and gives him an electric
shock. And then you go to the next word. You start with 15 volts
and increase the number of volts by 15 for each wrong answer.
The control board goes from 15 volts on one end to 450 volts on
the other. So that you know what you are doing, you get a test
shock yourself, at 45 volts. It hurts. To further keep you aware of
what you are doing to that man in there, the board has verbal
descriptions of the shock levels, ranging from "Slight Shock" at
the left-hand side, through "Intense Shock" in the middle, to
"Danger: Severe Shock" toward the far right. Finally, at the very
end, under 435- and 450-volt switches, there are three ambiguous
X's. If, at any point, you hesitate, Mr. Williams calmly tells you to
go on. If you still hesitate, he tells you again.

Except for some terrifying details, which will be explained in 15
a moment, this is the experiment. The object is to find the shock
level at which you disobey the experimenter and refuse to pull
the switch.

When Stanley Milgram first wrote this script, he took it to four- 16
teen Yale psychology majors and asked them what they thought
would happen. He put it this way: Out of one hundred persons in
the teacher's predicament, how would their breakoff points be distributed along the 15-to-450-volt scale? They thought a few would
break off very early, most would quit someplace in the middle and

a few would go all the way to the end. The highest estimate of the number out of one hundred who would go all the way to the end was three. Milgram then informally polled some of his fellow scholars in the psychology department. They agreed that very few would go to the end. Milgram thought so too.

17 "I'll tell you quite frankly," he says, "before I began this experiment, before any shock generator was built, I thought that most people would break off at 'Strong Shock' or 'Very Strong Shock.' You would get only a very, very small proportion of people going out to the end of the shock generator, and they would constitute a pathological fringe."

18 In his pilot experiments, Milgram used Yale students as subjects. Each of them pushed the shock switches, one by one, all the way to the end of the board.

19 So he rewrote the script to include some protests from the learner. At first, they were mild, gentlemanly, Yalie protests, but, "it didn't seem to have as much effect as I thought it would or should," Milgram recalls. "So we had more violent protestation on the part of the person getting the shock. All of the time, of course, what we were trying to do was not to create a macabre situation, but simply to generate disobedience. And that was one of the first findings. This was not only a technical deficiency of the experiment, that we didn't get disobedience. It really was the first finding: That obedience would be much greater than we had assumed it would be and disobedience would be much more difficult than we had assumed."

20 As it turned out, the situation did become rather macabre. The only meaningful way to generate disobedience was to have the victim protest with great anguish, noise, and vehemence. The protests were tape-recorded so that all the teachers ordinarily would hear the same sounds and nuances, and they started with a grunt at 75 volts, proceeded through a "Hey, that really hurts," at 125 volts, got desperate with, "I can't stand the pain, don't do that," at 180 volts, reached complaints of heart trouble at 195, an agonized scream at 285, a refusal to answer at 315, and only heartrending, ominous silence after that.

21 Still, sixty-five percent of the subjects, twenty- to fifty-year-old American males, everyday, ordinary people, like you and me,

obediently kept pushing those levers in the belief that they were shocking the mild-mannered learner, whose name was Mr. Wallace, and who was chosen for the role because of his innocent appearance, all the way up to 450 volts.

Milgram was now getting enough disobedience so that he had something he could measure. The next step was to vary the circumstances to see what would encourage or discourage obedience. 22

He put the learner in the same room with the teacher. He stopped strapping the learner's hand down. He rewrote the script so that at 150 volts the learner took his hand off the shock plate and declared that he wanted out of the experiment. He rewrote the script some more so that the experimenter then told the teacher to grasp the learner's hand and physically force it down on the plate to give Mr. Wallace his unwanted electric shock. 23

"I had the feeling that very few people would go on at that point, if any," Milgram says. "I thought that would be the limit of obedience that you would find in the laboratory." 24

It wasn't. 25

Although seven years have now gone by, Milgram still remembers the first person to walk into the laboratory in the newly rewritten script. He was a construction worker, a very short man. "He was so small," says Milgram, "that when he sat on the chair in front of the shock generator, his feet didn't reach the floor. When the experimenter told him to push the victim's hand down and give the shock, he turned to the experimenter, and he turned to the victim, his elbow went up, he fell down on the hand of the victim, his feet kind of tugged to one side, and he said, 'Like this, boss?' Zzumph!" 26

The experiment was played out to its bitter end. Milgram tried it with forty different subjects. And thirty percent of them obeyed the experimenter and kept on obeying. 27

"The protests of the victim were strong and vehement, he was screaming his guts out, he refused to participate, and you had to physically struggle with him in order to get his hand down on the shock generator," Milgram remembers. But twelve out of forty did it. 28

Milgram took his experiment out of New Haven. Not to Germany, just twenty miles down the road to Bridgeport. Maybe, 29 he reasoned, the people obeyed because of the prestigious setting of Yale University.

30   The new setting was a suite of three rooms in a run-down office building in Bridgeport. The only identification was a sign with a fictitious name: "Research Associates of Bridgeport." Questions about professional connections got only vague answers about "research for industry."

31   Obedience was less in Bridgeport. Forty-eight percent of the subjects stayed for the maximum shock, compared to sixty-five percent at Yale. But this was enough to prove that far more than Yale's prestige was behind the obedient behavior.

32   For more than seven years now, Stanley Milgram has been trying to figure out what makes ordinary American citizens so obedient. The most obvious answer—that people are mean, nasty, brutish and sadistic—won't do. The subjects who gave the shocks to Mr. Wallace to the end of the board did not enjoy it. They groaned, protested, fidgeted, argued, and in some cases, were seized by fits of nervous, agitated giggling.

33   "They even try to get out of it," says Milgram, "but they are somehow engaged in something from which they cannot liberate themselves. They are locked into a structure, and they do not have the skills or inner resources to disengage themselves."

34   Milgram's theory assumes that people behave in two different operating modes as different as ice and water. He does not rely on Freud or sex or toilet-training hang-ups for this theory. All he says is that ordinarily we operate in a state of autonomy, which means we pretty much have and assert control over what we do. But in certain circumstances, we operate under what Milgram calls a state of agency (after agent, *n* . . . one who acts for or in the place of another by authority from him; a substitute; a deputy— *Webster's Collegiate Dictionary*). A state of agency, to Milgram, is nothing more than a frame of mind.

35   "There's nothing bad about it, there's nothing good about it," he says. "It's a natural circumstance of living with other people. . . . I think of a state of agency as a real transformation of a person; if a person has different properties when he's in that state, just as water can turn to ice under certain conditions of temperature, a person can move to the state of mind that I call agency . . . the

critical thing is that you see yourself as the instrument of the execution of another person's wishes. You do not see yourself as acting on your own. And there's a real transformation, a real change of properties of the person."

So, for most subjects in Milgram's laboratory experiments, 36 the act of giving Mr. Wallace his painful shock was necessary, even though unpleasant, and besides they were doing it on behalf of somebody else and it was for science.

Stanley Milgram has his problems, too. He believes that in 37 the laboratory situation, he would not have shocked Mr. Wallace. His professional critics reply that in his real-life situation he has done the equivalent. He has placed innocent and naïve subjects under great emotional strain and pressure in selfish obedience to his quest for knowledge. When you raise this issue with Milgram, he has an answer ready. There is, he explains patiently, a critical difference between his naïve subjects and the man in the electric chair. The man in the electric chair (in the mind of the naïve subject) is helpless, strapped in. But the naïve subject is free to go at any time.

Immediately after he offers this distinction, Milgram antici- 38 pates the objection.

"It's quite true," he says, "that this is almost a philosophic 39 position, because we have learned that some people are psychologically incapable of disengaging themselves. But that doesn't relieve them of the moral responsibility."

The parallel is exquisite. "The tension problem was unex- 40 pected," says Milgram in his defense. But he went on anyway. The naïve subjects didn't expect the screaming protests from the strapped-in learner. But they went on.

"I had to make a judgment," says Milgram. "I had to ask 41 myself, was this harming the person or not? My judgment is that it was not. Even in the extreme cases, I wouldn't say that permanent damage results."

Sound familiar? "The shocks may be painful," the experi- 42 menter kept saying, "but they're not dangerous."

After the series of experiments was completed, Milgram sent 43 a report of the results to his subjects and a questionnaire, asking whether they were glad or sorry to have been in the experiment.

Eighty-three and seven-tenths percent said they were glad and only 1.3 percent were sorry; 15 percent were neither sorry nor glad. However, Milgram could not be sure at the time of the experiment that only 1.3 percent would be sorry.

44   Kurt Vonnegut Jr. put one paragraph in the preface to *Mother Night*, in 1966, which pretty much says it for the people with their fingers on the shock-generator switches, for you and me, and maybe even for Milgram. "If I'd been born in Germany," Vonnegut said, "I suppose I would have *been* a Nazi, bopping Jews and gypsies and Poles around, leaving boots sticking out of snow banks, warming myself with my sweetly virtuous insides. So it goes."

45   Just so. One thing that happened to Milgram back in New Haven during the days of the experiment was that he kept running into people he'd watched from behind the one-way glass. It gave him a funny feeling, seeing those people going about their everyday business in New Haven and knowing what they would do to Mr. Wallace if ordered to. Now that his research results are in and you've thought about it, you can get this funny feeling too. You don't need one-way glass. A glance in your own mirror may serve just as well.

1970

The Arrow of Time

K. C. Cole

1   It was about two months ago when I realized that entropy was getting the better of me. On the same day my car broke down (again), my refrigerator conked out and I learned that I needed root canal work in my right rear tooth. The windows in the bedroom were still leaking every time it rained and my son's baby sitter was still failing to show up every time I really needed her. My hair was turning gray and my typewriter was wearing out. The house needed paint and I needed glasses. My son's sneakers were developing holes and I was developing a deep sense of futility.

After all, what was the point of spending half of Saturday at ₂ the Laundromat if the clothes were dirty all over again the following Friday?

Disorder, alas, is the natural order of things in the universe. ₃ There is even a precise measure of the amount of disorder, called entropy. Unlike almost every other physical property (motion, gravity, energy), entropy does not work both ways. It can only increase. Once it's created it can never be destroyed. The road to disorder is a one-way street.

Because of its unnerving irreversibility, entropy has been ₄ called the arrow of time. We all understand this instinctively. Children's rooms, left on their own, tend to get messy, not neat. Wood rots, metal rusts, people wrinkle and flowers wither. Even mountains wear down; even the nuclei of atoms decay. In the city we see entropy in the rundown subways and worn-out sidewalks and torn-down buildings, in the increasing disorder of our lives. We know, without asking, what is old. If we were suddenly to see the paint jump back on an old building, we would know that something was wrong. If we saw an egg unscramble itself and jump back into its shell, we would laugh in the same way we laugh at a movie run backward.

Entropy is no laughing matter, however, because with every ₅ increase in entropy energy is wasted and opportunity is lost. Water flowing down a mountainside can be made to do some useful work on its way. But once all the water is at the same level it can work no more. That is entropy. When my refrigerator was working, it kept all the cold air ordered in one part of the kitchen and warmer air in another. Once it broke down the warm and cold mixed into a lukewarm mess that allowed my butter to melt, my milk to rot and my frozen vegetables to decay.

Of course the energy is not really lost, but it has diffused and ₆ dissipated into a chaotic caldron of randomness that can do us no possible good. Entropy is chaos. It is loss of purpose.

People are often upset by the entropy they seem to see in the ₇ haphazardness of their own lives. Buffeted about like so many molecules in my tepid kitchen, they feel that they have lost their sense of direction, that they are wasting youth and opportunity at every turn. It is easy to see entropy in marriages, when the

partners are too preoccupied to patch small things up, almost
guaranteeing that they will fall apart. There is much entropy in
the state of our country, in the relationships between nations—
lost opportunities to stop the avalanche of disorders that seems
ready to swallow us all.

8   Entropy is not inevitable everywhere, however. Crystals
and snowflakes and galaxies are islands of incredibly ordered
beauty in the midst of random events. If it was not for exceptions to entropy, the sky would be black and we would be able
to see where the stars spend their days; it is only because air
molecules in the atmosphere cluster in ordered groups that the
sky is blue.

9   The most profound exception to entropy is the creation of life.
A seed soaks up some soil and some carbon and some sunshine and
some water and arranges it into a rose. A seed in the womb takes
some oxygen and pizza and milk and transforms it into a baby.

10   The catch is that it takes a lot of energy to produce a baby. It
also takes energy to make a tree. The road to disorder is all downhill but the road to creation takes work. Though combating
entropy is possible, it also has its price. That's why it seems so
hard to get ourselves together, so easy to let ourselves fall apart.

11   Worse, creating order in one corner of the universe always
creates more disorder somewhere else. We create ordered energy
from oil and coal at the price of the entropy of smog.

12   I recently took up playing the flute again after an absence of
several months. As the uneven vibrations screeched through the
house, my son covered his ears and said, "Mom, what's wrong
with your flute?" Nothing was wrong with my flute, of course. It
was my ability to play it that had atrophied, or entropied, as the
case may be. The only way to stop that process was to practice
every day, and sure enough my tone improved, though only at
the price of constant work. Like anything else, abilities deteriorate
when we stop applying our energies to them.

13   That's why entropy is depressing. It seems as if just breaking
even is an uphill fight. There's a good reason that this should be
so. The mechanics of entropy are a matter of chance. Take any ice
cold air molecule milling around my kitchen. The chances that it
will wander in the direction of my refrigerator at any point are

exactly 50-50. The chances that it will wander away from my refrigerator are also 50-50. But take billions of warm and cold molecules mixed together, and the chances that all the cold ones will wander toward the refrigerator and all the warm ones will wander away from it are virtually nil.

Entropy wins not because order is impossible but because 14 there are always so many more paths toward disorder than toward order. There are so many more different ways to do a sloppy job than a good one, so many more ways to make a mess than to clean it up. The obstacles and accidents in our lives almost guarantee that constant collisions will bounce us on to random paths, get us off the track. Disorder is the path of least resistance, the easy but not the inevitable road.

Like so many others, I am distressed by the entropy I see 15 around me today. I am afraid of the randomness of international events, of the lack of common purpose in the world; I am terrified that it will lead into the ultimate entropy of nuclear war. I am upset that I could not in the city where I live send my child to a public school; that people are unemployed and inflation is out of control; that tensions between sexes and races seem to be increasing again; that relationships everywhere seem to be falling apart.

Social institutions—like atoms and stars—decay if energy is 16 not added to keep them ordered. Friendships and families and economies all fall apart unless we constantly make an effort to keep them working and well oiled. And far too few people, it seems to me, are willing to contribute consistently to those efforts.

Of course, the more complex things are, the harder it is. If 17 there were only a dozen or so air molecules in my kitchen, it would be likely—if I waited a year or so—that at some point the six coldest ones would congregate inside the freezer. But the more factors in the equation—the more players in the game—the less likely it is that their paths will coincide in an orderly way. The more pieces in the puzzle, the harder it is to put back together once order is disturbed. "Irreversibility," said a physicist, "is the price we pay for complexity."

1982

Shattered Sudan

Paul Salopek

1   The oldest civil war in the world is being fought, on one side, by men who wander like demented hospital orderlies across the primordial wastes of Africa.

2   I follow them one hot morning as they flee a government ambush in the oil fields of southern Sudan. One of their comrades has just been shot dead, his body abandoned on a parched savanna that hides nearly 20 billion dollars' worth of low-sulfur crude. We retreat for hours under a scalding sun, crossing in the process a vast, cauterized plain of cracked mud. I pause a moment to watch them: an ant-like column of rebels dressed in bizarre homemade uniforms of green cotton smocks and white plastic slippers, limping into the heat waves of distance. Five casualties bounce in stretchers. They suffer their bullet wounds in silence. A boy marching in front balances a car battery on his head. He is the radio operator's assistant. Every few hundred yards he puts the battery down and empties blood out of a shoe.

3   When we finally reach a tree line, the fighters strip off their clothes and jump into a bog. The water stinks. It is infested with larvae of guinea worms, which, once ingested, burrow painfully through the body to the legs, and are extracted by making a small incision; you reel the worm out slowly, day after day, by winding it on a small stick. All around us, half-naked people move feebly through the thorn forest: ethnic Dinka herders displaced from the contested oil fields by fighting between rebels and the central government based in the faraway capital, Khartoum. Their children, stunted and ginger-haired from malnutrition, clamber in the trees. They are collecting leaves to eat. This awful place, I learn, is called Biem—a safe haven, such as it is, of the 40,000-strong Sudan People's Liberation Army.

4   "You cannot reclaim what is lost," the sweating rebel commander says, squatting in the shade of an acacia, "so you just keep fighting for what little you have left."

5   He is trying to console himself. But I see little solace for the epic tragedy of Sudan. It is April 2002, and Africa's largest country is lurching into its 19th uninterrupted year of warfare—the latest

round of strife that has brutalized Sudan, off and on, for most of the past half century. More than two million Sudanese are dead. We just left the latest fatality sprawling back in the yellow grasses, a bullet through his brain. And thousands of scarecrow civilians stagger through the scrub, starving atop a lucrative sea of petroleum.

Numbly, I crawl inside an empty grass hut to be alone. Lying 6 flat on my back—depressed, exhausted, stewing in my own helplessness—I try to remind myself why I have returned to Sudan: Because peace is in the air. Because oil, newly tapped by the government, is shaking up the wretched status quo in Africa's most fractured nation. Because the long nightmare of Biem—and a thousand other places like it in Sudan—may soon be over.

Bulging like a gigantic hornet's nest against the shores of the Red 7 Sea, Sudan has rarely known stability. Civil war erupted even before the nation gained independence from Britain in 1956. (A frail peace lasted between 1972 and 1983.) The roots of the violence have never changed: British-ruled Sudan wasn't a country; it was two. The south is tropical, underdeveloped, and populated by Dinkas, Nuers, Azandes, and some hundred other ethnic groups of African descent. The north, by contrast, is drier, and wealthier—a Saharan world with strong links to the Muslim Middle East. Shackled together by lunatic colonial borders, these two groups—northern Arabs and southern blacks—have been at odds since the 19th century, when northern slave raiders preyed on the tribes of the south.

At present, the rebel Sudan People's Liberation Army, or 8 SPLA, controls much of the southern third of Sudan. Its insurgents sometimes carry spears as well as Kalashnikovs and are fighting for greater autonomy. The northern government in Khartoum, now dominated by Islamic fundamentalists, drops bombs on them from old Russian-made cargo planes and employs famines and modern-day slavery as crude weapons of mass destruction. So far the death toll—mostly among southern civilians—exceeds that of many of the world's recent conflicts combined, including Rwanda, the Persian Gulf war, the Balkans, and Chechnya. Four million Sudanese have been displaced by violence and starvation. Yet the calamity of Sudan unfolds largely without witnesses—an apocalypse in a vacuum. Until now.

9   Two factors are bringing new hope to Sudan. Neither has anything to do with the suffering of millions of Sudanese. Both involve the self-interest of outsiders.

10   First, the U.S. war on terrorism appears to be pressuring reforms in the northern Islamist regime. When a military coup backed by the radical National Islamic Front toppled Sudan's last democratically elected government in 1989, the country plunged into a new dark age. Independent newspapers were banned. Labor unions suppressed. The north's moderate Islamic parties were hounded into exile. The civil war escalated to the drumbeat of jihad—holy struggle against indigenous religions and Christianity in the south. Outlaws ranging from Osama bin Laden to Carlos the Jackal settled into mansions in Khartoum's sandy outskirts. And the fundamentalists' secret police, the feared *mukhabarat*, added a new word to the lexicon of political repression—the "ghost house," or unmarked detention center.

11   Recently, however, Khartoum's extremists have begun mellowing. Chafing under U.S. economic sanctions, they have begun cooperating with the global war on terror. Desperate to shed their pariah status, they have bowed to Western pressure to enter peace negotiations in the civil war. In October 2002 the government and the SPLA signed a fragile cease-fire.

12   The second—and perhaps more profound—force of change in Sudan is less noble. It is about something the whole world wants. It is about oil.

13   In May 1999 engineers in Khartoum opened the tap on a new thousand-mile-long pipeline that connects the Muglad Basin, a huge, petroleum-rich lowland in the south, to a gleaming new tanker terminal on the shores of the Red Sea. The Muglad Basin, a prehistoric lake bed, is said to hold some three billion barrels of crude—nearly half the amount of recoverable oil that lies under the Arctic National Wildlife Refuge in Alaska. This bonanza, pessimists say, is just one more prize for the warring parties to fight over. But oil also has fueled renewed international interest in Sudan. And diplomats are more optimistic.

14   "It's a no-brainer," says a U.S. expert familiar with Sudan's many woes. "The rebels control much of the oil country. The government has access to the sea. They need each other to get rich."

A Canadian geologist who is mapping the Muglad Basin 15
agrees: "Every Sudanese won't be driving a Mercedes tomorrow—
we're not talking about another Saudi Arabia here," he tells me,
"but the reserves are big enough to transform Sudan forever."

There are good reasons for skepticism. Sudan's grievances 16
are very old and complex. They confound even the Sudanese. For
many, the north-south war is rooted in the old toxic relationship
between Arab master and African servant. For the religious, it is
a contest between northern Islam and southern indigenous religions and Christianity. For the impoverished herdsmen on the
front lines, it is a local skirmish over a water hole or favorite pas-
tureland: Violent disputes among Sudan's hundreds of ethnic
groups have been inflamed—and manipulated—by the main
warring parties. Yet oil cuts, literally, across all of Sudan's over-
lapping wars. Better than any road, or river, or political theory,
the shining new pipeline leads the way through a labyrinth of
misery in the Horn of Africa that defies easy interpretation.

I have traveled before to Sudan. Like many journalists, I was 17
sent there to chronicle a freak show of human suffering: endless
civil war, recurrent droughts, mass starvation, slaving raids, and
epidemics of killing diseases. Today, however, I am on a different
mission. I will follow the flow of Sudan's oil wealth from the
implacable war zones of the south to an ultramodern export terminal on the Red Sea; to the country's future.

This will not be an easy journey. I will be forced to complete it 18
in disjointed segments, side-stepping battlefronts, accommodating
roadless deserts, avoiding suspicious bureaucrats—an erratic
process that mirrors life in Sudan.

I pressed my ear against the pipeline once: The Nile Blend 19
crude oozing inside emitted a faint liquid sigh. I listened hard,
sweating under a tropical sun, trying to discern some hidden
message—a clue as to whether 33 million Sudanese will stop
killing each other anytime soon.

We are sneaking into Unity State, the start of Sudan's pipeline, 20
some 450 miles northwest of the Kenyan border.

Flying into rebel-held southern Sudan from Kenya, you must 21
be prepared for certain compromises. First, the flight is illegal.

The central government in Khartoum disapproves of independent visits to its unseen war. Then there is the question of facilities. They simply don't exist. For almost four hours we drone over a landscape of impressive emptiness—a sea of grass that is burned and reburned by wildfires into a mottling of purplish grays, as if the muscles of the earth itself lay exposed. Later, a huge bruise darkens the western horizon: the famous Sudd, an enormous swamp clogging the flow of the White Nile. When the chartered Cessna finally touches down at a rebel airstrip, the pilot anxiously dumps my bags in the dust and leaves immediately for Nairobi. This is natural. His shiny airplane, a target for government bombers, stands out dangerously in the bleakest liberated zone in the world.

22   I have come to see George Athor Deng. Deng is a Dinka fighter, an SPLA commander of note. And he has promised, via shortwave radio, to show me what oil is doing to his people. He smiles sourly when I tell him what the diplomats say, that oil can bring all the Sudanese together.

23   "When has the north ever shared anything with the south?" he says of the government oil fields a two-day's walk across the front lines. "In the near future we will shut them down. Shut the oil down completely."

24   I meet Deng where he spends most of his days, issuing orders from a folding chair under a shady acacia. His headquarters, Biem, is like an engraving from another era—from the journals of Stanley and Livingstone. Stockades of elephant grass surround his crude huts. Food is precarious. His soldiers scavenge off the land and, when possible, skim UN rations dropped from airplanes for starving civilians. (His troops' canteens are empty plastic jugs marked "Canada-Aid Soy Milk.") There are at least 25,000 displaced people jammed into Deng's territory, virtually all of them Dinka herders fleeing the fighting in the nearby oil fields, and whenever groups of famished refugees trudge through Biem, begging for food, the commander dispatches a marksman to shoot a hippo.

25   According to Deng—and he is broadly backed up by human rights groups—oil has sparked some of the ugliest fighting Sudan has seen in years. Deng and other SPLA commanders mortar oil

rigs or shoot at oil company planes. And the Khartoum regime responds by striking back ferociously against local civilians. Government helicopters bought with new oil revenues strafe Dinka and Nuer villages. Sorghum crops are torched. And the dreaded *murahilin*, Muslim raiders armed by the Sudanese Army, sweep through porous rebel lines on horseback, sowing terror and taking slaves. Khartoum denies that it is targeting noncombatants, just as it has long rejected responsibility for slavery in Sudan; it calls these raids tribal abductions, and says they are beyond its control.

"It is simple," Deng declares. "The government is depopulating the area to make way for foreign oil companies." 26

Deng's outrage would inspire more sympathy if his own forces weren't so morally tainted. Traditionally, the SPLA has mistreated as much as defended Sudan's long marginalized southern peoples. Until the south's oil wealth helped forge a common cause, various rebel factions—especially the Dinka-dominated SPLA and a variety of ethnic Nuer militias—killed each other mercilessly, often with the encouragement of government bribes. Some commanders have kept civilians malnourished in order to "farm" UN aid. And the movement's political agenda has never really solidified. The SPLA's leader, an Iowa State University doctorate named John Garang, claims he is fighting for a secular, unified Sudan (as opposed to the north's theocracy), yet almost every field commander, Deng included, is gunning for full southern independence. 27

Knowing what I do about the SPLA, I am prepared to dislike Deng. Compact, scar-faced, blinded in one eye, he promenades around the refugee lean-tos of Biem with a lackey in tow, carrying his chair. Yet there is also an ineffable sadness about him. His entire family—a wife, child, and four brothers—have been wiped out in the current phase of the civil war, which erupted in 1983. Such stupefying losses pervade life in the south. They surface all the time in small, melancholy gestures. 28

Like the way Deng announces the name of his soldier who is killed, shot down and abandoned, on the ill-fated patrol that I attempt to accompany into the oil fields. "Mayak Arop," he sighs, waving a gnarled hand over a map of the expanding government oil roads, as if wishing to wipe them away. 29

30 Or, in the way a bowl-bellied Dinka girl stamps out a pretty little dance on a dusty path in Biem, oblivious to the thousands of haunted figures camped in the bush around her.

31 Or, in the answers to a simple question.

32 What color is oil?

33 "It's like cow urine," says Chan Akuei, an old herder at Biem with a belly wrinkled like elephant skin. Government troops have shot his cows, an incomprehensible crime in the Dinka universe. The Dinka adore their cattle. They rarely kill them for meat, and compose songs about their favorite animals. Akuei cannot stop talking about his murdered livestock.

34 "It is as clear as water," says a boy in Koch, a nearby frontline village. He is a member of an ethnic Nuer militia. The last I see of him, he is marching off at dawn to attack an oil road along with hundreds of other rebels—many of them children.

35 Nyanayule Arop Deng (the name Deng is common among the Dinka) doesn't know the color of oil. She sits by her skeletal husband, who is dying of kala-azar, a wasting disease that has killed tens of thousands in the oil zone. "All I know is the lights," she says dully. "They appear at night. We don't go near them."

36 The tower lights of Roll'n wildcat rig number 15 click on at dusk—an unexpectedly pretty sight as the sun drops behind the iron silhouettes of the thorn trees. The quest for oil is tireless, urgent, expensive. It is like a physical thirst—an around-the-clock obsession. Before the evening shift comes on, Terry Hoffman, a sweat-soaked driller from British Columbia, runs one last stand of pipe down into the skin of Sudan.

37 "Killer bees, cobras, and acid-spewing bugs that give you blisters!" Hoffman hollers over the rig's noisy generator, ticking off the dangers of roughnecking in Sudan. "Boredom's the worst, though. You can't even walk around this place."

38 Hoffman is a prisoner of his rig. He and his crew must eat their barbecued chicken and cherry pies, read their e-mail, and lift weights inside a Sudanese version of Fort Apache: a 15-foot-high berm has been bulldozed around the floodlit work site. Heavily armed government troops patrol the perimeter against the likes of

George Athor Deng. Deng is doubtless out there tonight, plotting under his tree.

The idea behind rig 15—a small component in a billion-dollar 39 complex of drilling equipment, dormitories, pumping stations, new roads, and prefabricated office buildings at Heglig, Sudan's torrid version of the North Slope—is visionary in its way.

At present, none of the Western energy majors dares to drill in 40 Sudan. Chevron suspended its exploration in 1984 after three of its employees were shot dead by rebels, and pulled out of the country altogether in 1990. (All American companies abandoned Sudan once the U.S. listed it as a supporter of terrorism and imposed sanctions in the 1990s.) Yet today an improbable mix of engineers from communist China, authoritarian Malaysia, democratic Canada, and Islamist Khartoum have cobbled together an experiment in globalization on the baleful plains of the Sahel. The Greater Nile Petroleum Operating Company, as it is called, pumps 240,000 barrels of crude a day out of a war zone. Two years from now that output is projected to nearly double. It may surge even higher should lasting peace return to Sudan, and the rebels allow French, Swedish, and Austrian companies to explore their concessions in the south.

"All these stories about us pushing out local people to pump 41 for oil? A total lie," says Bill, a rig supervisor with Talisman Energy, the Canadian partner in the Heglig project.

Bill wears cowboy boots and doesn't share his surname. Like 42 everyone else I meet in Heglig, he seems aggrieved. Talisman has come under fire from human rights groups for allegedly turning a blind eye to government atrocities in the oil patch. (Partly because of this bad publicity, Talisman will later sell its Sudan operation to an Indian oil company.) In response to the criticism, a wary company official in Khartoum lectures me on the value of free markets in reforming oppressive regimes. Supervisors drive me around Heglig in a pickup truck, pointing out unmolested villagers in the savanna. Few of these people are southerners. Most are Baggaras, northern Muslim pastoralists who vie with the Dinkas for grazing lands, and who have come to the oil fields to hack down trees for charcoal.

"TV at home shows these incredible stories—famines and war 43 in Sudan," says Bill. "Well, let me tell you, I've been in a 200-mile radius of this place, and I haven't seen that."

44   Bill may be willfully blind. But then so are his faraway customers. The only difference is, Bill must walk past a rebel bullet hole in his trailer wall every day and not see it. This is a difficult feat. But a common one in Sudan.

45 There is no fixed front line between SPLA territory and government-controlled Sudan. No walls. No razor wire fences. No permanent Thorn Curtain. The war is fluid. One army cedes power invisibly to another, and what changes across the no-man's-land are things far subtler and more profound than claims of political control. The round grass huts of Africa give way, slowly, to the square mud houses of desert dwellers. The hot blue dome of the tropical sky recedes behind a veil of white Saharan dust. As I travel north, the 21st century begins to reappear—roads are graded by machines, and human beings once more begin to congregate into towns. Some of these towns have sidewalks. The sight—concrete poured on the ground merely to ease walking—is mesmerizing; a surreal extravagance after the utter desolation of the south.

46   The oil pipeline rockets north from Heglig and crosses the eerie rock piles of the Nuba Mountains. The Nuba people, allied with the SPLA, have been fighting their own war of autonomy against Khartoum for years. A U.S.-brokered cease-fire is in place when I drive through. I see government trucks rolling up into the hills, loaded with satellite dishes. The equipment is meant for "peace clubs" designed to lure the stubborn Nubas down from their mountain strongholds and into areas of government control. "Many of them have never seen television before," a grinning official explains in the garrison town of Kadugli. "We give them 22 channels, including CNN. Their leaders are very irritated by this."

47   The pipeline burrows onward under a mound of raw earth—a monumental tribal scar creasing the barren landscape. Construction began in 1998 and was finished in 14 months by 2,000 Chinese laborers sweating through double shifts. Workers who died in Sudan were cremated on the spot, and their ashes shipped back to China.

48   I chase the 28-inch-wide steel tube on bad roads. Dilling. El Obeid. Rabak. The northern towns swell, turning into ramshackle mud cities. Two days north of Heglig, the pipeline disappears

into slums. A cratered highway leads me into an enormous traffic jam that backs up for miles. Buses nudge through herds of sheep. Donkey carts jockey with taxis so battered they look like the products of junkyard crushing machines. Pedestrians step unhurriedly among the stalled vehicles. Yet no one is angry or abusive. There are no honking horns, insults, threats, or curses. Silently, patiently, the drivers creep forward. They advance, inch by inch, into a city of waiting.

This is Khartoum.   49

"Please put your notebook away," advises Asim el Moghraby.   50
"We don't want any problems."

El Moghraby and I are perched in a borrowed motorboat,   51
bobbing in the middle of the Nile. I have joined el Moghraby expressly to avoid problems—to admire an overlooked natural wonder of Africa: the meeting of the Blue Nile and White Nile. The two majestic streams, tributaries of the world's longest river, swirl together in a mile-wide dance of light—one the hue of an evening sky and the other the color of a milky sunrise. Yet Sudan's troubles are insistent. El Moghraby, a retired University of Khartoum biologist and my unofficial guide in the city, is nervous. Western visitors are relatively rare in the city. And he worries that I will draw the attention of secret police. We are too close to shoreline government ministries. "The regime is loosening up," he says apologetically as we chug back to the marina, "but nobody knows how much."

Change is coming to Sudan, but few know if it is deep or real. 52
The thinking of the small cabal of generals and fundamentalists who run the country is largely opaque. Nevertheless, the virulence of their Islamic revolution began fading even before 1998, when the Clinton Administration launched cruise missiles at a pharmaceutical plant in Khartoum in retaliation for al Qaeda's terrorist bombings of two U.S. embassies in Africa. Eager to put those years behind them, Sudan's secretive rulers claim they have expelled some 3,000 foreigners linked with terror groups (bin Laden and Carlos included) and that they have released most political prisoners. Opposition parties have been invited back in from the cold, though they often remain marginalized.

53   Driving around Khartoum with el Moghraby—a lean, balding scholar who reminds me of a patient turtle, with his wrinkled neck and watchful eyes that dart behind wire-rimmed glasses—I see a crumbling metropolis of seven million that seems to be fluttering its dusty eyelids after a long slumber beneath the sands. Young couples hold hands on the banks of the Nile, unmolested by the morality police. Flashes of oil money glint off fleets of new Korean-made cars. And freshly painted Coke signs and a new BMW dealership have popped up in the city's shabby downtown.

54   Still, it is staggering to think that this insular, puritanical city—with its turbaned Arab rulers, domed mosques, and tea shops blaring pop music—is the capital of the bleeding African south. Yet the war is here too. On a blazing afternoon I visit Wad el Bashir, one of the miserable camps where some of the nearly two million southerners are sweating away their lives in and around Khartoum. Nubas and Dinkas accost me in the maze of dirt lanes. "They are taking our children!" they whisper, describing how their young men are being yanked off sidewalks and buses to fight for the Sudanese Army against their own people in the south. Behind their mud huts I spot my old companion, the pipeline. Its inert presence now seems malevolent.

55   Popular discontent—and profound war-weariness—is only slightly less palpable among northerners in Khartoum. University students complain about the loss of jobs and political freedoms under the Islamists. Arab businessmen bemoan Sudan's ruinous isolation. ("Please tell the world we are not all terrorists and bullyboys," pleads one wealthy trader.) And several middle-class men openly boast of evading the draft—they aren't buying jihad's promise of a direct ticket to heaven.

56   "What you are seeing is the northern front in Sudan's civil war," explains a human rights advocate named Osman Hummaida, when I share my surprise at the cynicism I find on Khartoum's streets. "Sudan is not just divided north-south. There is a broader struggle. It is the center against the periphery—a tiny Khartoum clique against everyone else, including fellow Arabs."

57   My tour guide, el Moghraby, is a casualty of this subtler northern war. Bullying his Land Rover through Khartoum's downtown one day, he points to a drab building and says,

"That one's mine"—meaning the old ghost house where he was
detained in 1992, along with his politically active lawyer. In
1995 he was arrested with his wife for producing a documen-
tary film critical of Sudan's environmental record. He was
imprisoned yet again, in 1999, for publicly questioning the
country's oil projects.

Like many disillusioned northern intellectuals, el Moghraby 58
has withdrawn from public life. He has retreated into private
enthusiasms—into the past. He takes me one day to see a weath-
ered colonial monument honoring the charge of the 21st Lancers,
a once famous skirmish in the British conquest of Sudan in 1898.
Wistfully, el Moghraby talks of an older, more cosmopolitan
Khartoum of electric trams, midnight cafés, and clean-swept
streets. This nostalgia is sad, especially given Britain's divisive
legacy in Sudan.

As a young soldier, Winston Churchill participated in the 59
charge of the 21st Lancers outside Khartoum. British horsemen
slammed into the ranks of defending Sudanese troops with such
force, he wrote, that "for perhaps ten wonderful seconds" all
sides simply staggered about in a daze. The beleaguered citizens
of Sudan's capital know this feeling well. They have endured it
for the better part of 50 years. It is not wonderful.

Where is undemocratic, underdeveloped, and oil-rich Sudan 60
headed? For answers I must leave the periphery. I go to the center.

Sudan's president, Lt. Gen. Omar al-Bashir, almost never 61
grants interviews. Hassan al-Turabi, the intellectual father of
Sudan's Islamist movement, is also not available, having been put
under house arrest by rivals in the government. (He has since
been locked up in Kober Prison.) So the task of explaining the
policies of the secretive National Islamic Front that rules Sudan
falls to Hasan Makki, an Islamic academic and one of the regime's
leading ideologues.

Makki greets me in a dazzling white djellaba, or Arab robe, in 62
his spacious home. He is a member of the elite "riverine" Arab
tribes who have monopolized power in Sudan for years. Like
most of Sudan's political inner circle, he is friendly, smart, and
chooses his words carefully.

63   On the war: "It is effectively over, my friend. The south already has lost. Millions of their people have moved up to join us in the north." Ignoring the detail that the refugees have not come by choice, he calls Khartoum "an American-style melting pot."

64   On Arab-black hostility: "How can there be racism? Look at my skin. No northern Sudanese is a pure Arab. For centuries our blood has mixed with Africans. We are brothers!"

65   On oil: "It is a blessing. It will hold Sudan together. Before oil, we northerners were tired of the south. Why lose our children there? Why fight for a wasteland? Oil has changed all that. Now our economic survival depends on it."

66   Regarding the unpopularity of the regime, Makki has little to say. He politely pours me another cup of tea and suggests that I go look at stones.

67 We have flown, walked, and driven more than 600 miles through Sudan.

68   The pipeline leads on—tireless and unerring, far more sure of itself in the turmoil of Sudan than I ever will be. Its oil is kept at 95 degrees Fahrenheit, the temperature required for it to be thin enough to flow freely. It tunnels through Khartoum's bleak refugee camps, then slips beneath the Nile. Emerging from the other side, it disappears north into an ocean of light: the Nubian Desert.

69   There, baking under the sun, are Makki's stones. They are the silent remains of ancient cities and temples.

70   At a city called Naga, a ruin of great beauty and stillness that juts from the eroding hills east of the Nile, I see a relief carved into an imposing temple wall. It depicts a queen grasping a handful of small, doomed captives. The queen is recognizably Nubian: Chiseled in pharaonic splendor, she is a mix of Egyptian elegance and full-hipped African beauty. Her prisoners too strike me as dead ringers. They look like the far-flung citizens of Sudan's modern fringe: fierce Beja nomads from the Red Sea Hills—or even Negroid Dinkas or Nubas from the south. Blinking sweat from my eyes, I stare in amazement at this antique blueprint for governance in Sudan—a 2,000-year-old political poster advertising the power of Nile-based elites over the weak periphery.

"Some things never change," says Dietrich Wildung, head of ₇₁
the Egyptian Museum and Papyrus Collection in Berlin and one
of the sunburned archaeologists working at Naga. "The north
always thinks itself supreme—Egypt over Sudan, Berlin over
Munich, New York over Alabama."

Wildung, an almost dauntingly effusive man, pads briskly ₇₂
around his digs in a flimsy pair of sneakers, pointing out details
on a half-excavated temple that make him exclaim with pure
delight. According to archaeologists, Sudan's northern deserts
hide one of the great civilizations not only of Africa but the world.
These Sudanic realms—variously known as Nubia, Kush, or
Meroë—were no mere appendages of neighboring Egypt, as was
sometimes thought. Their intelligentsia created an Egyptian-
derived writing system, Meroitic, for a still unintelligible language. And the "black pharaohs" of Sudan and their notorious
archers eventually gained such power that they briefly ruled all
of Egypt some 2,700 years ago.

Proudly, Wildung shows me his latest discovery: an altar ₇₃
excavated from beneath a fallen wall. Nile gods painted on its
plaster-covered pedestal indicate Egyptian influence, and the floral
designs are pure Africa—all exuberance, singing colors. Ancient
Greece reveals itself too in the classical flourishes on a figurine of
the Egyptian goddess Isis. Crouched over a hole in the earth, we
behold the unexpected beauty of Sudan's fractured nature, the art
of a continental crossroads.

Can oil dilute the age-old divisiveness of Sudan? The pipeline is ₇₄
my guide. But it is no oracle.

North of the city of Atbara, the steel artery is patrolled by ₇₅
wild-looking men in vehicles mounted with heavy machine guns:
mujahidin, or holy warriors, guarding the pipeline from being
blown up, as it was nearby in 1999. (That act of sabotage was carried out by northern opposition forces in alliance with the SPLA.)
The oil squirts across the Red Sea Hills at the pace of a fast walk.
Then it races 3,000 feet down to the devastatingly hot Sudanese
coast. To the Bashair Marine Terminal. To the end of the line.
When I visit the high-tech export facility, a Singapore-flagged
tanker is preparing to gulp a million barrels of crude.

76   "You are looking at our gateway to the world," a jump-suited technician tells me grandly in the sleek control room, some 950 miles from the oil wells pocking the savannas of Africa.

77   I hope he is right. I hope oil helps create a new era of stability in Sudan. I hope it prods international efforts, such as those of U.S. peacemaker John Danforth, to end the terrible civil war. I hope it bribes Sudan's cruel and insulated elites into abandoning selfish power struggles that have wreaked hell on millions of ordinary people. I hope it somehow lubricates relations with Egypt, the regional superpower, which exercises powerful inter-ests in Sudan: Egypt strongly opposes southern independence, fearing that such a development will threaten its access to the vital middle reaches of the Nile. Most of all, I hope Sudan's new oil revenues—more than two million dollars a day—do not end up stoking what one analyst calls a "perfect war," a conflict waged, at tolerable cost, indefinitely. Hope: a commodity Sudan could use more of, even, than oil.

78   Near the end of my journey, I camp for a few days in the parched wilderness of the Red Sea Hills. My host is Abu Fatna, an old Beja, a Muslim nomad whose ancestors have roamed the east-ern wastes of Sudan for the past 5,000 years. His tent is pegged only 40 miles west of the pipeline, yet his life is as detached from its power and wealth as those of the southern Dinkas dying at the opposite end of the oil trail. Drought has forced Fatna to sell his camels. Saudi hunters have slaughtered all the local wild ante-lope. He is skinny and poor, and he has only two teeth left in his head. But he still knows which desert stars to travel by. He can still handle a tribal broadsword.

79   When I leave, Fatna offers me a gift: He dances good-bye in the dust. The flapping of his scrawny arms, the dry snatches of song—these are meant as an honor, though they seem more like a lament. Driving back to the pipeline, I wonder if this sadness, too, somehow gets pumped out of Sudan. Along with commander Deng's bitter hand-waving over a crude map. Or el Moghraby's demoralized retreat from the world. Or the terrible absences of so many dead.

80   So much heartbreak, it seems, gets burned up in Sudan's oil.

2003

DNA as Destiny

David Ewing Duncan

I feel naked. Exposed. As if my skin, bone, muscle tissue, cells 1
have all been peeled back, down to a tidy swirl of DNA. It's the
basic stuff of life, the billions of nucleotides that keep me breathing, walking, craving, and just being. Eight hours ago, I gave a
few cells, swabbed from inside my cheek, to a team of geneticists.
They've spent the day extracting DNA and checking it for dozens
of hidden diseases. Eventually, I will be tested for hundreds more.
They include, as I will discover, a nucleic time bomb ticking inside
my chromosomes that might one day kill me.

For now I remain blissfully ignorant, awaiting the results in 2
an office at Sequenom, one of scores of biotech startups incubat-
ing in the canyons north of San Diego. I'm waiting to find out if I
have a genetic proclivity for cancer, cardiac disease, deafness,
Alzheimer's, or schizophrenia.

This, I'm told, is the first time a healthy human has ever been 3
screened for the full gamut of genetic-disease markers. Everyone
has errors in his or her DNA, glitches that may trigger a heart
spasm or cause a brain tumor. I'm here to learn mine.

Waiting, I wonder if I carry some sort of Pandora gene, a 4
hereditary predisposition to peek into places I shouldn't. Morbid
curiosity is an occupational hazard for a writer, I suppose, but
I've never been bothered by it before. Yet now I find myself growing nervous and slightly flushed. I can feel my pulse rising, a car-
diovascular response that I will soon discover has, for me, dire
implications.

In the coming days, I'll seek a second opinion, of sorts. 5
Curious about where my genes come from, I'll travel to Oxford
and visit an "ancestral geneticist" who has agreed to examine my
DNA for links back to progenitors whose mutations have been
passed on to me. He will reveal the seeds of my individuality and
the roots of the diseases that may kill me—and my children.

For now, I wait in an office at Sequenom, a sneak preview of a 6
trip to the DNA doctor, circa 2008. The personalized medicine being
pioneered here and elsewhere prefigures a day when everyone's

genome will be deposited on a chip or stored on a gene card tucked into a wallet. Physicians will forecast illnesses and prescribe preventive drugs custom-fitted to a patient's DNA, rather than the one-size-fits-all pharmaceuticals that people take today. Gene cards might also be used to find that best-suited career, or a DNA-compatible mate, or, more darkly, to deny someone jobs, dates, and meds because their nucleotides don't measure up. It's a scenario Andrew Niccol imagined in his 1997 film, *Gattaca*, where embryos in a not-too-distant future are bioengineered for perfection, and where genism—discrimination based on one's DNA—condemns the lesser-gened to scrubbing toilets.

7   The *Gattaca*-like engineering of defect-free embryos is at least 20 or 30 years away, but Sequenom and others plan to take DNA testing to the masses in just a year or two. The prize: a projected $5 billion market for personalized medicine by 2006, and billions, possibly hundreds of billions, more for those companies that can translate the errors in my genome and yours into custom pharmaceuticals.

8 Sitting across from me is the man responsible for my gene scan: Andi Braun, chief medical officer at Sequenom. Tall and sinewy, with a long neck, glasses, and short gray hair, Braun, 46, is both jovial and German. Genetic tests are already publicly available for Huntington's disease and cystic fibrosis, but Braun points out that these illnesses are relatively rare. "We are targeting diseases that impact millions," he says in a deep Bavarian accent, envisioning a day when genetic kits that can assay the whole range of human misery will be available at Wal-Mart, as easy to use as a home pregnancy test.

9   But a kit won't tell me if I'll definitely get a disease, just if I have a bum gene. What Sequenom and others are working toward is pinning down the probability that, for example, a colon cancer gene will actually trigger a tumor. To know this, Braun must analyze the DNA of thousands of people and tally how many have the colon cancer gene, how many actually get the disease, and how many don't. Once this data is gathered and crunched, Braun will be able to tell you, for instance, that if you have the defective DNA, you have a 40 percent chance, or maybe

a 75 percent chance, by age 50, or 90. Environmental factors such as eating right—or wrong—and smoking also weigh in. "It's a little like predicting the weather," says Charles Cantor, the company's cofounder and chief scientific officer.

Braun tells me that, for now, his tests offer only a rough 10 sketch of my genetic future. "We can't yet test for everything, and some of the information is only partially understood," he says. It's more of a peek through a rudimentary eyeglass than a Hubble Space Telescope. Yet I will be able to glimpse some of the internal programming bequeathed to me by evolution, and that I, in turn, have bequeathed to my children—Sander, Danielle, and Alex, ages 15, 13, and 7. They are a part of this story, too. Here's where I squirm, because as a father I pass on not only the ingredients of life to my children but the secret codes of their demise—just as I have passed on my blue eyes and a flip in my left brow that my grandmother called "a little lick from God." DNA is not only the book of life, it is also the book of death, says Braun: "We're all going to die, ja?"

Strictly speaking, Braun is not looking for entire genes, the long 11 strings of nucleotides that instruct the body to grow a tooth or create white blood cells to attack an incoming virus. He's after single nucleotide polymorphisms, or SNPs (pronounced "snips"), the tiny genetic variations that account for nearly all differences in humans.

Imagine DNA as a ladder made of rungs—3 billion in all— 12 spiraling upward in a double helix. Each step is a base pair, designated by two letters from the nucleotide alphabet of G, T, A, and C. More than 99 percent of these base pairs are identical in all humans, with only about one in a thousand SNPs diverging to make us distinct. For instance, you might have a CG that makes you susceptible to diabetes, and I might have a CC, which makes it far less likely I will get this disease.

This is all fairly well-known: Genetics 101. What's new is how 13 startups like Sequenom have industrialized the SNP identification process. Andi Braun and Charles Cantor are finding thousands of new SNPs a day, at a cost of about a penny each.

Braun tells me that there are possibly a million SNPs in each 14 person, though only a small fraction are tightly linked with common ailments. These disease-causing SNPs are fueling a

biotech bonanza; the hope is that after finding them, the discov-
erers can design wonder drugs. In the crowded SNP field,
Sequenom vies with Iceland-based deCode Genetics, American
companies such as Millennium Pharmaceuticals, Orchid
BioSciences, and Celera Genomics, as well as multinationals like
Eli Lilly and Roche Diagnostics. "It's the Oklahoma Land Grab
right now," says Toni Schuh, Sequenom's CEO.

15 The sun sets outside Braun's office as my results arrive, splayed
across his computer screen like tarot cards. I'm trying to maintain a
steely, reportorial facade, but my heart continues to race.

16   Names of SNPs pop up on the screen: connexin 26, implicated
in hearing loss; factor V leiden, which causes blood clots; and
alpha-1 antitrypsin deficiency, linked to lung and liver disease.
Beside each SNP are codes that mean nothing to me: 13q11-q12,
1q23, 14q32.1. Braun explains that these are addresses on the
human genome, the PO box numbers of life. For instance, 1q23 is
the address for a mutant gene that causes vessels to shrink and
impede the flow of blood—it's on chromosome 1. Thankfully, my
result is negative. "So, David, you will not get the varicose veins.
That's good, ja?" says Braun. One gene down, dozens to go.

17   Next up is the hemochromatosis gene. This causes one's blood
to retain too much iron, which can damage the liver. As Braun
explains it, somewhere in the past, an isolated human community
lived in an area where the food was poor in iron. Those who developed a mutation that stores high levels of iron survived, and those
who didn't became anemic and died, failing to reproduce.
However, in these iron-rich times, hemochromatosis is a liability.
Today's treatment? Regular bleeding. "You tested negative for this
mutation," says Braun. "You do not have to be bled."

18   I'm also clean for cystic fibrosis and for a SNP connected to
lung cancer.

19   Then comes the bad news. A line of results on Braun's monitor shows up red and is marked "MT," for mutant type. My
body's programming code is faulty. There's a glitch in my system.
Named ACE (for angiotensin-I converting enzyme), this SNP
means my body makes an enzyme that keeps my blood pressure
spiked. In plain English, I'm a heart attack risk.

My face drains of color as the news sinks in. I'm not only defec- ₂₀
tive, but down the road, every time I get anxious about my condition, I'll know that I have a much higher chance of dropping dead.
I shouldn't be surprised, since I'm told everyone has some sort of
disease-causing mutation. Yet I realize that my decision to take a
comprehensive DNA test has been based on the rather ridiculous
assumption that I would come out of this with a clean genetic bill of
health. I almost never get sick, and, at age 44, I seldom think about
my physical limitations, or death. This attitude is buttressed by a
family largely untouched by disease. The women routinely thrive
into their late eighties and nineties. One great-aunt lived to age 101;
she used to bake me cupcakes in her retirement home when I was a
boy. And some of the Duncan menfolk are pushing 90-plus. My parents, now entering their seventies, are healthy. In a flash of red MTs,
I'm glimpsing my own future; my own mortality. I'm slated to keel
over, both hands clutching at my heart.

"Do you have any history in your family of high blood pres- ₂₁
sure or heart disease?" asks Matthew McGinniss, a Sequenom
geneticist standing at Braun's side.

"No," I answer, trying to will the color back into my face. ₂₂
Then a second MT pops up on the screen—another high blood
pressure mutation. My other cardiac indicators are OK, which is
relatively good news, though I'm hardly listening now. I'm
already planning a full-scale assault to learn everything I can
about fighting heart disease—until McGinniss delivers an unexpected pronouncement. "These mutations are probably irrelevant," he says. Braun agrees: "It's likely that you carry a gene that
keeps these faulty ones from causing you trouble—DNA that we
have not yet discovered."

The SNPs keep rolling past, revealing more mutations, ₂₃
including a type-2 diabetes susceptibility, which tells me I may
want to steer clear of junk food. More bad news: I don't have a
SNP called CCR5 that prevents me from acquiring HIV, nor one
that seems to shield smokers from lung cancer. "Ja, that's my
favorite," says Braun, himself a smoker. "I wonder what Philip
Morris would pay for that."

By the time I get home, I realize that all I've really learned is I ₂₄
might get heart disease, and I could get diabetes. And I should

avoid smoking and unsafe sex—as if I didn't already know this. Obviously, I'll now watch my blood pressure, exercise more, and lay off the Cap'n Crunch. But beyond this, I have no idea what to make of the message Andi Braun has divined from a trace of my spit.

25 Looking for guidance, I visit Ann Walker, director of the Graduate Program for Genetic Counseling at the University of California at Irvine. Walker explains the whats and hows, and the pros and cons, of DNA testing to patients facing hereditary disease, pregnant couples concerned with prenatal disorders, and anyone else contemplating genetic evaluation. It's a tricky job because, as I've learned, genetic data is seldom clear-cut.

26   Take breast cancer, Walker says. A woman testing positive for BRCA1, the main breast cancer gene, has an 85 percent chance of actually getting the cancer by age 70, a wrenching situation, since the most effective method of prevention is a double mastectomy. What if a woman has the operation and it turns out she's among those 15 percent who carry the mutation but will never get the cancer? Not surprisingly, one study, conducted in Holland, found that half of healthy women whose mothers developed breast cancer opt not to be tested for the gene, preferring ignorance and closer monitoring. Another example is the test for APoE, the Alzheimer's gene. Since the affliction has no cure, most people don't want to know their status. But some do. A positive result, says Walker, allows them to put their affairs in order and prepare for their own dotage. Still, the news can be devastating. One biotech executive told me that a cousin of his committed suicide when he tested positive for Huntington's, having seen the disease slowly destroy his father.

27   Walker pulls out a chart and asks about my family's medical details, starting with my grandparents and their brothers and sisters: what they suffered and died from, and when. My Texas grandmother died at 92 after a series of strokes. My 91-year-old Missouri grandmom was headed to a vacation in Mexico with her 88-year-old second husband when she got her death sentence— ovarian cancer. The men died younger: my grandfathers in their late sixties, though they both have brothers still alive and healthy in their nineties. To the mix, Walker adds my parents and their

siblings, all of whom are alive and healthy in their sixties and seventies; then my generation; and finally our children. She looks up and smiles: "This is a pretty healthy group."

Normally, Walker says, she would send me home. Yet I'm sitting across from her not because my parents carry some perilous SNP, but as a healthy man who is after a forecast of future maladies. "We have no real training yet for this," she says, and tells me the two general rules of genetic counseling: No one should be screened unless there is an effective treatment or readily available counseling; and the information should not bewilder people or present them with unnecessary trauma.   28

Many worry that these prime directives may be ignored by Sequenom and other startups that need to launch products to survive. FDA testing for new drugs can take up to 10 years, and many biotech firms feel pressure to sell something in the interim. "Most of these companies need revenue," says the University of Pennsylvania's Arthur Caplan, a top bioethicist. "And the products they've got now are diagnostic. Whether they are good ones, useful ones, necessary ones, accurate ones, seems less of a concern than that they be sold." Caplan also notes that the FDA does not regulate these tests. "If it was a birth control test, the FDA would be all over it."   29

I ask Caplan about the *Gattaca* scenario of genetic discrimination. Will a woman dump me if she finds out about my ACE? Will my insurance company hike my rate? "People are denied insurance and jobs right now," he says, citing sickle-cell anemia, whose sufferers and carriers, mostly black, have faced job loss and discrimination. No federal laws exist to protect us from genism, or from insurers and employers finding out our genetic secrets. "Right now you're likely going to be more disadvantaged than empowered by genetic testing," says Caplan.   30

After probing my genetic future, I jet to England to investigate my DNA past. Who are these people who have bequeathed me this tainted bloodline? From my grandfather Duncan, an avid genealogist, I already know that my paternal ancestors came from Perth in south-central Scotland. We can trace the name back to an Anglican priest murdered in Glasgow in 1680 by a mob of Puritans.   31

His six sons escaped and settled in Shippensburg, Pennsylvania, where their descendants lived until my great-great-grandfather moved west to Kansas City in the 1860s.

32   In an Oxford restaurant, over a lean steak and a heart-healthy merlot, I talk with geneticist Bryan Sykes, a linebacker-sized 55-year-old with a baby face and an impish smile. He's a molecular biologist at the university's Institute of Molecular Medicine and the author of the best-selling *Seven Daughters of Eve.* Sykes first made headlines in 1994 when he used DNA to directly link a 5,000-year-old body discovered frozen and intact in an Austrian glacier to a 20th-century Dorset woman named Marie Mosley. This stunning genetic connection between housewife and hunter-gatherer launched Sykes' career as a globe-trotting genetic gumshoe. In 1995, he confirmed that bones dug up near Ekaterinburg, Russia, were the remains of Czar Nicholas II and his family, by comparing the body's DNA with that of the czar's living relatives, including Britain's Prince Philip. Sykes debunked explorer Thor Heyerdahl's *Kon-Tiki* theory by tracing Polynesian genes to Asia and not the Americas, and similarly put the lie to the *Clan of the Cave Bear* hypothesis, which held that the Neanderthal inter-bred with our ancestors, the Cro-Magnon, when the two subspecies coexisted in Europe 15,000 years ago.

33   Sykes explains to me that a bit of DNA called mtDNA is key to his investigations. A circular band of genes residing separately from the 23 chromosomes of the double helix, mtDNA is passed down solely through the maternal line. Sykes used mtDNA to discover something astounding: Nearly every European can be traced back to just seven women living 10,000 to 45,000 years ago. In his book, Sykes gives these seven ancestors hokey names and tells us where they most likely lived: Ursula, in Greece (circa 43,000 B.C.), and Velda, in northern Spain (circa 15,000 B.C.), to name two of the "seven daughters of Eve." (Eve was the ur-mother who lived 150,000 years ago in Africa.)

34   Sykes has taken swab samples from the cheeks of more than 10,000 people, charging $220 to individually determine a person's mtDNA type. "It's not serious genetics," Sykes admits, "but people like to know their roots. It makes genetics less scary and shows us that, through our genes, we are all very closely related."

He recently expanded his tests to include non-Europeans. The Asian daughters of Eve are named Emiko, Nene, and Yumio, and their African sisters are Lamia, Latifa, and Ulla, among others.

Before heading to England, I had mailed Sykes a swab of my 35 cheek cells. Over our desserts in Oxford he finally offers up the results. "You are descended from Helena," he pronounces. "She's the most common daughter of Eve, accounting for some 40 percent of Europeans." He hands me a colorful certificate, signed by him, that heralds my many-times-great-grandma and tells me that she lived 20,000 years ago in the Dordogne Valley of France. More interesting is the string of genetic letters from my mtDNA read-out that indicates I'm mostly Celtic, which makes sense. But other bits of code reveal traces of Southeast Asian DNA, and even a smidgen of Native American and African.

This doesn't quite have the impact of discovering that I'm 36 likely to die of a heart attack. Nor am I surprised about the African and Indian DNA, since my mother's family has lived in the American South since the 17th century. But Southeast Asian? Sykes laughs. "We are all mutts," he says. "There is no ethnic purity. Somewhere over the years, one of the thousands of ances-tors who contributed to your DNA had a child with someone from Southeast Asia." He tells me a story about a blond, blue-eyed surfer from Southern California who went to Hawaii to apply for monies awarded only to those who could prove native Hawaiian descent. The grant-givers laughed—until his DNA turned up traces of Hawaiian.

The next day, in Sykes' lab, we have one more test: running 37 another ancestry marker in my Y chromosome through a data-base of 10,000 other Ys to see which profile is closest to mine. If my father was in the database, his Y chromosome would be iden-tical, or possibly one small mutation off. A cousin might deviate by one tick. Someone descended from my native county of Perth might be two or three mutations removed, indicating that we share a common ancestor hundreds of years ago. Sykes tells me these comparisons are used routinely in paternity cases. He has another application. He is building up Y-chromosome profiles of surnames: men with the same last name whose DNA confirms that they are related to common ancestors.

38   After entering my mtDNA code into his laptop, Sykes looks intrigued, then surprised, and suddenly moves to the edge of his seat. Excited, he reports that the closest match is, incredibly, him—Bryan Sykes! "This has never happened," he says, telling me that I am a mere one mutation removed from him, and two from the average profile of a Sykes. He has not collected DNA from many other Duncans, he says, though it appears as if sometime in the past 400 years a Sykes must have ventured into Perth, and then had a child with a Duncan. "That makes us not-so-distant cousins," he says. We check a map of Britain on his wall, and sure enough, the Sykes family's homeland of Yorkshire is less than 200 miles south of Perth.

39   The fact that Sykes and I are members of the same extended family is just a bizarre coincidence, but it points to applications beyond simple genealogy. "I've been approached by the police to use my surnames data to match up with DNA from an unknown suspect found at a crime scene," says Sykes. Distinctive genetic markers can be found at the roots of many family trees. "This is possible, to narrow down a pool of suspects to a few likely surnames. But it's not nearly ready yet."

40   Back home in California, I'm sweating on a StairMaster at the gym, wondering about my heart. I wrap my hands around the grips and check my pulse: 129. Normal. I pump harder and top out at 158. Also normal. I think about my visit a few days earlier—prompted by my gene scan—to Robert Superko, a cardiologist. After performing another battery of tests, he gave me the all clear—except for one thing. Apparently, I have yet another lame-heart gene, the atherosclerosis susceptibility gene ATHS, a SNP that causes plaque in my cardiac bloodstream to build up if I don't exercise far more than average—which I do, these days, as a slightly obsessed biker and runner. "As long as you exercise, you'll be fine," Superko advised, a bizarre kind of life sentence that means that I must pedal and jog like a madman or face—what? A triple bypass?

41   Pumping on the StairMaster, I nudge the setting up a notch, wishing, in a way, that I either knew for sure I was going to die on, say, February 17, 2021, or that I hadn't been tested at all. As it

is, the knowledge that I have an ACE and ATHS deep inside me will be nagging me every time I get short of breath.

The last results from my DNA workup have also come in. [42] Andi Braun has tested me for 77 SNPs linked to lifespan in order to assess when and how I might get sick and die. He has given me a score of .49 on his scale. It indicates a lifespan at least 20 percent longer than that of the average American male who, statistically speaking, dies in his 74th year. I will likely live, then, to the age of 88. That's 44 years of StairMaster to go.

Braun warns that this figure does not take into account the [43] many thousands of other SNPs that affect my life, not to mention the possibility that a piano could fall on my head.

That night, I put my 7-year-old, Alex, to bed. His eyes droop [44] under his bright-white head of hair as I finish reading *Captain Underpants* aloud. Feeling his little heart beating as he lies next to me on his bed, I wonder what shockers await him inside his nucleotides, half of which I gave him. As I close the book and then sing him to sleep, I wonder if he has my culprit genes. I don't know, because he hasn't been scanned. For now, he and the rest of humanity are living in nearly the same blissful ignorance as Helena did in long-ago Dordogne. But I do know one thing: Alex has my eyebrow, the "lick of God." I touch his flip in the dark, and touch mine. He stirs, but it's not enough to wake him.

2002

9

Analogy

The Myth of the Cave

Plato

1   And now, I said, let me show in a figure how far our nature is enlightened or unenlightened:—Behold! human beings living in an underground den, which has a mouth open toward the light and reaching all along the den; here they have been from their childhood, and have their legs and necks chained so that they cannot move, and can only see before them, being prevented by the chains from turning round their heads. Above and behind them a fire is blazing at a distance, and between the fire and the prisoners there is a raised way; and you will see, if you look, a low wall built along the way, like the screen which marionette players have in front of them, over which they show the puppets.

2   I see.

3   And do you see, I said, men passing along the wall carrying all sorts of vessels, and statues and figures of animals made of wood and stone and various materials, which appear over the wall? Some of them are talking, others silent.

4   You have shown me a strange image, and they are strange prisoners.

5   Like ourselves, I replied; and they see only their own shadows, or the shadows of one another, which the fire throws on the opposite wall of the cave?

6   True, he said; how could they see anything but the shadows if they were never allowed to move their heads?

7   And of the objects which are being carried in like manner they would only see the shadows?

Yes, he said. 8

And if they were able to converse with one another, would they 9
not suppose that they were naming what was actually before them?

Very true. 10

And suppose further that the prison had an echo which came 11
from the other side, would they not be sure to fancy when one of
the passers-by spoke that the voice which they heard came from
the passing shadow?

No question, he replied. 12

To them, I said, the truth would be literally nothing but the 13
shadows of the images.

That is certain. 14

And now look again, and see what will naturally follow if the 15
prisoners are released and disabused of their error. At first, when
any of them is liberated and compelled suddenly to stand up and
turn his neck round and walk and look toward the light, he will
suffer sharp pains; the glare will distress him, and he will be
unable to see the realities of which in his former state he had seen
the shadows; and then conceive someone saying to him, that what
he saw before was an illusion, but that now, when he is approaching nearer to being and his eye is turned toward more real existence, he has a clearer vision—what will be his reply? And you
may further imagine that his instructor is pointing to the objects as
they pass and requiring him to name them—will he not be perplexed? Will he not fancy that the shadows which he formerly saw
are truer than the objects which are now shown to him?

Far truer. 16

And if he is compelled to look straight at the light, will he not 17
have a pain in his eyes which will make him turn away to take
refuge in the objects of vision which he can see, and which he will
conceive to be in reality clearer than the things which are now
being shown to him?

True, he said. 18

And suppose once more, that he is reluctantly dragged up a 19
steep and rugged ascent, and held fast until he is forced into the
presence of the sun himself, is he not likely to be pained and irritated?
When he approaches the light his eyes will be dazzled, and he will
not be able to see anything at all of what are now called realities.

20   Not all in a moment, he said.

21   He will require to grow accustomed to the sight of the upper world. And first he will see the shadows best, next the reflections of men and other objects in the water, and then the objects themselves; then he will gaze upon the light of the moon and the stars and the spangled heaven; and he will see the sky and the stars by night better than the sun or the light of the sun by day?

22   Certainly.

23   Last of all he will be able to see the sun, and not mere reflections of him in the water, but he will see him in his own proper place, and not in another; and he will contemplate him as he is.

24   Certainly.

25   He will then proceed to argue that this is he who gives the season and the years, and is the guardian of all that is in the visible world, and in a certain way the cause of all things which he and his fellows have been accustomed to behold?

26   Clearly, he said, he would first see the sun and then reason about him.

27   And when he remembered his old habitation, and the wisdom of the den and his fellow-prisoners, do you not suppose that he would felicitate himself on the change, and pity them?

28   Certainly, he would.

29   And if they were in the habit of conferring honors among themselves on those who were quickest to observe the passing shadows and to remark which of them went before, and which followed after, and which were together; and who were therefore best able to draw conclusions as to the future, do you think that he would care for such honors and glories, or envy the possessors of them? Would he not say with Homer,

        Better to be the poor servant of a poor master,

and to endure anything, rather than think as they do and live after their manner?

30   Yes, he said, I think that he would rather suffer anything than entertain these false notions and live in this miserable manner.

31   Imagine once more, I said, such a one coming suddenly out of the sun to be replaced in his old situation; would he not be certain to have his eyes full of darkness?

To be sure, he said.   32

And if there were a contest, and he had to compete in mea-   33
suring the shadows with the prisoners who had never moved out
of the den, while his sight was still weak, and before his eyes had
become steady (and the time which would be needed to acquire
this new habit of sight might be very considerable), would he not
be ridiculous? Men would say of him that up he went and down
he came without his eyes; and that it was better not even to think
of ascending and if any one tried to loose another and lead him
up to the light, let them only catch the offender, and they would
put him to death.

No question, he said.   34

This entire allegory, I said, you may now append, dear   35
Glaucon, to the previous argument; the prison-house is the world
of sight, the light of the fire is the sun, and you will not misap-
prehend me if you interpret the journey upwards to be the ascent
of the soul into the intellectual world according to my poor
belief, which, at your desire, I have expressed—whether rightly
or wrongly God knows. But, whether true or false, my opinion is
that in the world of knowledge the idea of good appears last of all,
and is seen only with an effort; and, when seen, is also inferred to
be the universal author of all things beautiful and right, parent of
light and of the lord of light in this visible world, and the immediate source of reason and truth in the intellectual; and that this is
the power upon which he who would act rationally either in public or private life must have his eye fixed.

I agree, he said, as far as I am able to understand you.   36

Moreover, I said, you must not wonder that those who attain   37
to this beatific vision are unwilling to descend to human affairs;
for their souls are ever hastening into the upper world where they
desire to dwell; which desire of theirs is very natural, if our allegory may be trusted.

Yes, very natural.   38

And is there anything surprising in one who passes from   39
divine contemplations to the evil state of man, misbehaving himself in a ridiculous manner; if, while his eyes are blinking and
before he has become accustomed to the surrounding darkness,
he is compelled to fight in courts of law, or in other places, about

the images or the shadows of images of justice, and is endeavoring to meet the conceptions of those who have never yet seen absolute justice?

40   Anything but surprising, he replied.

41   Anyone who has common sense will remember that the bewilderments of the eyes are of two kinds, and arise from two causes, either from coming out of the light or from going into the light, which is true of the mind's eye, quite as much as of the bodily eye; and he who remembers this when he sees anyone whose vision is perplexed and weak, will not be too ready to laugh; he will first ask whether that soul of man has come out of the brighter life, and is unable to see because unaccustomed to the dark, or having turned from darkness to the day is dazzled by excess of light. And he will count the one happy in his condition and state of being, and he will pity the other; or, if he have a mind to laugh at the soul which comes from below into the light, there will be more reason in this than in the laugh which greets him who returns from above out of the light into the den.

42   That, he said, is a very just distinction.

ca. 373 B.C.

Am I Blue?

Alice Walker

1   For about three years my companion and I rented a small house in the country that stood on the edge of a large meadow that appeared to run from the end of our deck straight into the mountains. The mountains, however, were quite far away, and between us and them there was, in fact, a town. It was one of the many pleasant aspects of the house that you never really were aware of this.

2   It was a house of many windows, low, wide, nearly floor to ceiling in the living room, which faced the meadow, and it was from one of these that I first saw our closest neighbor, a large white horse, cropping grass, flipping its mane, and ambling

about—not over the entire meadow, which stretched well out of sight of the house, but over the five or so fenced-in acres that were next to the twenty-odd that we had rented. I soon learned that the horse, whose name was Blue, belonged to a man who lived in another town, but was boarded by our neighbors next door. Occasionally, one of the children, usually a stocky teenager, but sometimes a much younger girl or boy, could be seen riding Blue. They would appear in the meadow, climb up on his back, ride furiously for ten or fifteen minutes, then get off, slap Blue on the flanks, and not be seen again for a month or more.

There were many apple trees in our yard, and one by the 3 fence that Blue could almost reach. We were soon in the habit of feeding him apples, which he relished, especially because by the middle of summer the meadow grasses—so green and succulent since January—had dried out from lack of rain, and Blue stumbled about munching the dried stalks half-heartedly. Sometimes he would stand very still just by the apple tree, and when one of us came out he would whinny, snort loudly, or stamp the ground. This meant, of course: I want an apple.

It was quite wonderful to pick a few apples, or collect those 4 that had fallen to the ground overnight, and patiently hold them, one by one, up to his large, toothy mouth. I remained as thrilled as a child by his flexible dark lips, huge, cubelike teeth that crunched the apples, core and all, with such finality, and his high, broadbreasted *enormity;* beside which, I felt small indeed. When I was a child, I used to ride horses, and was especially friendly with one named Nan until the day I was riding and my brother deliberately spooked her and I was thrown, head first, against the trunk of a tree. When I came to, I was in bed and my mother was bending worriedly over me; we silently agreed that perhaps horseback riding was not the safest sport for me. Since then I have walked, and prefer walking to horseback riding—but I had forgotten the depth of feeling one could see in horses' eyes.

I was therefore unprepared for the expression in Blue's. Blue 5 was lonely. Blue was horribly lonely and bored. I was not shocked that this should be the case; five acres to tramp by yourself, endlessly, even in the most beautiful of meadows—and his was—cannot provide many interesting events, and once rainy season turned to dry that was about it. No, I was shocked that I had forgotten that human animals and nonhuman animals can communicate quite well; if we are brought up around animals as children we take this for granted. By the time we are adults we no longer remember. However, the animals have not changed. They are in fact *completed* creations (at least they seem to be, so much more than we) who are not likely to change; it is their nature to express themselves. What else are they going to express? And they do. And, generally speaking, they are ignored.

6   After giving Blue the apples, I would wander back to the house, aware that he was observing me. Were more apples not forthcoming then? Was that to be his sole entertainment for the day? My partner's small son had decided he wanted to learn how to piece a quilt; we worked in silence on our respective squares as I thought . . .

7   Well, about slavery: About white children, who were raised by black people, who knew their first all-accepting love from black women, and then, when they were twelve or so, were told they must "forget" the deep levels of communication between themselves and "mammy" that they knew. Later they would be able to relate quite calmly, "My old mammy was sold to another good family." "My old mammy was _____ _____." Fill in the blank. Many more years later a white woman would say: "I can't understand these Negroes, these blacks. What do they want? They're so different from us."

8   And about the Indians, considered to be "like animals" by the "settlers" (a very benign euphemism for what they actually were), who did not understand their description as a compliment.

9   And about the thousands of American men who marry Japanese, Korean, Filipina, and other non-English-speaking women and of how happy they report they are, "*blissfully*," until their brides learn to speak English, at which point the marriages tend to fall apart. What then did the men see, when they looked into the eyes of the women they married, before they could speak English? Apparently only their own reflections.

10   I thought of society's impatience with the young. "Why are they playing the music so loud?" Perhaps the children have listened to much of the music of oppressed people their parents danced to before they were born, with its passionate but soft cries for acceptance and love, and they have wondered why their parents failed to hear.

I do not know how long Blue had inhabited his five beautiful, 11
boring acres before we moved into our house; a year after we had
arrived—and had also traveled to other valleys, other cities, other
worlds—he was still there.

But then, in our second year at the house, something happened 12
in Blue's life. One morning, looking out the window at the fog that
lay like a ribbon over the meadow, I saw another horse, a brown
one, at the other end of Blue's field. Blue appeared to be afraid of it,
and for several days made no attempt to go near. We went away for
a week. When we returned, Blue had decided to make friends and
the two horses ambled or galloped along together, and Blue did not
come nearly as often to the fence underneath the apple tree.

When he did, bringing his new friend with him, there was a dif- 13
ferent look in his eyes. A look of independence, of self-possession,
of inalienable *horse*ness. His friend eventually became pregnant.
For months and months there was, it seemed to me, a mutual
feeling between me and the horses of justice, of peace. I fed
apples to them both. The look in Blue's eyes was one of
unabashed "this is *it*ness."

It did not, however, last forever. One day, after a visit to the 14
city, I went out to give Blue some apples. He stood waiting, or so
I thought, though not beneath the tree. When I shook the tree and
jumped back from the shower of apples, he made no move. I carried some over to him. He managed to half-crunch one. The rest
he let fall to the ground. I dreaded looking into his eyes—because
I had of course noticed that Brown, his partner, had gone—but I
did look. If I had been born into slavery, and my partner had been
sold or killed, my eyes would have looked like that. The children
next door explained that Blue's partner had been "put with him"
(the same expression that old people used, I had noticed, when
speaking of an ancestor during slavery who had been impregnated by her owner) so that they could mate and she conceive.
Since that was accomplished, she had been taken back by her
owner, who lived somewhere else.

Will she be back? I asked. 15
They didn't know. 16

Blue was like a crazed person. Blue *was*, to me, a crazed person. 17
He galloped furiously, as if he were being ridden, around and
around his five beautiful acres. He whinnied until he couldn't.

He tore at the ground with his hooves. He butted himself against his single shade tree. He looked always and always toward the road down which his partner had gone. And then, occasionally, when he came up for apples, or I took apples to him, he looked at me. It was a look so piercing, so full of grief, a look so *human*, I almost laughed (I felt too sad to cry) to think there are people who do not know that animals suffer. People like me who have forgotten, and daily forget, all that animals try to tell us. "Everything you do to us will happen to you; we are your teachers, as you are ours. We are one lesson" is essentially it, I think. There are those who never once have even considered animals' rights: Those who have been taught that animals actually want to be used and abused by us, as small children "love" to be frightened, or women "love" to be mutilated and raped. . . . They are the great-grandchildren of those who honestly thought, because someone taught them this: "Women can't think," and "niggers can't faint." But most disturbing of all, in Blue's large brown eyes was a new look more painful than the look of despair: The look of disgust with human beings, with life; the look of hatred. And it was odd what the look of hatred did. It gave him, for the first time, the look of a beast. And what that meant was that he had put up a barrier within to protect himself from further violence; all the apples in the world wouldn't change that fact.

18   And so Blue remained, a beautiful part of our landscape, very peaceful to look at from the window, white against the grass. Once a friend came to visit and said, looking out on the soothing view: "And it *would* have to be a *white* horse; the very image of freedom." And I thought, yes, the animals are forced to become for us merely "images" of what they once so beautifully expressed. And we are used to drinking milk from containers showing "contented" cows, whose real lives we want to hear nothing about, eating eggs and drumsticks from "happy" hens, and munching hamburgers advertised by bulls of integrity who seem to command their fate.

19   As we talked of freedom and justice one day for all, we sat down to steaks. I am eating misery, I thought, as I took the first bite. And spit it out.

1986

Body Ritual among the Nacirema

Horace Miner

The anthropologist has become so familiar with the diversity of 1
ways in which different peoples behave in similar situations that he
is not apt to be surprised by even the most exotic customs. In fact, if
all of the logically possible combinations of behavior have not been
found somewhere in the world, he is apt to suspect that they must
be present in some yet undescribed tribe. This point has, in fact,
been expressed with respect to clan organization by Murdock.[1] In
this light, the magical beliefs and practices of the Nacirema present
such unusual aspects that it seems desirable to describe them as an
example of the extremes to which human behavior can go.

Professor Linton first brought the ritual of the Nacirema to 2
the attention of anthropologists twenty years ago, but the culture
of this people is still very poorly understood. They are a North
American group living in the territory between the Canadian
Cree, the Yaqui and Tarahumare of Mexico, and the Carib and
Arawak of the Antilles.[2] Little is known of their origin, although
tradition states that they came from the east. . . .

Nacirema culture is characterized by a highly developed 3
market economy which has evolved in a rich natural habitat.
While much of the people's time is devoted to economic pursuits,
a large part of the fruits of these labors and a considerable portion
of the day are spent in ritual activity. The focus of this activity is
the human body, the appearance and health of which loom as a
dominant concern in the ethos of the people. While such a concern is certainly not unusual, its ceremonial aspects and associated philosophy are unique.

The fundamental belief underlying the whole system appears 4
to be that the human body is ugly and that its natural tendency is
to debility and disease. Incarcerated in such a body, man's only
hope is to avert these characteristics through the use of the
powerful influences of ritual and ceremony. Every household has

[1]American anthropologist George Peter Murdock, authority on primitive cultures.
[2]Native American tribes formerly inhabiting the Saskatchewan region of Canada,
the Sonora region of Mexico, and the West Indies.

one or more shrines devoted to this purpose. The more powerful
individuals in the society have several shrines in their houses
and, in fact, the opulence of a house is often referred to in terms
of the number of such ritual centers it possesses. Most houses are
of wattle and daub construction, but the shrine rooms of the more
wealthy are walled with stone. Poorer families imitate the rich by
applying pottery plaques to their shrine walls.

5   While each family has at least one such shrine, the rituals associated with it are not family ceremonies but are private and secret.
The rites are normally only discussed with children, and then only
during the period when they are being initiated into these mysteries.
I was able, however, to establish sufficient rapport with the natives
to examine these shrines and to have the rituals described to me.

6   The focal point of the shrine is a box or chest which is built
into the wall. In this chest are kept the many charms and magical
potions without which no native believes he could live. These
preparations are secured from a variety of specialized practitioners. The most powerful of these are the medicine men, whose
assistance must be rewarded with substantial gifts. However, the
medicine men do not provide the curative potions for their
clients, but decide what the ingredients should be and then write
them down in an ancient and secret language. This writing is
understood only by the medicine men and by the herbalists who,
for another gift, provide the required charm.

7   The charm is not disposed of after it has served its purpose,
but is placed in the charm-box of the household shrine. As these
magical materials are specific for certain ills, and the real or imagined maladies of the people are many, the charm-box is usually
full to overflowing. The magical packets are so numerous that
people forget what their purposes were and fear to use them
again. While the natives are very vague on this point, we can only
assume that the idea in retaining all the old magical materials is
that their presence in the charm-box, before which the body rituals are conducted, will in some way protect the worshipper.

8   Beneath the charm-box is a small font. Each day every member
of the family, in succession, enters the shrine room, bows his head
before the charm-box, mingles different sorts of holy water in the
font, and proceeds with a brief rite of ablution. The holy waters are

secured from the Water Temple of the community, where the priests conduct elaborate ceremonies to make the liquid ritually pure.

In the hierarchy of magical practitioners, and below the medi- 9 cine men in prestige, are specialists whose designation is best translated "holy-mouth-men." The Nacirema have an almost pathological horror of and fascination with the mouth, the condition of which is believed to have a supernatural influence on all social relationships. Were it not for the rituals of the mouth, they believe that their teeth would fall out, their gums bleed, their jaws shrink, their friends desert them, and their lovers reject them. They also believe that a strong relationship exists between oral and moral characteristics. For example, there is a ritual ablution of the mouth for children which is supposed to improve their moral fiber.

The daily body ritual performed by everyone includes a 10 mouth-rite. Despite the fact that these people are so punctilious about care of the mouth, this rite involves a practice which strikes the uninitiated stranger as revolting. It was reported to me that the ritual consists of inserting a small bundle of hog hairs into the mouth, along with certain magical powders, and then moving the bundle in a highly formalized series of gestures.

In addition to the private mouth-rite, the people seek out a 11 holy-mouth-man once or twice a year. These practitioners have an impressive set of paraphernalia, consisting of a variety of augers, awls, probes, and prods. The use of these objects in the exorcism of the evils of the mouth involves almost unbelievable ritual torture of the client. The holy-mouth-man opens the client's mouth and, using the above mentioned tools, enlarges any holes which decay may have created in the teeth. Magical materials are put into these holes. If there are not naturally occurring holes in the teeth, large sections of one or more teeth are gouged out so that the supernatural substance can be applied. In the client's view, the purpose of these ministrations is to arrest decay and to draw friends. The extremely sacred and traditional character of the rite is evident in the fact that the natives return to the holy-mouth-men year after year, despite the fact that their teeth continue to decay.

It is to be hoped that, when a thorough study of the Nacirema 12 is made, there will be careful inquiry into the personality structure of these people. One has but to watch the gleam in the eye of a holy-mouth-man, as he jabs an awl into an exposed nerve, to suspect that a certain amount of sadism is involved. If this can be established, a very interesting pattern emerges, for most of the population shows definite masochistic tendencies. It was to these that Professor Linton referred in discussing a distinctive part of the daily body ritual which is performed only by men. This part of the rite involves scraping and lacerating the surface of the face with a sharp instrument. Special women's rites are performed only four times during each lunar month, but what they lack in frequency is made up in barbarity. As part of this ceremony, women bake their heads in small ovens for about an hour. The theoretically interesting point is that what seems to be a preponderantly masochistic people have developed sadistic specialists.

13   The medicine men have an imposing temple, or latipso, in every community of any size. The more elaborate ceremonies required to treat very sick patients can only be performed at this temple. These ceremonies involve not only the thaumaturge but a permanent group of vestal maidens who move sedately about the temple chambers in distinctive costume and headdress.

14   The latipso ceremonies are so harsh that it is phenomenal that a fair proportion of the really sick natives who enter the temple even recover. Small children whose indoctrination is still incomplete have been known to resist attempts to take them to the temple because "that is where you go to die." Despite this fact, sick adults are not only willing but eager to undergo the protracted ritual purification, if they can afford to do so. No matter how ill the supplicant or how grave the emergency, the guardians of many temples will not admit a client if he cannot give a rich gift to the custodian. Even after one has gained admission and survived the ceremonies, the guardians will not permit the neophyte to leave until he makes still another gift.

15   The supplicant entering the temple is first stripped of all his or her clothes. In everyday life the Nacirema avoids exposure of his body and its natural functions. Bathing and excretory acts are performed only in the secrecy of the household shrine, where they are ritualized as part of the body-rites. Psychological shock results from the fact that body secrecy is suddenly lost upon entry into the latipso. A man, whose own wife has never seen him in an

excretory act, suddenly finds himself naked and assisted by a vestal maiden while he performs his natural functions into a sacred vessel. This sort of ceremonial treatment is necessitated by the fact that the excreta are used by a diviner to ascertain the course and nature of the client's sickness. Female clients, on the other hand, find their naked bodies are subjected to the scrutiny, manipulation and prodding of the medicine men.

Few supplicants in the temple are well enough to do anything 16 but lie on their hard beds. The daily ceremonies, like the rites of the holy-mouth-men, involve discomfort and torture. With ritual precision, the vestals awaken their miserable charges each dawn and roll them about on their beds of pain while performing ablutions, in the formal movements of which the maidens are highly trained. At other times they insert magic wands in the supplicant's mouth or force him to eat substances which are supposed to be healing. From time to time the medicine men come to their clients and jab magically treated needles into their flesh. The fact that these temple ceremonies may not cure, and may even kill the neophyte, in no way decreases the people's faith in the medicine men.

There remains one other kind of practitioner, known as a 17 "listener." This witchdoctor has the power to exorcise the devils that lodge in the heads of people who have been bewitched. The Nacirema believe that parents bewitch their own children. Mothers are particularly suspected of putting a curse on children while teaching them the secret body rituals. The counter-magic of the witchdoctor is unusual in its lack of ritual. The patient simply tells the "listener" all his troubles and fears, beginning with the earliest difficulties he can remember. The memory displayed by the Nacirema in these exorcism sessions is truly remarkable. It is not uncommon for the patient to bemoan the rejection he felt upon being weaned as a babe, and a few individuals even see their troubles going back to the traumatic effects of their own birth.

In conclusion, mention must be made of certain practices which 18 have their base in native esthetics but which depend upon the pervasive aversion to the natural body and its functions. There are ritual fasts to make fat people thin and ceremonial feasts to make thin people fat. Still other rites are used to make women's breasts larger if they are small, and smaller if they are large. General dissatisfaction with breast shape is symbolized in the fact that the ideal form is virtually outside the range of human variation. A few women afflicted with almost inhuman hypermammary development are so idolized that they make a handsome living by simply going from village to village and permitting the natives to stare at them for a fee.

19   Reference has already been made to the fact that excretory functions are ritualized, routinized, and relegated to secrecy. Natural reproductive functions are similarly distorted. Intercourse is taboo as a topic and scheduled as an act. Efforts are made to avoid pregnancy by the use of magical materials or by limiting intercourse to certain phases of the moon. Conception is actually very infrequent. When pregnant, women dress so as to hide their condition. Parturition takes place in secret, without friends or relatives to assist, and the majority of women do not nurse their infants.

20   Our review of the ritual life of the Nacirema has certainly shown them to be a magic-ridden people. It is hard to understand how they have managed to exist so long under the burdens which they have imposed upon themselves. But even such exotic customs as these take on real meaning when they are viewed with the insight provided by Malinowski when he wrote:

21   "Looking from far and above, from our high places of safety in the developed civilization, it is easy to see all the crudity and irrelevance of magic. But without its power and guidance early man could not have mastered his practical difficulties as he has done, nor could man have advanced to the higher stages of civilization."

1956

The Cosmic Prison

Loren Eiseley

1   "A name is a prison, God is free," once observed the Greek poet Nikos Kazantzakis. He meant, I think, that valuable though language is to man, it is by very necessity limiting, and creates for man an invisible prison. Language implies boundaries. A word spoken creates a dog, a rabbit, a man. It fixes their nature before

our eyes; henceforth their shapes are, in a sense, our own creation. They are no longer part of the unnamed shifting architecture of the universe. They have been transfixed as if by sorcery, frozen into a concept, a word. Powerful though the spell of human language has proven itself to be, it has laid boundaries upon the cosmos.

No matter how far-ranging some of the mental probes that   2 man has philosophically devised, by his own created nature he is forced to hold the specious and emerging present and transform it into words. The words are startling in their immediate effectiveness, but at the same time they are always finally imprisoning because man has constituted himself a prison keeper. He does so out of no conscious intention, but because for immediate purposes he has created an unnatural world of his own, which he calls the cultural world, and in which he feels at home. It defines his needs and allows him to lay a small immobilizing spell upon the nearer portions of his universe. Nevertheless, it transforms that universe into a cosmic prison house which is no sooner mapped than man feels its inadequacy and his own.

He seeks then to escape, and the theory of escape involves   3 bodily flight. Scarcely had the first moon landing been achieved before one U.S. senator boldly announced: "We are the masters of the universe. We can go anywhere we choose." This statement was widely and editorially acclaimed. It is a striking example of the comfort of words, also of the covert substitutions and mental projections to which they are subject. The cosmic prison is not made less so by a successful journey of some two hundred and forty thousand miles in a cramped and primitive vehicle.

To escape the cosmic prison man is poorly equipped. He has   4 to drag portions of his environment with him, and his life span is that of a mayfly in terms of the distances he seeks to penetrate. There is no possible way to master such a universe by flight alone. Indeed such a dream is a dangerous illusion. This may seem a heretical statement, but its truth is self-evident if we try seriously to comprehend the nature of time and space that I sought to grasp when held up to view the fiery messenger that flared across the zenith in 1910. "Seventy-five years," my father had whispered in my ear, "seventy-five years and it will be racing homeward. Perhaps you will live to see it again. Try to remember."

5   And so I remembered. I had gained a faint glimpse of the size of our prison house. Somewhere out there beyond a billion miles in space, an entity known as a comet had rounded on its track in the black darkness of the void. It was surging homeward toward the sun because it was an eccentric satellite of this solar system. If I lived to see it it would be but barely, and with the dimmed eyes of age. Yet it, too, in its long traverse, was but a flitting mayfly in terms of the universe the night sky revealed.

6   So relative is the cosmos we inhabit that, as we gaze upon the outer galaxies available to the reach of our telescopes, we are placed in about the position that a single white blood cell in our bodies would occupy, if it were intelligently capable of seeking to understand the nature of its own universe, the body it inhabits. The cell would encounter rivers ramifying into miles of distance seemingly leading nowhere. It would pass through gigantic structures whose meaning it could never grasp—the brain, for example. It could never know there was an outside, a vast being on a scale it could not conceive of and of which it formed an infinitesimal part. It would know only the pouring tumult of the creation it inhabited, but of the nature of that great beast, or even indeed that it was a beast, it could have no conception whatever. It might examine the liquid in which it floated and decide, as in the case of the fall of Lucretius's atoms, that the pouring of obscure torrents had created its world.

7   It might discover that creatures other than itself swam in the torrent. But that its universe was alive, had been born and was destined to perish, its own ephemeral existence would never allow it to perceive. It would never know the sun; it would explore only through dim tactile sensations and react to chemical stimuli that were borne to it along the mysterious conduits of the arteries and veins. Its universe would be centered upon a great arborescent tree of spouting blood. This, at best, generations of white blood cells by enormous labor and continuity might succeed, like astronomers, in charting.

8   They could never, by any conceivable stretch of the imagination, be aware that their so-called universe was, in actuality, the prowling body of a cat or the more time-enduring body of a philosopher, himself engaged upon the same quest in a more

gigantic world and perhaps deceived proportionately by greater vistas. What if, for example, the far galaxies man observes make up, across void spaces of which even we are atomically composed, some kind of enormous creature or cosmic snowflake whose exterior we will never see? We will know more than the phagocyte in our bodies, but no more than that limited creature can we climb out of our universe, or successfully enhance our size or longevity sufficiently to thrust our heads through the confines of the universe that terminates our vision.

Some further "outside" will hover elusively in our thought, but upon its nature, or even its reality, we can do no more than speculate. The phagocyte might observe the salty turbulence of an eternal river system, Lucretius the fall of atoms creating momentary living shapes. We suspiciously sense, in the concept of the expanding universe derived from the primordial atom— the monobloc—some kind of oscillating universal heart. At the instant of its contraction we will vanish. It is not given us, nor can our science recapture, the state beyond the monobloc, nor whether we exist in the diastole of some inconceivable being. We know only a little more extended reality than the hypothetical creature below us. Above us may lie realms it is beyond our power to grasp.

1970

Living Like Weasels

Annie Dillard

A Weasel is Wild. Who knows what he thinks? He sleeps in his underground den, his tail draped over his nose. Sometimes he lives in his den for two days without leaving. Outside, he stalks rabbits, mice, muskrats, and birds, killing more bodies than he can eat warm, and often dragging the carcasses home. Obedient to instinct, he bites his prey at the neck, either splitting the jugular vein at the throat or crunching the brain at the base of the skull, and he does not let go. One naturalist refused to kill a weasel who was socketed into his hand deeply as a rattlesnake. The man could in no way pry the tiny weasel off, and he had to walk half a mile to water, the weasel dangling from his palm, and soak him off like a stubborn label.

2   And once, says Ernest Thompson Seton—once, a man shot an eagle out of the sky. He examined the eagle and found the dry skull of a weasel fixed by the jaws to his throat. The supposition is that the eagle had pounced on the weasel and the weasel swiveled and bit as instinct taught him, tooth to neck, and nearly won. I would like to have seen that eagle from the air a few weeks or months before he was shot: was the whole weasel still attached to his feathered throat, a fur pendant? Or did the eagle eat what he could reach, gutting the living weasel with his talons before his breast, bending his beak, cleaning the beautiful airborne bones?

3   I have been reading about weasels because I saw one last week. I startled a weasel who startled me, and we exchanged a long glance.

4   Twenty minutes from my house, through the woods by the quarry and across the highway, is Hollins Pond, a remarkable piece of shallowness, where I like to go at sunset and sit on a tree trunk. Hollins Pond is also called Murray's Pond; it covers two acres of bottomland near Tinker Creek with six inches of water and six thousand lily pads. In winter, brown-and-white steers stand in the middle of it, merely dampening their hooves; from the distant shore they look like miracle itself, complete with miracle's nonchalance. Now, in summer, the steers are gone. The water lilies have blossomed and spread to a green horizontal plane that is terra firma to plodding blackbirds, and tremulous ceiling to black leeches, crayfish, and carp.

5   This is, mind you, suburbia. It is a five-minute walk in three directions to rows of houses, though none is visible here. There's a 55 mph highway at one end of the pond, and a nesting pair of wood ducks at the other. Under every bush is a muskrat hole or a beer can. The far end is an alternating series of fields and woods, fields and woods, threaded everywhere with motorcycle tracks— in whose bare clay wild turtles lay eggs.

So, I had crossed the highway, stepped over two low barbed- 6
wire fences, and traced the motorcycle path in all gratitude
through the wild rose and poison ivy of the pond's shoreline up
into high grassy fields. Then I cut down through the woods to the
mossy fallen tree where I sit. This tree is excellent. It makes a dry,
upholstered bench at the upper, marshy end of the pond, a plush
jetty raised from the thorny shore between a shallow blue body of
water and a deep blue body of sky.

The sun had just set. I was relaxed on the tree trunk, 7
ensconced in the lap of lichen, watching the lily pads at my feet
tremble and part dreamily over the thrusting path of a carp. A
yellow bird appeared to my right and flew behind me. It caught
my eye; I swiveled around—and the next instant, inexplicably, I
was looking down at a weasel, who was looking up at me.

Weasel! I'd never seen one wild before. He was ten inches 8
long, thin as a curve, a muscled ribbon, brown as fruitwood, soft-
furred, alert. His face was fierce, small and pointed as a lizard's;
he would have made a good arrowhead. There was just a dot of
chin, maybe two brown hairs' worth, and then the pure white fur
began that spread down his underside. He had two black eyes I
didn't see, any more than you see a window.

The weasel was stunned into stillness as he was emerging 9
from beneath an enormous shaggy wild rose bush four feet away.
I was stunned into stillness twisted backward on the tree trunk.
Our eyes locked, and someone threw away the key.

Our look was as if two lovers, or deadly enemies, met unex- 10
pectedly on an overgrown path when each had been thinking of
something else: a clearing blow to the gut. It was also a bright
blow to the brain, or a sudden beating of brains, with all the
charge and intimate grate of rubbed balloons. It emptied our
lungs. It felled the forest, moved the fields, and drained the pond;
the world dismantled and tumbled into that black hole of eyes. If
you and I looked at each other that way, our skulls would split
and drop to our shoulders. But we don't. We keep our skulls. So.

He disappeared. This was only last week, and already I don't 11
remember what shattered the enchantment. I think I blinked, I
think I retrieved my brain from the weasel's brain, and tried to

memorize what I was seeing, and the weasel felt the yank of separation, the careening splash-down into real life and the urgent current of instinct. He vanished under the wild rose. I waited motionless, my mind suddenly full of data and my spirit with pleadings, but he didn't return.

12   Please do not tell me about "approach-avoidance conflicts." I tell you I've been in that weasel's brain for sixty seconds, and he was in mine. Brains are private places, muttering through unique and secret tapes—but the weasel and I both plugged into another tape simultaneously, for a sweet and shocking time. Can I help it if it was a blank?

13   What goes on in his brain the rest of the time? What does a weasel think about? He won't say. His journal is tracks in clay, a spray of feathers, mouse blood and bone: uncollected, unconnected, loose-leaf, and blown.

14   I would like to learn, or remember, how to live. I come to Hollins Pond not so much to learn how to live as, frankly, to forget about it. That is, I don't think I can learn from a wild animal how to live in particular—shall I suck warm blood, hold my tail high, walk with my footprints precisely over the prints of my hands?—but I might learn something of mindlessness, something of the purity of living in the physical senses and the dignity of living without bias or motive. The weasel lives in necessity and we live in choice, hating necessity and dying at the last ignobly in its talons. I would like to live as I should, as the weasel lives as he should. And I suspect that for me the way is like the weasel's: open to time and death painlessly, noticing everything, remembering nothing, choosing the given with a fierce and pointed will.

15   I missed my chance. I should have gone for the throat. I should have lunged for that streak of white under the weasel's chin and held on, held on through mud and into the wild rose, held on for a dearer life. We could live under the wild rose wild as weasels, mute and uncomprehending. I could very calmly go wild. I could live two days in the den, curled, leaning on mouse fur, sniffing bird bones, blinking, licking, breathing musk, my hair tangled in the roots of grasses. Down is a good place to go,

where the mind is single. Down is out, out of your ever-loving mind and back to your careless senses. I remember muteness as a prolonged and giddy fast, where every moment is a feast of utterance received. Time and events are merely poured, unremarked, and ingested directly, like blood pulsed into my gut through a jugular vein. Could two live that way? Could two live under the wild rose, and explore by the pond, so that the smooth mind of each is as everywhere present to the other, and as received and as unchallenged, as falling snow?

We could, you know. We can live any way we want. People 16 take vows of poverty, chastity, and obedience—even of silence— by choice. The thing is to stalk your calling in a certain skilled and supple way, to locate the most tender and live spot and plug into that pulse. This is yielding, not fighting. A weasel doesn't "attack" anything; a weasel lives as he's meant to, yielding at every moment to the perfect freedom of single necessity.

I think it would be well, and proper, and obedient, and pure, 17 to grasp your one necessity and not let it go, to dangle from it limp wherever it takes you. Then even death, where you're going no matter how you live, cannot you part. Seize it and let it seize you up aloft even, till your eyes burn out and drop; let your musky flesh fall off in shreds, and let your very bones unhinge and scatter, loosened over fields, over fields and woods, lightly, thoughtless, from any height at all, from as high as eagles.

1982

10

Argument and Persuasion

ARGUMENT

Economics and Social Responsibility

A Step Back to the Workhouse?

Barbara Ehrenreich

1 The commentators are calling it a "remarkable consensus." Workfare, as programs to force welfare recipients to work are known, was once abhorred by liberals as a step back toward the 17th-century workhouse or—worse—slavery. But today no political candidate dares step outdoors without some plan for curing "welfare dependency" by putting its hapless victims to work—if necessary, at the nearest Burger King. It is as if the men who run things, or who aspire to run things (and we are, unfortunately, talking mostly about men when we talk about candidates), had gone off and caucused for a while and decided on the one constituency that could be safely sacrificed in the name of political expediency and "new ideas," and that constituency is poor women.

2 Most of the arguments for workfare are simply the same indestructible stereotypes that have been around, in one form or another, since the first public relief program in England 400 years ago: That the poor are poor because they are lazy and dissolute, and that they are lazy and dissolute because they are suffering from "welfare dependency." Add a touch of modern race and gender stereotypes and you have the image that haunts the

294

workfare advocates: A slovenly, overweight, black woman who produces a baby a year in order to augment her welfare checks.

But there is a new twist to this season's spurt of welfare-bash- 3 ing: Workfare is being presented as a kind of *feminist* alternative to welfare. As [the late] Senator Daniel Patrick Moynihan (D.-N.Y.) has put it, "A program that was designed to pay mothers to stay at home with their children [i.e., welfare, or Aid to Families with Dependent Children] cannot succeed when we now observe most mothers going out to work." Never mind the startling illogic of this argument, which is on a par with saying that no woman should stay home with her children because other women do not, or that a laid-off male worker should not receive unemployment compensation because most men have been observed holding jobs. We are being asked to believe that pushing destitute moth- ers into the work force (in some versions of workfare, for no other compensation than the welfare payments they would have received anyway) is consistent with women's strivings toward self-determination.

Now I will acknowledge that most women on welfare—like 4 most unemployed women in general—would rather have jobs. And I will further acknowledge that many of the proponents of workfare, possibly including Senator Moynihan and the Democratic presidential candidates, have mounted the band- wagon with the best of intentions. Welfare surely needs reform. But workfare is not the solution, because "dependency"—with all its implications of laziness and depravity—is not the problem. The problem is poverty, which most women enter in a uniquely devastating way—with their children in tow.

Let me introduce a real person, if only because real people, as 5 opposed to imaginative stereotypes, never seem to make an appearance in the current rhetoric on welfare. "Lynn," as I will call her, is a friend and onetime neighbor who has been on wel- fare for two years. She is also about as unlike the stereotypical "welfare mother" as one can get—which is to say that she is a fairly typical welfare recipient. She has only one child, which puts her among the 74 percent of welfare recipients who have only one or two children. She is white (not that that should matter), as are almost half of welfare recipients. Like most welfare recipients, she is not herself the daughter of a welfare recipient, and hence not part of anything that could be called an "intergenerational cycle of dependency." And like every woman on welfare I have ever talked to, she resents the bureaucratic hassles that are the psychic price of welfare. But, for now, there are no alternatives.

6   When I first met Lynn, she seemed withdrawn and disoriented. She had just taken the biggest step of her 25 years; she had left an abusive husband and she was scared: Scared about whether she could survive on her own and scared of her estranged husband. He owned a small restaurant; she was a high school dropout who had been a waitress when she met him. During their three years of marriage he had beaten her repeatedly. Only after he threw her down a flight of stairs had she realized that her life was in danger and moved out. I don't think I fully grasped the terror she had lived in until one summer day when he chased Lynn to the door of my house with a drawn gun.

7   Gradually Lynn began to put her life together. She got a divorce and went on welfare; she found a pediatrician who would accept Medicaid and a supermarket that would take food stamps. She fixed up her apartment with secondhand furniture and flea market curtains. She was, by my admittedly low standards, a compulsive housekeeper and an overprotective mother; and when she wasn't waxing her floors or ironing her two-year-old's playsuits, she was studying the help-wanted ads. She spent a lot of her time struggling with details that most of us barely notice—the price of cigarettes, mittens, or of a bus ticket to the welfare office—yet, somehow, she regained her sense of humor. In fact, most of the time we spent together was probably spent laughing—over the foibles of the neighbors, the conceits of men, and the snares of welfare and the rest of "the system."

8   Yet for all its inadequacies, Lynn was grateful for welfare. Maybe if she had been more intellectually inclined she would have found out that she was suffering from "welfare dependency," a condition that is supposed to sap the will and demolish the work ethic. But "dependency" is not an issue when it is a choice between an abusive husband and an impersonal government. Welfare had given Lynn a brief shelter in a hostile world, and as far as she was concerned, it was her ticket to *independence*.

Suppose there had been no welfare at the time when Lynn 9
finally summoned the courage to leave her husband. Suppose she
had gone for help and been told she would have to "work off" her
benefits in some menial government job (restocking the toilet
paper in rest rooms is one such "job" assigned to New York
women in a current workfare program). Or suppose, as in some
versions of workfare, she had been told she would have to take
the first available private sector job, which (for a non-high school
graduate like Lynn) would have paid near the minimum wage, or
$3.35 an hour. How would she have been able to afford child
care? What would she have done for health insurance (as a welfare recipient she had Medicaid, but most low-paying jobs offer
little or no coverage)? Would she have ever made the decision to
leave her husband in the first place?

As Ruth Sidel points out in *Women and Children Last* (Viking), 10
most women who are or have been on welfare have stories like
Lynn's. They go onto welfare in response to a crisis—divorce, illness, loss of a job, the birth of an additional child to feed—and
they remain on welfare for two years or less. They are not victims
of any "welfare culture," but of a society that increasingly
expects women to both raise and support children—and often on
wages that would barely support a woman alone. In fact, even
some of the most vociferous advocates of replacing welfare with
workfare admit that, in their own estimation, only about 15 percent
of welfare recipients fit the stereotype associated with "welfare
dependency": Demoralization, long-term welfare use, lack of
drive, and so on.

But workfare will not help anyone, not even the presumed 11
15 percent of "bad apples" for whose sake the majority will be
penalized. First, it will not help because it does not solve the problem that drives most women into poverty in the first place: How to
hold a job *and* care for children. Child care in a licensed, professionally run center can easily cost as much as $100 a week per child—
more than most states now pay in welfare benefits (for two
children) and more than most welfare recipients could expect
to earn in the work force. Any serious effort to get welfare recipients
into the work force would require child care provisions at a price
that would probably end up higher than the current budget for

AFDC. But none of the workfare advocates are proposing that sort of massive public commitment to child care.

12   Then there is the problem of jobs. So far, studies show that existing state workfare programs have had virtually no success in improving their participants' incomes or employment rates. Small wonder: Nearly half the new jobs generated in recent years pay poverty-level wages; and most welfare recipients will enter jobs that pay near the minimum wage, which is $6,900 a year—26 percent less than the poverty level for a family of three. A menial, low-wage job may be character-building (from a middle-class vantage point), but it will not lift anyone out of poverty.

13   Some of my feminist activist friends argue that it is too late to stop the workfare juggernaut. The best we can do, they say, is to try to defeat the more pernicious proposals: Those that are over-coercive, that do not offer funds for child care, or that would relegate work clients to a "subemployee" status unprotected by federal labor and civil rights legislation. Our goal, the pragmatists argue, should be to harness the current enthusiasm for workfare to push for services welfare recipients genuinely need, such as child care and job training and counseling.

14   I wish the pragmatists well, but for me, it would be a betrayal of women like Lynn to encourage the workfare band-wagon in any way. Most women, like Lynn, do not take up wel-fare as a career, but as an emergency measure in a time of personal trauma and dire need. At such times, the last thing they need is to be hustled into a low-wage job, and left to piece together child care, health insurance, transportation, and all the other ingredients of survival. In fact, the main effect of work-fare may be to discourage needy women from seeking any help at all—a disastrous result in a nation already suffering from a child poverty rate of nearly 25 percent. Public policy should be aimed at giving impoverished mothers (and, I would add, fathers) the help they so urgently need—not only in the form of job opportunities, but sufficient income support to live on until a job worth taking comes along.

15   Besides, there is an ancient feminist principle at stake. The premise of all the workfare proposals—the more humane as

well as the nasty—is that single mothers on welfare are not *working.* But, to quote the old feminist bumper sticker, EVERY MOTHER IS A WORKING MOTHER. And those who labor to raise their children in poverty—to feed and clothe them on meager budgets and to nurture them in an uncaring world—are working the hardest. The feminist position has never been that all women must pack off their children and enter the work force, but that all women's work—in the home or on the job—should be valued and respected.

1987

Barbara Ehrenreich's essay stimulated a lively response from Ms. *readers. The following letters were published in the February 1988 issue.*

I was absolutely thrilled when I read Barbara Ehrenreich's 16 article on workfare ("A Step Back to the Workhouse?" November 1987). As a single mother who received welfare for several years (with no child support) I'm against everything that workfare stands for. I belong to an organization called Women, Work, and Welfare, a group of current and former welfare recipients trying to empower ourselves and become a part of the decisions that affect our lives as poor women. It seems as if everybody but the welfare recipient herself has a hand in the decisions that are made.

CHERI HONKALA
Minneapolis, Minn.

I arrived in Chicago in 1952 with a husband and two children 17 from a camp in Europe. I had another child in 1953, lost a newborn in 1954, had a miscarriage, a hysterectomy, and a divorce in 1955. I never received child support. My ex-husband was remarried within two months.

18   I *never* received welfare. I worked in another culture, while in very bad health. I found a two-room flat, had no furniture and slept for years on the floor. I even went back to school at night and had to contend with companies like Gulf Oil Corp., which did not believe in promoting women. But I just slugged on.

19   By the end of the sixties, I had two daughters in college, and I had bought a house. My total earnings for 1970 from three jobs came to a whopping $8,000.

20   A full-time minimum wage job *can* support one adult and one child. One just has to learn how to do it.

URRSULA SCHRAMM
Hurley, Wis.

21   I found myself agreeing with the problems that Barbara Ehrenreich outlines in the present workfare program.

22   Yet deep inside a protesting rumbling exploded when I read that impoverished mothers should receive sufficient income support to live on "until a job worth taking comes along." *Bullshit!* Sure, we all should have the right to only work a job we love, but how many of us can afford to wait for it? That we are often forced to work at jobs that are not fulfilling says a lot about our society in which more needs to be changed than just the welfare system!

23   My mother was forced to go to work when I was nine years old. Our family was in dire financial straits and at the age of 50 she took a job in a factory. Was that job "worth taking"? Did it utilize her unique talents? *No!* Did it bring her personal fulfillment? *No!* Did it prevent the bank from foreclosing on our home? *Yes!* Did it give my mother the power to overcome our financial crisis and maintain her autonomy? *Yes!* You tell me if it was "worth taking." That depends on what your self-respect is worth to you.

GAIL FREI
Newtown Square, Pa.

Barbara Ehrenreich omitted a major element in her discussion 24
of the victimization of welfare families: The inability or unwill-
ingness of the legal system to award *and enforce* realistic child support. Until it stops being easier to abandon your children than to
default on that car loan, women and those who depend on them
will be welfare/workfare victims.

SUSAN MARTIN RYNARD
Durham, N.C.

I went on welfare when my daughter was three, when I left 25
my husband. I had a high school education, but had always
wanted to go to college. I was 25.

So, with the help of the government, I got my B.S. in nursing. 26
I worked for several years as an R.N. and then returned to school
for my master's degree. For graduate school, I lived on savings,
loans, and grants. The loans ($19,000 for undergrad and graduate
in all) will be paid off in less than a year, in time for my daughter
to begin college!

KATHRYN REID
Silverado, Calif.

Although I share Barbara Ehrenreich's concerns about 27
workfare and the plight of her friend Lynn, the conclusions she
draws strike me as misguided. We live in a society where the
myths of the work ethic and self-help are deeply embedded in
the popular culture; where resort to the dole is frowned upon
unless the need is temporary or arises from disability; where
the middle-class majority feels inequitably taxed, as compared
to the wealthy, to support a system that directly benefits few of
its members.

28   Feminists and other liberals should acknowledge the swelling demand for welfare reform. Our support should be conditional upon the incorporation in any welfare reform plan of provision for *quality* childcare facilities; upon the minimization of coercion; and upon further efforts to compel ex-spouses to pay their fair share of support. Nothing in this approach rules out our going ahead simultaneously with other, parallel efforts to question the mystique of work or to expose the links between welfare and poverty, on the one hand, and capitalism and the subordination of women, on the other.

DAVID G. BECKER
Hanover, N.H.

29   California is serious about workfare, but we call it GAIN (Greater Avenues for Independence). It offers welfare recipients vocational counseling, up to two years of vocational training, and workshops in how to get and hold a job.

30   GAIN also pays for child care and transportation. No job need be accepted by the recipient unless she/he will *net* at least as much as their AFDC grant, *including* child care, transportation, and medical insurance. And even then, they will receive funds to cover these costs for three months after they begin working to help them make the transition to the work force.

JANE KIRCHMAN
Guerneville, Calif.

Lifeboat Ethics: The Case Against Helping the Poor

Garrett Hardin

Environmentalists use the metaphor of the Earth as a "spaceship" 1
in trying to persuade countries, industries and people to stop
wasting and polluting our natural resources. Since we all share
life on this planet, they argue, no single person or institution has
the right to destroy, waste, or use more than a fair share of its
resources.

But does everyone on Earth have an equal right to an equal 2
share of its resources? The spaceship metaphor can be dangerous
when used by misguided idealists to justify suicidal policies for
sharing our resources through uncontrolled immigration and
foreign aid. In their enthusiastic but unrealistic generosity, they
confuse the ethics of a spaceship with those of a lifeboat.

A true spaceship would have to be under the control of a 3
captain, since no ship could possibly survive if its course were
determined by committee. Spaceship Earth certainly has no
captain; the United Nations is merely a toothless tiger, with little
power to enforce any policy upon its bickering members.

If we divide the world crudely into rich nations and poor 4
nations, two thirds of them are desperately poor, and only one
third comparatively rich, with the United States the wealthiest of
all. Metaphorically each rich nation can be seen as a lifeboat full of
comparatively rich people. In the ocean outside each lifeboat
swim the poor of the world, who would like to get in, or at least to
share some of the wealth. What should the lifeboat passengers do?

First, we must recognize the limited capacity of any lifeboat. 5
For example, a nation's land has a limited capacity to support a
population and as the current energy crisis has shown us, in some
ways we have already exceeded the carrying capacity of our land.
So here we sit, say 50 people in our lifeboat. To be generous, let us
assume it has room for 10 more, making a total capacity of 60.
Suppose the 50 of us in the lifeboat see 100 others swimming
in the water outside, begging for admission to our boat or for

handouts. We have several options: We may be tempted to try to live by the Christian ideal of being "our brother's keeper," or by the Marxist ideal of "to each according to his needs." Since the needs of all in the water are the same, and since they can all be seen as our "brothers," we could take them all into our boat, making a total of 150 in a boat designed for 60. The boat swamps; everyone drowns. Complete justice, complete catastrophe.

6   Since the boat has an unused excess capacity of 10 more passengers, we could admit just 10 more to it. But which 10 do we let in? How do we choose? Do we pick the best 10, the neediest 10, "first come, first served"? And what do we say to the 90 we exclude? If we do let an extra 10 into our lifeboat, we will have lost our "safety factor," an engineering principle of critical importance. For example, if we don't leave room for excess capacity as a safety factor in our country's agriculture, a new plant disease or a bad change in the weather could have disastrous consequences.

7   Suppose we decide to preserve our small safety factor and admit no more to the lifeboat. Our survival is then possible, although we shall have to be constantly on guard against boarding parties.

8   While this last solution clearly offers the only means of our survival, it is morally abhorrent to many people. Some say they feel guilty about their good luck. My reply is simple: "Get out and yield your place to others." This may solve the problem of the guilt-ridden person's conscience, but it does not change the ethics of the lifeboat. The needy person to whom the guilt-ridden person yields his place will not himself feel guilty about his good luck. If he did, he would not climb aboard. The net result of conscience-stricken people giving up their unjustly held seats is the elimination of that sort of conscience from the lifeboat.

9   This is the basic metaphor within which we must work out our solutions. Let us now enrich the image, step by step, with substantive additions from the real world, a world that must solve real and pressing problems of overpopulation and hunger.

10   The harsh ethics of the lifeboat become even harsher when we consider the reproductive differences between the rich nations and the poor nations. The people inside the lifeboats are

doubling in numbers every 87 years; those swimming around outside are doubling, on the average, every 35 years, more than twice as fast as the rich. And since the world's resources are dwindling, the difference in prosperity between the rich and the poor can only increase.

As of 1973, the United States had a population of 210 million 11 people, who were increasing by 0.8 percent per year. Outside our lifeboat, let us imagine another 210 million people (say the combined populations of Colombia, Ecuador, Venezuela, Morocco, Pakistan, Thailand, and the Philippines), increasing at a rate of 3.3 percent per year. Put differently, the doubling time for this aggregate population was 21 years, compared to 87 years for the United States.

Now suppose the United States agreed to pool its resources 12 with those seven countries, with everyone receiving an equal share. Initially the ratio of Americans to non-Americans in this model would be one-to-one. But consider what the ratio would be after 87 years, by which time the Americans would have doubled to a population of 420 million. By then, doubling every 21 years, the other group would have swollen to 3.54 billion. Each American would have to share the available resources with more than eight people.

But, one could argue, this discussion assumes that current 13 population trends will continue, and they may not. Quite so. Most likely the rate of population increase will decline much faster in the United States than it will in the other countries, and there does not seem to be much we can do about it. In sharing with "each according to his needs," we must recognize that needs are determined by population size, which is determined by the rate of reproduction, which at present is regarded as a sovereign right of every nation, poor or not. This being so, the philanthropic load created by the sharing ethic of the spaceship can only increase.

The fundamental error of spaceship ethics, and the sharing it 14 requires, is that it leads to what I call "the tragedy of the commons." Under a system of private property, people who own property recognize their responsibility to care for it, for if they don't they will eventually suffer. A farmer, for instance, will allow no more cattle in a pasture than its carrying capacity justifies. If he overloads it, erosion sets in, weeds take over, and he loses the use of the pasture.

15   If a pasture becomes a commons open to all, the right of each to use it may not be matched by a corresponding responsibility to protect it. Asking everyone to use it with discretion will hardly do, for the considerate herdsman who refrains from overloading the commons suffers more than a selfish one who says his needs are greater. If everyone would restrain himself, all would be well; but it takes only one less than everyone to ruin a system of voluntary restraint. In a crowded world of less than perfect human beings, mutual ruin is inevitable if there are no controls. This is the tragedy of the commons.

16   One of the major tasks of education today should be the creation of such an acute awareness of the dangers of the commons that people will recognize its many varieties. For example, the air and water have become polluted because they are treated as commons. Further growth in the population or per-capita conversion of natural resources into pollutants will only make the problem worse. The same holds true for the fish of the oceans. Fishing fleets have nearly disappeared in many parts of the world; technological improvements in the art of fishing are hastening the day of complete ruin. Only the replacement of the system of the commons with a responsible system of control will save the land, air, water and oceanic fisheries.

17   In recent years there has been a push to create a new commons called a World Food Bank, an international depository of food reserves to which nations would contribute according to their abilities and from which they would draw according to their needs. This humanitarian proposal received support from many liberal international groups, and from such prominent citizens as Margaret Mead, the U.N. Secretary General, and Senator Edward Kennedy.

18   A world food bank appeals powerfully to our humanitarian impulses. But before we rush ahead with such a plan, let us ask if such a program would actually do more good than harm, not only momentarily but also in the long run. Those who propose a food bank usually refer to a current "emergency" or "crisis" in

terms of world food supply. But what is an emergency? Although they may be infrequent and sudden, everyone knows that emergencies will occur from time to time. A well-run family, company, organization or country prepares for the likelihood of accidents and emergencies. It expects them, it budgets for them, it saves for them.

What happens if some organizations or countries budget for accidents and others do not? If each country is solely responsible for its own well-being, poorly managed ones will suffer. But they can learn from experience. They may mend their ways, and learn to budget for infrequent but certain emergencies. For example, the weather varies from year to year, and periodic crop failures are certain. A wise and competent government saves out of the production of the good years in anticipation of bad years to come. Joseph taught this policy to Pharaoh in Egypt more than 2,000 years ago. Yet the great majority of the governments in the world today do not follow such a policy. They lack either the wisdom or the competence, or both. Should those nations that do manage to put something aside be forced to come to the rescue each time an emergency occurs among the poor nations?

"But it isn't their fault!" some kind-hearted liberals argue. "How can we blame the poor people who are caught in an emergency? Why must they suffer for the sins of their governments?" The concept of blame is simply not relevant here. The real question is, what are the operational consequences of establishing a world food bank? If it is open to every country every time a need develops, slovenly rulers will not be motivated to take Joseph's advice. Someone will always come to their aid. Some countries will deposit food in the world food bank, and others will withdraw it. There will be almost no overlap. As a result of such solutions to food shortage emergencies, the poor countries will not learn to mend their ways, and will suffer progressively greater emergencies as their populations grow.

On the average, poor countries undergo a 2.5 percent increase in population each year; rich countries, about 0.6 percent. Only rich countries have anything in the way of food reserves set aside, and even they do not have as much as they should. Poor countries have none. If poor countries received no food from the outside, the rate of their population growth would be periodically checked by crop failures and famines. But if they can always draw on a world food bank in time of need, their population can continue to grow unchecked, and so will their "need" for aid. In the short run, a world food bank may diminish that need, but in the long run it actually increases the need without limit.

22   Without some system of worldwide food sharing, the proportion of people in the rich and poor nations might eventually stabilize. The overpopulated poor countries would decrease in numbers while the rich countries that had room for more people would increase. But with a well-meaning system of sharing, such as a world food bank, the growth differential between the rich and the poor countries will not only persist, it will increase. Because of the higher rate of population growth in the poor countries of the world, 88 percent of today's children are born poor, and only 12 percent rich. Year by year the ratio becomes worse as the fast-reproducing poor outnumber the slow-reproducing rich.

23   A world food bank is thus a commons in disguise: People will have more motivation to draw from it than to add to any common store. The less provident and less able will multiply at the expense of the abler and more provident, bringing eventual ruin upon all who share in the commons. Besides, any system of "sharing" that amounts to foreign aid from the rich nations to the poor nations will carry the taint of charity, which will contribute little to the world peace so devoutly desired by those who support the idea of a world food bank.

24   As past U.S. foreign-aid programs have amply and depressingly demonstrated, international charity frequently inspires mistrust and antagonism rather than gratitude on the part of the recipient nation.

25   The modern approach to foreign aid stresses the export of technology and advice, rather than money and food. As an ancient Chinese proverb goes: "Give a man a fish and he will eat for a day; teach him how to fish and he will eat for the rest of his days." Acting on this advice, the Rockefeller and Ford Foundations have financed a number of programs for improving agriculture in the hungry nations. Known as the "Green Revolution," these programs have led to the development of

"miracle rice" and "miracle wheat," new strains that offer bigger harvests and greater resistance to crop damage.

Whether or not the Green Revolution can increase food pro- 26 duction as much as its champions claim is a debatable but possibly irrelevant point. Those who support this well-intended humanitarian effort should first consider some of the fundamentals of human ecology. Ironically, one man who did was the late Alan Gregg, a vice president of the Rockefeller Foundation. Two decades ago he expressed strong doubts about the wisdom of such attempts to increase food production. He likened the growth and spread of humanity over the surface of the Earth to the spread of cancer in the human body, remarking that "cancerous growths demand food, but, as far as I know, they have never been cured by getting it."

Every human born constitutes a draft on all aspects of the 27 environment: Food, air, water, forests, beaches, wildlife, scenery and solitude. Food can, perhaps, be significantly increased to meet a growing demand. But what about clean beaches, unspoiled forests, and solitude? If we satisfy a growing population's need for food, we necessarily decrease its per capita supply of the other resources needed by people.

India, for example, now has a population of 600 million, 28 which increases by 15 million each year. This population already puts a huge load on a relatively impoverished environment. The country's forests are now only a small fraction of what they were three centuries ago, and floods and erosion continually destroy the insufficient farmland that remains. Every one of the 15 million new lives added to India's population puts an additional burden on the environment, and increases the economic and social costs of crowding. However humanitarian our intent, every Indian life saved through medical or nutritional assistance from abroad diminishes the quality of life for those who remain, and for subsequent generations. If rich countries make it possible, through foreign aid, for 600 million Indians to swell to 1.2 billion in a mere 28 years, as their current growth rate threatens, will future generations of Indians thank us for hastening the destruction of their environment? Will our good intentions be sufficient excuse for the consequences of our actions?

29   Without a true world government to control reproduction and the use of available resources, the sharing ethic of the spaceship is impossible. For the foreseeable future, our survival demands that we govern our actions by the ethics of a lifeboat, harsh though they may be. Posterity will be satisfied with nothing less.

1974

The Details of Life

Jonathan Kozol

1   "Peter's dog ate Jefferson's cat," says Mother Martha in a letter I received from the South Bronx.

2   Mother Martha is the priest of St. Ann's Church in the Mott Haven neighborhood, still the poorest section of the Bronx and, as physicians tell me, one of the most unhealthy places for a child to grow up in this or any other country of the Western world, with pediatric asthma rates and HIV infection rates for females in their older teenage years believed to be the highest in the nation.

3   St. Ann's is an Episcopal church. Martha Overall, a spirited and gutsy graduate of Radcliffe, used to practice law with the noted trial attorney Louis Nizer but gave up the law during the eighties and now, as the pastor of St. Ann's, she spends most of her days and nights surrounded by young children. Peter is a 10-year-old who lives above a store on St. Ann's Avenue directly opposite the garden of the church. His cousin Jefferson is living with him now, because the 7-year-old's mother has been seriously ill. She will be ill, as it turns out, for a long time and is for now, according to the priest, at Lincoln Hospital.

4   "First his mother. Then his cat!" says Mother Martha. "When I found him here this morning he was sitting on the front steps of the church. The cat, or what remained of her, was in a cardboard box. I sat there with him and we had a long talk about animals, because

I think you know that some denominations don't believe that animals have souls, and he's been told a number of conflicting things.

"After our talk we found a cookie tin. Armando dressed in [5] black for the occasion. Jefferson and Armando dug the hole. We said a prayer and sprinkled water on the cookie tin, and then the little ones threw dirt into the hole. I think that he was pleased, because he kept on bringing people out to see the grave. He dug her up three times to show his friends."

Armando is the sports director at the church. He tries, as do [6] most people on the staff, to give emotional support to kids like Jefferson when they have troubles in their home. Jefferson doesn't open up to many grown-ups, though. He's rather bashful and has melancholy eyes. When things are going well with him, he likes to race around the churchyard with the pastor and her dog. When things are going badly, he hardly talks at all. He gets a hunted look, like that of a small rabbit frozen by the headlights of a car. Mother Martha says he chose the prayer they read during the burial. Later, he found two sticks and made a cross to stand above the grave. When warmer weather came, he went back to the grave and planted flowers in the grass. "The dog who ate his cat," says Mother Martha, "is named Diesel—a good name, if you ask me, for an antisocial character who eats his friends."

Jefferson is one of six or seven children from the neighbor- [7] hood who spend hours of their time with Mother Martha and for whom she sweeps away appointments with all types of visitors, to the dismay of many who have often traveled a long way to get some time with her. Four of them are boys, and two or three, depending on the season or the year, are girls who are their sisters or their cousins. Katrice, a woman from the neighborhood who runs the free-food pantry at the church, refers to them as "Mother Martha's gang" and disapproves of how they pester and pursue the priest all day. "Look at how they pull her clothes!" she says when they surround her as she's coming from her car.

Jefferson brings animals he finds around the neighborhood [8] into the garden of St. Ann's. He seems happy with the animals, more than he sometimes seems to be with people. He likes to hang around at night with Mother Martha and her dog before it's time for him to go across the street to sleep.

9   Why does this story about Jefferson set off some warning signals for me as a writer? Perhaps simply because I know the fairly hard-nosed attitudes that govern social policy in urban neighborhoods today and can anticipate that this may be perceived as a preposterous distraction from the bottom-line concerns with "discipline" and "rigor" and "job preparation" and "high standards" and what is now known as "high-stakes testing" and the rest of the severe agenda that has recently been put in place for inner-city kids. Burials for cats somehow don't fit into this picture.

10   Then, too, in the business-minded ethos of our age, any money we may spend on children of poor people must be proven to be economically utilitarian and justifiable in cost-effective terms. But much of what goes on around St. Ann's cannot be justified in terms like these. You could not prove to anyone in Washington that Mother Martha's talk with Jefferson about the possibilities of an afterlife for animals will have "a positive effect" upon his reading scores or make him more employable a decade later.

11   Those, however, are the usual criteria for budgeting decisions in most programs that serve children. "Productivity" is almost everything. Elements of childhood that bear no possible connection to the world of enterprise and profit get no honor in the pedagogic world right now, nor do they in the economic universe to which it seems increasingly subservient.

12   Now and then I'm asked to go to conferences of urban school officials, corporation leaders and consultants, and the representatives of agencies that serve (or, as the jargon now requires, "service") inner-city youth. The atmosphere is very different at these sessions than it was only about ten years ago. The dialogue is managerial and structural, and its vocabulary tends to be impersonal and technocratic, weighted down by hyphenated words such as "performance-referenced," "outcome-oriented," "competency-centered." One hears a lot of economics, many references to competition and "delivery of product" and, of course, high standards and exams. Questions that concern the inner health of children, or their happiness or sadness, or their personalities as complicated, unpredictable and interesting little people don't come up at all, or if they do, are often treated as a genteel

afterthought and handled with dispatch and even traces of deri-
sion. The settings for these gatherings, which business leaders
sometimes underwrite, are generally extravagant. Guests are
inundated with expensively produced materials: shoulder bags
embossed with corporate logos, loose-leaf notebooks filled with
corporate position papers. The feeling of a public school is far
removed from all of this. People rarely speak of children; you
hear of "cohort groups" and "standard variations," but you don't
hear much of boys who miss their cats or 6-year-olds who have
to struggle with potato balls. If a bunch of kids like Elio and
Pineapple—two of the lively children I have known at St. Ann's
Church for many years—were seated at the table, it would seem
a comical anomaly. Statistical decorum would be undermined
by the particularities of all these uncontrollable and restless little variables.

13   The relentless emphasis at these events is on the future economic worth that low-income children may or may not have for
our society. Policy discussions seem to view them less as children
who have fingers, elbows, stomachaches and emotions than as
"economic units"—pint-sized deficits or assets in blue jeans and
jerseys, some of whom may prove to be a burden to society, others of whom may have some limited utility.

14   "The right kind of investment," says the former CEO of a
large corporation that sells toothpaste and detergent, "from conception to age 5, will pay back every dollar we spent at least four
for one, plus interest, plus inflation. I don't know of a factor anybody can build that will give that kind of return." However
intended, it seems a peculiar way to speak of children.

15   The trouble with this is that "investment values," whether in
petroleum, in soy or in the children of poor people, rise and fall.
What if a future generation of geneticists, economists or both
should come to the conclusion that the children of St. Ann's don't
offer a sufficient payoff to a corporation's bottom line to warrant
serious investment? We hear the stirrings of such notions even
now in writings that allude to IQ differentials between racial and
religious subgroups of the population. The subgroup living in
Mott Haven does not stand too high within these rankings. If
investment value is the governing determination here, black and

Hispanic boys and girls like Elio and Pineapple are certain to be given less of almost everything that can bring purpose or fulfillment to existence than the seemingly "more valuable" white and Asian children who get into schools like Stuyvesant, New York's most famous high school for the academic elite. Advocates for children, most of whom dislike this ethos, nonetheless play into it in efforts to obtain financial backing from the world of business.

16   "A dollar spent on Head Start," they repeat time and again, "will save our government six dollars over twenty years" in lowered costs for juvenile detention and adult incarceration. It's a point worth making if it's true, although it's hard to prove; and, still, it is a pretty dreadful way to have to think about 4-year-olds. The fact that such a program allows a child the size of Mariposa—one of the littlest children at St. Ann's and one of many in the neighborhood who suffer from chronic asthma—several hundred mornings with warmhearted people in a safe and friendly pastel-painted setting seems to be regarded as too "soft," too sentimental, to be mentioned in the course of these discussions. "We should invest in kids like these," we're told, "because it will be more expensive not to." Why does our natural compassion or religious inclination need to find a surrogate in dollar savings to be voiced or acted on? Why not give these kids the best we have because we are a wealthy nation and they're children and deserve to have some fun while they're still less than four feet high?

17   Or is the point here that we don't believe this? Sometimes it seems that "having fun" is seen as a luxurious entitlement that cannot be accorded to the child of a woman who relies on welfare lest it make dependent status too enjoyable. It seems at times that happiness itself is viewed as an extravagance and that our sole concerns in dealing with such children must be discipline, efficiency and future worth.

18   The problem is not only that low-income children are devalued by these mercantile criteria; childhood itself is also redefined. It ceases to hold value for its own sake but is valued only as a "necessary prologue" to utilitarian adulthood. The first ten, twelve or fifteen years of life are excavated of inherent moral worth in order to accommodate a regimen of basic training for the

adult years that many of the poorest children may not even live
to know. There is no reference to investing in the present—in the
childhood of children—only in a later incarnation of the child as
a "product" or "producer."

"We must start to think about these inner-city children as our 19
future entry-level workers," we are told by business leaders as
they forge their various alliances and partnerships with poorly
funded urban schools. It's fair to ask why we are being urged to
see "these" children in that quite specific way. Why are we to look
at Elio and see a future entry-level worker rather than to see him,
as we see our own kids, as perhaps a future doctor, dancer, artist,
poet, priest, psychologist or teacher, or whatever else he might
someday desire to be? Why not, for that matter, look at him and
see the only thing he really is: a 7-year-old child? Mariposa is not
simply thirty-seven pounds of raw material that wants a certain
"processing" and "finishing" before she can be shipped to market
and considered to have value. She is of value now, and if she dies
of a disease or accident when she is 12 years old, the sixth year of
her life will not as a result be robbed of meaning.

St. Ann's runs an excellent afterschool and literacy program 20
for approximately eighty children. Civic leaders from the downtown business world stop by at times to meet the children and for
conversations with the priest. They often get more than they bar-
gained for.

Mother Martha is a fearless woman who speaks truth to 21
power and does not allow her strong political beliefs to be subdued or suffocated by the pretense of civility so common in the
upper reaches of the press and power structure in New York. She
cuts right through the philanthropic piety of many visitors.
"Charity is not a substitute for justice," she says frequently. She's
unsparing also in her reference to the seemingly eternalized
apartheid of New York—99.8 percent of children in the schools
that serve this neighborhood are black or brown, and she does not
let visitors forget this. Even the most tough-minded CEOs look
shaken sometimes after they have talked with her.

But the presence and the sheer vitality of all these children 22
have a powerful effect upon the visitors as well. Once they're
here, it seems, their ideologies disintegrate. An intimate reality

does often have this power to collapse or modify belief. Nobody seems to want to advocate a "lean and mean" approach to public services for children while they're sitting in the chapel of St. Ann's with Elio or being drilled with questions by Pineapple.

23   The parents and staff at St. Ann's aren't naive about the world of economic competition that their children will be forced to enter in a few more years. The pedagogic program at the afterschool is rigorous. The women and men who run the program have a lot of love and hot sauce in their style, but they also have a realistic recognition of the academic needs of children. The church is also forced to pay attention to the newly instituted tests the children have to pass in public school. No one here, no matter how benighted they may think these tests are, has any hesitation about working hard with children on test-taking skills, because they know that children in rich neighborhoods receive this preparation as a matter of routine, often in expensive private programs.

24   Intensive academics aren't the whole of what goes on here at the afterschool, however. If they were, the children wouldn't come here with such eagerness when they leave public school. Amid the pressures and the tensions about school promotion policies (and nonpromotion policies, which recently have come to be capricious and severe) and reading skills, percentile "norms," math exams and high school applications or rejections, and the rest of what makes up the pedagogic battlefield—which is not now, and never was, a level field for children in poor neighborhoods like the South Bronx—the grown-ups here have also managed somehow to leave room for innocence.

25   The pastor here has her three degrees: in economics (as an undergraduate at Radcliffe), then in law, and then theology. She also has a bracelet made of jelly beans that Jefferson's sister gave her as a present before Easter. It is, she told me once when I was looking at the brightly colored jelly beans that Jefferson's sister somehow linked together with a needle and a piece of string, the only bracelet anyone has given her since childhood—"more beautiful," she said with pride, "than finest pearls." In an age of drills and skills and endless lists of reinvented standards and a multitude of new and sometimes useful but too often frankly punitive

exams, it's nice to find a place where there is still some room for things of no cash value—oddball humor, silliness and whim, a child's love, a grown-up's gratitude and joy—that never in a hundred years would show up as a creditable number on one of those all-important state exams.

Competitive skills are desperately needed by poor children 26 in America, and realistic recognition of the economic roles that they may someday have an opportunity to fill is obviously important too. But there is more to life, and there ought to be much more to childhood, than readiness for economic functions. Childhood ought to have at least a few entitlements that aren't entangled with utilitarian considerations. One of them should be the right to a degree of unencumbered satisfaction in the sheer delight and goodness of existence in itself. Another ought to be the confidence of knowing that one's presence on this earth is taken as an unconditioned blessing that is not contaminated by the economic uses that a nation does or does not have for you. What I admire most about the programs and the atmosphere of daily life here at the church is that these diverse goals are reconciled in relatively seamless ways that make it possible for children to regard the world, and life itself, as something that, though difficult and often filled with pain and tears, is also sometimes good, and sometimes bountiful in foolishness, and therefore beautiful.

I recognize that jelly beans will not be seen by all 27 Episcopalian officials as appropriate adornments for the vicar of an urban church, but it means something to Jefferson's sister when she sees the pastor wear that bracelet as she stands before the cross to celebrate the mass. The details of life renew our faith in life. In the busy ministries of grief the detailed things—the Band-Aids and the skinned knees and the handiwork of children's fingers—are too easily dismissed or relegated to the margins of consideration. I've been thankful that the detailed things are not forgotten in the course of all the solemn matters that preoccupy the pastor of St. Ann's.

People ask me why I keep on going back to visit at this 28 church when there are other churches in New York that operate effective programs that teach children useful skills each afternoon when they are done with school. I don't usually answer. If I did, I know I wouldn't say too much about the writing program and test-preparation program and computer classes. They're good programs, but a "program," even one that has some provable success, would not have brought me back into a church in the South Bronx nearly 200 times. If I had to answer, I would say that I go back for all the things that can't be calibrated by exams. Elio's imagination and his curiosity and tenderness are part of this, and Pineapple's unselfishness, and Jefferson's shyness and sweet sadness, and his closeness to the priest, and Jefferson's cat.

29   Two years have passed. On quiet afternoons the boy with melancholy eyes goes by himself sometimes into the chapel of St. Ann's and kneels down on the floor to say prayers for his mother and his cat. Mother Martha sometimes prays beside him. I have never asked the pastor what she prays for.

2000

Free Speech

Should This Student Have Been Expelled?

Nat Hentoff

> *The day that Brown denies any student freedom of speech*
> *is the day I give up my presidency of the university.*
> —Vartan Gregorian, president of Brown University,
>   February 20, 1991

1   Doug Hann, a varsity football player at Brown, was also concentrating on organizational behavior and management and business economics. On the night of October 18, 1990, Hann, a junior, was celebrating his twenty-first birthday, and in the process had imbibed a considerable amount of spirits.

At one point, Hann shouted into the air, "Fuck you, nig- 2 gers!" It was aimed at no one in particular but apparently at all black students at Brown. Or in the world. A freshman leaned out a dormitory window and asked him to stop being so loud and offensive.

Hann, according to reporters on the *Brown Daily Herald,* looked 3 up and yelled, "What are you, a faggot?" Hann then noticed an Israeli flag in the dorm. "What are you, a Jew?" he shouted. "Fucking Jew!"

Hann had achieved the hat trick of bigotry. (In hockey, the 4 hat trick is scoring three goals in a game.) In less than a minute, Hann had engaged in racist, anti-Semitic, and homophobic insults.

He wasn't through. As reported by Smita Nerula in the *Brown* 5 *Daily Herald,* the freshman who had asked Hann to cool it recruited a few people from his dorm "and followed Hann and his friends."

"This resulted in a verbal confrontation outside of Wayland 6 Arch. At this time, [Hann] was said to have turned to one of the freshman's friends, a black woman, and shouted, 'My parents own your people.'"

To the Jewish student, or the student he thought was Jewish, 7 Hann said, "Happy Hanukkah."

There are reports that at this juncture Hann tried to fight 8 some of the students who had been following him. But, the *Brown Daily Herald* reports, he "was held back by one of his friends, while [another] friend stretched his arm across the Wayland Gates to keep the students from following Hann."

John Howard Crouch—a student and Brown chapter secre- 9 tary of the American Civil Liberties Union there—tells me that because Hann had friends restraining him, "nobody seriously expected fighting, regardless of anyone's words."

Anyway, there was no physical combat. Just words. Awful 10 words, but nothing more than speech. (Nor were there any threats.)

This was not the first time Hann's disgraceful drunken lan- 11 guage had surfaced at Brown. Two years before, in an argument with a black student at a fraternity bar, Hann had called the student a "nigger." Thereupon he had been ordered to attend a race relations workshop and to get counseling for possible alcohol abuse. Obviously, he has not been rehabilitated.

12   Months went by after Hann's notorious birthday celebration as Brown's internal disciplinary procedures cranked away. (To steal a phrase from Robert Sherrill, Brown's way of reaching decisions in these matters is to due process as military music is to music. But that's true of any college or university I know anything about.)

13   At last, the Undergraduate Disciplinary Council (five faculty or administration members and five students) ruled that Doug Hann was to leave the university forevermore. Until two years ago, it was possible for a Brown student to be dismissed, which meant that he or she could reapply after a decent period of penance. But now, Brown has enshrined the sentence of expulsion. You may go on to assist Mother Teresa in caring for the dying or you may teach a course in feminism to 2 Live Crew, but no accomplishments, no matter how noble, will get you back into Brown once you have been expelled.

14   Doug Hann will wander the Earth without a Brown degree for the rest of his days.

15   The president of Brown, Vartan Gregorian—formerly the genial head of the New York Public Library—had the power to commute or even reverse the sentence. But the speech code under which Hann was thrown out had been proposed by Gregorian himself shortly after he was inaugurated in 1989, so he was hardly a detached magistrate.

16   On January 25, 1991, Vartan Gregorian affirmed, with vigor, the expulsion decision by the Undergraduate Disciplinary Council.

17   Hann became a historic figure. Under all the "hate speech" codes enacted around the country in recent years, he is the first student to actually be expelled for violating one of the codes.

18   The *New York Times* (February 12) reported that "Howard Ehrlich, the research director of the National Institute Against Prejudice and Violence, said that he did not know of any other such expulsions, but that he was familiar with cases in which students who had harassed others were moved to other dormitories or ordered to undergo counseling."

But that takes place in *educational* institutions, whose presi- 19
dents recognize that there are students who need help, not
exile.

At first, there didn't seem to be much protest among the stu- 20
dent body at Brown on free speech grounds—except for members
of the Brown chapter of the ACLU and some free thinkers on the
student paper, as well as some unaffiliated objectors to expelling
students for what they say, not for what they do. The number of
these dissenters is increasing, as we shall see.

At the student paper, however, the official tone has changed 21
from the libertarian approach of Vernon Silver, who was editor-
in-chief last semester. A February 13 *Brown Daily Herald* editorial
was headed: *"Good Riddance."*

It began: "Doug Hann is gone, and the university is well to be 22
rid of him."

But President Gregorian has been getting a certain amount of 23
flack and so, smiting his critics hip and thigh, he wrote a letter to
the *New York Times*. Well, that letter (printed on February 21) was
actually a press release, distributed by the Brown University
News Bureau to all sorts of people, including me, on February 12.
There were a few changes—and that *Brown Daily Herald* editorial
was attached to it—but Gregorian's declaration was clearly not
written exclusively for the *Times*.

Is this a new policy at the *Times*—taking public relations 24
handouts for the letters page?

Next week I shall include a relentlessly accurate analysis of 25
President Gregorian's letter by the executive director of the
Rhode Island ACLU. But first, an account of what Gregorian said
in that letter to the *Times*.

President Gregorian indignantly denies that Brown has ever 26
expelled "anyone for the exercise of free speech, nor will it ever
do so." Cross his heart.

He then goes into self-celebration: "My commitment to free 27
speech and condemnation of racism and homophobia are well
known. . . .

"The university's code of conduct does not prohibit speech; it 28
prohibits *actions*."

Now watch this pitiable curve ball: 29

30   "Offense III [of the Brown code]—which deals with harassment—prohibits inappropriate, abusive, threatening, or demeaning actions based on race, religion, gender, handicap, ethnicity, national origin, or sexual orientation."

31   In the original press release, Gregorian underlined the word *actions*. There, and in the letter to the *Times*—lest a dozing reader miss the point—Gregorian emphasizes that "The rules do not proscribe words, epithets, or slanders, they proscribe behavior." Behavior that "shows flagrant disrespect for the well-being of others or is unreasonably disruptive of the University community."

32   Consider the overbreadth and vagueness of these penalty-bearing provisions. What are the definitions of "harassment," "inappropriate," "demeaning," "flagrant," "disrespect," "wellbeing," "unreasonably"?

33   Furthermore, with regard to Brown's termination of Doug Hann with extreme prejudice, Gregorian is engaging in the crudest form of Orwellian newspeak. Hann was kicked out for *speech,* and only speech—not for *actions,* as Gregorian huffily insists. As for behavior, the prickly folks whose burning of the American flag was upheld by the Supreme Court were indeed engaged in behavior, but that behavior was based entirely on symbolic speech. So was Hann's. He didn't punch anybody or vandalize any property. He brayed.

34   Art Spitzer, legal director of the ACLU's National Capital Area affiliate, wrote a personal letter to Gregorian:

35   "There is a very simple test for determining whether a person is being punished for his actions or his speech. You just ask whether he would have received the same punishment if he had spoken different words while engaging in the same conduct."

36   "Thus, would your student have been expelled if he had gotten drunk and stood in the same courtyard at the same hour of the night, shouting at the same decibel level, 'Black is Beautiful!' 'Gay is Good!' or 'Go Brown! Beat Yale!' or even 'Nuke Baghdad! Kill Saddam!'?

37   "I am confident," Spitzer said, that "he would not have been expelled for such 'actions.' If that is correct, it follows that *he was expelled for the unsavory content of his speech,* and not for his actions. I have no doubt that you can understand this distinction. (Emphasis added.)

"Now, you are certainly entitled to believe that it is appropri- 38 ate to expel a student for the content of his speech when that content is sufficiently offensive to the 'university community.' . . .

"If that is your position, why can't you deliver it forthrightly? 39 Then the university community can have an open debate about which opinions it finds offensive, and ban them. Perhaps this can be done once a year, so that the university's rules can keep pace with the tenor of the times—after all, it wouldn't do to have outmoded rules banning procommunist or blasphemous speech still on the books, now that it's 1991. Then students and teachers applying for admission or employment at Brown will know what they are getting into.

"Your recent statements, denying the obvious, are just 40 hypocritical. . . ."

And what did the *New York Times*—in a stunningly fatuous 41 February 21 editorial—say of Vartan Gregorian's sending Doug Hann into permanent exile? "A noble attempt both to govern and teach."

The *Times* editorials should really be signed, so that the rest of 42 the editorial board isn't blamed for such embarrassments.

1991

How Much Hate to Tolerate

New York Times editorial (February 21, 1991)

Free speech and human relations seemed to collide last month at 1 Brown University when it expelled a student for racial and religious harassment. In fact, however, to judge by all that is publicly known, the school walked a fine line with sensitivity toward its complex mission.

One mission of a university is to send into the world gradu- 2 ates who are tolerant of many races, faiths and cultures. Another mission is to teach the value of free expression and tolerance even for hateful ideas. But should such tolerance cover racist, sexist or homophobic speech that makes the learning environment intolerable for racial and religious minorities, women and other targets of abuse? Brown found a reasonable basis for saying, clearly, no.

3   Douglas Hann, white, a junior and a varsity football player, had previously been disciplined for alcohol abuse and for racial insults against a black fellow student. Then, one evening last fall, he shouted racial insults in a university courtyard. A Jewish student who opened a dormitory window and called for quiet was answered with a religious insult. Later that evening Mr. Hann directed a racial insult at a black undergraduate.

4   The student-faculty discipline committee found him guilty of three violations of student rules, including another count of alcohol abuse. Vartan Gregorian, the university's president, upheld the student's expulsion last month. He had a sound basis for doing so. If the facts are reported correctly, Mr. Hann crossed the line between merely hateful speech and hateful speech that directly confronted and insulted other undergraduates.

5   Some courts have found that public universities are bound by the First Amendment's ban on state censorship and thus may not punish students for expressing politically incorrect or socially distasteful ideas. Brown, like other private schools, is less directly bound by the Constitution but committed to its precepts. It is trying to avoid censorship but draws a line between strong language and what the courts often call "fighting words."

6   In the adjacent Letters column today, Mr. Gregorian insists that Brown does not punish unruly speech as such but will decide case-by-case whether a student has passed "the point at which speech becomes behavior" that flagrantly disregards the well-being of others or "subjects someone to abusive or demeaning actions."

7   That formula is a noble attempt both to govern and teach. It offers a principled basis for disciplinary action against Mr. Hann for his direct, confrontational conduct.

8   The lines may not be so clearly drawn in other cases. There may also be more of them in the present climate of evidently increasing student intolerance. But when bigots attack other students with ugly invective, universities, whether public or private, need not remain silent. Their presidents, like Mr. Gregorian, may denounce indecency and, in so doing, protect tolerance.

Brown Expulsion Not About Free Speech

New York Times letter to the editor (February 21, 1991)

To the Editor:

"Student at Brown Is Expelled Under a Rule Barring 'Hate- 1
Speech'" (news article, Feb. 12) suggests I have instituted "hate-
speech" prohibitions at Brown University and that the expulsion
of a student who shouted racial and homophobic epithets on
campus last October is the first such in the nation based on restrictions of free speech. Brown University has never expelled anyone
for free speech, nor will it ever do so.

My commitment to free speech and condemnation of racism 2
and homophobia are well known. In April 1989, several students
were subjected to a cowardly attack of racial and homophobic
graffiti. The words and slogans scrawled anonymously on doors
in one of our dormitories were vicious attacks threatening the
well-being and security of Brown students.

I condemned that anonymous poisoning of our community 3
and said I would prosecute vigorously and seek the expulsion of
those who incite hatred or perpetuate such acts of vandalism.
Nothing I said then or have done since should be construed as
limiting anyone's freedom of speech, nor have I revised the university's code of conduct to that effect.

The university's code of conduct does not prohibit speech; it 4
prohibits actions, and these include behavior that "shows flagrant
disrespect for the well-being of others or is unreasonably disruptive of the university community."

Offense III, which deals with harassment, prohibits inappro- 5
priate, abusive, threatening or demeaning actions based on race,
religion, gender, handicap, ethnicity, national origin or sexual orientation.

"The Tenets of Community Behavior," which outline com- 6
munity standards for acceptable behavior at Brown, have been
read for more than 10 years by entering students, who agree in
writing to abide by them.

The rules do not proscribe words, epithets or slanders; they 7
proscribe behavior. The point at which speech becomes behavior

and the degree to which that behavior shows flagrant disrespect for the well-being of others (Offense II), subjects someone to abusive or demeaning actions (Offense III) or is related to drug or alcohol use (Offense IV) is determined by a hearing to consider the circumstances of each case. The student is entitled to an appeal, which includes review by a senior officer and a decision by the president.

8   I cannot and will not comment about any specific case. I regret the release of any student's name in connection with a disciplinary hearing and the exposure any case may receive in *The Brown Herald*.

9   Freedom-of-speech questions lie at the heart of any academic community. The very nature of the academic enterprise necessitates that universities remain partisans of heterodoxy, of a rich and full range of opinions, ideas and expression. Imposed orthodoxies of all sorts, including what is called "politically correct" speech, are anathema to our enterprise.

10   The university's most compelling challenge is to achieve a balance between the right of its individual members to operate and speak freely, and fostering respect for and adherence to community values and standards of conduct.

VARTAN GREGORIAN
President, Brown University
Providence, R.I., Feb. 21, 1991

Shouting "Fire!"

Alan M. Dershowitz

1   When the Reverend Jerry Falwell learned that the Supreme Court had reversed his $200,000 judgment against *Hustler* magazine for the emotional distress that he had suffered from an outrageous parody, his response was typical of those who seek to censor speech: "Just as no person may scream 'Fire!' in a crowded theater when there is no fire, and find cover under the First Amendment,

likewise, no sleazy merchant like Larry Flynt should be able to use the First Amendment as an excuse for maliciously and dishonestly attacking public figures, as he has so often done."

Justice Oliver Wendell Holmes's classic example of unprotected speech—falsely shouting "Fire!" in a crowded theater—has been invoked so often, by so many people, in such diverse contexts, that it has become part of our national folk language. It has even appeared—most appropriately—in the theater: In Tom Stoppard's play *Rosecrantz and Guildenstern Are Dead* a character shouts at the audience, "Fire!" He then quickly explains: "It's all right—I'm demonstrating the misuse of free speech." Shouting "Fire!" in the theater may well be the only jurisprudential analogy that has assumed the status of a folk argument. A prominent historian recently characterized it as "the most brilliantly persuasive expression that ever came from Holmes's pen." But in spite of its hallowed position in both the jurisprudence of the First Amendment and the arsenal of political discourse, it is and was an inapt analogy, even in the context in which it was originally offered. It has lately become—despite, perhaps even because of, the frequency and promiscuousness of its invocation—little more than a caricature of logical argumentation.

The case that gave rise to the "Fire!"-in-a-crowded-theater analogy, *Schenck v. United States,* involved the prosecution of Charles Schenck, who was the general secretary of the Socialist Party in Philadelphia, and Elizabeth Baer, who was its recording secretary. In 1917 a jury found Schenck and Baer guilty of attempting to cause insubordination among soldiers who had been drafted to fight in the First World War. They and other party members had circulated leaflets urging draftees not to "submit to intimidation" by fighting in a war being conducted on behalf of "Wall Street's chosen few."

Schenck admitted, and the Court found, that the intent of the pamphlets' "impassioned language" was to "influence" drafters to resist the draft. Interestingly, however, Justice Holmes noted that nothing in the pamphlet suggested that the draftees should use unlawful or violent means to oppose conscription: "In form at least [the pamphlet] confined itself to peaceful measures, such as petition for the repeal of the act" and an exhortation to exercise "your right to assert your opposition to the draft." Many of its most impassioned words were quoted directly from the Constitution.

5   Justice Holmes acknowledged that "in many places and in ordinary times the defendants, in saying all that was said in the circular, would have been within their constitutional rights." "But," he added, "the character of every act depends upon the circumstances in which it is done." And to illustrate that truism he went on to say:

> The most stringent protection of free speech would not protect a man in falsely shouting fire in a theater, and causing panic. It does not even protect a man from an injunction against uttering words that may have all the effect of force.

6   Justice Holmes then upheld the convictions in the context of a wartime draft, holding that the pamphlet created "a clear and present danger" of hindering the war effort while our soldiers were fighting for their lives and our liberty.

7   The example of shouting "Fire!" obviously bore little relationship to the facts of the *Schenck* case. The Schenck pamphlet contained a substantive political message. It urged its draftee readers to *think* about the message and then—if they so chose—to act on it in a lawful and nonviolent way. The man who shouts "Fire!" in a crowded theater is neither sending a political message nor inviting his listener to think about what he has said and decide what to do in a rational, calculated manner. On the contrary, the message is designed to force action *without* contemplation. The message "Fire!" is directed not to the mind and the conscience of the listener but, rather, to his adrenaline and his feet. It is a stimulus to immediate *action*, not thoughtful reflection. It is—as Justice Holmes recognized in his follow-up sentence—the functional equivalent of "uttering words that may have all the effect of force."

8   Indeed, in that respect the shout of "Fire!" is not even speech, in any meaningful sense of the term. It is a *clang* sound, the equivalent of setting off a nonverbal alarm. Had Justice Holmes been more honest about his example, he would have said that freedom of speech does not protect a kid who pulls a fire alarm

in the absence of a fire. But that obviously would have been irrelevant to the case at hand. The proposition that pulling an alarm is not protected speech certainly leads to the conclusion that shouting the word "fire" is also not protected. But the core analogy is the nonverbal alarm, and the derivative example is the verbal shout. By cleverly substituting the derivative shout for the core alarm, Holmes made it possible to analogize one set of words to another—as he could not have done if he had begun with the self-evident proposition that setting off an alarm bell is not free speech.

The analogy is thus not only inapt but also insulting. Most 9 Americans do not respond to political rhetoric with the same kind of automatic acceptance expected of schoolchildren responding to a fire drill. Not a single recipient of the Schenck pamphlet is known to have changed his mind after reading it. Indeed, one draftee, who appeared as a prosecution witness, was asked whether reading a pamphlet asserting that the draft law was unjust would make him "immediately decide that you must erase that law." Not surprisingly, he replied, "I do my own thinking." A theatergoer would probably not respond similarly if asked how he would react to a shout of "Fire!"

Another important reason why the analogy is inapt is that 10 Holmes emphasizes the factual falsity of the shout "Fire!" The Schenck pamphlet, however, was not factually false. It contained political opinions and ideas about the causes of the war and about appropriate and lawful responses to the draft. As the Supreme Court recently reaffirmed (in *Falwell v. Hustler*), "The First Amendment recognizes no such thing as a 'false' idea." Nor does it recognize false opinions about the causes of or cures for war.

A closer analogy to the facts of the *Schenck* case might have 11 been provided by a person's standing outside a theater, offering the patrons a leaflet advising them that in his opinion the theater was structurally unsafe, and urging them not to enter but to complain to the building inspectors. That analogy, however, would not have served Holmes's argument for punishing Schenck. Holmes needed an analogy that would appear relevant to Schenck's political speech but that would invite the conclusion that censorship was appropriate.

12   Unsurprisingly, a war-weary nation—in the throes of a know-nothing hysteria over immigrant anarchists and socialists—welcomed the comparison between what was regarded as a seditious political pamphlet and a malicious shout of "Fire!" Ironically, the "Fire!" analogy is nearly all that survives from the *Schenck* case; the ruling itself is almost certainly not good law. Pamphlets of the kind that resulted in Schenck's imprisonment have been circulated with impunity during subsequent wars.

13   Over the past several years I have assembled a collection of instances—cases, speeches, arguments—in which proponents of censorship have maintained that the expression at issue is "just like" or "equivalent to" falsely shouting "Fire!" in a crowded theater and ought to be banned, "just as" shouting "Fire!" ought to be banned. The analogy is generally invoked, often with self-satisfaction, as an absolute argument-stopper. It does, after all, claim the high authority of the great Justice Oliver Wendell Holmes. I have rarely heard it invoked in a convincing, or even particularly relevant, way. But that, too, can claim lineage from the great Holmes.

14   Not unlike Falwell, with his silly comparison between shouting "Fire!" and publishing an offensive parody, courts and commentators have frequently invoked "Fire!" as an analogy to expression that is not an automatic stimulus to panic. A state supreme court held that "Holmes's aphorism . . . applies with equal force to pornography"—in particular to the exhibition of the movie *Carmen Baby* in a drive-in theater in close proximity to highways of a secondary boycott" to shouting "Fire!" because in both instances "speech and conduct are brigaded." In the famous Skokie case one of the judges argued that allowing Nazis to march through a city where a large number of Holocaust survivors live "just might fall into the same category as one's 'right' to cry fire in a crowded theater."

15   Outside court the analogies become even more badly stretched. A spokesperson for the New Jersey Sports and Exposition Authority complained that newspaper reports to the effect that a large number of football players had contracted cancer

after playing in the Meadowlands—a stadium atop a landfill—were the "journalistic equivalent of shouting fire in a crowded theater." An insect researcher acknowledged that his prediction that a certain amusement park might become roach-infested "may be tantamount to shouting fire in a crowded theater." The philosopher Sidney Hook, in a letter to the *New York Times* bemoaning a Supreme Court decision that required a plaintiff in a defamation action to prove that the offending statement was actually false, argued that the First Amendment does not give the press carte blanche to accuse innocent persons "any more than the First Amendment protects the right of someone falsely to shout fire in a crowded theater."

Some close analogies to shouting "Fire!" or setting off an 16 alarm are, of course, available: Calling in a false bomb threat; dialing 911 and falsely describing an emergency; making a loud, gun-like sound in the presence of the President; setting off a voice-activated sprinkler system by falsely shouting "Fire!" In one case in which the "Fire!" analogy was directly to the point, a creative defendant tried to get around it. The case involved a man who calmly advised an airline clerk that he was "only here to hijack the plane." He was charged, in effect, with shouting "Fire!" in a crowded theater, and his rejected defense—as quoted by the court—was as follows: "If we built fire-proof theaters and let people know about this, then the shouting of 'Fire!' would not cause panic."

Here are some more-distant but still related examples: The 17 recent incident of the police slaying in which some members of an onlooking crowd urged a mentally ill vagrant who had taken an officer's gun to shoot the officer; the screaming of racial epithets during a tense confrontation; shouting down a speaker and preventing him from continuing his speech.

Analogies are, by their nature, matters of degree. Some are 18 closer to the core example than others. But any attempt to analogize political ideas in a pamphlet, ugly parody in a magazine, offensive movies in a theater, controversial newspaper articles, or any of the other expressions and actions catalogued above to the very different act of shouting "Fire!" in a crowded theater is either self-deceptive or self-serving.

19   The government does, of course, have some arguably legitimate bases for suppressing speech which bear no relationship to shouting "Fire!" It may ban the publication of nuclear-weapon codes, of information about troop movements, and of the identity of undercover agents. It may criminalize extortion threats and conspiratorial agreements. These expressions may lead directly to serious harm, but the mechanisms of causation are very different from those at work when an alarm is sounded. One may also argue—less persuasively, in my view—against protecting certain forms of public obscenity and defamatory statements. Here, too, the mechanisms of causation are very different. None of these exceptions to the First Amendment's exhortation that the government "shall make no law . . . abridging the freedom of speech, or of the press" is anything like falsely shouting "Fire!" in a crowded theater; they all must be justified on other grounds.

20   A comedian once told his audience, during a stand-up routine, about the time he was standing around a fire with a crowd of people and got in trouble for yelling "Theater, theater!" That, I think, is about as clever and productive a use as anyone has ever made of Holmes's flawed analogy.

1989

Cloning

Embryo Police

Brendan I. Koerner

1 For Alan and Louise Masterton, the death of their daughter, Nicole, had a uniquely cruel twist. It was terrible enough that the 3-year-old succumbed to burns suffered in an accident at the family's Monifieth, Scotland, home in 1999. But for the Mastertons, Nicole was more than just a cherished child—she was a chromosomal miracle. The couple had spent 15 years trying to conceive a girl, bearing four sons in the process.

When Nicole finally arrived in 1995, the Mastertons considered their prayers answered and their family complete. Louise had her tubes tied.

A month after Nicole's death, a heartbroken Alan began 2 posting messages on Usenet's fertility groups. "We know that if we had another 100 children, none could replace Nicole," he wrote. "But she has left such a huge emptiness in all our hearts, we feel (possibly selfishly) desperate to have another little girl to love and cherish, to let her live the life that Nicole was so cruelly denied." The Mastertons wanted another go at parenthood, provided they could be guaranteed a female child. The note ended with an appeal for leads on in vitro fertilization clinics that could identify an embryo's sex prior to implantation in the womb.

Had the Mastertons lived in the United States, the Wild West 3 of reproductive medicine, their quest would have sparked little outcry. Fertility clinics in the US aren't subject to government licensing—unlike, say, tattoo parlors, veterinary hospitals, and, of course, individual doctors. Any family with $30,000 to spend can order a lab-concocted boy or girl.

The British, however, are more cautious about meddling in 4 Nature's affairs. In the United Kingdom, a government panel known as the Human Fertilization and Embryology Authority tightly regulates the fertility industry. The HFEA, the world's first official overseer of reproductive technology, forbids human bioengineering for "social purposes," a catchall ban that largely disallows gender selection. If the Mastertons wished to proceed, they would need to change the HFEA's mind.

Currently, the HFEA is unique to Britain—but not for long. 5 Canada's national health service, Health Canada, is considering a biotech jury based on the HFEA. Japan, Australia, and several European nations also have inquired about transplanting the authority's model. Ruth Deech, the HFEA's chair, spent last October in Japan, lecturing on the finer points of IVF regulation. There has even been a spark of interest in the freewheeling US: James Childress, a bioethicist from the University of Virginia, lauded the HFEA at a September Senate hearing, noting that "Congress might consider that model for our society as well."

6   Much of the admiration stems from the HFEA's willingness to confront even the stickiest moral quandaries with a cold, rational eye. As Britain's de facto guardian of the human blueprint, the HFEA takes seriously its obligation to look past emotional appeals in the interest of the big picture. "We are sympathetic to the difficulties of these couples, of course," says Jane Denton, a former nurse and one of the authority's 21 members. "But we do have to look at the overall principle of whether or not it's appropriate to allow some of these techniques. Because if it goes ahead in one particular case, it is eventually going to become widespread."

7   Most of all, the HFEA fears the slippery slope, a long-debated Ethics 101 concept best summed up in this case as "Today sex-specific children, tomorrow a bioengineered master race." Perhaps allowing the Mastertons to manufacture a substitute daughter would be a first step toward a *Gattaca*-like future of made-to-order babies, scrubbed clean of diseases and endowed with sparkling blue eyes—a world in which eugenics is just another branch of science.

8   Alan Masterton was primed for the challenge of persuading the HFEA. A feisty Scot who bears more than a passing resemblance to tough-guy actor Brian Dennehy, Masterton likes to point out his family's motto: *Ea quibus credimus defendimus, dum ceciderit ultimus,* or "We fight for what we believe in, until the last of us falls." In the past, the HFEA has approved sex selection, but only in rare cases involving genetic diseases that strike a particular gender. Families with a history of hemophilia, for example, are given permission to specify female, because only males are afflicted with the illness. To Masterton, making a similar exception for mental-health reasons didn't seem like much of a stretch. "The void that Nicole has left in our home and in our hearts can never be filled," he says. "But another female child would help us all heal a little bit better."

9   A Dundee University law student at the time, Masterton spent three months compiling a 30-page pamphlet containing his point-by-point argument in favor of sex selection. On the cover was a picture of a smiling, pigtailed Nicole and an inscription: "The joy and happiness she brought into our lives, her spirit, her

place in our family and our hearts are the driving force behind this appeal." Masterton had 21 copies bound—one for each HFEA member—and sent them to London, hoping that the snapshot of a smiling Nicole would melt some hearts.

Unlike the US, Britain was relatively well prepared for the genetics revolution. The UK was the site of the first test-tube baby, Louise Brown, in 1978, and ever since has been trying to divine the murky implications of bioengineering. In 1984, the government-appointed Warnock Committee released a prescient report on the long-term problems that might arise from reproductive technology, everything from snake-oil treatments and dangerous implantation procedures to the ethics of designer kids. "And then that committee suggested setting up another committee, which tends to be a very British way of doing things," says Deech, the HFEA's chair since '94 and an Oxford University administrator. The bioethics panel was created in 1991 to license and inspect IVF clinics, with an eye toward preventing rogue experimentation. Fertility doctors who are discovered engaging in unapproved practices—implanting too many embryos in patients, skirting the rules on sex selection—risk losing their licenses. Those who dare soldier on without licenses risk prison terms.

The wielders of this extraordinary power are, for the most part, ordinary folks. The HFEA's charter requires that at least half of the panel's members come from outside the medical community. And neither the chair nor vice chair can have any connection to the fertility industry. Current ranks include a journalist, an Anglican bishop, an accountant, a social worker, and a retired customs official. "People know we're not just a bunch of mad, profit-seeking doctors running around in white coats," says Sara Nathan, an ex-BBC producer and a member since 1998. "The laypeople are there to make sure the doctors don't let science run ahead of what society wants."

Members are recruited via newspaper ads, and hundreds of applications flood the national Department of Health. A rigorous interview process follows, designed to weed out the merely curious from the passionate. "Sometimes we feel we need a child psychologist, or someone with experience in counseling, or an ethicist, or a philosopher, or a clergyman," says Deech, who assists in the selection process. "We also look for people who do not have any sort of emotional baggage—I think it would be a mistake to have a member who would be crusading for a particular point of view."

13   Those who are accepted receive three-year, renewable terms, along with a packed schedule of committee powwows and inspection tours. Though most members work full-time at other jobs, they are expected to dedicate at least one day per week to their HFEA duties. The panel meets monthly at the agency's headquarters near London's Liverpool Street.

14   Passions often flare around the huge oval table, as on this day, when members debate whether new fertility treatments merit the HFEA's seal of approval. The gatherings are closed to the public; only skeletal minutes are published, and individual comments are not recorded. Nathan admits "the meetings can get heated." She recalls her first one, which focused on egg sharing, an arrangement by which an infertile (usually wealthy) woman offers to pay for another woman's IVF procedure in exchange for a few spare ova. Skeptics at the table argued that such arrangements violated a fundamental principle of egg donation—that it should be altruistic—and could pave the way for a black market in gametes. "We spent a long time drawing up egg-sharing guidelines," says Nathan, "to protect women from overly enthusiastic medical staff."

15   In addition, members supervise inspection teams, which monitor the nation's 74 licensed fertility clinics. At least once a year, an HFEA squad will visit each clinic to see that records are up-to-date and gametes are safely stored. The inspectors also make sure the clinic isn't inflating its success rate to impress potential clients. Even under the best of circumstances, only 25 percent of infertility patients will ever give birth.

16   The HFEA's task was difficult enough during its early-'90s infancy, when the fertility industry was a rather simple affair. But as the number of British couples seeking treatment doubled over the decade to more than 30,000 annually, the panel's scope broadened. Few Britons had heard of the authority before 1995, the year a man named Stephen Blood contracted a fatal case of

meningitis. Moments before his death, his wife, Diane, persuaded doctors to use a technique known as electro ejaculation to extract his sperm. She insisted the couple had talked of starting a family, and she hoped to create his children posthumously. But because Diane was unable to obtain explicit consent from her comatose husband, the HFEA tried to block her reproductive efforts, forbidding any UK clinic to impregnate her with the frozen sperm.

"Here was a man in a coma, at death's door," says Deech. 17 "He didn't know that his sperm was being taken from him. . . . If there is one fundamental principle in common law, it is that you never do anything to a person when they are unconscious and without consent." Diane Blood's plight generated a tremendous amount of public sympathy, and she contested the HFEA's decision according to a European treaty that permits freedom of movement for medical reasons. She was eventually allowed to take her husband's gametes to Belgium, where she was impregnated.

Deech views the Blood case as emblematic of the fertility 18 industry's evolution and of the HFEA's as well. "When IVF started, I think it was imagined that we would be dealing with infertile couples who needed a baby to complete their families," says Deech. "But around about the early to mid-'90s, it began to move beyond that. Clinicians and patients could see the possibilities of extending fertility beyond menopause, of freezing sperm or embryos, posthumous babies, and so on. And it moved away from just treatment of infertility to, if you like, matters of convenience."

Now, with the human genome a more or less open book, Deech 19 foresees the HFEA grappling with a new era. "We have now just moved on to a third phase, which is genetic engineering," she says. "Are these techniques going to be used for the improvement—or, some would say, the manipulation—of babies?"

Fertility technology is developing at a relentless pace. Ten years 20 ago, an infertile male's odds of siring children were nil. Now, a procedure known as intra-cytoplasmic sperm injection, in which a single sperm is directly injected into an egg, gives 95 percent of those afflicted a shot at genetic fatherhood. With improved hormonal regimens, IVF enables women in their fifties, even their sixties, to bear children. A few mavericks are freezing the testicular or ovarian tissue of terminally ill prepubescents, in the hope that technology might someday allow for the creation of sex cells.

21   The struggle to overcome infertility has brought researchers to the cusp of altering humanity's genetic heritage. As academics bicker over cloning, more efficacious technologies are quietly changing the rules of reproduction. One such method is cytoplasmic transfer, a process by which the damaged eggs of older women are repaired with injections of cytoplasm—the "jacket" that surrounds the egg—harvested from younger women. Since cytoplasm contains mitochondrial DNA, the resultant child inherits genetic material from several sources—the father, the mother, and the cytoplasm donor (or donors). Jacques Cohen, a researcher at the Institute for Reproductive Medicine and Science of Saint Barnabas, a New Jersey fertility clinic, has supervised the creation of 15 such multiparent babies over the past three years. In the March 2001 issue of the journal *Human Reproduction,* he boasted that his experiment was "the first case of human germline genetic modification resulting in normal, healthy children." He failed to note that cytoplasmic transfer negates the most basic equation of mammalian reproduction—one male plus one female equals offspring.

22   Then there are the rodents. In March 2000, Japanese and American researchers announced that they had transplanted human ovaries into mice. Their goal was to "create an egg bank for patients suffering from infantile cancer who may survive into adulthood and want to have a child," explains project leader Akiyasu Mizukami. The breakthrough followed the 1999 claim of Nikolaos Sofikitis, a Greek doctor, who said he'd grown human sperm in rat testes.

23   Some bioethicists fear these pioneers are pushing humanity down that infamous slippery slope. One nightmare scenario was popularized by Princeton University molecular biologist Lee Silver in his 1998 book *Remaking Eden: How Genetic Engineering and Cloning Will Transform the American Family.* Silver predicted that

wealthy families would have their offspring crafted in IVF clinics, where the tykes would be outfitted with genes that confer advantages in intelligence, health, and appearance. These "GenRich" would lord over the unendowed masses, the "Naturals," who would provide menial labor. "The GenRich class and the Natural class will become entirely separate species with no ability to cross-breed," Silver prophesied, "and with as much romantic interest in each other as a current human would have in a chimpanzee."

That split seems distant, but inklings of a remade Eden are 24 beginning to appear. Last January, scientists at the Oregon Regional Primate Research Center reported that they'd succeeded in endowing a rhesus monkey, nicknamed ANDi, with jellyfish genes. They did so by injecting viruses laden with jellyfish DNA into the mother's unfertilized eggs. ANDi was a first, small step toward allowing doctors to imbue human eggs with genes that confer disease resistance, or even enhanced mental and physical traits.

The standard media reaction to ANDi's birth was horror—a 25 *Saturday Night Live* sketch joshed that the discovery would "be reported in the *New England Journal of Evil.*" But what loving parents wouldn't resist the chance to enhance their child's prospects for health and happiness? Lori Andrews, author of *Future Perfect: Confronting Decisions About Genetics,* cites a Boston University Medical School study that found that 12 percent of women say they would abort a fetus with a genetic predisposition to obesity. And American IVF clinics are attracting well-heeled clients by selling gametes derived from Nobel laureates or Yale graduates, services that could conjure up a new tort. "If a woman gets sperm from a Nobel sperm bank," says Andrews, "and $E = mc^2$ isn't the first thing out of the child's mouth, will they sue?"

That legal question is typical of the Solomonic dilemmas 26 wrought by the new technology. One of the HFEA's prime directives, for example, states that authority decisions must take into account both the welfare of the embryo and the welfare of existing children. But things get murky when those two obligations conflict, as is the situation with Raj and Shahana Hashmi, a couple whose case is being reviewed by the HFEA. Their 2-year-old son, Zain, suffers from beta thalassemia major, a rare blood disorder that is invariably fatal. Zain endures a harsh treatment regimen of four blood transfusions and five marathon drug-infusion sessions per week. Yet his condition is worsening, and he'll soon die without a stem-cell transplant.

27   The national registry contains no suitable donors, so the Hashmis are considering a revolutionary IVF procedure to help their son. Using a pre-implantation genetic diagnosis, a doctor would select an embryo with compatible tissue from among Shahana's many fertilized eggs, and then harvest the stem cells for Zain from the resulting child's umbilical cord. This seems to have worked for a Colorado couple, the Nashes, whose daughter, Molly, suffers from Fanconi anemia, a blood disease that leads to bone marrow failure. The Nashes used in vitro fertilization and PGD to select a tissue-matched son, Adam, who was born last October; an infusion of stem cells from her brother has given Molly a 90 percent chance of survival.

28   Despite the time-sensitive nature of the case, the HFEA is being judicious. Panelists consider the Hashmi decision fraught with ethical perils, most of them related to a frightful vision of babies rolling off a conveyor belt and being stamped SPARE PARTS. "If the first child needed a bone marrow transfusion, for example, or needed another organ, would compatibility mean the second child was always expected to provide these things?" asks the Right Reverend Michael Nazir-Ali, an HFEA member and the bishop of Rochester. One potential solution the HFEA has considered is making the tissue-matched offspring a ward of the court, thereby curtailing the parents' harvesting powers. A final decision is expected early this year, but in the meantime, the HFEA has denied the Hashmis' request to freeze eggs in anticipation of the ruling.

29   Though no polls have been taken, panel members claim that the majority of Britons support their go-slow approach. "What we do is certainly made easier by the fact that we have so much support from the general public," says Peter Mills, a spokesperson for the HFEA and one of 34 full-time staffers assigned to it. Clinicians, however, frequently rail against the panel, saying it's overly timid. Doctors howled when the authority held up the approval of intracytoplasmic sperm injection due to anecdotal evidence that the ensuing babies are prone to chromosomal abnormalities (likely inherited from their infertile fathers). The HFEA tarried despite

the procedure's acceptance in the US and Europe, which played host to hundreds of British "fertility tourists" throughout the 1990s. "The problem with the HFEA is that they have to be certain everything is safe before it is used," grumbles Simon Fishel, director of the Nottingham-based Centres for Assisted Reproduction. "If everybody else was inhibited in the same way, no progress would be made. Indeed, some would argue that Louise Brown would never have come into existence with the current act."

The HFEA's influence over a controversial field of medicine, 30 coupled with the secrecy of its deliberations, has made it a particularly inviting target in the press. Tom Utley, a popular *Daily Telegraph* columnist, wrote in November 1999: "It is hardly an exaggeration to say that, every time these 21 people meet, they are required to make decisions that in an earlier age were left to God."

The Fleet Street tabs were similarly unkind to the Mastertons, 31 accusing the couple of reviving Nazi eugenics and treating kids like consumer items. "How long before every child born in Britain is as, one to another, a foil-wrapped pack of tomatoes?" wrote one *Daily Mail* scribe. Alan Masterton couldn't understand the fuss—he's heard of cases in which Britons discovered a fetus' gender via amniocentesis and then aborted. Why should Louise be denied the opportunity to select the sex of her child merely because she required IVF?

Alan made repeated requests—26 by his count—to state his 32 case in person. HFEA rules bar public participation at the panel's meetings, but chief executive Suzanne McCarthy assured him that his case would be considered. Finally, in January 2000, the issue came up at the authority's monthly conclave. The committee decided, in effect, not to hear the case at all. If the Mastertons wanted the HFEA to reconsider the use of PGD for sex selection, they would have to persuade a British clinic to file a licensing application on their behalf. "We sorted out the law," says Deech, "which was that they should really make their case to a clinic. And if a clinic really wants to espouse it, they should apply to us."

The decision left the Mastertons in a tight spot. They needed 33 to find a clinic willing to challenge the HFEA's ruling. However, obtaining a license is an arduous process that few clinics would undertake without being fairly certain their application would be accepted—and, in this case, such an outcome was highly unlikely. Alan Masterton was enraged. "I was promised right up to the day before the meeting that my case would be seen by all 21 members of the committee," says Masterton, who accuses Deech of making the decision unilaterally. She denies this. With no formal appeals process, the family's options were limited. They requested a parliamentary investigation, and last May an ombudsman concluded that the HFEA did err in promising the Mastertons that an individual appeal would be heard. But the ombudsman has no power to force reconsideration.

34   The HFEA based its ruling on a technicality, but it's clear that many members harbored qualms about the Masterton case. Nazir-Ali believes the sex-selection boundary is best left uncrossed. "There's a fear that sex selection for social purposes will discriminate against women, in effect," he says. "There is also the fear that a child may be treated as a means to an end, rather than an end in itself, particularly if that child is seen as replacing a child who died in tragic circumstances. It's a heavy burden to bear if you're there as a replacement, not for your own sake."

35   Still desperate for a daughter, the Mastertons joined the hordes of British fertility tourists who go elsewhere for treatments deemed too risky or offensive back home. The richest travel to the United States; those of lesser means head to Italy, also an unregulated frontier of reproductive medicine. In July of 2000, with £6,000 borrowed from friends, the Mastertons visited Biogenesi, a Roman clinic, where doctors removed three eggs from Louise's ovaries. Two of the eggs were immature so they couldn't be used—a common complication for a woman in her forties. The surviving ovum was successfully fertilized with Alan's sperm, and then screened to ensure that the telltale Y chromosome was absent.

36   No dice. It was a male. And it was the last straw.

37   Lacking funds for another treatment cycle, the Mastertons donated the embryo to an infertile couple. And then they headed home, exhausted and broke. They've retained a London lawyer to research whether the family can file an appeal in accordance with Britain's Human Rights Act, which guarantees a fair judicial review. Alan knows it's a long shot, and his natural optimism has

been supplanted with bitterness. "These people are coldhearted, uncaring bastards," he says, his Scottish brogue thickening with anger. "They look after their own asses and care not a jot for anyone else. Because of the shabby way my family has been treated by these deceitful people, I will crusade against the way this organization operates until it is changed to be more people-friendly and accountable."

The HFEA's handling of the Masterton case still riles Simon 38 Fishel too, who favors a regulatory body staffed by more seasoned scientists in addition to laypersons. "If you and your medical practitioner want to do some chemical jiggery-pokery for you to have the gift of your own child, who else should have a say in that decision?" he asks. "Does it matter that your next-door neighbor has an opinion on how you reproduce?"

Absolutely, says HFEA member Sara Nathan. "Fertility doc- 39 tors are not just curing somebody's arm ache—they're creating new people," she says. "And those people are going to live in society, and they'll have mutual responsibilities with society. That's why we need regulation that is both scientific and ethical."

The next big test for that credo will likely be the use of PGD 40 for science beyond sex selection. By analyzing a sliver of embryonic cells, doctors can now determine whether an embryo contains genetic flaws, and then refrain from implanting it in the womb. Of the 10,000 or so genetic disorders that can afflict an embryo, only a few are currently subject to tests—primarily grave conditions such as cystic fibrosis or Duchenne's muscular dystrophy. But if the evolution of pre-implantation genetic diagnosis mirrors that of other reproductive technologies, doctors could soon be able to identify whether a child is predisposed to middle-aged cancer, late-onset deafness, or even premature baldness.

Nevertheless, if there were a test developed that could detect 41 a propensity for severe late-onset diseases, the ever-cautious HFEA would be disinclined to approve its use. "By the time a person is 45, there might be a cure for heart disease, or that person may be a Beethoven who's written I don't know how many symphonies, or married and had beautiful children who are free of heart disease," says Deech. "People are fearful of the search for perfection, and in the public's mind there is a broad distinction between avoidance of a very serious disease that a parent would dread, and trying to choose an embryo who will be perfect."

42   That philosophy baffles Simon Fishel. "You either have to be on the side of medicine and scientific development, or on the side of natural selection. You cannot just say, well, with regard to appendicitis, it's OK to intervene, but in regard to human reproduction, we should just leave it up to divine providence." If bioengineering can spare a human the burden of, say, diabetes, Fishel cannot imagine a good reason for not taking action. And if this science can also be used to select a baby's gender, then so be it.

43   But what about sparing a toddler the dangers of asthma? Or an adult the horrors of clinical depression? The thorniness of these questions has opened a debate in the United States about whether to let fertility doctors act as sole arbiters of what's best for humanity. There are federal agencies that regulate airwaves, power plants, highways, even harbor buoys. Why not a biotech jury to safeguard life itself? It all seems so sensible.

44   Not to everyone, though. "I am aware that your government has been discussing possibly following the HFEA model," says Alan Masterton, turning a bit gruff. "My heartfelt advice, born of experience, is don't do it."

2002

Symposium: Should Congress Use Tax Dollars to Fund Therapeutic Cloning?

James Greenwood and Sam Brownback

1 James Greenwood: Yes: Important medical advances could be achieved that currently are beyond our imagination.

2   A young woman is thrown from her horse. The fall breaks her back, severing her spine and paralyzing her from the neck down. She is a paraplegic for life. Only with the greatest effort can she form the words to ask her attendant to carry her to the bathroom.

Imagine instead that her doctors take a few cells from the ₃ inside of her cheek and expose them to protein-growth factors that convert them to stem cells. These stem cells are, in turn, mixed with different growth factors that change them into spine cells. These spine cells are injected into the damaged portion of her spine. Because these cells are made from her own DNA, her body does not reject them. Her life miraculously is returned to her.

This is not science fiction. In our lifetimes researchers will ₄ enable physicians to repair damage to our brains, livers, hearts and other organs with specialized cells transmuted from healthy cells taken from other parts of our bodies. Cell therapy will free us from Alzheimer's, Parkinson's, diabetes and a potentially limitless list of other dread diseases that torture children, the elderly and everyone in between.

Scientists will discover the growth factors that cause our bod- ₅ ies' cells to develop from specialized somatic cells into pluripotent stem cells and vice versa by observing embryonic stem cells and cells developed from somatic-cell nuclear transfer, otherwise known as therapeutic cloning—if the politicians stay out of their laboratories.

This is what the stem-cell debate is all about. Stem cells are ₆ derived primarily from embryos that are created at in vitro fertilization clinics. At these clinics, to help infertile couples achieve a pregnancy, more embryos are created than will be implanted in a woman's womb. This is because it normally is necessary to implant more than one embryo to ensure a pregnancy. The small number of embryos that are created but not implanted are frozen and stored. If these couples choose not to have additional children, these embryos generally either are discarded or donated for scientific research purposes. Thousands, if not hundreds of thousands, of these embryos are destroyed in this country every year.

Recently, the National Institutes of Health (NIH), at the ₇ request of the Bush administration, completed an extensive study on the recent scientific research and the potential of stem-cell research. This study suggests that stem cells "present immense research opportunities for potential therapy." The report also suggests that, while it is early in the scientific cycle of research on this subject, it is unclear which type of stem cell will meet our needs best and, therefore, "the answers clearly lie in conducting more research."

8   A significant part of this research lies in immunorejection, the rejection of transplanted cells. As in an organ transplant, there is a likelihood that transplanted cells from a donor would be subject to rejection by the patient. The standard set of immunosuppressive drugs that make transplants possible may not be feasible.

9   For this reason, I believe that there is even greater potential in the study of somatic-cell nuclear transfer. In this research, the 23 chromosomes of DNA are extracted from the nucleus of an unfertilized egg cell, making it an enucleated egg. In its place, the nuclei of a somatic cell, containing all 46 chromosomes required for a complete human DNA structure, are taken from an individual and inserted into the enucleated egg. An electric shock or chemicals are added to stimulate the egg to start dividing. If the process is successful, this new egg begins dividing into undifferentiated, pluripotent stem cells.

10   Somatic-cell nuclear-transfer research is essential if we are to achieve our goals in regenerative medicine. We must understand the biological properties of the egg cell that cause a differentiated-cell nucleus to act like one in a pluripotent cell. This process is called "reprogramming"—and scientists still are not sure how it works. That's why we need to continue to perform research.

11   Once we understand how cells transform themselves from somatic to stem cells and back to somatic cells, we will not need any more embryonic material. We will not need any cloned eggs. We will have discovered the proteins and the growth factors that let us take the DNA of our own bodies to cure that which tortures us.

12   Since this therapy could replace damaged or dead cells with healthy, vigorous, new and transplantable cells from one's own body, it potentially could reduce the need for costly and dangerous organ transplants and end the danger of rejection and reliance on toxic immunosuppressive drugs.

An important distinction must be made here. I completely 13
oppose human reproductive cloning. It is unsafe and unethical.
According to scientists who have worked on animal-cloning
research, including members of the team that successfully cloned
"Dolly" the sheep, there would be 999 miscarriages, deformities
and birth defects for every one cloned human. This failure rate is
unacceptable. A caring society cannot condone that level of
human suffering.

But somatic-cell nuclear transfer should not be banned, 14
given the promise of reducing rejection problems from cellular
therapies.

Besides embryonic stem cells, adult stem cells also have been 15
the focus of much debate and research. These stem cells exist in
the body at low concentration and, according to the NIH report,
are difficult to distinguish from partially differentiated progeni-
tor cells.

Many opponents of stem-cell research suggest that adult stem 16
cells may hold out great therapeutic promise. Unfortunately, the
evidence does not support this claim. The NIH report concludes,
"Current evidence indicates that the capability of adult stem cells
to give rise to many different specialized cell types is more limited than that of embryonic stem cells; a single adult stem cell has
not been shown to have the same degree of pluripotency as
embryonic stem cells." While I believe that we should certainly
continue to research the possible uses of adult stem cells, it
should not take the place of embryonic stem cells.

Recently, President George W. Bush announced that his 17
administration would support federal funding for stem-cell
research on approximately 60 existing cell lines. This highly publicized decision to overturn existing policy is disappointing. The
NIH report clearly states that more research needs to be done, and
the president's decision creates only a narrow window of availability for federally funded research in this area. This research
needs federal support in order to have the greatest breadth and
availability of our vast scientific expertise.

Given the NIH's recent announcement that identified the 18
cell lines that would be eligible for federal funding, I am very
concerned that the research sponsored by federal dollars

achieve its intended ends. At present, the scientific literature reflects some 10 stem-cell lines, not the 60 indicated by the president. Most of the 60 stem-cell lines are located outside the United States: Fully one-third are located in Sweden, and 10 are located in India. Furthermore, these stem-cell lines are owned by various private and public organizations; as a result, they may or may not have proprietary value and therefore may not be available for research.

19   Clearly, we can and must do better. There is positive, substantive research that must continue that will benefit all of us through further rigorous investigation on stem cells. Federal support must be made broadly available to the greatest number of researchers possible in the United States if we are to achieve these hoped-for medical breakthroughs. Sadly, the president's current approach will not allow that result.

20   In pursuing this path, we cannot be unmindful of the uneasy relationship between science and religion that lies behind so much of the advance of civilized man. Perhaps the most well-known example of the collision between science and religion is the attempt of Galileo to show that the Earth revolves around the sun. Galileo paid a high price for his courage, but he left us with a great legacy as well. "I do not feel obliged," he wrote, "to believe that the same God who has endowed us with sense, reason and intellect has intended us to forgo their use." What is at stake is nothing less than whether we will permit ourselves to achieve medical advances beyond our present imagination.

21 Sam Brownback: No: It is immoral to create human embryos and then kill them for the purposes of science.

22   The nation currently is faced with monumental bioethics issues—destructive embryo and embryonic-stem-cell research, cloning and the special creation of embryos for research purposes. They are all closely related. President George W. Bush's decision to fund limited embryonic-stem-cell research is not the end of our national bioethics debate—it is the beginning. The debate shifts to the workability of the guidelines proposed by the president as well as the need to prevent the destruction of more innocent human lives.

There are two dimensions to this debate that demand closer 23
scrutiny by our policymakers. The first is the widespread availability and clinical use of adult stem cells—a fact that makes the
so-called "need" for embryonic stem cells highly questionable.
The second is the recognition of the very close link between
destructive embryonic-stem-cell research and the issue of
human cloning.

The advances being made in adult-stem-cell research con- 24
tinue to show great promise. Not only are we beginning to treat
the myriad diseases that plague humanity, but we are continuing to find that we can do so without the use of controversial
techniques or research that relies on the death of another
human being.

In fact, Dr. Neil Theise of the New York University School of 25
Medicine recently commented that "it had been thought only
embryonic stem cells had such wide-ranging potential.
However, this study provides the strongest evidence yet that the
adult body harbors stem cells that are as flexible as embryonic
stem cells." (See "Researchers Discover in Bone Marrow an
Adult Stem Cell That Can Transform Itself Into Almost Any
Organ in Body," New York University Medical Center, posted on
Ascribe Newswire, May 9.)

The notion that we have to end one life to find cures for oth- 26
ers is a false trade-off that has been presented to the American
people in what seems to be total disregard of the advances being
made in the promising fields of alternative nonembryonic sources
of stem cells. As our national bioethics debate progresses, we
must continue closely to monitor the advances being made in the
field of adult-stem-cell research.

As we continue to debate this issue that is so fundamental to 27
the meaning and the essence of what it means to be a human
being, we must consider very carefully the moral implications
associated with the issue of human cloning.

This issue demands the public's attention because it implic- 28
itly revolves around the meaning of human dignity and the
inalienable rights that belong to every person. The creation of any
child is a gift that is given to a man and woman. A child, whether
at the one-celled zygote stage or when fully born, is not and can

never be an object. A child is a precious and unmerited gift, not a right. Human cloning treats children as objects and as pieces of property that can be disposed of at will by the technicians that create and manipulate its young developing life.

29   Human cloning distorts the relationship between man and woman by negating the necessity of either one in the creation of new life. Fundamentally, it alters the view of the child to the world in such a way that the child is seen as something that can fulfill the needs of an individual physically, emotionally or spiritually—whether through the child's birth or through its willful destruction. This is an incorrect view in part because it reduces a child to a means to an end and denies him the dignity he deserves to be treated not as a means but as an end in and of himself.

30   And this notion is precisely where much of the disagreement on this issue exists. Some will argue that the issue simply needs to be studied before any research begins—a notion that does not rest on the supposition of a child as a gift. There is no research that can justify the willful technological manipulation and creation of human life through the process of human cloning. Some do not want a permanent ban—they want a limited ban on "reproductive" cloning but not on so-called "therapeutic" cloning.

31   The notion that human cloning can be "therapeutic" is both misleading and disingenuous. Therapeutic cloning, as some of the proponents of cloning in the biotech industry refer to it, is really the process by which an embryo is specially created for the directly intended purpose of subsequently killing it for its stem cells. Some proponents of human cloning claim that an embryo created in this manner will have cells that are a genetic match to the patient being cloned and thus the cells would not be rejected by the patient's immune system.

32   But to describe the process of destructive human cloning as "therapeutic," when the intent is to create a human embryo that is destined for its virtually immediate destruction, is deeply misleading.

33   Supporters of therapeutic cloning believe there may be a use for this technology as it relates to the issue of destructive

embryonic-stem-cell research. The act of cloning a human being for the purposes of study, to make "designer" replacement cells or for the purpose of bringing new life into the world is intrinsically wrong. It turns a child into property. The child's sole purpose in creation is to be destroyed for someone else's benefit. This is no way to operate in a civil society, especially in the United States, which leads the world in human-rights concerns.

Many proponents of destructive embryo research now are 34 advocating the use of therapeutic cloning. At a recent hearing on the issue of human cloning both the president of the Biotechnology Industry Organization (BIO) and a representative from the American Society for Cell Biology emphasized their strong support for therapeutic cloning as the ultimate source of embryonic stem cells that won't be subject to rejection.

Carl Feldman, the president of BIO, declared that the special 35 creation of human embryos by cloning will be critical to efforts to take embryonic stem cells into human treatments. The cloning technique used to make "Dolly" the sheep, he said, "allows cells to be produced that are uniquely yours or uniquely mine, that would not be rejected."

This testimony demonstrates that for possible future clinical 36 applications, particularly to avoid tissue rejection, human cloning is the logical next step. This means that live embryos created by researchers can be experimented on and killed at the leisure of researchers for the purported benefit of the patient.

Surprisingly, while almost everyone involved in the stem-cell 37 debate has rejected the special creation of embryos for research, the biotech interests are rushing to embrace it.

Medical researchers and biotech firms argue special cre- 38 ation is necessary to avoid immune-response rejection of stem cells. If that is their real interest, the explosion of favorable results in the field of adult stem cells appears to offer much more promise of yielding near- and long-term benefits while avoiding the ethical dilemmas involved in embryonic-stem-cell research.

The slippery slope of embryonic-stem-cell research, which is 39 in itself deeply immoral, ultimately leads to cloning. It's a slippery slope because the current proposals dismiss any principled limitation by rejecting true principle. The principle being denied in this case is the dignity of the young human, effectively making the human embryo equal to animal life, livestock or property, to be disposed of according to human choice governed by legal and pragmatic considerations.

40   Even as we continue to debate these issues in the Congress, many experts question whether there are any benefits to "therapeutic cloning." The Coalition of Americans for Research Ethics reports on its Website (www.stemcellresearch.org) that an article by Peter Aldhous in the journal *Nature* ("Can They Rebuild Us?" April 5) shows that cloning human embryos to harvest their stem cells is being abandoned by many researchers as inefficient, costly and unnecessary: "'[I]t may come as a surprise that many experts do not now expect therapeutic cloning to have a large clinical impact many researchers have come to doubt whether therapeutic cloning will ever be efficient enough to be commercially viable. It would be astronomically expensive,' says James Thomson of the University of Wisconsin in Madison, who led the team that first isolated Embryonic Stem cells from human blastocysts."

41   The article continues: "[M]ammalian cloning is inefficient, even in the hands of the most skilled scientists. Of the 277 cells from Dolly's mother that were fused with donor egg cells, less than 30 developed to the blastocyst stage. At the time experts believed efficiency would improve. But despite feverish efforts by groups worldwide, progress has been disappointing. 'We don't at the moment have any real handle on how to greatly increase the efficiency,' admits Alan Coleman of PPL Therapeutics near Edinburgh [Scotland], the company involved in the Dolly experiments."

42   It is important that as we continue to engage this national dialogue, we strive to do so in a way that grasps the profound mystery and infinite worth of every human being from the moment of conception until natural death. It is a debate well worth having. Our own humanity depends upon it.

2001

PERSUASION

A Modest Proposal

Jonathan Swift

It is a melancholy object to those who walk through this great 1
town or travel in the country, when they see the streets, the roads,
and cabin doors, crowded with beggars of the female sex, followed by three, four, or six children, all in rags and importuning
every passenger for an alms. These mothers, instead of being able
to work for their honest livelihood, are forced to employ all their
time in strolling to beg sustenance for their helpless infants: Who
as they grow up either turn thieves for want of work, or leave
their dear native country to fight for the Pretender in Spain, or sell
themselves to the Barbadoes.

I think it is agreed by all parties that this prodigious number 2
of children in the arms, or on the backs, or at the heels of their
mothers, and frequently of their fathers, is in the present
deplorable state of the kingdom a very great additional griev-
ance; and, therefore, whoever could find out a fair, cheap, and
easy method of making these children sound, useful members of
the commonwealth, would deserve so well of the public as to
have his statue set up for a preserver of the nation.

But my intention is very far from being confined to provide 3
only for the children of professed beggars; it is of a much greater
extent, and shall take in the whole number of infants at a certain
age who are born of parents in effect as little able to support them
as those who demand our charity in the streets.

As to my own part, having turned my thoughts for many years 4
upon this important subject, and maturely weighed the several
schemes of our projectors, I have always found them grossly mistaken in their computation. It is true, a child just dropped from its
dam may be supported by her milk for a solar year, with little other
nourishment; at most not above the value of 2s., which the mother
may certainly get, or the value in scraps, by her lawful occupation

of begging; and it is exactly at one year old that I propose to provide for them in such a manner as instead of being a charge upon
their parents or the parish, or wanting food and raiment for the rest
of their lives, they shall on the contrary contribute to the feeding,
and partly to the clothing, of many thousands.

5   There is likewise another great advantage in my scheme, that
it will prevent those voluntary abortions, and that horrid practice
of women murdering their bastard children, alas! too frequent
among us! sacrificing the poor innocent babes I doubt more to
avoid the expense than the shame, which would move tears and
pity in the most savage and inhuman breast.

6   The number of souls in this kingdom being usually reckoned one million and a half, of these I calculate there may be
about 200,000 couples whose wives are breeders; from which
number I subtract 30,000 couples who are able to maintain their
own children (although I apprehend there cannot be so many,
under the present distress of the kingdom); but this being
granted, there will remain 170,000 breeders. I again subtract
50,000 for those women who miscarry, or whose children die by
accident or disease within the year. There only remain 120,000
children of poor parents annually born. The question therefore
is, how this number shall be reared and provided for? which, as
I have already said, under the present situation of affairs, is
utterly impossible by all the methods hitherto proposed. For we
can neither employ them in handicraft or agriculture; we neither
build houses (I mean live in the country) nor cultivate land; they
can very seldom pick up a livelihood by stealing, till they arrive
at six years old, except where they are of towardly parts;
although I confess they learn the rudiments much earlier; during which time they can, however, be properly looked upon
only as probationers; as I have been informed by a principal
gentleman in the county of Cavan, who protested to me that he
never knew above one or two instances under the age of six,
even in a part of the kingdom so renowned for the quickest pro-
ficiency in that art.

7   I am assured by our merchants, that a boy or a girl before
twelve years old is no saleable commodity; and even when they
come to this age they will not yield above 3l. or 3l.2s. 6d. at most

on the exchange; which cannot turn to account either to the parents or kingdom, the charge of nutriment and rags having been at least four times that value.

I shall now therefore humbly propose my own thoughts, [8] which I hope will not be liable to the least objection.

I have been assured by a very knowing American of my [9] acquaintance in London, that a young healthy child well nursed is at a year old a most delicious, nourishing, and wholesome food, whether stewed, roasted, baked, or broiled; and I make no doubt that it will equally serve in a fricassee or a ragout.

I do therefore humbly offer it to public consideration that of [10] the 120,000 children already computed, 20,000 may be reserved for breed, whereof only one-fourth part to be males; which is more than we allow to sheep, black cattle, or swine; and my reason is, that these children are seldom the fruits of marriage, a circumstance not much regarded by our savages; therefore one male will be sufficient to serve four females. That the remaining 100,000 may, at a year old, be offered in sale to the persons of quality and fortune through the kingdom; always advising the mother to let them suck plentifully in the last month, so as to render them plump and fat for a good table. A child will make two dishes at an entertainment for friends; and when the family dines alone, the fore or hind quarter will make a reasonable dish, and seasoned with a little pepper or salt will be very good boiled on the fourth day, especially in winter.

I have reckoned upon a medium that a child just born will [11] weigh 12 pounds, and in a solar year, if tolerably nursed, will increase to 28 pounds.

I grant this food will be somewhat dear, and therefore very [12] proper for landlords, who, as they have already devoured most of the parents, seem to have the best title to the children.

Infant's flesh will be in season throughout the year, but more [13] plentiful in March, and a little before and after; for we are told by a grave author, an eminent French physician, that fish being a prolific diet, there are more children born in Roman Catholic countries about nine months after Lent than at any other season; therefore, reckoning a year after Lent, the markets will be more glutted than usual, because the number of popish infants is at least three to one in this kingdom: and therefore it will have one other collateral advantage, by lessening the number of papists among us.

14   I have already computed the charge of nursing a beggar's child (in which list I reckon all cottagers, laborers, and four-fifths of the farmers) to be about 2s. per annum, rags included; and I believe no gentleman would repine to give 10s. for the carcass of a good fat child, which, as I have said, will make four dishes of excellent nutritive meat, when he has only some particular friend or his own family to dine with him. Thus the squire will learn to be a good landlord, and grow popular among the tenants; the mother will have 8s. net profit, and be fit for work till she produces another child.

15   Those who are more thrifty (as I must confess the times require) may flay the carcass; the skin of which artificially dressed will make admirable gloves for ladies, and summer boots for fine gentlemen.

16   As to our city of Dublin, shambles may be appointed for this purpose in the most convenient parts of it, and butchers we may be assured will not be wanting: although I rather recommend buying the children alive, and dressing them hot from the knife as we do roasting pigs.

17   A very worthy person, a true lover of his country, and whose virtues I highly esteem, was lately pleased in discoursing on this matter to offer a refinement upon my scheme. He said that many gentlemen of this kingdom, having of late destroyed their deer, he conceived that the want of venison might be well supplied by the bodies of young lads and maidens, not exceeding fourteen years of age nor under twelve; so great a number of both sexes in every country being now ready to starve for want of work and service; and these to be disposed of by their parents, if alive, or otherwise by their nearest relations. But with due deference to so excellent a friend and so deserving a patriot, I cannot be altogether in his sentiments; for as to the males, my American acquaintance assured me from frequent experience that their flesh was generally tough and lean, like that of our schoolboys by continual exercise, and their taste disagreeable; and to fatten them would not

answer the charge. Then as to the females, it would, I think, with humble submission be a loss to the public, because they soon would become breeders themselves; and besides, it is not improbable that some scrupulous people might be apt to censure such a practice (although indeed very unjustly), as a little bordering upon cruelty; which, I confess, has always been with me the strongest objection against any project, how well so-ever intended.

But in order to justify my friend, he confessed that this 18 expedient was put into his head by the famous Psalmanazar, a native of the island Formosa, who came from thence to London about twenty years ago: And in conversation told my friend, that in his country when any young person happened to be put to death, the executioner sold the carcass to persons of quality as a prime dainty; and that in his time the body of a plump girl of fifteen, who was crucified for an attempt to poison the emperor, was sold to his imperial majesty's prime minister of state, and other great mandarins of the court, in joints from the gibbet, at 400 crowns. Neither indeed can I deny, that if the same use were made of several plump young girls in this town, who without one single groat to their fortunes cannot stir without a chair, and appear at the playhouse and assemblies in foreign fineries which they never will pay for, the kingdom would not be the worse.

Some persons of a desponding spirit are in great concern 19 about that vast number of poor people, who are aged, diseased, or maimed, and I have been desired to employ my thoughts what course may be taken to ease the nation of so grievous an encumbrance. But I am not in the least pain upon that matter, because it is very well known that they are every day dying and rotting by cold and famine, and filth and vermin, as fast as can be reasonably expected. And as to the young laborers, they are now in as hopeful a condition: they cannot get work, and consequently pine away for want of nourishment, to a degree that if at any time they are accidentally hired to common labor, they have not strength to perform it; and thus the country and themselves are happily delivered from the evils to come.

20   I have too long digressed, and therefore shall return to my subject. I think the advantages by the proposal which I have made are obvious and many, as well as of the highest importance.

21   For first, as I have already observed, it would greatly lessen the number of papists, with whom we are yearly overrun, being the principal breeders of the nation as well as our most dangerous enemies; and who stay at home on purpose to deliver the kingdom to the Pretender, hoping to take their advantage by the absence of so many good Protestants, who have chosen rather to leave their country than stay at home and pay tithes against their conscience to an Episcopal curate.

22   Secondly, the poor tenants will have something valuable of their own, which by law may be made liable to distress and help to pay their landlord's rent, their corn and cattle being already seized, and money a thing unknown.

23   Thirdly, whereas the maintenance of 100,000 children from two years old and upward, cannot be computed at less than 10s. apiece per annum, the nation's stock will be thereby increased £50,000 per annum, beside the profit of a new dish introduced to the tables of all gentlemen of fortune in the kingdom who have any refinement in taste. And the money will circulate among ourselves, the goods being entirely of our own growth and manufacture.

24   Fourthly, the constant breeders beside the gain of 8s. sterling per annum by the sale of their children, will be rid of the charge of maintaining them after the first year.

25   Fifthly, this food would likewise bring great custom to taverns, where the vintners will certainly be so prudent as to procure the best recipes for dressing it to perfection, and consequently have their houses frequented by all the fine gentlemen, who justly value themselves upon their knowledge in good eating; and a skilful cook who understands how to oblige his guests, will contrive to make it as expensive as they please.

26   Sixthly, this would be a great inducement to marriage, which all wise nations have either encouraged by rewards or enforced by laws and penalties. It would increase the care and tenderness of mothers toward their children, when they were sure of a settlement for life to the poor babes, provided in some sort by the

public, to their annual profit instead of expense. We should see an honest emulation among the married women, which of them would bring the fattest child to the market. Men would become as fond of their wives during the time of their pregnancy as they are now of their mares in foal, their cows in calf, their sows when they are ready to farrow; nor offer to beat or kick them (as is too frequent a practice) for fear of a miscarriage.

Many other advantages might be enumerated. For instance, 27 the addition of some thousand carcasses in our exportation of barreled beef, the propagation of swine's flesh, and improvement in the art of making good bacon, so much wanted among us by the great destruction of pigs, too frequent at our table; which are no way comparable in taste or magnificence to a well-grown, fat, yearling child, which roasted whole will make a considerable figure at a lord mayor's feast or any other public entertainment. But this and many others I omit, being studious of brevity.

Supposing that 1,000 families in this city would be constant 28 customers for infants' flesh, besides others who might have it at merry-meetings, particularly at weddings and christenings, I compute that Dublin would take off annually about 20,000 carcasses; and the rest of the kingdom (where probably they will be sold somewhat cheaper) the remaining 80,000.

I can think of no one objection that will possibly be raised 29 against this proposal, unless it should be urged that the number of people will be thereby much lessened in the kingdom. This I freely own, and it was indeed one principal design in offering it to the world. I desire the reader will observe, that I calculate my remedy for this one individual kingdom of Ireland and for no other than ever was, is, or I think ever can be upon Earth. Therefore let no man talk to me of other expedients: Of taxing our absentees at 5s. a pound: Of using neither clothes nor household furniture except what is of our own growth and manufacture: Of utterly rejecting the materials and instruments that promote foreign luxury: Of curing the expensiveness of pride, vanity, idleness, and gaming in our women: Of introducing a vein of parsimony, prudence, and temperance: Of learning to love our country, in the want of which we differ even from Laplander and the inhabitants of Topinamboo: Of quitting our animosities and factions, nor acting any longer like the Jews, who were murdering one another at the very moment their city was taken: Of being a little cautious not to sell our country and conscience for nothing: Of teaching landlords to have at least one degree of mercy toward their tenants: Lastly, of putting a spirit of honesty, industry, and skill into our shopkeepers; who, if a resolution could now be taken to buy only our native goods, would immediately unite to cheat and exact upon us in the price, the measure, and the goodness, nor could ever yet be brought to make one fair proposal of just dealing, though often and earnestly invited to it.

30   Therefore I repeat, let no man talk to me of these and the like expedients, till he has at least some glimpse of hope that there will be ever some hearty and sincere attempt to put them in practice.

31   But as to myself, having been wearied out for many years with offering vain, idle, visionary thoughts, and at length utterly despairing of success, I fortunately fell upon this proposal; which, as it is wholly new, so it has something solid and real, of no expense and little trouble, full in our own power, and whereby we can incur no danger in disobliging England. For this kind of commodity will not bear exportation, the flesh being of too tender a consistence to admit a long continuance in salt, although perhaps I could name a country which would be glad to eat up our whole nation without it.

32   After all, I am not so violently bent upon my own opinion as to reject any offer proposed by wise men, which shall be found equally innocent, cheap, easy, and effectual. But before something of that kind shall be advanced in contradiction to my scheme, and offering a better, I desire the author or authors will be pleased maturely to consider two points. First, as things now stand, how they will be able to find food and raiment for 100,000 useless mouths and backs. And secondly, there being a round million of creatures in human figure throughout this kingdom, whose subsistence put into a common stock would leave them in debt 2,000,000*l*. sterling, adding those who are beggars by profession to the bulk of farmers, cottagers, and laborers, with the wives and children who are beggars in effect; I desire those politicians who

dislike my overture, and may perhaps be so bold as to attempt an answer, that they will first ask the parents of these mortals, whether they would not at this day think it a great happiness to have been sold for food at a year old in the manner I prescribe, and thereby have avoided such a perpetual scene of misfortunes as they have since gone through by the oppression of landlords, the impossibility of paying rent without money or trade, the want of common sustenance, with neither house nor clothes to cover them from the inclemencies of the weather, and the most inevitable prospect of entailing the like or greater miseries upon their breed for ever.

I profess, in the sincerity of my heart, that I have not the least 33 personal interest in endeavoring to promote this necessary work, having no other motive than the public good of my country, by advancing our trade, providing for infants, relieving the poor, and giving some pleasure to the rich. I have no children by which I can propose to get a single penny; the youngest being nine years old, and my wife past childbearing.

1714

I Have a Dream

Martin Luther King, Jr.

Five score years ago, a great American, in whose symbolic 1 shadow we stand, signed the Emancipation Proclamation. This momentous decree came as a great beacon light of hope to millions of Negro slaves who had been seared in the flames of withering injustice. It came as a joyous daybreak to end the long night of captivity.

But one hundred years later, we must face the tragic fact that 2 the Negro is still not free. One hundred years later, the life of the Negro is still sadly crippled by the manacles of segregation and the chains of discrimination. One hundred years later, the Negro lives on a lonely island of poverty in the midst of a vast ocean of material prosperity. One hundred years later, the Negro is still languishing in the corners of American society and finds himself an exile in his own land. So we have come here today to dramatize an appalling condition.

3   In a sense we have come to our nation's capital to cash a check. When the architects of our republic wrote the magnificent words of the Constitution and the Declaration of Independence, they were signing a promissory note to which every American was to fall heir. This note was a promise that all men would be guaranteed the unalienable rights of life, liberty, and the pursuit of happiness.

4   It is obvious today that America has defaulted on this promissory note insofar as her citizens of color are concerned. Instead of honoring this sacred obligation, America has given the Negro people a bad check; a check which has come back marked "insufficient funds." But we refuse to believe that the bank of justice is bankrupt. We refuse to believe that there are insufficient funds in the great vaults of opportunity of this nation. So we have come to cash this check—a check that will give us upon demand the riches of freedom and the security of justice. We have also come to this hallowed spot to remind America of the fierce urgency of *now.* This is no time to engage in the luxury of cooling off or to take the tranquilizing drugs of gradualism. *Now* is the time to make real the promises of Democracy. *Now* is the time to rise from the dark and desolate valley of segregation to the sunlit path of racial justice. *Now* is the time to open the doors of opportunity to all of God's children. *Now* is the time to lift our nation from the quicksands of racial injustice to the solid rock of brotherhood.

5   It would be fatal for the nation to overlook the urgency of the moment and to underestimate the determination of the Negro. This sweltering summer of the Negro's legitimate discontent will not pass until there is an invigorating autumn of freedom and equality. 1963 is not an end, but a beginning. Those who hope that the Negro needed to blow off steam and will now be content will have a rude awakening if the nation returns to business as usual. There will be neither rest nor tranquility in America until the Negro is granted his citizenship rights. The whirlwinds of revolt

will continue to shake the foundations of our nation until the bright day of justice emerges.

But there is something that I must say to my people who 6 stand on the warm threshold which leads into the palace of justice. In the process of gaining our rightful place we must not be guilty of wrongful deeds. Let us not seek to satisfy our thirst for freedom by drinking from the cup of bitterness and hatred. We must forever conduct our struggle on the high plane of dignity and discipline. We must not allow our creative protest to degenerate into physical violence. Again and again we must rise to the majestic heights of meeting physical force with soul force. The marvelous new militancy which has engulfed the Negro community must not lead us to a distrust of all white people, for many of our white brothers, as evidenced by their presence here today, have come to realize that their destiny is tied up with our destiny and their freedom is inextricably bound to our freedom. We cannot walk alone.

And as we walk, we must make the pledge that we shall 7 march ahead. We cannot turn back. There are those who are asking the devotees of civil rights, "When will you be satisfied?" We can never be satisfied as long as the Negro is the victim of the unspeakable horrors of police brutality. We can never be satisfied as long as our bodies, heavy with the fatigue of travel, cannot gain lodging in the motels of the highways and the hotels of the cities. We cannot be satisfied as long as the Negro's basic mobility is from a smaller ghetto to a larger one. We can never be satisfied as long as a Negro in Mississippi cannot vote and a Negro in New York believes he has nothing for which to vote. No, no, we are not satisfied, and we will not be satisfied until justice rolls down like waters and righteousness like a mighty stream.

I am not unmindful that some of you have come here out of 8 great trials and tribulations. Some of you have come fresh from narrow jail cells. Some of you have come from areas where your quest for freedom left you battered by the storms of persecution and staggered by the winds of police brutality. You have been the veterans of creative suffering. Continue to work with the faith that unearned suffering is redemptive.

9   Go back to Mississippi, go back to Alabama, go back to South Carolina, go back to Georgia, go back to Louisiana, go back to the slums and ghettos of our northern cities, knowing that somehow this situation can and will be changed. Let us not wallow in the valley of despair.

10   I say to you today, my friends, that in spite of the difficulties and frustrations of the moment I still have a dream. It is a dream deeply rooted in the American dream.

11   I have a dream that one day this nation will rise up and live out the true meaning of its creed: "We hold these truths to be self-evident; that all men are created equal."

12   I have a dream that one day on the red hills of Georgia the sons of former slaves and the sons of former slaveowners will be able to sit down together at the table of brotherhood.

13   I have a dream that one day even the state of Mississippi, a desert state sweltering with the heat of injustice and oppression, will be transformed into an oasis of freedom and justice.

14   I have a dream that my four little children will one day live in a nation where they will not be judged by the color of their skin but by the content of their character.

15   I have a dream today.

16   I have a dream that one day the state of Alabama, whose governor's lips are presently dripping with the words of inter-position and nullification, will be transformed into a situation where little black boys and black girls will be able to join hands with little white boys and white girls and walk together as sisters and brothers.

17   I have a dream today.

18   I have a dream that one day every valley shall be exalted, every hill and mountain shall be made low, the rough places will be made plain, and the crooked places will be made straight, and the glory of the Lord shall be revealed, and all flesh shall see it together.

19   This is our hope. This is the faith with which I return to the South. With this faith we will be able to hew out of the mountain of despair a stone of hope. With this faith we will be able to transform the jangling discords of our nation into a beautiful symphony of brotherhood. With this faith we will be able to work

together, to pray together, to struggle together, to go to jail together, to stand up for freedom together, knowing that we will be free one day.

This will be the day when all of God's children will be able to 20 sing with new meaning

> My country, 'tis of thee,
> Sweet land of liberty,
>   Of thee I sing:
> Land where my fathers died,
> Land of the pilgrims' pride,
> From every mountain-side
>   Let freedom ring.

And if America is to be a great nation this must become true. 21 So let freedom ring from the prodigious hilltops of New Hampshire. Let freedom ring from the mighty mountains of New York. Let freedom ring from the heightening Alleghenies of Pennsylvania!

Let freedom ring from the snowcapped Rockies of 22 Colorado!

Let freedom ring from the curvaceous peaks of California! 23

But not only that; let freedom ring from Stone Mountain of 24 Georgia!

Let freedom ring from Lookout Mountain of Tennessee! 25

Let freedom ring from every hill and molehill of 26 Mississippi.

From every mountainside, let freedom ring.

When we let freedom ring, when we let it ring from every 27 village and every hamlet, from every state and every city, we will be able to speed up that day when all of God's children, black men and white men, Jews and Gentiles, Protestants and Catholics, will be able to join hands and sing in the words of the old Negro spiritual, "Free at last! free at last! thank God almighty, we are free at last!"

1963

Bilingual Education:
Outdated and Unrealistic

Richard Rodriguez

1   How shall we teach the dark-eyed child *ingles?* The debate continues much as it did two decades ago.

2   Bilingual education belongs to the 1960s, the years of the black civil rights movement. Bilingual education became the official Hispanic demand; as a symbol, the English-only classroom was intended to be analogous to the segregated lunch counter; the locked school door. Bilingual education was endorsed by judges and, of course, by politicians well before anyone knew the answer to the question: Does bilingual education work?

3   Who knows? *Quien sabe?*

4   The official drone over bilingual education is conducted by educationalists with numbers and charts. Because bilingual education was never simply a matter of pedagogy, it is too much to expect educators to resolve the matter. Proclamations concerning bilingual education are weighted at bottom with Hispanic political grievances and, too, with middle-class romanticism.

5   No one will say it in public; in private, Hispanics argue with me about bilingual education and every time it comes down to memory. Everyone remembers going to that grammar school where students were slapped for speaking Spanish. Childhood memory is offered as parable; the memory is meant to compress the gringo's long history of offenses against Spanish, Hispanic culture, Hispanics.

6   It is no coincidence that, although all of America's ethnic groups are implicated in the policy of bilingual education, Hispanics, particularly Mexican-Americans, have been its chief advocates. The English words used by Hispanics in support of bilingual education are words such as "dignity," "heritage," "culture." Bilingualism becomes a way of exacting from gringos a grudging admission of contrition—for the 19th-century theft of

the Southwest, the relegation of Spanish to a foreign tongue, the injustice of history. At the extreme, Hispanic bilingual enthusiasts demand that public schools "maintain" a student's sense of separateness.

Hispanics may be among the last groups of Americans who 7 still believe in the 1960s. Bilingual-education proposals still serve the romance of that decade, especially of the late 60s, when the heroic black civil rights movement grew paradoxically wedded to its opposite—the ethnic revival movement. Integration and separatism merged into twin, possible goals.

With integration, the black movement inspired middle-class 8 Americans to imitations—the Hispanic movement; the Gray Panthers; feminism; gay rights. Then there was withdrawal, with black glamour leading a romantic retreat from the anonymous crowd.

Americans came to want it both ways. They wanted in and 9 they wanted out. Hispanics took to celebrating their diversity, joined other Americans in dancing rings around the melting pot.

MYTHIC METAPHORS

More intently than most, Hispanics wanted the romance of 10 their dual cultural allegiance backed up by law. Bilingualism became proof that one could have it both ways, could be a full member of public America and yet also separate, privately Hispanic. "Spanish" and "English" became mythic metaphors like country and city, describing separate islands of private and public life.

Ballots, billboards, and, of course, classrooms in Spanish. 11 For nearly two decades now, middle-class Hispanics have had it their way. They have foisted a neat ideological scheme on working-class children. What they want to believe about themselves, they wait for the child to prove, that it is possible to be two, that one can assume the public language (the public life) of America, even while remaining what one was, existentially separate.

Adulthood is not so neatly balanced. The tension between 12 public and private life is intrinsic to adulthood—certainly middle-class adulthood. Usually the city wins because the city pays. We are mass people for more of the day than we are with our intimates. No Congressional mandate or Supreme Court decision can diminish the loss.

13   I was talking the other day to a carpenter from Riga, in the Soviet Republic of Latvia. He has been here six years. He told me of his having to force himself to relinquish the "luxury" of reading books in Russian or Latvian so he could begin to read books in English. And the books he was able to read in English were not of a complexity to satisfy him. But he was not going back to Riga.

14   Beyond any question of pedagogy there is the simple fact that a language gets learned as it gets used, fills one's mouth, one's mind, with the new names for things.

15   The civil rights movement of the 1960s taught Americans to deal with forms of discrimination other than economic—racial, sexual. We forget class. We talk about bilingual education as an ethnic issue; we forget to notice that the program mainly touches the lives of working-class immigrant children. Foreign-language acquisition is one thing for the upper-class child in a convent school learning to curtsy. Language acquisition can only seem a loss for the ghetto child, for the new language is psychologically awesome, being, as it is, the language of the bus driver and Papa's employer. The child's difficulty will turn out to be psychological more than linguistic because what he gives up are symbols of home.

PAIN AND GUILT

16   I was that child! I faced the stranger's English with pain and guilt and fear. Baptized to English in school, at first I felt myself drowning—the ugly sounds forced down my throat—until slowly, slowly (held in the tender grip of my teachers), suddenly the conviction took; English was my language to use.

17   What I yearn for is some candor from those who speak about bilingual education. Which of its supporters dares speak of the price a child pays—the price of adulthood—to make the journey

from a working-class home into a middle-class schoolroom? The real story, the silent story of the immigrant child's journey is one of embarrassments in public; betrayal of all that is private; silence at home; and at school the hand tentatively raised.

Bilingual enthusiasts bespeak an easier world. They seek a [18] linguistic solution to a social dilemma. They seem to want to believe that there is an easy way for the child to balance private and public, in order to believe that there is some easy way for themselves.

Ten years ago, I started writing about the ideological implica- [19] tions of bilingual education. Ten years from now some newspaper may well invite me to contribute another Sunday supplement essay on the subject. The debate is going to continue. The bilingual establishment is now inside the door. Jobs are at stake. Politicians can only count heads; growing numbers of Hispanics will ensure the compliance of politicians.

Publicly, we will continue the fiction. We will solemnly [20] address this issue as an educational question, a matter of pedagogy. But privately, Hispanics will still seek from bilingual education an admission from the gringo that Spanish has value and presence. Hispanics of middle class will continue to seek the romantic assurance of separateness. Experts will argue. Dark-eyed children will sit in the classroom. Mute

1985

To Any Would-Be Terrorists
Naomi Shihab Nye

I am sorry I have to call you that, but I don't know how else to get [1] your attention. I hate that word. Do you know how hard some of us have worked to get rid of that word, to deny its instant connection to the Middle East? And now look. Look what extra work we have. Not only did your colleagues kill thousands of innocent, international people in those buildings and scar their families forever, they wounded a huge community of people in the Middle East, in the United States, and all over the world. If that's what they wanted to do, please know the mission was a terrible success, and you can stop now.

2   Because I feel a little closer to you than many Americans could possibly feel, or ever want to feel, I insist that you listen to me. Sit down and listen. I know what kinds of foods you like. I would feed them to you if you were right here, because it is very very important that you listen. I am humble in my country's pain and I am furious.

3   My Palestinian father became a refugee in 1948. He came to the United States as a college student. He is 74 years old now and still homesick. He has planted fig trees. He has invited all the Ethiopians in his neighborhood to fill their little paper sacks with his figs. He has written columns and stories saying the Arabs are not terrorists, he has worked all his life to defy that word. Arabs are businessmen and students and kind neighbors. There is no one like him and there are thousands like him— gentle Arab daddies who make everyone laugh around the dinner table, who have a hard time with headlines, who stand outside in the evenings with their hands in their pockets staring toward the far horizon.

4   I am sorry if you did not have a father like that. I wish everyone could have a father like that.

5   My hard-working American mother has spent 50 years trying to convince her fellow teachers and choir mates not to believe stereotypes about the Middle East. She always told them, there is a much larger story. If you knew the story, you would not jump to conclusions from what you see in the news. But now look at the news. What a mess has been made. Sometimes I wish everyone could have parents from different countries or ethnic groups so they would be forced to cross boundaries, to believe in mixtures, every day of their lives. Because this is what the world calls us to do. Wake up!

6   The Palestinian grocer in my Mexican-American neighborhood paints pictures of the Palestinian flag on his empty cartons. He paints trees and rivers. He gives his paintings away. He says, "Don't insult me" when I try to pay him for a lemonade.

Arabs have always been famous for their generosity. Remember? My half-Arab brother with an Arabic name looks more like an Arab than many full-blooded Arabs do and he has to fly every week.

My Palestinian cousins in Texas have beautiful brown little 7 boys. Many of them haven't gone to school yet. And now they have this heavy word to carry in their backpacks along with the weight of their papers and books. I repeat, the mission was a terrible success. But it was also a complete, total tragedy and I want you to think about a few things.

1. Many people, thousands of people, perhaps even millions 8 of people, in the United States are very aware of the long unfairness of our country's policies regarding Israel and Palestine. We talk about this all the time. It exhausts us and we keep talking. We write letters to newspapers, to politicians, to each other. We speak out in public even when it is uncomfortable to do so, because that is our responsibility. Many of these people aren't even Arabs. Many happen to be Jews who are equally troubled by the inequity. I promise you this is true. Because I am Arab-American, people always express these views to me and I am amazed how many understand the intricate situation and have strong, caring feelings for Arabs and Palestinians even when they don't have to. Think of them, please: All those people who have been standing up for Arabs when they didn't have to. But as ordinary citizens we don't run the government and don't get to make all our government's policies, which makes us sad sometimes. We believe in the power of the word and we keep using it, even when it seems no one large enough is listening. That is one of the best things about this country: the free power of free words. Maybe we take it for granted too much. Many of the people killed in the World Trade Center probably believed in a free Palestine and were probably talking about it all the time.

But this tragedy could never help the Palestinians. 9 Somehow, miraculously, if other people won't help them more, they are going to have to help themselves. And it will be peace, not violence, that fixes things. You could ask any one of the kids

in the Seeds of Peace organization and they would tell you that.
Do you ever talk to kids? Please, please, talk to more kids.

10   **2.** Have you noticed how many roads there are? Sure you
have. You must check out maps and highways and small alternate routes just like anyone else. There is no way everyone on
earth could travel on the same road, or believe in exactly the
same religion. It would be too crowded, it would be dumb. I
don't believe you want us all to be Muslims. My Palestinian
grandmother lived to be 106 years old, and did not read or
write, but even she was much smarter than that. The only place
she ever went beyond Palestine and Jordan was to Mecca, by
bus, and she was very proud to be called a Hajji and to wear
white clothes afterward. She worked very hard to get stains out
of everyone's dresses—scrubbing them with a stone. I think she
would consider the recent tragedies a terrible stain on her religion and her whole part of the world. She would weep. She was
scared of airplanes anyway. She wanted people to worship God
in whatever ways they felt comfortable. Just worship. Just
remember God in every single day and doing. It didn't matter
what they called it. When people asked her how she felt about
the peace talks that were happening right before she died, she
puffed up like a proud little bird and said, in Arabic, "I never
lost my peace inside." To her, Islam was a welcoming religion.
After her home in Jerusalem was stolen from her, she lived in a
small village that contained a Christian shrine. She felt very tender toward the people who would visit it. A Jewish professor
tracked me down a few years ago in Jerusalem to tell me she
changed his life after he went to her village to do an oral history
project on Arabs. "Don't think she only mattered to you!" he
said. "She gave me a whole different reality to imagine—yet it
was amazing how close we became. Arabs could never be just a
'project' after that."

11   Did you have a grandmother or two? Mine never wanted
people to be pushed around. What did yours want? Reading
about Islam since my grandmother died, I note the "tolerance" that
was "typical of Islam" even in the old days. The Muslim leader
Khalid ibn al-Walid signed a Jerusalem treaty which declared, "In
the name of God, you have complete security for your churches

which shall not be occupied by the Muslims or destroyed." It is the new millennium in which we should be even smarter than we used to be, right? But I think we have fallen behind.

3. Many Americans do not want to kill any more innocent people anywhere in the world. We are extremely worried about military actions killing innocent people. We didn't like this in Iraq, we never liked it anywhere. We would like no more violence, from us as well as from you. HEAR US! We would like to stop the terrifying wheel of violence, just stop it, right on the road, and find something more creative to do to fix these huge problems we have. Violence is not creative, it is stupid and scary and many of us hate all those terrible movies and TV shows made in our own country that try to pretend otherwise. Don't watch them. Everyone should stop watching them. An appetite for explosive sounds and toppling buildings is not a healthy thing for anyone in any country. The USA should apologize to the whole world for sending this trash out into the air and for paying people to make it.

But here's something good you may not know—one of the best-selling books of poetry in the United States in recent years is the Coleman Barks translation of Rumi, a mystical Sufi poet of the 13th century, and Sufism is Islam and doesn't that make you glad?

Everyone is talking about the suffering that ethnic Americans are going through. Many will no doubt go through more of it, but I would like to thank everyone who has sent me a consolation card. Americans are usually very kind people. Didn't your colleagues find that out during their time living here? It is hard to imagine they missed it. How could they do what they did, knowing that?

4. We will all die soon enough. Why not take the short time we have on this delicate planet and figure out some really interesting things we might do together? I promise you, God would be happier. So many people are always trying to speak for God—I know it is a very dangerous thing to do. I tried my whole life not to do it. But this one time is an exception. Because there are so many people crying and scarred and confused and complicated and exhausted right now—it is as if we have all had a giant simultaneous breakdown. I beg you, as your distant Arab cousin, as your American neighbor, listen to me. Our hearts are broken, as yours may also feel broken in some ways we can't understand, unless you tell us in words. Killing people won't tell us. We can't read that message. Find another way to live. Don't expect others to be like you. Read Rumi. Read Arabic poetry. Poetry humanizes us in a way that news, or even religion, has a harder time doing. A great Arab scholar, Dr. Salma Jayyusi, said, "If we read one another, we won't kill one another." Read American poetry. Plant mint. Find a friend who is so different from you, you can't believe how much you have in common. Love them. Let them love you. Surprise people in gentle ways, as friends do. The rest of us will try harder too. Make our family proud.

2001

Why I Want a Wife

Judy Brady

1 I belong to that classification of people known as wives. I am A Wife. And, not altogether incidentally, I am a mother.

2   Not too long ago a male friend of mine appeared on the scene fresh from a recent divorce. He had one child, who is, of course, with his ex-wife. He is looking for another wife. As I thought about him while I was ironing one evening, it suddenly occurred to me that I, too, would like to have a wife. Why do I want a wife?

3   I would like to go back to school so that I can become economically independent, support myself, and, if need be, support

those dependent upon me. I want a wife who will work and send me to school. And while I am going to school I want a wife to take care of my children. I want a wife to keep track of the children's doctor and dentist appointments. And to keep track of mine, too. I want a wife to make sure my children eat properly and are kept clean. I want a wife who will wash the children's clothes and keep them mended. I want a wife who is a good nurturant attendant to my children, who arranges for their school, makes sure that they have an adequate social life with their peers, takes them to the park, the zoo, etc. I want a wife who takes care of the children when they are sick, a wife who arranges to be around when the children need special care, because, of course, I cannot miss classes at school. My wife must arrange to lose time at work and not lose the job. It may mean a small cut in my wife's income from time to time, but I guess I can tolerate that. Needless to say, my wife will arrange and pay for the care of the children while my wife is working.

I want a wife who will take care of *my* physical needs. I 4 want a wife who will keep my house clean. A wife who will pick up after my children, a wife who will pick up after me. I want a wife who will keep my clothes clean, ironed, mended, replaced when need be, and who will see to it that my personal things are kept in their proper place so that I can find what I need the minute I need it. I want a wife who cooks the meals, a wife who is a *good* cook. I want a wife who will plan the menus, do the necessary grocery shopping, prepare the meals, serve them pleasantly, and then do the cleaning up while I do my studying. I want a wife who will care for me when I am sick and sympathize with my pain and loss of time from school. I want a wife to go along when our family takes a vacation so that someone can continue to care for me and my children when I need a rest and change of scene.

I want a wife who will not bother me with rambling com- 5 plaints about a wife's duties. But I want a wife who will listen to me when I feel the need to explain a rather difficult point I have come across in my course of studies. And I want a wife who will type my papers for me when I have written them.

6   I want a wife who will take care of the details of my social life. When my wife and I are invited out by my friends, I want a wife who will take care of the babysitting arrangements. When I meet people at school that I like and want to entertain, I want a wife who will have the house clean, will prepare a special meal, serve it to me and my friends, and not interrupt when I talk about things that interest me and my friends. I want a wife who will have arranged that the children do not bother us. I want a wife who takes care of the needs of my guests so that they feel comfortable, who makes sure that they have an ashtray, that they are passed the hors d'oeuvres, that they are offered a second helping of the food, that their wine glasses are replenished when necessary, that the coffee is served to them as they like it. And I want a wife who knows that sometimes I need a night out by myself.

7   I want a wife who is sensitive to my sexual needs, a wife who makes love passionately and eagerly when I feel like it, a wife who makes sure that I am satisfied. And, of course, I want a wife who will not demand sexual attention when I am not in the mood for it. I want a wife who assumes the complete responsibility for birth control, because I do not want more children. I want a wife who will remain sexually faithful to me so that I do not have to clutter up my intellectual life with jealousies. And I want a wife who understands that *my* sexual needs may entail more than strict adherence to monogamy. I must, after all, be able to relate to people as fully as possible.

8   If, by chance, I find another person more suitable as a wife than the wife I already have, I want the liberty to replace my present wife with another one. Naturally, I will expect a fresh, new life; my wife will take the children and be solely responsible for them so that I am left free.

9   When I am through with school and have a job, I want my wife to quit working and remain at home so that my wife can more fully and completely take care of a wife's duties.

10   My God, who *wouldn't* want a wife?

1970

An Indian Father's Plea

Medicine Grizzlybear Lake

Dear teacher:

I would like to introduce you to my son, Wind-Wolf. He is 1 probably what you would consider a typical Indian kid. He was born and raised on the reservation. He has black hair, dark brown eyes, and an olive complexion. And like so many Indian children his age, he is shy and quiet in the classroom. He is five years old, in kindergarten, and I cannot understand why you have already labeled him a "slow learner."

At the age of five, he has already had quite an education com- 2 pared with his peers in Western society. As his first introduction into this world, he was bonded to his mother and to the Mother Earth in a traditional native childbirth ceremony. And he has been continuously cared for by his mother, father, sisters, cousins, aunts, uncles, grandparents, and extended tribal family since this ceremony.

From his mother's loving arms, Wind-Wolf was placed in a 3 secure and specially designed Indian baby basket. His father and the medicine elders conducted another ceremony to bond him with the essence of his genetic father, the Great Spirit, the Grandfather Sun, and the Grandmother Moon. This was all done in order to introduce him into the natural world, and to protect his soul. It is our people's way of showing the newborn respect, ensuring that he starts life on the path of spirituality.

The traditional Indian baby basket became his "turtle's shell" 4 and served as the first seat for his classroom. He was strapped in for safety, protected from injury by the willow roots and hazelwood construction. The basket was made by a tribal elder who had gathered her materials with prayer. It is specially designed to provide the child with the knowledge and experience he will need in order to survive in his culture and environment.

Wind-Wolf was strapped in snuggly with a deliberate restric- 5 tion upon his arms and legs. Although you in Western society may argue that such a method serves to hinder motor-skill development and abstract reasoning, we believe it forces the child to first develop his intuitive faculties, rational intellect, symbolic thinking, and five senses. Wind-Wolf was with his mother constantly, closely bonded, as she carried him on her back or held him in front while breast feeding. She carried him everywhere she went, and every night he slept with both parents. Because of this, Wind-Wolf's educational setting was not only "secure," but also colorful, complicated, and diverse. He has been with his mother at the ocean at daybreak when she made her prayers and gathered fresh seaweed from the rocks, he has sat with his uncles in a rowboat on the river while they fished with gill nets, and he has watched and listened to elders as they told creation stories and animal legends and sang songs around the campfires.

6   He has attended the sacred White Deerskin Dance of his people and is well acquainted with the cultures and languages of other tribes. He has been with his mother when she gathered herbs for healing and watched his tribal aunts and grandmothers gather and prepare traditional foods such as acorn, smoked salmon, and deer meat. He has played with abalone shells, pine nuts, iris grass string, and leather while watching the women make traditional regalia. He has had many opportunities to watch his father, uncles, and ceremonial leaders use different kinds of colorful feathers and sing different kinds of songs while preparing for the sacred dances and rituals.

7   As he grew older, Wind-Wolf began to crawl out of the baby basket and explore the world around him. When frightened or sleepy, he could always return to the basket, as a turtle withdraws into its shell. Such an inward journey allows one to reflect in privacy on what he has learned and to carry the new knowledge deeply into the unconscious and the soul. Shapes, sizes, colors, texture, sound, smell, feeling, taste, and the learning process are therefore integrated—the physical and spiritual, matter and energy, conscious and unconscious, individual and social.

8   Wind-Wolf was with his mother in South Dakota while she danced for seven days straight in the hot sun, in the sacred Sun Dance Ceremony of a distant tribe. He has been doctored in a number of different healing ceremonies by medicine men and women from places ranging from Alaska and Arizona to New York and California. He has been in more than twenty different sacred sweat lodge rituals—used by native tribes to purify mind,

body, and soul—since he was three years old, and he has already been exposed to many different religions of his racial brothers: Protestant, Catholic, Asian Buddhist, and Tibetan Lamaist.

It takes a long time to absorb and reflect on these kinds of experiences, so maybe that is why you think my Indian child is a slow learner. His aunts and grandmothers taught him to count while they sorted out the materials used to make the abstract designs in native baskets. He learned his basic numbers by helping his father count and sort the rocks to be used in the sweat lodge—seven rocks for a medicine sweat, say, or thirteen for the summer solstice ceremony. And he was taught mathematics by counting the sticks we use in our traditional native hand game. So I realize he may be slow in grasping the methods that you are now using in your classroom, but I hope you will be patient with him. It takes time to adjust to a new cultural system.

He is not culturally "disadvantaged," but he is culturally "different." If you ask him how many months there are in a year, he will probably tell you thirteen. He will respond this way not because he doesn't know how to count properly, but because he has been taught by our traditional people that there are thirteen full moons in a year according to the native tribal calendar and thirteen tail feathers on a perfectly balanced eagle.

But he also knows that some eagles may only have twelve tail feathers, or seven. He knows that the flicker has exactly ten tail feathers; that they are red and black, representing east and west, life and death, and that this bird is a "fire" bird, a power used in native healing. He can probably count more than forty different kinds of birds, tell you what kind of bird each is and where it lives, the seasons in which it appears, and how it is used in a sacred ceremony. He may have trouble writing his name on a piece of paper, but he knows how to say it and many other things in several different Indian languages. He is not fluent yet because he is only five years old and required by law to attend your educational system, learn your language, your values, your ways of thinking, and your methods of teaching.

So you see, all of these influences together make him somewhat shy and quiet—and perhaps "slow" according to your standards. But if Wind-Wolf was not prepared for his first tentative foray into your world, neither were you appreciative of his culture. On the first day of class, you had difficulty with his name. You wanted to call him "Wind"—insisting that Wolf somehow must be his middle name. The students in the class laughed at him, causing him embarrassment.

13   While you are trying to teach him your new methods, he may be looking out the window as if daydreaming. Why? Because he has been taught to watch and study the changes in nature. It is hard for him to switch from the right to the left hemisphere of the brain when he sees the leaves turning bright colors, the geese heading south, and the squirrels scurrying to get ready for winter. In his heart, in his young mind, and almost by instinct, he knows that this is the time of year he is supposed to be with his people gathering and preparing fish, deer meat, and plants and herbs, and learning his assigned tasks in this role. He is caught between two worlds.

14   Yesterday, for the third time in two weeks, he came home crying and said he wanted to have his hair cut. He said he doesn't have any friends at school because they make fun of his long hair. I tried to explain to him that in our culture, long hair is a sign of masculinity and balance and is a source of power. But he remained adamant in his position.

15   To make matters worse, he recently encountered his first harsh case of racism. Wind-Wolf had managed to adopt at least one good school friend. On the way home from school one day, he asked his new pal if he wanted to come home to play with him until supper. That was okay with Wind-Wolf's mother, who was walking with them. When they got to the friend's house, the two boys ran inside to ask permission while Wind-Wolf's mother waited. But the other boy's mother lashed out: "It is okay if you have to play with him at school, but we don't allow that kind of people in our house!" When my wife asked why not, the other boy's mother answered, "Because you are Indians and we are white, and I don't want my kids growing up with your kind of people."

16   So now my young Indian child does not want to go to school anymore (even though his hair is cut). He feels that he does not belong. He is the only Indian child in your class, and instead of being proud of his race, heritage, and culture, he now feels ashamed. When he watches television, he asks why white people

hate us so much and always kill our people in the movies and why they take everything from us. He asks why the other kids in school are not taught about the power, beauty, and essence of nature. Now he refuses to sing his native songs, play with his Indian artifacts, learn his language, or participate in his sacred ceremonies. When I ask him to go to an urban pow-wow or help me with a sacred sweat lodge ritual, he says no because "that's weird."

So, dear teacher, I want to introduce you to my son, Wind-Wolf. 17 He stems from a long line of hereditary chiefs, medicine men and women, and ceremonial leaders whose knowledge is still being studied and recorded in contemporary books. He has seven different tribal systems flowing through his blood; he is even part white. I want my child to succeed in school and in life. I don't want him to be a dropout or to end up on drugs and alcohol because he is made to feel inferior or because of discrimination. I want him to be proud of his rich culture, and I would like him to succeed in both cultures. But I need your help.

What you say and what you do in the classroom has a signif- 18 icant effect on my child. All I ask is that you work with me to help educate my child in the best way. If you don't have the knowledge and experience to deal with culturally different children, I am willing to help you with the few resources I have or direct you to other resources.

Millions of dollars have been appropriated by Congress each 19 year for "Indian Education." All you have to do is encourage your school to use these resources. My Indian child has a constitutional right to learn and maintain his culture. By the same token I believe that non-Indian children have a constitutional right to learn about our Native American heritage and culture, because Indians play a significant part in the history of Western society.

My son, Wind-Wolf, is not an empty glass coming into your 20 class to be filled. He is a full basket coming into a different society with something special to share. Please let him share his knowledge, heritage, and culture with you and his peers.

1995

Mixed Strategies

Sex, Drugs, Disasters, and the Extinction of Dinosaurs

Stephen Jay Gould

1 Science, in its most fundamental definition, is a fruitful mode of inquiry, not a list of enticing conclusions. The conclusions are the consequence, not the essence.

2 My greatest unhappiness with most popular presentations of science concerns their failure to separate fascinating claims from the methods that scientists use to establish the facts of nature. Journalists, and the public, thrive on controversial and stunning statements. But science is, basically, a way of knowing—in P. B. Medawar's apt words, "the art of the soluble." If the growing corps of popular science writers would focus on *how* scientists develop and defend those fascinating claims, they would make their greatest possible contribution to public understanding.

3 Consider three ideas, proposed in perfect seriousness to explain that greatest of all titillating puzzles—the extinction of dinosaurs. Since these three notions invoke the primally fascinating themes of our culture—sex, drugs, and violence—they surely reside in the category of fascinating claims. I want to show why two of them rank as silly speculation, while the other represents science at its grandest and most useful.

4 Science works with testable proposals. If, after much compilation and scrutiny of data, new information continues to affirm a hypothesis, we may accept it provisionally and gain confidence as further evidence mounts. We can never be completely sure that

a hypothesis is right, though we may be able to show with confidence that it is wrong. The best scientific hypotheses are also generous and expansive: They suggest extensions and implications that enlighten related, and even far distant, subjects. Simply consider how the idea of evolution has influenced virtually every intellectual field.

Useless speculation, on the other hand, is restrictive. It generates no testable hypothesis, and offers no way to obtain potentially refuting evidence. Please note that I am not speaking of truth or falsity. The speculation may well be true; still, if it provides, in principle, no material for affirmation or rejection, we can make nothing of it. It must simply stand forever as an intriguing idea. Useless speculation turns in on itself and leads nowhere; good science, containing both seeds for its potential refutation and implications for more and different testable knowledge, reaches out. But, enough preaching. Let's move on to dinosaurs, and the three proposals for their extinction.

1. **Sex:** Testes function only in a narrow range of temperature (those of mammals hang externally in a scrotal sac because internal body temperatures are too high for their proper function). A worldwide rise in temperature at the close of the Cretaceous period caused the testes of dinosaurs to stop functioning and led to their extinction by sterilization of males.

2. **Drugs:** Angiosperms (flowering plants) first evolved toward the end of the dinosaurs' reign. Many of these plants contain psychoactive agents, avoided by mammals today as a result of their bitter taste. Dinosaurs had neither means to taste the bitterness nor livers effective enough to detoxify the substances. They died of massive overdoses.

3. **Disasters:** A large comet or asteroid struck the Earth some 65 million years ago, lofting a cloud of dust into the sky and blocking sunlight, thereby suppressing photosynthesis and so drastically lowering world temperatures that dinosaurs and hosts of other creatures became extinct.

Before analyzing these three tantalizing statements, we must establish a basic ground rule often violated in proposals for the dinosaurs' demise. *There is no separate problem of the extinction of dinosaurs.* Too often we divorce specific events from their wider contexts and systems of cause and effect. The fundamental fact of dinosaur extinction is its synchrony with the demise of so many other groups across a wide range of habitats, from terrestrial to marine.

7   The history of life has been punctuated by brief episodes of mass extinction. A recent analysis by University of Chicago paleontologists Jack Sepkoski and Dave Raup, based on the best and most exhaustive tabulation of data ever assembled, shows clearly that five episodes of mass dying stand well above the "background" extinctions of normal times (when we consider all mass extinctions, large and small, they seem to fall in a regular 26-million-year cycle). The Cretaceous debacle, occurring 65 million years ago and separating the Mesozoic and Cenozoic eras of our geological time scale, ranks prominently among the five. Nearly all the marine plankton (single-celled floating creatures) died with geological suddenness; among marine invertebrates, nearly 15 percent of all families perished, including many previously dominant groups, especially the ammonites (relatives of squids in coiled shells). On land, the dinosaurs disappeared after more than 100 million years of unchallenged domination.

8   In this context, speculations limited to dinosaurs alone ignore the larger phenomenon. We need a coordinated explanation for a system of events that includes the extinction of dinosaurs as one component. Thus it makes little sense, though it may fuel our desire to view mammals as inevitable inheritors of the Earth, to guess that dinosaurs died because small mammals ate their eggs (a perennial favorite among untestable speculations). It seems most unlikely that some disaster peculiar to dinosaurs befell these massive beasts—and that the debacle happened to strike just when one of history's five great dyings had enveloped the Earth for completely different reasons.

9   The testicular theory, an old favorite from the 1940s, had its root in an interesting and thoroughly respectable study of temperature tolerances in the American alligator, published in the staid *Bulletin of the American Museum of Natural History* in 1946 by three experts on living and fossil reptiles—E. H. Colbert, my own first teacher in paleontology; R. B. Cowles; and C. M. Bogert.

The first sentence of their summary reveals a purpose 10 beyond alligators: "This report describes an attempt to infer the reactions of extinct reptiles, especially the dinosaurs, to high temperatures as based upon reactions observed in the modern alligator." They studied, by rectal thermometry, the body temperatures of alligators under changing conditions of heating and cooling. (Well, let's face it, you wouldn't want to try sticking a thermometer under a 'gator's tongue.) The predictions under test go way back to an old theory first stated by Galileo in the 1630s—the unequal scaling of surfaces and volumes. As an animal, or any object, grows (provided its shape doesn't change), surface areas must increase more slowly than volumes—since surfaces get larger as length squared, while volumes increase much more rapidly, as length cubed. Therefore, small animals have high ratios of surface to volume, while large animals cover themselves with relatively little surface.

Among cold-blooded animals lacking any physiological 11 mechanism for keeping their temperatures constant, small creatures have a hell of a time keeping warm—because they lose so much heat through their relatively large surfaces. On the other hand, large animals, with their relatively small surfaces, may lose heat so slowly that, once warm, they may maintain effectively constant temperatures against ordinary fluctuations of climate. (In fact, the resolution of the "hot-blooded dinosaur" controversy that burned so brightly a few years back may simply be that, while large dinosaurs possessed no physiological mechanism for constant temperature, and were not therefore warm-blooded in the technical sense, their large size and relatively small surface area kept them warm.)

Colbert, Cowles, and Bogert compared the warming rates of 12 small and large alligators. As predicted, the small fellows heated up (and cooled down) more quickly. When exposed to a warm sun, a tiny 50-gram (1.76-ounce) alligator heated up one degree Celsius every minute and a half, while a large alligator, 260 times bigger at 13,000 grams (28.7 pounds), took seven and a half minutes to gain a degree. Extrapolating up to an adult 10-ton dinosaur, they concluded that a one-degree rise in body temperature would take eighty-six hours. If large animals absorb heat so slowly (through their relatively small surfaces), they will also be unable to shed any excess heat gained when temperatures rise above a favorable level.

13   The authors then guessed that large dinosaurs lived at or near their optimum temperatures; Cowles suggested that a rise in global temperatures just before the Cretaceous extinction caused the dinosaurs to heat up beyond their optimal tolerance—and, being so large, they couldn't shed the unwanted heat. (In a most unusual statement within a scientific paper, Colbert and Bogert then explicitly disavowed this speculative extension of their empirical work on alligators.) Cowles conceded that this excess heat probably wasn't enough to kill or even to enervate the great beasts, but since testes often function only within a narrow range of temperature, he proposed that this global rise might have sterilized all the males, causing extinction by natural contraception.

14   The overdose theory has recently been supported by UCLA psychiatrist Ronald K. Siegel. Siegel has gathered, he claims, more than 2,000 records of animals who, when given access, administer various drugs to themselves—from a mere swig of alcohol to massive doses of the big H. Elephants will swill the equivalent of twenty beers at a time, but do not like alcohol in concentrations greater than seven percent. In a silly bit of anthropocentric speculation, Siegel states that "elephants drink, perhaps, to forget . . . the anxiety produced by shrinking rangeland and the competition for food."

15   Since fertile imaginations can apply almost any hot idea to the extinction of dinosaurs, Siegel found a way. Flowering plants did not evolve until late in the dinosaurs' reign. These plants also produced an array of aromatic, amino-acid-based alkaloids—the major group of psychoactive agents. Most mammals are "smart" enough to avoid these potential poisons. The alkaloids simply don't taste good (they are bitter); in any case, we mammals have livers happily supplied with the capacity to detoxify them. But, Siegel speculates, perhaps dinosaurs could neither taste the bitterness nor detoxify the substances once ingested. He recently told members of the American Psychological Association: "I'm not suggesting that all dinosaurs OD'd on plant drugs, but it certainly was a factor." He also argued that death by overdose

may help explain why so many dinosaur fossils are found in contorted positions. (Do not go gentle into that good night.)

Extraterrestrial catastrophes have long pedigrees in the popular literature of extinction, but the subject exploded again in 1979, after a long lull, when the father-son, physicist-geologist team of Luis and Walter Alvarez proposed that an asteroid, some 10 km in diameter, struck the Earth 65 million years ago. (Comets, rather than asteroids, have since gained favor. Good science is self-corrective.) 16

The force of such a collision would be immense, greater by far than the megatonnage of all the world's nuclear weapons. In trying to reconstruct a scenario that would explain the simultaneous dying of dinosaurs on land and so many creatures in the sea, the Alvarezes proposed that a gigantic dust cloud, generated by particles blown aloft in the impact, would so darken the Earth that photosynthesis would cease and temperatures drop precipitously. (Rage, rage against the dying of the light.) The single-celled photosynthetic oceanic plankton, with life cycles measured in weeks, would perish outright, but land plants might survive through the dormancy of their seeds. (Land plants were not much affected by the Cretaceous extinction, and any adequate theory must account for the curious pattern of differential survival.) Dinosaurs would die by starvation and freezing; small, warm-blooded mammals, with more modest requirements for food and better regulation of body temperature, would squeak through. "Let the bastards freeze in the dark," as bumper stickers of our chauvinistic neighbors in sunbelt states proclaimed several years ago during the Northeast's winter oil crisis. 17

All three theories, testicular malfunction, psychoactive overdosing, and asteroidal zapping, grab our attention mightily. As pure phenomenology, they rank about equally high on any hit parade of primal fascination. Yet one represents expansive science, the others restrictive and untestable speculation. The proper criterion lies in evidence and methodology; we must probe behind the superficial fascination of particular claims. 18

How could we possibly decide whether the hypothesis of testicular frying is right or wrong? We would have to know things that the fossil record cannot provide. What temperatures 19 were optimal for dinosaurs? Could they avoid the absorption of excess heat by staying in the shade, or in caves? At what temperatures did their testicles cease to function? Were late Cretaceous climates ever warm enough to drive the internal temperatures of dinosaurs close to this ceiling? Testicles simply don't fossilize, and how could we infer their temperature tolerances even if they did? In short, Cowles's hypothesis is only an intriguing speculation leading nowhere. The most damning statement against it appeared right in the conclusion of Colbert, Cowles, and Bogert's paper, when they admitted: "It is difficult to advance any definite arguments against the hypothesis." My statement may seem paradoxical—isn't a hypothesis really good if you can't devise any arguments against it? Quite the contrary. It is simply untestable and unusable.

20   Siegel's overdosing has even less going for it. At least Cowles extrapolated his conclusion from some good data on alligators. And he didn't completely violate the primary guideline of siting dinosaur extinction in the context of a general mass dying—for rise in temperature could be the root cause of a general catastrophe, zapping dinosaurs by testicular malfunction and different groups for other reasons. But Siegel's speculation cannot touch the extinction of ammonites or oceanic plankton. (Diatoms make their own food with good sweet sunlight; they don't OD on the chemicals of terrestrial plants.) It is simply a gratuitous, attention-grabbing guess. It cannot be tested, for how can we know what dinosaurs tasted and what their livers could do? Livers don't fossilize any better than testicles.

21   The hypothesis doesn't even make any sense in its own context. Angiosperms were in full flower ten million years before dinosaurs went the way of all flesh. Why did it take so long? As for the pains of a chemical death recorded in contortions of fossils, I regret to say (or rather I'm pleased to note for the dinosaurs' sake) that Siegel's knowledge of geology must be a bit deficient: Muscles contract after death and geological strata rise and fall with motions of the Earth's crust after burial—more than enough reason to distort a fossil's pristine appearance.

22   The impact story, on the other hand, has a sound basis in evidence. It can be tested, extended, refined, and, if wrong, disproved.

The Alvarezes did not just construct an arresting guess for public consumption. They proposed their hypothesis after laborious geochemical studies with Frank Asaro and Helen Michael had revealed a massive increase of iridium in rocks deposited right at the time of extinction. Iridium, a rare metal of the platinum group, is virtually absent from indigenous rocks of the Earth's crust; most of our iridium arrives on extraterrestrial objects that strike the Earth.

The Alvarez hypothesis bore immediate fruit. Based originally 23 on evidence from two European localities, it led geochemists throughout the world to examine other sediments of the same age. They found abnormally high amounts of iridium everywhere— from continental rocks of the western United States to deep sea cores from the South Atlantic.

Cowles proposed his testicular hypothesis in the mid-1940s. 24 Where has it gone since then? Absolutely nowhere, because scientists can do nothing with it. The hypothesis must stand as a curious appendage to a solid study of alligators. Siegel's overdose scenario will also win a few press notices and fade into oblivion. The Alvarezes' asteroid falls into a different category altogether, and much of the popular commentary has missed this essential distinction by focusing on the impact and its attendant results, and forgetting what really matters to a scientist—the iridium. If you talk just about asteroids, dust, and darkness, you tell stories no better and no more entertaining than fried testicles or terminal trips. It is the iridium—the source of testable evidence— that counts and forges the crucial distinction between speculation and science.

The proof, to twist a phrase, lies in the doing. Cowles's 25 hypothesis has generated nothing in thirty-five years. Since its proposal in 1979, the Alvarez hypothesis has spawned hundreds of studies, a major conference, and attendant publications. Geologists are fired up. They are looking for iridium at all other extinction boundaries. Every week exposes a new wrinkle in the scientific press. Further evidence that the Cretaceous iridium represents extraterrestrial impact and not indigenous volcanism continues to accumulate. As I revise this essay in November 1984 (this paragraph will be out of date when the book is published), new data include chemical "signatures" of other isotopes indicating unearthly provenance, glass spherules of a size and sort produced by impact and not by volcanic eruptions, and high-pressure varieties of silica formed (so far as we know) only under the tremendous shock of impact.

26 My point is simply this: Whatever the eventual outcome (I suspect it will be positive), the Alvarez hypothesis is exciting, fruitful science because it generates tests, provides us with things to do, and expands outward. We are having fun, battling back and forth, moving toward a resolution, and extending the hypothesis beyond its original scope.

27 As just one example of the unexpected, distant cross-fertilization that good science engenders, the Alvarez hypothesis made a major contribution to a theme that has riveted public attention in the past few months—so-called nuclear winter. In a speech delivered in April 1982, Luis Alvarez calculated the energy that a ten-kilometer asteroid would release on impact. He compared such an explosion with a full nuclear exchange and implied that all-out atomic war might unleash similar consequences.

28 This theme of impact leading to massive dust clouds and falling temperatures formed an important input to the decision of Carl Sagan and a group of colleagues to model the climatic consequences of nuclear holocaust. Full nuclear exchange would probably generate the same kind of dust cloud and darkening that may have wiped out the dinosaurs. Temperatures would drop precipitously and agriculture might become impossible. Avoidance of nuclear war is fundamentally an ethical and political imperative, but we must know the factual consequences to make firm judgments. I am heartened by a final link across disciplines and deep concerns—another criterion, by the way, of science at its best. A recognition of the very phenomenon that made our evolution possible by exterminating the previously dominant dinosaurs and clearing a way for the evolution of large mammals, including us, might actually help to save us from joining those magnificent beasts in contorted poses among the strata of the Earth.

1984

Mother Tongue

Amy Tan

I am not a scholar of English or literature. I cannot give you much ₁
more than personal opinions on the English language and its
variations in this country or others.

I am a writer. And by that definition, I am someone who has ₂
always loved language. I am fascinated by language in daily
life. I spend a great deal of my time thinking about the power of
language—the way it can evoke an emotion, a visual image, a
complex idea, or a simple truth. Language is the tool of my
trade. And I use them all—all the Englishes I grew up with.

Recently, I was made keenly aware of the different Englishes ₃
I do use. I was giving a talk to a large group of people, the same
talk I had already given to half a dozen other groups. The nature
of the talk was about my writing, my life, and my book *The Joy
Luck Club*. The talk was going along well enough, until I remembered one major difference that made the whole talk sound
wrong. My mother was in the room. And it was perhaps the first
time she had heard me give a lengthy speech, using the kind of
English I have never used with her. I was saying things like, "The
intersection of memory upon imagination" and "There is an
aspect of my fiction that relates to thus-and-thus"—a speech
filled with carefully wrought grammatical phrases, burdened, it
suddenly seemed to me, with nominalized forms, past perfect
tenses, conditional phrases, all the forms of standard English that
I had learned in school and through books, the forms of English I
did not use at home with my mother.

Just last week, I was walking down the street with my ₄
mother, and I again found myself conscious of the English I was
using, the English I do use with her. We were talking about the
price of new and used furniture and I heard myself saying this:
"Not waste money that way." My husband was with us as well,
and he didn't notice any switch in my English. And then I realized why. It's because over the twenty years we've been
together I've often used that same kind of English with him, and
sometimes he even uses it with me. It has become our language

of intimacy, a different sort of English that relates to family talk, the language I grew up with.

5   So you'll have some idea of what this family talk I heard sounds like, I'll quote what my mother said during a recent conversation which I videotaped and then transcribed. During this conversation, my mother was talking about a political gangster in Shanghai who had the same last name as her family's, Du, and how the gangster in his early years wanted to be adopted by her family, which was rich by comparison. Later, the gangster became more powerful, far richer than my mother's family, and one day showed up at my mother's wedding to pay his respects. Here's what she said in part:

6   "Du Yusong having business like fruit stand. Like off the street kind. He is Du like Du Zong—but not Tsung-ming Island people. The local people call putong, the river east side, he belong to that side local people. That man want to ask Du Zong father take him in like become own family. Du Zong father wasn't look down on him, but didn't take seriously, until that man big like become a mafia. Now important person, very hard to inviting him. Chinese way, came only to show respect, don't stay for dinner. Respect for making big celebration, he shows up. Mean gives lots of respect. Chinese custom. Chinese social life that way. If too important won't have to stay too long. He come to my wedding. I didn't see, I heard it. I gone to boy's side, they have YMCA dinner. Chinese age I was nineteen."

7   You should know that my mother's expressive command of English belies how much she actually understands. She reads the *Forbes* report, listens to *Wall Street Week,* converses daily with her stockbroker, reads all of Shirley MacLaine's books with ease—all kinds of things I can't begin to understand. Yet some of my friends tell me they understand 50 percent of what my mother says. Some say they understand 80 to 90 percent. Some say they understand none of it, as if she was speaking pure Chinese. But to me, my mother's English is perfectly clear, perfectly natural. It's my mother tongue. Her language, as I hear it, is vivid, direct, full of observation and imagery. That was the language that helped shape the way I saw things, expressed things, made sense of the world.

Lately, I've been giving more thought to the kind of English my 8
mother speaks. Like others, I have described it to people as
"broken" or "fractured" English. But I wince when I say that. It
has always bothered me that I can think of no way to describe it
other than "broken," as if it were damaged and needed to be
fixed, as if it lacked a certain wholeness and soundness. I've
heard other terms used, "limited English," for example. But they
seem just as bad, as if everything is limited, including people's
perceptions of the limited English speaker.

I know this for a fact, because when I was growing up, my 9
mother's "limited" English limited *my* perception of her. I was
ashamed of her English. I believed that her English reflected the
quality of what she had to say. That is, because she expressed
them imperfectly her thoughts were imperfect. And I had plenty
of empirical evidence to support me: the fact that people in
department stores, at banks, and at restaurants did not take her
seriously, did not give her good service, pretended not to understand her, or even acted as if they did not hear her.

My mother has long realized the limitations of her English as 10
well. When I was fifteen, she used to have me call people on the
phone to pretend I was she. In this guise, I was forced to ask for
information or even to complain and yell at people who had been
rude to her. One time it was a call to her stockbroker in New York.
She had cashed out her small portfolio and it just so happened we
were going to go to New York the next week, our very first trip
outside California. I had to get on the phone and say in an adolescent voice that was not very convincing, "This is Mrs. Tan."

And my mother was standing in the back whispering loudly, 11
"Why he don't send me check, already two weeks late. So mad he
lie to me, losing me money."

And then I said in perfect English, "Yes, I'm getting rather 12
concerned. You had agreed to send the check two weeks ago, but
it hasn't arrived."

Then she began to talk more loudly. "What he want, I come to 13
New York tell him front of his boss, you cheating me?" And I was
trying to calm her down, make her be quiet, while telling the
stockbroker, "I can't tolerate any more excuses. If I don't receive
the check immediately, I am going to have to speak to your manager

when I'm in New York next week." And sure enough, the follow-ing week there we were in front of this astonished stockbroker, and I was sitting there red-faced and quiet, and my mother, the real Mrs. Tan, was shouting at his boss in her impeccable broken English.

14   We used a similar routine just five days ago, for a situation that was far less humorous. My mother had gone to the hospital for an appointment, to find out about a benign brain tumor a CAT scan had revealed a month ago. She said she had spoken very good English, her best English, no mistakes. Still, she said, the hospital did not apologize when they said they had lost the CAT scan and she had come for nothing. She said they did not seem to have any sympathy when she told them she was anxious to know the exact diagnosis, since her husband and son had both died of brain tumors. She said they would not give her any more infor-mation until the next time and she would have to make another appointment for that. So she said she would not leave until the doctor called her daughter. She wouldn't budge. And when the doctor finally called her daughter, me, who spoke in perfect Eng-lish—lo and behold—we had assurances the CAT scan would be found, promises that a conference call on Monday would be held, and apologies for any suffering my mother had gone through for a most regrettable mistake.

15   I think my mother's English almost had an effect on limiting my possibilities in life as well. Sociologists and linguists probably will tell you that a person's developing language skills are more influenced by peers. But I do think that the language spoken in the family, especially in immigrant families which are more insu-lar, plays a large role in shaping the language of the child. And I believe that it affected my results on achievements tests, IQ tests, and the SAT. While my English skills were never judged as poor, compared to math, English could not be considered my strong suit. In grade school I did moderately well, getting perhaps Bs, sometimes B-pluses, in English and scoring perhaps in the sixtieth or seventieth percentile on achievement tests. But those scores were not good enough to override the opinion that my true abilities lay in math and science, because in those areas I achieved As and scored in the ninetieth percentile or higher.

This was understandable. Math is precise; there is only one 16
correct answer. Whereas, for me at least, the answers on English
tests were always a judgment call, a matter of opinion and personal experience. Those tests were constructed around items like
fill-in-the-blank sentence completion, such as: "Even though Tom
was _____, Mary thought he was _____." And the correct answer
always seemed to be the most bland combinations of thoughts,
for example, "Even though Tom was shy, Mary thought he was
charming," with the grammatical structure "even though" limiting the correct answer to some sort of semantic opposites, so you
wouldn't get answers like, "Even though Tom was foolish, Mary
thought he was ridiculous." Well, according to my mother, there
were very few limitations as to what Tom could have been and
what Mary might have thought of him. So I never did well on
tests like that.

The same was true with word analogies, pairs of words in 17
which you were supposed to find some sort of logical, semantic relationship—for example, "*Sunset* is to *nightfall* as _____ is
to _____." And here you would be presented with a list of our
possible pairs, one of which showed the same kind of relation-
ship: *red* is to *stoplight*, *bus* is to *arrival*, *chills* is to *fever*, *yawn* is to
boring. Well, I could never think that way. I knew what the tests
were asking, but I could not block out of my mind the images
already created by the first pair, "*sunset* is to *nightfall*"—and I
would see a burst of colors against a darkening sky, the moon rising, the lowering of a curtain of stars. And all the other pairs of
words—red, bus, stoplight, boring—just threw up a mass of confusing images, making it impossible for me to sort out something
as logical as saying: "A sunset precedes nightfall" is the same as
"a chill precedes a fever." The only way I would have gotten that
answer right would have been to imagine an associative situation, for example, my being disobedient and staying out past sunset, catching a chill at night, which turns into feverish pneumonia
as punishment, which indeed did happen to me.

I have been thinking about all this lately, about my mother's Eng- 18
lish, about achievement tests. Because lately I've been asked, as a
writer, why there are not more Asian Americans represented in

American literature. Why are there few Asian Americans enrolled in creative writing programs? Why do so many Chinese students go into engineering? Well, these are broad sociological questions I can't begin to answer. But I have noticed in surveys—in fact, just last week—that Asian students, as a whole, always do significantly better on math achievement tests than in English. And this makes me think that there are other Asian-American students whose English spoken in the home might also be described as "broken" or "limited." And perhaps they also have teachers who are steering them away from writing and into math and science, which is what happened to me.

19   Fortunately, I happen to be rebellious in nature and enjoy the challenge of disproving assumptions made about me. I became an English major my first year in college, after being enrolled as premed. I started writing nonfiction as a freelancer the week after I was told by my former boss that writing was my worst skill and I should hone my talents toward account management.

20   But it wasn't until 1985 that I finally began to write fiction. And at first I wrote using what I thought to be wittily crafted sentences, sentences that would finally prove I had mastery over the English language. Here's an example from the first draft of a story that later made its way into *The Joy Luck Club*, but without this line: "That was my mental quandary in its nascent state." A terrible line, which I can barely pronounce.

21   Fortunately, for reasons I won't get into today, I later decided I should envision a reader for the stories I would write. And the reader I decided upon was my mother, because these were stories about mothers. So with this reader in mind—and in fact she did read my early drafts—I began to write stories using all the Englishes I grew up with: the English I spoke to my mother, which for lack of a better term might be described as "simple"; the English she used with me, which for lack of a better term might be described as "broken"; my translation of her Chinese, which could certainly be described as "watered down"; and what I imagined to be her translation of her Chinese if she could speak in perfect English, her internal language, and for that I sought to preserve the essence, but neither an English nor a Chinese structure. I wanted to capture what language ability tests can never reveal:

her intent, her passion, her imagery, the rhythms of her speech and the nature of her thoughts.

Apart from what any critic had to say about my writing, I knew I had succeeded where it counted when my mother finished reading my book and gave me her verdict: "So easy to read." 22

1990

On Dumpster Diving

Lars Eighner

Long before I began Dumpster diving I was impressed with Dumpsters, enough so that I wrote the Merriam-Webster research service to discover what I could about the word *Dumpster.* I learned from them that it is a proprietary word belonging to the Dempster Dumpster company. Since then I have dutifully capitalized the word, although it was lowercased in almost all the citations Merriam-Webster photocopied for me. Dempster's word is too apt. I have never heard these things called anything but Dumpsters. I do not know anyone who knows the generic name for these objects. From time to time I have heard a wino or hobo give some corrupted credit to the original and call them Dipsy Dumpsters. 1

I began Dumpster diving about a year before I became homeless. 2

I prefer the word *scavenging* and use the word *scrounging* when I mean to be obscure. I have heard people, evidently meaning to be polite, use the word *foraging,* but I prefer to reserve that word for gathering nuts and berries and such, which I do also according to the season and the opportunity. *Dumpster diving* seems to me to be a little too cute and, in my case, inaccurate because I lack the athletic ability to lower myself into the Dumpsters as the true divers do, much to their increased profit. 3

I like the frankness of the word *scavenging,* which I can hardly think of without picturing a big black snail on an aquarium wall. I live from the refuse of others. I am a scavenger. I think it a sound 4 and honorable niche, although if I could I would naturally prefer to live the comfortable consumer life, perhaps—and only perhaps—as a slightly less wasteful consumer, owing to what I have learned as a scavenger.

5   While Lizbeth [Eighner's dog] and I were still living in the shack on Avenue B as my savings ran out, I put almost all my sporadic income into rent. The necessities of daily life I began to extract from Dumpsters. Yes, we ate from them. Except for jeans, all my clothes came from Dumpsters. Boom boxes, candles, bedding, toilet paper, a virgin male love doll, medicine, books, a typewriter, dishes, furnishing, and change, sometimes amounting to many dollars—I acquired many things from the Dumpsters.

6   I have learned much as a scavenger. I mean to put some of what I have learned down here, beginning with the practical art of Dumpster diving and proceeding to the abstract.

7   What is safe to eat?

8   After all, the finding of objects is becoming something of an urban art. Even respectable employed people will sometimes find something tempting sticking out of a Dumpster or standing beside one. Quite a number of people, not all of them of the bohemian type, are willing to brag that they found this or that piece in the trash. But eating from Dumpsters is what separates the dilettanti from the professionals. Eating safely from the Dumpsters involves three principles: using the senses and common sense to evaluate the condition of the found materials, knowing the Dumpsters of a given area and checking them regularly, and seeking always to answer the question "Why was this discarded?"

9   Perhaps everyone who has a kitchen and a regular supply of groceries has, at one time or another, made a sandwich and eaten half of it before discovering mold on the bread or got a mouthful of milk before realizing the milk had turned. Nothing of the sort is likely to happen to a Dumpster diver because he is constantly reminded that most food is discarded for a reason. Yet a lot of perfectly good food can be found in Dumpsters.

10   Canned goods, for example, turn up fairly often in the Dumpsters I frequent. All except the most phobic people would be willing to eat from a can, even if it came from a Dumpster. Canned

goods are among the safest of foods to be found in Dumpsters but are not utterly foolproof.

Although very rare with modern canning methods, botulism 11 is a possibility. Most other forms of food poisoning seldom do lasting harm to a healthy person, but botulism is almost certainly fatal and often the first symptom is death. Except for carbonated beverages, all canned goods should contain a slight vacuum and suck air when first punctured. Bulging, rusty, and dented cans and cans that spew when punctured should be avoided, especially when the contents are not very acidic or syrupy.

Heat can break down the botulin, but this requires much 12 more cooking than most people do to canned goods. To the extent that botulism occurs at all, of course, it can occur in cans on pantry shelves as well as in cans from Dumpsters. Need I say that home-canned goods are simply too risky to be recommended.

From time to time one of my companions, aware of the 13 source of my provisions, will ask, "Do you think these crackers are really safe to eat?" For some reason it is most often the crackers they ask about.

This question has always made me angry. Of course I would 14 not offer my companion anything I had doubts about. But more than that, I wonder why he cannot evaluate the condition of the crackers for himself. I have no special knowledge and I have been wrong before. Since he knows where the food comes from, it seems to me he ought to assume some of the responsibility for deciding what he will put in his mouth. For myself I have few qualms about dry foods such as crackers, cookies, cereal, chips, and pasta if they are free of visible contaminates and still dry and crisp. Most often such things are found in the original packaging, which is not so much a positive sign as it is the absence of a negative one.

Raw fruits and vegetables with intact skins seem perfectly 15 safe to me, excluding of course the obviously rotten. Many are discarded for minor imperfections that can be pared away. Leafy vegetables, grapes, cauliflower, broccoli, and similar things may be contaminated by liquids and may be impractical to wash.

Candy, especially hard candy, is usually safe if it has not 16 drawn ants. Chocolate is often discarded only because it has become discolored as the cocoa butter de-emulsified. Candying, after all, is one method of food preservation because pathogens do not like very sugary substances.

17   All of these foods might be found in any Dumpster and can be evaluated with some confidence largely on the basis of appearance. Beyond these are foods that cannot be correctly evaluated without additional information.

18   I began scavenging by pulling pizzas out of the Dumpster behind a pizza delivery shop. In general, prepared food requires caution, but in this case I knew when the shop closed and went to the Dumpster as soon as the last of the help left.

19   Such shops often get prank orders; both the orders and the products made to fill them are called *bogus*. Because help seldom stays long at these places, pizzas are often made with the wrong topping, refused on delivery for being cold, or baked incorrectly. The products to be discarded are boxed up because inventory is kept by counting boxes: A boxed pizza can be written off; an unboxed pizza does not exist.

20   I never placed a bogus order to increase the supply of pizzas and I believe no one else was scavenging in this Dumpster. But the people in the shop became suspicious and began to retain their garbage in the shop overnight. While it lasted I had a steady supply of fresh, sometimes warm pizza. Because I knew the Dumpster I knew the source of the pizza, and because I visited the Dumpster regularly I knew what was fresh and what was yesterday's.

21   The area I frequent is inhabited by many affluent college students. I am not here by chance; the Dumpsters in this area are very rich. Students throw out many good things, including food. In particular they tend to throw everything out when they move at the end of a semester, before and after breaks, and around midterm, when many of them despair of college. So I find it advantageous to keep an eye on the academic calendar.

22   Students throw food away around breaks because they do not know whether it has spoiled or will spoil before they return. A typical discard is a half jar of peanut butter. In fact, nonorganic peanut butter does not require refrigeration and is unlikely to spoil in any reasonable time. The student does not know that, and since it is Daddy's money, the student decides not to take a chance. Opened containers require caution and some attention to

the question, "Why was this discarded?" But in the case of discards from student apartments, the answer may be that the item was thrown out through carelessness, ignorance, or wastefulness. This can sometimes be deduced when the item is found with many others, including some that are obviously perfectly good.

Some students, and others, approach defrosting a freezer by 23 chucking out the whole lot. Not only do the circumstances of such a find tell the story, but also the mass of frozen goods stays cold for a long time and items may be found still frozen or freshly thawed.

Yogurt, cheese, and sour cream are items that are often 24 thrown out while they are still good. Occasionally I find a cheese with a spot of mold, which of course I just pare off, and because it is obvious why such a cheese was discarded, I treat it with less suspicion than an apparently perfect cheese found in similar circumstances. Yogurt is often discarded, still sealed, only because the expiration date on the carton had passed. This is one of my favorite finds because yogurt will keep for several days, even in warm weather.

Students throw out canned goods and staples at the end of 25 semesters and when they give up college at midterm. Drugs, pornography, spirits, and the like are often discarded when parents are expected—Dad's Day, for example. And spirits also turn up after big party weekends, presumably discarded by the newly reformed. Wine and spirits, of course, keep perfectly well even once opened, but the same cannot be said of beer.

My test for carbonated soft drinks is whether they still fizz 26 vigorously. Many juices or other beverages are too acidic or too syrupy to cause much concern, provided they are not visibly contaminated. I have discovered nasty molds in vegetable juices, even when the product was found under its original seal; I recommend that such products be decanted slowly into a clear glass. Liquids always require some care. One hot day I found a large jug of Pat O'Brien's Hurricane mix. The jug had been opened but was still ice cold. I drank three large glasses before it became apparent to me that someone had added the rum to the mix, and not a little rum. I never tasted the rum, and by the time I began to feel the effects I had already ingested a very large quantity of the beverage. Some divers would have considered this a boon, but being suddenly intoxicated in a public place in the early afternoon is not my idea of a good time.

27   I have heard of people maliciously contaminating discarded food and even handouts, but mostly I have heard of this from people with vivid imaginations who have had no experience with the Dumpsters themselves. Just before the pizza shop stopped discarding its garbage at night, jalapeños began showing up on most of the thrown-out pizzas. If indeed this was meant to discourage me, it was a wasted effort because I am a native Texan.

28   For myself, I avoid game, poultry, pork, and egg-based foods, whether I find them raw or cooked. I seldom have the means to cook what I find, but when I do I avail myself of plentiful supplies of beef, which is often in very good condition. I suppose fish becomes disagreeable before it becomes dangerous. Lizbeth is happy to have any such thing that is past its prime and, in fact, does not recognize fish as food until it is quite strong.

29   Home leftovers, as opposed to surpluses from restaurants, are very often bad. Evidently, especially among students, there is a common type of personality that carefully wraps up even the smallest leftover and shoves it into the back of the refrigerator for six months or so before discarding it. Characteristic of this type are the reused jars and margarine tubs to which the remains are committed. I avoid ethnic foods I am unfamiliar with. If I do not know what it is supposed to look like when it is good, I cannot be certain I will be able to tell if it is bad.

30   No matter how careful I am I still get dysentery at least once a month, oftener in warm weather. I do not want to paint too romantic a picture. Dumpster diving has serious drawbacks as a way of life.

31   I learned to scavenge gradually, on my own. Since then I have initiated several companions into the trade. I have learned that there is a predictable series of stages a person goes through in learning to scavenge.

32   At first the new scavenger is filled with disgust and self-loathing. He is ashamed of being seen and may lurk around, trying to duck behind things, or he may try to dive at night. (In fact, most people instinctively look away from a scavenger. By skulking around, the novice calls attention to himself and arouses suspicion. Diving at night is ineffective and needlessly messy.)

Every grain of rice seems to be a maggot. Everything seems ₃₃ to stink. He can wipe the egg yolk off the found can, but he cannot erase from his mind the stigma of eating garbage.

That stage passes with experience. The scavenger finds a pair ₃₄ of running shoes that fit and look and smell brand-new. He finds a pocket calculator in perfect working order. He finds pristine ice cream, still frozen, more than he can eat or keep. He begins to understand: People throw away perfectly good stuff, a lot of perfectly good stuff.

At this stage, Dumpster shyness begins to dissipate. The ₃₅ diver, after all, has the last laugh. He is finding all manner of good things that are his for the taking. Those who disparage his profession are the fools, not he.

He may begin to hang on to some perfectly good things for ₃₆ which he has neither a use nor a market. Then he begins to take note of the things that are not perfectly good but are nearly so. He mates a Walkman with broken earphones and one that is missing a battery cover. He picks up things that he can repair.

At this stage he may become lost and never recover. Dump- ₃₇ sters are full of things of some potential value to someone and also of things that never have much intrinsic value but are interesting. All the Dumpster divers I have known come to the point of trying to acquire everything they touch. Why not take it, they reason, since it is all free? This is, of course, hopeless. Most divers come to realize that they must restrict themselves to items of relatively immediate utility. But in some cases the diver simply cannot control himself. I have met several of these pack-rat types. Their ideas of the values of various pieces of junk verge on the psychotic. Every bit of glass may be a diamond, they think, and all that glistens, gold.

I tend to gain weight when I am scavenging. Partly this is ₃₈ because I always find far more pizza and doughnuts than water-packed tuna, nonfat yogurt, and fresh vegetables. Also I have not developed much faith in the reliability of Dumpsters as a food source, although it has been proven to me many times. I tend to eat as if I have no idea where my next meal is coming from. But mostly I just hate to see food go to waste and so I eat much more than I should. Something like this drives the obsession to collect junk.

39   As for collecting objects, I usually restrict myself to collecting one kind of small object at a time, such as pocket calculators, sunglasses, or campaign buttons. To live on the street I must anticipate my needs to a certain extent: I must pick up and save warm bedding I find in August because it will not be found in Dumpsters in November. As I have no access to health care, I often hoard essential drugs, such as antibiotics and antihistamines. (This course can be recommended only to those with some grounding in pharmacology. Antibiotics, for example, even when indicated are worse than useless if taken in insufficient amounts.) But even if I had a home with extensive storage space, I could not save everything that might be valuable in some contingency.

40   I have proprietary feelings about my Dumpsters. As I have mentioned, it is no accident that I scavenge from ones where good finds are common. But my limited experience with Dumpsters in other areas suggests to me that even in poorer areas, Dumpsters, if attended with sufficient diligence, can be made to yield a livelihood. The rich students discard perfectly good kiwifruit; poorer people discard perfectly good apples. Slacks and Polo shirts are found in the one place; jeans and T-shirts in the other. The population of competitors rather than the affluence of the dumpers most affects the feasibility of survival by scavenging. The large number of competitors is what puts me off the idea of trying to scavenge in places like Los Angeles.

41   Curiously, I do not mind my direct competition, other scavengers, so much as I hate the can scroungers.

42   People scrounge cans because they have to have a little cash. I have tried scrounging cans with an able-bodied companion. Afoot a can scrounger simply cannot make more than a few dollars a day. One can extract the necessities of life from the Dumpsters directly with far less effort than would be required to accumulate the equivalent value in cans. (These observations may not hold in places with container redemption laws.)

43   Can scroungers, then, are people who must have small amounts of cash. These are drug addicts and winos, mostly the latter because the amounts are so small. Spirits and drugs do, like all other commodities, turn up in Dumpsters and the scavenger will

from time to time have a half bottle of a rather good wine with his dinner. But the wino cannot survive on these occasional finds; he must have his daily dose to stave off the DTs. All the cans he can carry will buy about three bottles of Wild Irish Rose.

I do not begrudge them the cans, but can scroungers tend to 44 tear up the Dumpsters, mixing the contents and littering the area. They become so specialized that they can see only cans. They earn my contempt by passing up change, canned goods, and readily hockable items.

There are precious few courtesies among scavengers. But it is 45 common practice to set aside surplus items: pairs of shoes, clothing, canned goods, and such. A true scavenger hates to see good stuff go to waste, and what he cannot use he leaves in good condition in plain sight.

Can scroungers lay waste to everything in their path and will 46 stir one of a pair of good shoes to the bottom of a Dumpster, to be lost or ruined in the muck. Can scroungers will even go through individual garbage cans, something I have never seen a scavenger do.

Individual garbage cans are set out on the public easement 47 only on garbage days. On other days going through them requires trespassing close to a dwelling. Going through individual garbage cans without scattering litter is almost impossible. Litter is likely to reduce the public's tolerance of scavenging. Individual cans are simply not as productive as Dumpsters; people in houses and duplexes do not move so often and for some reason do not tend to discard as much useful material. Moreover, the time required to go through one garbage can that serves one household is not much less than the time required to go through a Dumpster that contains the refuse of twenty apartments.

But my strongest reservation about going through individual 48 garbage cans is that this seems to me a very personal kind of invasion to which I would object if I were a householder. Although many things in Dumpsters are obviously meant never to come to light, a Dumpster is somehow less personal.

I avoid trying to draw conclusions about the people who 49 dump in the Dumpsters I frequent. I think it would be unethical to do so, although I know many people will find the idea of scavenger ethics too funny for words.

50   Dumpsters contain bank statements, correspondence, and other documents, just as anyone might expect. But there are less obvious sources of information. Pill bottles, for example. The labels bear the name of the patient, the name of the doctor, and the name of the drug. AIDS drugs and antipsychotic medicines, to name but two groups, are specific and are seldom prescribed for any other disorders. The plastic compacts for birth-control pills usually have complete label information.

51   Despite all of this sensitive information, I have had only one apartment resident object to my going through the Dumpster. In that case it turned out the resident was a university athlete who was taking bets and who was afraid I would turn up his wager slips.

52   Occasionally a find tells a story. I once found a small paper bag containing some unused condoms, several partial tubes of flavored sexual lubricants, a partially used compact of birth-control pills, and the torn pieces of a picture of a young man. Clearly she was through with him and planning to give up sex altogether.

53   Dumpster things are often sad—abandoned teddy bears, shredded wedding books, despaired-of sales kits. I find many pets lying in state in Dumpsters. Although I hope to get off the streets so that Lizbeth can have a long and comfortable old age, I know this hope is not very realistic. So I suppose when her time comes she too will go into a Dumpster. I will have no better place for her. And after all, it is fitting, since for most of her life her livelihood has come from the Dumpster. When she finds something I think is safe that has been spilled from a Dumpster, I let her have it. She already knows the route around the best ones. I like to think that if she survives me she will have a chance of evading the dog catcher and of finding her sustenance on the route.

54   Silly vanities also come to rest in the Dumpsters. I am a rather accomplished needleworker. I get a lot of material from the Dumpsters. Evidently sorority girls, hoping to impress someone, perhaps themselves, with their mastery of a womanly art, buy a lot of embroider-by-number kits, work a few stitches horribly, and eventually discard the whole mess. I pull out their stitches, turn the canvas over, and work an original design. Do not think I refrain from chuckling as I make gifts from these kits.

I find diaries and journals. I have often thought of compiling a 55 book of literary found objects. And perhaps I will one day. But what I find is hopelessly commonplace and bad without being, even unconsciously, camp. College students also discard their papers. I am horrified to discover the kind of paper that now merits an A in an undergraduate course. I am grateful, however, for the number of good books and magazines the students throw out.

In the area I know best I have never discovered vermin in the 56 Dumpsters, but there are two kinds of kitty surprise. One is alley cats whom I meet as they leap, claws first, out of Dumpsters. This is especially thrilling when I have Lizbeth in tow. The other kind of kitty surprise is a plastic garbage bag filled with some ponderous, amorphous mass. This always proves to be used cat litter.

City bees harvest doughnut glaze and this makes the Dumpster 57 at the doughnut shop more interesting. My faith in the instinctive wisdom of animals is always shaken whenever I see Lizbeth attempt to catch a bee in her mouth, which she does wherever bees are present. Evidently some birds find Dumpsters profitable, for birdie surprise is almost as common as kitty surprise of the first kind. In hunting season all kinds of small game turn up in Dumpsters, some of it, sadly, not entirely dead. Curiously, summer and winter, maggots are uncommon.

The worst of the living and near-living hazards of the Dump- 58 sters are the fire ants. The food they claim is not much of a loss, but they are vicious and aggressive. It is very easy to brush against some surface of the Dumpster and pick up half a dozen or more fire ants, usually in some sensitive area such as the underarm. One advantage of bringing Lizbeth along as I make Dumpster rounds is that, for obvious reasons, she is very alert to ground-based fire ants. When Lizbeth recognizes a fire-ant infestation around our feet, she does the Dance of the Zillion Fire Ants. I have learned not to ignore this warning from Lizbeth, whether I perceive the tiny ants or not, but to remove ourselves at Lizbeth's first pas de bourée. All the more so because the ants are the worst in the summer months when I wear flip-flops if I have them. (Perhaps someone will misunderstand this. Lizbeth does the Dance of the Zillion Fire Ants when she recognizes more fire ants than she cares to eat, not when she is being bitten. Since I have learned to react promptly, she does not get bitten at all. It is the isolated patrol of fire ants that falls in Lizbeth's range that deserves pity. She finds them quite tasty.)

59   By far the best way to go through a Dumpster is to lower yourself into it. Most of the good stuff tends to settle at the bottom because it is usually weightier than the rubbish. My more athletic companions have often demonstrated to me that they can extract much good material from a Dumpster I have already been over.

60   To those psychologically or physically unprepared to enter a Dumpster, I recommend a stout stick, preferable with some barb or hook at one end. The hook can be used to grab plastic garbage bags. When I find canned goods or other objects loose at the bottom of a Dumpster, I lower a bag into it, roll the desired object into the bag, and then hoist the bag out—a procedure more easily described than executed. Much Dumpster diving is a matter of experience for which nothing will do except practice.

61   Dumpster diving is outdoor work, often surprisingly pleasant. It is not entirely predictable; things of interest turn up every day and some days there are finds of great value. I am always very pleased when I can turn up exactly the thing I most wanted to find. Yet in spite of the element of chance, scavenging more than most other pursuits tends to yield returns in some proportion to the effort and intelligence brought to bear. It is very sweet to turn up a few dollars in change from a Dumpster that has just been gone over by a wino.

62   The land is now covered with cities. The cities are full of Dumpsters. If a member of the canine race is ever able to know what it is doing, then Lizbeth knows that when we go around to the Dumpsters, we are hunting. I think of scavenging as a modern form of self-reliance. In any event, after having survived nearly ten years of government service, where everything is geared to the lowest common denominator, I find it refreshing to have work that rewards initiative and effort. Certainly I would be happy to have a sinecure again, but I am no longer heartbroken that I left one.

63   I find from the experience of scavenging two rather deep lessons. The first is to take what you can use and let the rest go by. I have come to think that there is no value in the abstract. A thing I cannot use or make useful, perhaps by trading, has no value however rare or fine it may be. I mean useful in a broad sense—some art I would find useful and some otherwise.

I was shocked to realize that some things are not worth acquir- 64
ing, but now I think it is so. Some material things are white elephants that eat up the possessor's substance. The second lesson is
the transience of material being. This has not quite converted me
to a dualist, but it has made some headway in that direction. I do
not suppose that ideas are immortal, but certainly mental things
are longer lived than other material things.

Once I was the sort of person who invests objects with senti- 65
mental value. Now I no longer have those objects, but I have the
sentiments yet.

Many times in our travels I have lost everything but the 66
clothes I was wearing and Lizbeth. The things I find in Dumpsters, the love letters and rag dolls of so many lives, remind me of
this lesson. Now I hardly pick up a thing without envisioning the
time I will cast it aside. This I think is a healthy state of mind.
Almost everything I have now has already been cast out at least
once, proving that what I own is valueless to someone.

Anyway, I find my desire to grab for the gaudy bauble has 67
been largely sated. I think this is an attitude I share with the very
wealthy—we both know there is plenty more where what we
have came from. Between us are the rat-race millions who nightly
scavenge the cable channels looking for they know not what.

I am sorry for them.   68

1993

This Is a Religious War

Andrew Sullivan

Perhaps the most admirable part of the response to the conflict 1
that began on September 11 has been a general reluctance to call it
a religious war. Officials and commentators have rightly stressed
that this is not a battle between the Muslim world and the West,
that the murderers are not representative of Islam. President Bush
went to the Islamic Center in Washington to reinforce the point.

At prayer meetings across the United States and throughout the world, Muslim leaders have been included alongside Christians, Jews, and Buddhists.

2   The only problem with this otherwise laudable effort is that it doesn't hold up under inspection. The religious dimension of this conflict is central to its meaning. The words of Osama bin Laden are saturated with religious argument and theological language. Whatever else the Taliban regime [was] in Afghanistan, it [was] fanatically religious. Although some Muslim leaders have criticized the terrorists, and even Saudi Arabia's rulers have distanced themselves from the militants, other Muslims in the Middle East and elsewhere have not denounced these acts, have been conspicuously silent, or have indeed celebrated them. The terrorists' strain of Islam is clearly not shared by most Muslims and is deeply unrepresentative of Islam's glorious, civilized, and peaceful past. But it surely represents a part of Islam—a radical, fundamentalist part—that simply cannot be ignored or denied.

3   In that sense, this surely is a religious war—but not of Islam versus Christianity and Judaism. Rather, it is a war of fundamentalism against faiths of all kinds that are at peace with freedom and modernity. This war even has far gentler echoes in America's own religious conflicts between newer, more virulent stands of Christian fundamentalism and mainstream Protestantism and Catholicism. These conflicts have ancient roots, but they seem to be gaining new force as modernity spreads and deepens. They are our new wars of religion—and their victims are in all likelihood going to mount with each passing year.

4   Osama bin Laden himself couldn't be clearer about the religious underpinnings of his campaign of terror. In 1998, he told his followers, "The call to wage war against America was made because America has spearheaded the crusade against the Islamic nation, sending tens of thousands of its troops to the land of the two holy mosques over and above its meddling in its affairs and its politics and its support of the oppressive, corrupt and tyrannical regime that is in control." Notice the use of the word "crusade," an explicitly religious term, and one that simply ignores the fact that the last few major American interventions

abroad—in Kuwait, Somalia, and the Balkans—were all conducted in defense of Muslims.

Notice also that as bin Laden understands it, the "crusade" 5
America is alleged to be leading is not against Arabs but against
the Islamic nation, which spans many ethnicities. This nation
knows no nation-states as they actually exist in the region—
which is why this form of Islamic fundamentalism is also so worrying to the rulers of many Middle Eastern states. Notice also that
bin Laden's beef is with American troops defiling the land of
Saudi Arabia—"the land of the two holy mosques," in Mecca and
Medina. In 1998, he also told followers that his terrorism was
"of the commendable kind, for it is directed at the tyrants and the
aggressors and the enemies of Allah." He has a litany of grievances against Israel as well, but his concerns are not primarily
territorial or procedural. "Our religion is under attack," he said
baldly. The attackers are Christians and Jews. When asked to sum
up his message to the people of the West, bin Laden couldn't have
been clearer: "Our call is the call of Islam that was revealed to
Muhammad. It is a call to all mankind. We have been entrusted
with good cause to follow in the footsteps of the messenger and
to communicate his message to all nations."

This is a religious war against "unbelief and unbelievers," in 6
bin Laden's words. Are these cynical words designed merely to
use Islam for nefarious ends? We cannot know the precise
motives of bin Laden, but we can know that he would not use
these words if he did not think they had salience among the people
he wishes to inspire and provoke. This form of Islam is not restricted
to bin Laden alone.

Its roots lie in an extreme and violent strain in Islam that 7
emerged in the eighteenth century in opposition to what was seen
by some Muslims as Ottoman decadence but has gained greater
strength in the twentieth. For the past two decades, this form of
Islamic fundamentalism has racked the Middle East. It has tar-
geted almost every regime in the region and, as it failed to make
progress, has extended its hostility into the West. From the assassination of Anwar Sadat to the fatwa against Salman Rushdie to
the decade-long campaign of bin Laden to the destruction of
ancient Buddhist statues and the hideous persecution of women

and homosexuals by the Taliban to the World Trade Center massacre, there is a single line. That line is a fundamentalist, religious one. And it is an Islamic one.

8   Most interpreters of the Koran find no arguments in it for the murder of innocents. But it would be naïve to ignore in Islam a deep thread of intolerance toward unbelievers, especially if those unbelievers are believed to be a threat to the Islamic world. There are many passages in the Koran urging mercy toward others, tolerance, respect for life, and so on. But there are also passages as violent as this: "And when the sacred months are passed, kill those who join other gods with God wherever ye shall find them; and seize them, besiege them, and lay wait for them with every kind of ambush." And this: "Believers! Wage war against such of the infidels as are your neighbors, and let them find you rigorous." Bernard Lewis, the great scholar of Islam, writes of the dissonance within Islam: "There is something in the religious culture of Islam which inspired, in even the humblest peasant or peddler, a dignity and a courtesy toward others never exceeded and rarely equaled in other civilizations. And yet, in moments of upheaval and disruption, when the deeper passions are stirred, this dignity and courtesy toward others can give way to an explosive mixture of rage and hatred which impels even the government of an ancient and civilized country—even the spokesman of a great spiritual and ethical religion—to espouse kidnapping and assassination, and try to find, in the life of their prophet, approval and indeed precedent for such actions." Since Muhammad was, unlike many other religious leaders, not simply a sage or a prophet but a ruler in his own right, this exploitation of his politics is not as great a stretch as some would argue.

9   This use of religion for extreme repression, and even terror, is not, of course, restricted to Islam. For most of its history, Christianity has had a worse record. From the Crusades to the Inquisition to the bloody religious wars of the sixteenth and seventeenth centuries, Europe saw far more blood spilled for religion's sake than the Muslim world did. And given how expressly nonviolent the teachings of the Gospels are, the perversion of Christianity in this respect was arguably greater than bin Laden's selective use of Islam. But it is there nonetheless. It seems almost as if there is

something inherent in religious monotheism that lends itself to this kind of terrorist temptation. And our bland attempts to ignore this—to speak of this violence as if it did not have religious roots—is some kind of denial. We don't want to denigrate religion as such, and so we deny that religion is at the heart of this. But we would understand this conflict better, perhaps, if we first acknowledged that religion is responsible in some way, and then figured out how and why.

The first mistake is surely to condescend to fundamentalism. 10 We may disagree with it, but is has attracted millions of adherents for centuries, and for a good reason. It elevates and comforts. It provides a sense of meaning and direction to those lost in a disorienting world. The blind recourse to texts embraced as literal truth, the injunction to follow the commandments of God before anything else, the subjugation of reason and judgment and even conscience to the dictates of dogma: these can be exhilarating and transformative. They have led human beings to perform extraordinary acts of both good and evil. And they have an internal logic to them. If you believe that there is an eternal afterlife and that endless indescribable torture awaits those who disobey God's law, then it requires no huge stretch of imagination to make sure that you not only conform to each diktat but that you also encourage and, if necessary, coerce others to do the same. The logic behind this is impeccable. Sin begets sin. The sin of others can corrupt you as well. The only solution is to construct a world in which such sin is outlawed and punished and constantly purged—by force if necessary. It is not crazy to act this way if you believe these things strongly enough. In some ways, it's crazier to believe these things and not act this way.

In a world of absolute truth, in matters graver than life and 11 death, there is no room for dissent and no room for theological doubt. Hence the reliance on literal interpretations of texts—because interpretation can lead to error, and error can lead to damnation. Hence also the ancient Catholic insistence on absolute church authority. Without infallibility, there can be no guarantee of truth. Without such a guarantee, confusion can lead to hell.

Dostoyevsky's Grand Inquisitor makes the case perhaps as 12 well as anyone. In the story told by Ivan Karamazov in *The Brothers*

Karamazov, Jesus returns to earth during the Spanish Inquisition. On a day when hundreds have been burned at the stake for heresy, Jesus performs miracles. Alarmed, the Inquisitor arrests Jesus and imprisons him with the intent of burning him at the stake as well. What follows is a conversation between the Inquisitor and Jesus. Except it isn't conversation because Jesus says nothing. It is really a dialogue between two modes of religion, an exploration of the tension between the extraordinary, transcendent claims of religion and human beings, inability to live up to them, or even fully believe them.

13   According to the Inquisitor, Jesus' crime was revealing that salvation was possible but still allowing humans the freedom to refuse it. And this, to the Inquisitor, was a form of cruelty. When the truth involves the most important things imaginable—the meaning of life, the fate of one's eternal soul, the difference between good and evil—it is not enough to premise it on the capacity of human choice. That is too great a burden. Choice leads to unbelief or distraction or negligence or despair. What human beings really need is the certainty of truth, and they need to see it reflected in everything around them—in the cultures in which they live, enveloping them in a seamless fabric of faith that helps them resist the terror of choice and the abyss of unbelief. This need is what the Inquisitor calls the "fundamental secret of human nature." He explains: "These pitiful creatures are concerned not only to find what one or the other can worship, but to find something that all would believe in and worship; what is essential is that all may be together in it. This craving for community of worship is the chief misery of every man individually and of all humanity since the beginning of time."

14   This is the voice of fundamentalism. Faith cannot exist alone in a single person. Indeed, faith needs others for it to survive—and the more complete the culture of faith, the wider it is, and the more total its infiltration of the world the better. It is hard for us to wrap our minds around this today, but it is quite clear from the accounts of the Inquisition and, indeed, of the religious wars that continued to rage in Europe for nearly three centuries, that many of the fanatics who burned human beings at the stake were acting out of what they genuinely thought were the best interests of the victims.

With the power of the state, they used fire, as opposed to simple execution, because it was thought to be spiritually cleansing. A few minutes of hideous torture on earth were deemed a small price to pay for helping such souls avoid eternal torture in the afterlife. Moreover, the example of such government-sponsored executions helped create a culture in which certain truths were reinforced and in which it was easier for more weak people to find faith. The burden of this duty to uphold that faith lay on the men required to torture, persecute, and murder the unfaithful. And many of them believed, as no doubt some Islamic fundamentalists believe, that they were acting out of mercy and godliness.

This is the authentic voice of the Taliban. It also finds itself 15 replicated in secular form. What, after all, were the totalitarian societies of Nazi Germany or Soviet Russia if not an exact replica of this kind of fusion of politics and ultimate meaning? Under Lenin's and Stalin's rules, the imminence of salvation through revolutionary consciousness was in perpetual danger of being undermined by those too weak to have faith—the bourgeois or the kulaks or the intellectuals. So they had to be liquidated or purged. Similarly, it is easy for us to dismiss the Nazis as evil, as they surely were. It is harder for us to understand that in some twisted fashion, they truly believed that they were creating a new dawn for humanity, a place where all the doubts that freedom brings could be dispelled in a rapture of racial purity and destiny. Hence the destruction of all dissidents and the Jews—carried out by fire as the Inquisitors had before, an act of purification different merely in its scale, efficiency, and Godlessness.

Perhaps the most important thing for us to realize today is 16 that the defeat of each of these fundamentalisms required a long and arduous effort. The conflict with Islamic fundamentalism is likely to take as long. For unlike Europe's religious wars, which taught Christians the futility of fighting to the death over something beyond human understanding and so immune to any definitive resolution, there has been no such educative conflict in the Muslim world. Only Iran and Afghanistan have experienced the full horror of revolutionary fundamentalism, and only Iran has so far seen reason to moderate to some extent. From everything we see, the lessons Europe learned in its bloody history have yet to be absorbed within the Muslim world. There, as in sixteenth-century Europe, the promise of purity and salvation seems far more enticing than the mundane allure of mere peace. That means that we are not at the end of this conflict but in its very early stages.

17   America is not a neophyte in this struggle. The United States has seen several waves of religious fervor since its founding. But American evangelicalism has always kept its distance from governmental power. The Christian separation between what is God's and what is Caesar's—drawn from the Gospels—helped restrain the fundamentalist temptation. The last few decades have proved an exception, however. As modernity advanced, and the certitudes of fundamentalist faith seemed mocked by an increasingly liberal society, evangelicals mobilized and entered politics. Their faith sharpened, their zeal intensified, the temptation to fuse political and religious authority beckoned more insistently.

18   Mercifully, violence has not been a significant feature of this trend but it has not been absent. The murders of abortion providers show what such zeal can lead to. And indeed, if people truly believe that abortion is the same as mass murder, then you can see the awful logic of the terrorism it has spawned. This is the same logic as bin Laden's. If faith is that strong, and it dictates a choice between action or eternal damnation, then violence can easily be justified. In retrospect, we should be amazed not that violence has occurred—but that it hasn't occurred more often.

19   The critical link between Western and Middle Eastern fundamentalism is surely the pace of social change. If you take your beliefs from books written more than a thousand years ago, and you believe in these texts literally, then the appearance of the modern world must truly terrify. If you believe that women should be consigned to polygamous, concealed servitude, then Manhattan must appear like Gomorrah. If you believe that homosexuality is a crime punishable by death, as both fundamentalist Islam and the Bible dictate, then a world of same-sex marriage is surely Sodom. It is not a big step to argue that such centers of evil should be destroyed or undermined, as bin Laden does, or to believe that their destruction is somehow a consequence of their sin, as Jerry Falwell argued. Look again at Falwell's now infamous

words in the wake of September 11: "I really believe that the pagans, and the abortionists, and the feminists, and the gays and lesbians who are actively trying to make that an alternative lifestyle, the A.C.L.U., People for the American Way—all of them who have tried to secularize America—I point the finger in their face and say, 'You helped this happen.'"

And why wouldn't he believe that? He has subsequently 20 apologized for the insensitivity of the remark but not for its theological underpinning. He cannot repudiate the theology—because it is the essence of what he believes in and must believe in for his faith to remain alive.

The other critical aspect of this kind of faith is insecurity. 21 American fundamentalists know they are losing the culture war. They are terrified of failure and of the Godless world they believe is about to engulf or crush them. They speak and think defensively. They talk about renewal, but in their private discourse they expect damnation for an America that has lost sight of the fundamentalist notion of God.

Similarly, Muslims know that the era of Islam's imperial tri- 22 umph has long since gone. For many centuries, the civilization of Islam was the center of the world. It eclipsed Europe in the Dark Ages, fostered great learning and expanded territorially well into Europe and Asia. But it has all been downhill from there. From the collapse of the Ottoman Empire onward, it has been on the losing side of history. The response to this has been an intermittent flirtation with Westernization but far more emphatically a reaffirmation of the most irredentist and extreme forms of the culture under threat. Hence the odd phenomenon of Islamic extremism beginning in earnest only in the last 200 years.

With Islam, this has worse implications than for other cul- 23 tures that have had rises and falls. For Islam's religious tolerance has always been premised on its own power. It was tolerant when it controlled the territory and called the shots. When it lost territory and saw itself eclipsed by the West in power and civilization, tolerance evaporated. To cite Lewis again on Islam: "What is truly evil and unacceptable is the domination of infidels over true believers. For true believers to rule misbelievers is proper and natural, since this provides for the maintenance of the holy law and gives the misbelievers both the opportunity and the incentive to embrace the true faith. But for misbelievers to rule over true believers is blasphemous and unnatural, since it leads to the corruption of religion and morality in society and to the flouting or even the abrogation of God's law."

24   Thus the horror at the establishment of the State of Israel, an infidel country in Muslim lands, is a bitter reminder of the eclipse of Islam in the modern world. Thus also the revulsion at American bases in Saudi Arabia. While colonialism of different degrees is merely political oppression for some cultures, for Islam it was far worse. It was blasphemy that had to be avenged and countered.

25   I cannot help thinking of this defensiveness when I read stories of the suicide bombers sitting poolside in Florida or racking up a $48 vodka tab in an American restaurant. We tend to think that this assimilation into the West might bring Islamic fundamentalists around somewhat, temper their zeal. But in fact, the opposite is the case. The temptation of American and Western culture—indeed, the very allure of such culture—may well require a repression all the more brutal if it is to be overcome. The transmission of American culture into the heart of what bin Laden calls the Islamic nation requires only two responses— capitulation to unbelief or a radical strike against it. There is little room in the fundamentalist psyche for a moderate accommodation. The very psychological dynamics that lead repressed homosexuals to be viciously homophobic or that entice sexually tempted preachers to inveigh against immorality are the very dynamics that lead vodka-drinking fundamentalists to steer planes into buildings. It is not designed to achieve anything, construct anything, argue anything. It is a violent acting out of internal conflict.

26   And America is the perfect arena for such acting out. For the question of religious fundamentalism was not only familiar to the founding fathers. In many ways, it was the central question that led to America's existence. The first American immigrants, after all, were refugees from the religious wars that engulfed England and that intensified under England's Taliban, Oliver Cromwell. One central influence on the founders' political thought

was John Locke, the English liberal who wrote the now famous "Letter on Toleration." In it, Locke argued that true salvation could not be a result of coercion, that faith had to be freely chosen to be genuine and that any other interpretation was counter to the Gospels. Following Locke, the founders established as a central element of the new American order a stark separation of church and state, ensuring that no single religion could use political means to enforce its own orthodoxies.

We cite this as a platitude today without absorbing or even 27 realizing its radical nature in human history—and the deep human predicament it was designed to solve. It was an attempt to answer the eternal human question of how to pursue the goal of religious salvation for ourselves and others and yet also maintain civil peace. What the founders and Locke were saying was that the ultimate claims of religion should simply not be allowed to interfere with political and religious freedom. They did this to preserve peace above all—but also to preserve true religion itself.

The security against an American Taliban is therefore relatively 28 simple: it's the Constitution. And the surprising consequence of this separation is not that it led to a collapse of religious faith in America—as weak human beings found themselves unable to believe without social and political reinforcement, but that it led to one of the most vibrantly religious civil societies on earth. No other country has achieved this. And it is this achievement that the Taliban and bin Laden have now decided to challenge. It is a living, tangible rebuke to everything they believe in.

That is why this coming conflict is indeed as momentous and 29 as grave as the last major conflicts, against Nazism and Communism, and why it is not hyperbole to see it in these epic terms. What is at stake is yet another battle against a religion that is succumbing to the temptation Jesus refused in the desert—to rule by force. The difference is that this conflict is against a more formidable enemy than Nazism or Communism. The secular totalitarianisms of the twentieth century were, in President Bush's memorable words, "discarded lies." They were fundamentalisms built on the very weak intellectual conceits of a master race and a Communist revolution.

30   But Islamic fundamentalism is based on a glorious civilization and a great faith. It can harness and coopt and corrupt true
and good believers if it has a propitious and toxic enough environment. It has a more powerful logic than either Stalin's or
Hitler's Godless ideology, and it can serve as a focal point for all
the other societies in the world, whose resentment of Western
success and civilization comes more easily than the arduous task
of accommodation to modernity. We have to somehow defeat this
without defeating or even opposing a great religion that is
nonetheless more powerful faiths. It is hard to underestimate the
extreme delicacy and difficulty of this task.

31   In this sense, the symbol of this conflict should not be Old
Glory, however stirring it is. What is really at issue here is the
simple but immensely difficult principle of the separation of politics and religion. We are fighting not for our country as such or
for our flag. We are fighting for the universal principles of our
Constitution—and the possibility of free religious faith it guarantees. We are fighting for religion against one of the deepest
strains in religion there is. And not only our lives but our souls
are at stake.

2001

Only Daughter

Sandra Cisneros

1 Once, several years ago, when I was just starting out my writing
career, I was asked to write my own contributor's note for an
anthology I was part of. I wrote: "I am the only daughter in a family of six sons. *That* explains everything."

Well, I've thought about that ever since, and yes, it explains a lot   2
to me, but for the reader's sake I should have written: "I am the only
daughter in a *Mexican* family of six sons." Or even: "I am the
only daughter of a Mexican father and a Mexican-American
mother." Or: "I am the only daughter of a working-class family of
nine." All of these had everything to do with who I am today.

I was/am the only daughter and *only* a daughter. Being an   3
only daughter in a family of six sons forced me by circumstance
to spend a lot of time by myself because my brothers felt it
beneath them to play with a *girl* in public. But that aloneness, that
loneliness, was good for a would-be writer—it allowed me time
to think and think, to imagine, to read and prepare myself.

Being only a daughter for my father meant my destiny would   4
lead me to become someone's wife. That's what he believed. But
when I was in the fifth grade and shared my plans for college with
him, I was sure he understood. I remember my father saying, "*Que
bueno, mi'ja,* that's good." That meant a lot to me, especially since
my brothers thought the idea hilarious. What I didn't realize was
that my father thought college was good for girls—good for finding a husband. After four years in college and two more in graduate school, and still no husband, my father shakes his head even
now and says I wasted all that education.

In retrospect, I'm lucky my father believed daughters were   5
meant for husbands. It meant it didn't matter if I majored in something silly like English. After all, I'd find a nice professional eventually, right? This allowed me the liberty to putter about embroidering
my little poems and stories without my father interrupting with so
much as a "What's that you're writing?"

But the truth is, I wanted him to interrupt. I wanted my father   6
to understand what it was I was scribbling, to introduce me as
"My only daughter, the writer." Not as "This is only my daughter. She teaches." *Es maestra*—teacher. Not even *professora.*

In a sense, everything I have ever written has been for him, to   7
win his approval even though I know my father can't read English
words, even though my father's only reading includes the brown-
ink *Esto* sports magazine from Mexico City and the bloody
¡*Alarma!* magazines that feature yet another sighting of *La Virgen*

de Guadalupe on a tortilla or a wife's revenge on her philandering husband by bashing his skull in with a *molcajete* (a kitchen mortar made of volcanic rock). Or the *fotonovelas*, the little picture paper-backs with tragedy and trauma erupting from the characters' mouths in bubbles.

8   My father represents, then, the public majority. A public who is disinterested in reading, and yet one whom I am writing about and for, and privately trying to woo.

9   When we were growing up in Chicago, we moved a lot because of my father. He suffered bouts of nostalgia. Then we'd have to let go our flat, store the furniture with mother's relatives, load the station wagon with baggage and bologna sandwiches and head south. To Mexico City:

10   We came back, of course. To yet another Chicago flat, another Chicago neighborhood, another Catholic school. Each time, my father would seek out the parish priest in order to get a tuition break, and complain or boast: "I have seven sons."

11   He meant *siete hijos,* seven children, but he translated it as "sons." "I have seven sons." To anyone who would listen. The Sears Roebuck employee who sold us the washing machine. The short-order cook where my father ate his ham-and-eggs breakfasts. "I have seven sons." As if he deserved a medal from the state.

12   My papa. He didn't mean anything by that mistranslation, I'm sure. But somehow I could feel myself being erased. I'd tug my father's sleeve and whisper: "Not seven sons. Six! and *one daughter.*"

13   When my oldest brother graduated from medical school, he fulfilled my father's dream that we study hard and use this—our heads, instead of this—our hands. Even now my father's hands are thick and yellow, stubbed by a history of hammer and nails and twine and coils and springs. "Use this," my father said, tapping his head, "and not this," showing us those hands. He always looked tired when he said it.

14   Wasn't college an investment? And hadn't I spent all those years in college? And if I didn't marry, what was it all for? Why would anyone go to college and then choose to be poor? Especially someone who had always been poor.

15   Last year, after ten years of writing professionally, the financial rewards started to trickle in. My second National Endowment for

the Arts Fellowship. A guest professorship at the University of California, Berkeley. My book, which sold to a major New York publishing house.

At Christmas, I flew home to Chicago. The house was throb- 16 bing, same as always; hot *tamales* and sweet *tamales* hissing in my mother's pressure cooker, and everybody—my mother, six broth- ers, wives, babies, aunts, cousins—talking too loud and at the same time, like in a Fellini film, because that's just how we are.

I went upstairs to my father's room. One of my stories had 17 just been translated into Spanish and published in an anthology of Chicano writing, and I wanted to show it to him. Ever since he recovered from a stroke two years ago, my father likes to spend his leisure hours horizontally. And that's how I found him, watching a Pedro Infante movie on Galavisión and eating rice pudding.

There was a glass filmed with milk on the bedside table. 18 There were several vials of pills and balled Kleenex. And on the floor, one black sock and a plastic urinal that I didn't want to look at but looked at anyway. Pedro Infante was about to burst into song, and my father was laughing.

I'm not sure if it was because my story was translated into 19 Spanish, or because it was published in Mexico, or perhaps because the story dealt with Topeyac, the *colonia* my father was raised in and the house he grew up in, but at any rate, my father punched the mute button on his remote control and read my story.

I sat on the bed next to my father and waited. He read it very 20 slowly. As if he were reading each line over and over. He laughed at all the right places and read lines he liked out loud. He pointed and asked questions: "Is this So-and-so?" "Yes," I said. He kept reading.

When he was finally finished, after what seemed like hours, 21 my father looked up and asked: "Where can we get more copies of this for the relatives?"

Of all the wonderful things that happened to me last year, 22 that was the most wonderful.

1990

Coyote vs. Acme

Ian Frazier

In the United States District Court,
Southwestern District,
Tempe, Arizona
Case No. B19294,
Judge Joan Kujava, Presiding
Wile E. Coyote, Plaintiff
—v.—
Acme Company, Defendant

1 Opening Statement of Mr. Harold Schoff, attorney for Mr. Coyote: My client, Mr. Wile E. Coyote, a resident of Arizona and contiguous states, does hereby bring suit for damages against the Acme Company, manufacturer and retail distributor of assorted merchandise, incorporated in Delaware and doing business in every state, district, and territory. Mr. Coyote seeks compensation for personal injuries, loss of business income, and mental suffering caused as a direct result of the actions and/or gross negligence of said company, under Title 15 of the United States Code, Chapter 47, section 2072, subsection (a), relating to product liability.

2   Mr. Coyote states that on eighty-five separate occasions he has purchased of the Acme Company (hereinafter, "Defendant"), through that company's mail-order department, certain products which did cause him bodily injury due to defects in manufacture or improper cautionary labelling. Sales slips made out to Mr. Coyote as proof of purchase are at present in the possession of the Court, marked Exhibit A. Such injuries sustained by Mr. Coyote have temporarily restricted his ability to make a living in his profession of predator. Mr. Coyote is self-employed and thus not eligible for Workmen's Compensation.

3   Mr. Coyote states that on December 13th he received of Defendant via parcel post one Acme Rocket Sled. The intention of Mr. Coyote was to use the Rocket Sled to aid him in pursuit of his prey. Upon receipt of the Rocket Sled Mr. Coyote removed it from its wooden shipping crate and, sighting his prey in the distance,

activated the ignition. As Mr. Coyote gripped the handlebars, the Rocket Sled accelerated with such sudden and precipitate force as to stretch Mr. Coyote's forelimbs to a length of fifty feet. Subsequently, the rest of Mr. Coyote's body shot forward with a violent jolt, causing severe strain to his back and neck and placing him unexpectedly astride the Rocket Sled. Disappearing over the horizon at such speed as to leave a diminishing jet trail along its path, the Rocket Sled soon brought Mr. Coyote abreast of his prey. At that moment the animal he was pursuing veered sharply to the right. Mr. Coyote vigorously attempted to follow this maneuver but was unable to, due to poorly designed steering on the Rocket Sled and a faulty or nonexistent braking system. Shortly thereafter, the unchecked progress of the Rocket Sled brought it and Mr. Coyote into collision with the side of a mesa.

Paragraph One of the Report of Attending Physician 4 (Exhibit B), prepared by Dr. Ernest Grosscup, M.D., D.O., details the multiple fractures, contusions, and tissue damage suffered by Mr. Coyote as a result of this collision. Repair of the injuries required a full bandage around the head (excluding the ears), a neck brace, and full or partial casts on all four legs.

Hampered by these injuries, Mr. Coyote was nevertheless 5 obliged to support himself. With this in mind, he purchased of Defendant as an aid to mobility one pair of Acme Rocket Skates. When he attempted to use this product, however, he became involved in an accident remarkably similar to that which occurred with the Rocket Sled. Again, Defendant sold over the counter, without caveat, a product which attached powerful jet engines (in this case, two) to inadequate vehicles, with little or no provision for passenger safety. Encumbered by his heavy casts, Mr. Coyote lost control of the Rocket Skates soon after strapping them on, and collided with a roadside billboard so violently as to leave a hole in the shape of his full silhouette.

Mr. Coyote states that on occasions too numerous to list in 6 this document he has suffered mishaps with explosives purchased of Defendant: the Acme "Little Giant" Firecracker, the Acme Self-Guided Aerial Bomb, etc. (For a full listing, see the Acme Mail Order Explosives Catalogue and attached deposition, entered in evidence as Exhibit C.) Indeed, it is safe to say that not once has an explosive purchased of Defendant by Mr. Coyote performed in an expected manner. To cite just one example: At the expense of much time and personal effort, Mr. Coyote constructed around the outer rim of a butte a wooden trough beginning at the top of the butte and spiralling downward around it to some few feet above a black X painted on the desert floor. The trough was designed in such a way that a spherical explosive of the type sold by Defendant would roll easily and swiftly down to the point of detonation indicated by the X. Mr. Coyote placed a generous pile of birdseed directly on the X, and then, carrying the spherical Acme Bomb (Catalogue #78-832), climbed to the top of the butte. Mr. Coyote's prey, seeing the birdseed, approached, and Mr. Coyote proceeded to light the fuse. In an instant, the fuse burned down to the stem, causing the bomb to detonate.

7   In addition to reducing all Mr. Coyote's careful preparations to naught, the premature detonation of Defendant's product resulted in the following disfigurements to Mr. Coyote:

1. Severe singeing of the hair on the head, neck, and muzzle.
2. Sooty discoloration.
3. Fracture of the left ear at the stem, causing the ear to dangle in the aftershock with a creaking noise.
4. Full or partial combustion of whiskers, producing kinking, frazzling, and ashy disintegration.
5. Radical widening of the eyes, due to brow and lid charring.

8   We come now to the Acme Spring-Powered Shoes. The remains of a pair of these purchased by Mr. Coyote on June 23rd are Plaintiff's Exhibit D. Selected fragments have been shipped to the metallurgical laboratories of the University of California at Santa Barbara for analysis, but to date no explanation has been found for this product's sudden and extreme malfunction. As advertised by Defendant, this product is simplicity itself: two wood-and-metal sandals, each attached to milled-steel springs of high tensile strength and compressed in a tightly coiled position by a cocking device with a lanyard release. Mr. Coyote believed that this product would enable him to pounce upon his prey in the initial moments of the chase, when swift reflexes are at a premium.

To increase the shoes' thrusting power still further, Mr. Coyote 9
affixed them by their bottoms to the side of a large boulder. Adjacent to the boulder was a path which Mr. Coyote's prey was known
to frequent. Mr. Coyote put his hind feet in the wood-and-metal
sandals and crouched in readiness, his right forepaw holding
firmly to the lanyard release. Within a short time Mr. Coyote's prey
did indeed appear on the path coming toward him. Unsuspecting,
the prey stopped near Mr. Coyote, well within range of the springs
at full extension. Mr. Coyote gauged the distance with care and
proceeded to pull the lanyard release.

At this point, Defendant's product should have thrust 10
Mr. Coyote forward and away from the boulder. Instead, for reasons yet unknown, the Acme Spring-Powered Shoes thrust the
boulder away from Mr. Coyote. As the intended prey looked on
unharmed, Mr. Coyote hung suspended in air. Then the twin
springs recoiled, bringing Mr. Coyote to a violent feet-first collision with the boulder, the full weight of his head and forequarters
falling upon his lower extremities.

The force of this impact then caused the springs to rebound, 11
whereupon Mr. Coyote was thrust skyward. A second recoil and
collision followed. The boulder, meanwhile, which was roughly
ovoid in shape, had begun to bounce down a hillside, the coiling
and recoiling of the springs adding to its velocity. At each bounce,
Mr. Coyote came into contact with the boulder, or the boulder
came into contact with Mr. Coyote, or both came into contact with
the ground. As the grade was a long one, this process continued
for some time.

The sequence of collisions resulted in systemic physical dam- 12
age to Mr. Coyote, viz., flattening of the cranium, sideways dis-
placement of the tongue, reduction of length of legs and upper
body, and compression of vertebrae from base of tail to head. Rep-
etition of blows along a vertical axis produced a series of regular horizontal folds in Mr. Coyote's body tissues—a rare and
painful condition which caused Mr. Coyote to expand upward and
contract downward alternately as he walked, and to emit an off-
key accordionlike wheezing with every step. The distracting and
embarrassing nature of this symptom has been a major impedi-
ment to Mr. Coyote's pursuit of a normal social life.

13   As the Court is no doubt aware, Defendant has a virtual monopoly of manufacture and sale of goods required by Mr. Coyote's work. It is our contention that Defendant has used its market advantage to the detriment of the consumer of such specialized products as itching powder, giant kites, Burmese tiger traps, anvils, and two-hundred-foot-long rubber bands. Much as he has come to mistrust Defendant's products, Mr. Coyote has no other domestic source of supply to which to turn. One can only wonder what our trading partners in Western Europe and Japan would make of such a situation, where a giant company is allowed to victimize the consumer in the most reckless and wrongful manner over and over again.

14   Mr. Coyote respectfully requests that the Court regard these larger economic implications and assess punitive damages in the amount of seventeen million dollars. In addition, Mr. Coyote seeks actual damages (missed meals, medical expenses, days lost from professional occupation) of one million dollars; general damages (mental suffering, injury to reputation) of twenty million dollars; and attorney's fees of seven hundred and fifty thousand dollars. Total damages: thirty-eight million seven hundred and fifty thousand dollars. By awarding Mr. Coyote the full amount, this Court will censure Defendant, its directors, officers, shareholders, successors, and assigns, in the only language they understand, and reaffirm the right of the individual predator to equal protection under the law.

1996

Test Day

Frank Bures

1 From the doorway, I can see the last of my students walking up the dirt road into the school grounds. They're late as usual, but Mr. Ndyogi isn't here to beat them, so no one is running. Their crisp blue and white uniforms move slowly beneath the outline of Mt. Meru. I can see they're even less eager for class to begin than normal, less enthused about English grammar than ever.

They know, as they drag their feet through the dust, that ₂
today is test day.

The last students straggle into class as I write the final ques- ₃
tions on the blackboard. When the talking and the scraping of
wooden chairs dies down, I tell them to put their notebooks away
and begin.

Testing is a futile exercise in so many ways. For most of these ₄
students, all 47 of them on a good day, English is their third language, after Swahili and Maasai. My own Swahili is very bad and
even though we've been working on prepositions for some time,
I still have no idea what the Swahili word for preposition is, or if
there is one.

Instead, I'm reduced to crude hand gestures and bad draw- ₅
ings on the board. Walking around the room, glancing at the
papers, I can see this hasn't worked as well as I thought it would.
Instead, judging from their writing, preposition roulette is the
favorite strategy once again.

"Go apologize to your brother *by* punching him in the nose." ₆
"Where should I get *inward* the bus?" ₇
"What sort of things are you interested *nothing?*" ₈

Our school is a small one, not far from Arusha, the semi- ₉
cosmopolitan urban center of northern Tanzania. We have eight
classrooms, which are staggered at intervals down a hill. The students begin at the top and after a four-year downhill slide, they
end up with their "certificate." My students are about mid-slide,
in Form III. I'm here for the year on a mostly self-funded teaching
program, the idea being that, as an English speaker I should have
enough grasp of it to pass it along. This, in other words, is test day
for me too.

The walls of our classroom are whitewashed and the room is ₁₀
packed tight with desks and stools. The blackboard at the front is
badly chipped and overhead are corrugated iron sheets, with one
plastic panel to allow the sunshine through. Our school is called
"Ekenywa," which in Maasai means "Sunrise," because (as our
headmaster told us) with education, the area around the school is
waking up.

If some of my students would wake up, they might do better ₁₁
on this test.

12   My only real ambition here has been to leave them with a few practical English skills—how to write a letter, for example, or what the plot of "No Longer at Ease" is. Something to help them get a job in town, or at least to pass their national exam.

13   On test day, walking between the desks, I see how far we are from such lofty goals. Take, for example, their "Letter to a friend." I don't know how many times I told them—how many times I made them write in their notebooks—to end a letter, any letter, with, "Yours sincerely."

14   Around the room, there are many interpretations of this: "Your thinthially," "you thinkfully," "Yours sincefully," "Your sincilier," "your sceneially," "Senceally," "Your friendly," "Yours be love friend." A few students do get the basics. John signs his, "Yours in the Building of the Nation," which I'm quite happy with. But mostly test day is the day I wonder why I'm here.

15   My students wonder this too. Imani even writes in his letter: "The aim of sending this letter to you is to tell you about my exam I do. The test I taking was very hard. I try to think, but I am not understand anything in this test. The teacher who make this test was not like the Form III to go in the Form IV."

16   A good effort, and not a bad letter, as they go. Rukia takes a more flattering tack.

17   "I study in Ekenywa Secondary School, and the teacher is the very good and the teacher of English is come from America so they teach very well." Or, "Frank was teach me English very well. I like it because I trie to speak English and I want to go some o my town to teach a young girl and boy, like Frenck teach me." Or, "I will get 18 points on this test are very big points."

18   Her points, I'm afraid, will be the same size as everyone else's. But they try so hard, in spite of everything working against them. At primary school everything is taught in Swahili. Then they hit secondary school and suddenly all their classes are taught in English. In this kind of immersion, most students drown. The school provides no life rafts either, such as dictionaries or grammar books or workbooks. Never mind school supplies. Some days there aren't even any teachers.

19   Nonetheless, the Ministry of Education sets a huge task before them. Form III students, it says, should "develop the habit

of reading for pleasure and for information," as well as to increase reading speed. It says they should complete 13 books during the third year.

But our school only has five of the books on the syllabus, and 20 enough copies of only three to actually use.

Of the two we finally read—"Things Fall Apart" and "No 21 Longer at Ease," both by Chinua Achebe—we had 14 and 23 copies, and only a handful in good condition. These were shared by groups of three and four students. But actually reading them would be like me reading "Don Quixote" in Spanish. Impossible.

Of course, this shows on test day. We spent several weeks going 22 over these books, and I wrote explicit outlines of everything that happened on the board, which I watched them copy down.

But on test day, students who once seemed to have mastered 23 the plot, or at least memorized the characters, answer questions about Obi and his grandfather, Okonkwo, like this:

"Okonkwo Obi is falling apart."   24

"Obi is republic."   25

"Clara was very dislike because Obi's parents they don't 26 want Clara to be wife of Obi. So Clara want to kill himself for that. THIS IS NOT GOD TO WANT TO KILL YOURSELF. EVEN YOU MR. FRANK."

Hmm. The thought hadn't crossed my mind. But with many 27 more days like this, it just might.

On the other hand, sometimes on test day, a previously 28 illiterate student mysteriously becomes a brilliant literary critic.

"Okonkwo," writes Godson, "through his fears, becomes 29 exiled from his tribe and returns only to be forced in the ignonimy of suicide to escape the results of his rash courage against the white man."

Godson is the class Rastafarian and knows the words to every 30 Bob Marley song. I know he doesn't know anything about Okonkwo.

"Obi Okonkwo," writes Tumaini in suspiciously good Eng- 31 lish, "returns from his studies in England to try to live up to the expectations of his family and his tribe and at the same time to breathe the heady atmosphere of Lagos."

Such is the heady atmosphere of test day. Martin writes in 32 his letter, "Just a quick note to let you know that I've had a rather serious accident in my holiday, and my leg is now in plaster. The doctor said that I've fractured it, and that I'll be laid up for about six weeks. After that I should be right as rain. I will tell you more in another letter. For now, let me end here. Yours ever, Martin Paul."

33 There are about three students in the class who might be able to write something like this. Martin is not one of them. He is one of the other 44 who come to school, sit, talk, use cheat sheets I can never find, and don't pay attention, except on days when I give up on grammar and answer questions about America.

34 "Is it true," they would ask, "that the government gives every American a gun at age 18?" "Is it true that even the poorest Americans have 12 cars?" "What's up, man?" they would ask. "Hey," I'd say. "Not much."

35 Those days were the best of all, the days when I felt that I really had something to offer, something they wanted to know. These were the days we connected. These were the days when they sat rapt, as I unlocked the secrets of America, and they, in turn, unlocked their own country, giving me all the street lingo I could use.

36 But there was no slang on the national syllabus, and it didn't help them on test day.

37 "So," I ask again as we go over the test (we've been over the material before), "Obi and Christopher went out with some Irish girls. Does anyone know what Irish means?"

38 "Irish potatoes!" someone shouts.

39 "Yes," I say, "like Irish potatoes. But what does Irish mean?"

40 "Beautiful!" someone else shouts.

41 Next question: "So, the girl tried to bribe Obi with sex. What . . ."

42 Suddenly they are all fluent. "Explain! Explain!" they yell.

43 "No!" says Seuri, "don't explain in words. Give demonstration so we can see."

44 The students hand in the tests, and the scores are abysmal again. I'm not even sure how to grade them. If I make it on a curve, it will be a very small bump. The hardest part is that I know they could do it if they had chance, if they had some hope. But there are too many obstacles and too few incentives. Most of

my students will be married off or end up putting their certificate to work in the fields.

Yet as with so many things in Tanzania, we move on. Life is 45
hard here, but giving up is even harder, and it's not really an option. So we go forward, to the next test, the next lesson. Along the way, we look for hope and laughter and comfort where there is little, and make our own where there is none.

As class finishes, wooden chairs scrape across the floor again 46
as the students stand up to leave with their tests. I too move to the door, but accidentally step on Matthew's foot.

"Oh, sorry," I say.   47
"It's cool," he says.   48
"Where did you learn that?" I ask.   49
He looks at me and smiles.   50
"You."   51

2003

Permissions Acknowledgments

Abbey, Edward. "The Serpents of Paradise" from *Desert Solitaire: A Season in the Wilderness* by Edward Abbey. Reprinted by permission of Don Congdon Associates, Inc. Copyright © 1968 by Edward Abbey, renewed 1996 by Clarke Abbey.

Ackerman, Diane. "Where Fall Color Comes From" from *A Natural History of the Senses* by Diane Ackerman, copyright © 1990 by Diane Ackerman. Used by permission of Random House, Inc.

Angelou, Maya. "Grandmother's Victory," copyright © 1969 and renewed 1997 by Maya Angelou, from *I Know Why the Caged Bird Sings* by Maya Angelou. Used by permission of Random House, Inc.

Baldwin, James. "Fifth Avenue Uptown: A Letter from Harlem" by James Baldwin. Originally published in Esquire. Copyright © 1960 by James Baldwin. Copyright renewed. Collected in *Nobody Knows My Name*, published by Vintage Books. Reprinted by arrangement with the James Baldwin Estate.

Brady, Judith. "Why I Want a Wife." Copyright © 1970 by Judith Brady. Reprinted by permission of the author.

Britt, Suzanne. "Neat People vs. Sloppy People" from *Show and Tell* by Suzanne Britt. Copyright © 1982 by Suzanne Britt. Reprinted by permission of the author.

Bures, Frank. "Test Day" by Frank Bures as appeared in *World Hum*, September 10, 2003. Reprinted by permission of Frank Bures.

Byers, Michael. "Monuments to Our Better Nature" by Michael Byers. Originally appeared in *Preservation*, January/February 2003. Reprinted by permission of Michael Byers.

Catton, Bruce. "Grant and Lee: A Study in Contrasts" from *The American Story* by Bruce Catton. Copyright U.S. Capitol Historical Society; all rights reserved. Reprinted by permission.

435

King, Martin Luther, Jr. "I Have a Dream" reprinted by arrangement with the Estate of Martin Luther King Jr., c/o Writer's House as agent for the proprietor, New York, NY.

Koerner, Brendan. "Embryo Police" by Brendan Koerner from *Wired*, February 2002. Copyright © 2002 Conde Nast Publications. All rights reserved. Originally published in *Wired*. Reprinted by permission.

Kozol, Jonathan. "The Details of Life" by Jonathan Kozol. Reprinted by permission from the May 22, 2000 issue of *The Nation*. For subscription information, call 1-800-333-8536. Portions of each week's *Nation* magazine can be accessed at http://www.thenation.com.

Lake, Medicine Grizzlybear. "An Indian Father's Plea" by Medicine Grizzlybear Lake (a/k/a Robert G. Lake-Thom) as appeared in *Orion* magazine, Autumn 1995. Reprinted by permission of the author.

Lame Deer, John (Fire) and Richard Erdoes. "Alone on the Hilltop" reprinted with the permission of Simon & Schuster Adult Publishing Group from *Lame Deer Seeker of Visions* by John (Fire) Lame Deer and Richard Erdoes. Copyright © 1972 by John (Fire) Lame Deer and Richard Erdoes.

Lethem, Jonathan. "9 Failures of the Imagination." Copyright © 2002 by Jonathan Lethem. Distributed by The New York Times Special Features.

Lightman, Alan. "Smile" from *Dance for Two* by Alan Lightman, copyright © 1996 by Alan Lightman. Used by permission of Pantheon Books, a division of Random House, Inc.

Lutz, William. "Doublespeak" from *Doublespeak* by William Lutz. Copyright © 1989 by Blonde Bear, Inc. Reprinted by permission of Jean V. Naggar Literary Agency.

Marius, Richard. Pages 45–48 from "Writing Drafts" in *The Writer's Companion, 2E* by Richard Marius. Copyright © 1984. Reprinted by permission of The McGraw-Hill Companies.

McPhee, John. "Silk Parachute" by John McPhee. Reprinted by permission; © 1997 John McPhee. Originally published in *The New Yorker*, May 12, 1997. All Rights Reserved.

Meyer, Philip. "If Hitler Asked You to Electrocute a Stranger, Would You? Probably." Originally published in *Esquire*. Copyright © 1970 by Philip Meyer. Reprinted by permission of Philip Meyer. Excerpt from *Obedience* by Stanley Milgram copyright © 1965 by Stanley Milgram and distributed by Penn State Media Sales.

Miner, Horace. "Body Ritual among the Nacirema." *American Anthropologist, 58*(3), 1959.

Index